T. H. GREEN
Lectures on the Princi
Political Obligatio

This book contains the political writing of T. H. Green and selections from those of his ethical writing which bear on his political philosophy. Green's best known work, *Lectures on the Principles of Political Obligation*, is included in full, as are the essay on freedom and the lecture 'Liberal Legislation and Freedom of Contract'. There are also extracts from Green's lectures on the English Revolution and from the *Prologomena to Ethics*, and a number of previously unpublished essays and notes. All the texts have been corrected against Green's manuscripts, held in Balliol College. The editors have provided a list of variants, full notes and an introductory essay on the importance of Green's form of revitalised liberalism.

The volume will be a valuable sourcebook for students of Green's thought and the history of nineteenth-century liberation.

T. H. GREEN
Lectures on the Principles of Political Obligation
and Other Writings

Edited by
PAUL HARRIS and JOHN MORROW
Victoria University of Wellington
New Zealand

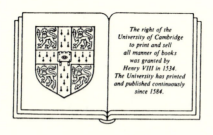

The right of the
University of Cambridge
to print and sell
all manner of books
was granted by
Henry VIII in 1534.
The University has printed
and published continuously
since 1584.

CAMBRIDGE UNIVERSITY PRESS
CAMBRIDGE
LONDON   NEW YORK   NEW ROCHELLE
MELBOURNE   SYDNEY

Published by the Press Syndicate of the University of Cambridge
The Pitt Building, Trumpington Street, Cambridge CB2 1RP
32 East 57th Street, New York, NY 10022, USA
10 Stamford Road, Oakleigh, Melbourne 3166, Australia

First published 1986

British Library cataloguing in publication data
Green, T. H.
Lectures on the principles of political
obligation and other writings.
1. Political science
I. Title   II. Harris, Paul   III. Morrow, John
320'.01   JC223.G78

Library of Congress cataloguing in publication data
Green, Thomas Hill, 1836–1882.
T. H. Green: Lectures on the principles of
political obligation, and other writings.
Bibliography: p.
Includes index.
1. Liberty – Addresses, essays, lectures.
2. Natural law – Addresses, essays, lectures.
3. Political science – Addresses, essays, lectures.
I. Harris, Paul, Ph. D.   II. Morrow, John, Ph. D.
III. Title.
JC571.G78122   1985   320'.01'1   85–7816

ISBN 0 521 26035 3 hard covers
ISBN 0 521 27810 4 paperback

Transferred to digital printing 1999

CONTENTS

===

v

PREFACE

In selecting and preparing the texts for this volume of Green's political philosophy, we have tried to cater for the needs of graduate and undergraduate students on the one hand, and scholars on the other. Although Green's social and political thought is inseparable from his metaphysics, his epistemology, and his religious thought, we have not been able to include any of Green's writings in these areas but have used notes to point to relevant passages in the *Works*.

The texts of the previously unpublished writings are taken from Green's manuscripts, now held in the Balliol College Library. We have supplied the 'Fragments' with titles and have divided them into sections; the 'Undergraduate essays' are as Green wrote them. We have based our texts of Green's published works on those prepared by the original editors, and we have retained their titles and their divisions into sections and chapters, although we have not been able to include their useful analytic tables of contents. We have, however, corrected their versions against Green's manuscripts. Where the original editors have significantly misread or unjustifiably altered what Green wrote, we have restored Green's words and noted their version in the Variants (see pp. 367–72). In addition, where there is an unresolved choice in the manuscript between two words or phrases (usually written one above the other), we have included the one not used in the Variants, prefixed '*alt.*' We have not noted minor alterations to the text, nor changes in punctuation and spelling, the insertion or deletion of definite articles, the completion of abbreviations, or the restoration of Green's emphasis of a word or phrase. We have checked Green's quotations from other authors and corrected errors, usually without comment. Material in square brackets has been added by the present editors. Green's quotations in Latin, Greek, and German have been replaced by English translations. Foreign words and phrases have had a translation supplied on the first occurrence in each chapter, and Greek has been transliterated. Numbered notes with asterisks are Green's own; all other notes are the present editors'. A list of the abbreviations used in the notes is on p. ix.

We have received advice and assistance from many sources during our work on this book. We are particularly grateful to the Master and Fellows of Balliol College, Oxford, for permission to use the Green Papers, and to the College's Library staff for their considerable help. We acknowledge assistance received from the Leave Committee and the Internal Research Committee of Victoria University, and from the staffs of the following libraries: Victoria University, the British Library, the Senate House Library of the University of London, and the British Library of Political and Economic Science at the London School of Economics. We are grateful to Oxford University Press for permission to quote from Benedict de Spinoza, *The Political Works*, translated and edited by A. G. Wernham (1958), and to Martin Robertson Ltd for allowing us to see the proofs of *Philosophy, Politics and Citizenship: Idealism and the Welfare State* by Andrew Vincent and Raymond Plant. Marion Beardsmore, Jenny Berry, and Coula Pastelides typed and retyped with accuracy and good humour. We are glad of this opportunity to recognise the help we have received from Peter Nicholson, of the University of York; Mark Francis, of the University of Canterbury, New Zealand; and Patrick Conway, J. C. Davis, David Hamer, Peter McPhee, and Arthur Pomeroy, all of Victoria University. Finally, we wish to acknowledge our special and considerable debt to our colleague Chris Parkin, who was always willing to set aside other burdens in order to help us.

PAUL HARRIS
JOHN MORROW

Wellington, New Zealand
September 1984

ABBREVIATIONS

Collected Coleridge	*Collected Works of Samuel Taylor Coleridge*, 16 vols., ed. Katherine Coburn (London and Princeton, 1969–).
'English Revolution'	T. H. Green, 'Four Lectures on the English Revolution', *Works*, III, pp. 277–364; selections below, pp. 213–27.
D.N.B.	*Dictionary of National Biography*
'Freedom'	Green, 'On the Different Senses of "Freedom" as Applied to the Will and to the Moral Progress of Man', below pp. 228–49.
Lectures	Green, *Lectures on the Principles of Political Obligation*, below pp. 13–193.
'Liberal Legislation'	Green, 'Lecture on "Liberal Legislation and Freedom of Contract"', below pp. 194–212.
Memoir	R. L. Nettleship, 'Memoir', *Works*, III, pp. xi–clxi.
Political Economy	John Stuart Mill, *The Principles of Political Economy with some of their Applications to Social Philosophy*, 2 vols., introd. V. W. Bladen, ed. J. M. Robson, *The Collected Works of J. S. Mill* (London and Toronto, 1965), vols. 2–3.
Prolegomena	Green, *Prolegomena to Ethics*, ed. A. C. Bradley (Oxford, 1883). Selections below, pp. 250–301.
Richter	Melvin Richter, *The Politics of Conscience: T. H. Green and His Age* (London, 1964).
Rodman	*The Political Theory of T. H. Green: Selected Writings*, ed. John R. Rodman (New York, 1964).
Works	*Works of Thomas Hill Green*, 3 vols., ed. R. L. Nettleship (London, 1885–8).

INTRODUCTION

I

The writings collected in this volume represent the political *oeuvre* of a philosopher who exerted an important influence on late nineteenth- and early twentieth-century life. Although lacking the somewhat austere glamour that surrounds John Stuart Mill, Green acquired a standing among political practitioners unmatched by any later British political philosopher, and a reputation among professional political philosophers which survived well into the twentieth century.[1] This social and political impact was particularly evident in two areas. First, and most immediately, Green's form of politicised Christianity was important in encouraging members of the upper and middle classes to see disinterested social service as a particularly significant field for the exercise of Christian virtue. The most well documented example is Green's inspirational role in the Settlement Movement designed to provide young university graduates with opportunities for living among and improving the material, intellectual, and moral well-being of London's poor.[2] Secondly, Green's moral conception of politics – his idea of the common good and his positive conception of the state – became the common premises of those members of the late nineteenth- and early twentieth-century Liberal Party who wished to justify new departures in state activity in order to secure what they regarded as the minimum social and economic conditions necessary for harmonious and just social existence. Although the precise nature of the relationship between Green's political theory and the 'New Liberalism' is a matter of some contention, there is little doubt that some of the most important of the New Liberals portrayed themselves as heirs to the tradition established by Green.[3]

Green's inspirational and ideological importance in this period is sufficient to justify an interest in his political writings by those concerned with English social and political history. But Green was more than a political writer; he was also a philosopher who occupies an important place in the history of political thought, in two major respects. In the first place, Green was the leading exponent of 'British' Idealism and of its political implications. This movement flourished in British universities for about fifty years from 1870, and was marked by a clear and quite conscious antipathy to the empiricism of Locke, Hume and the Utilitarians and by an attempt to awaken British philosophy to the thought of Kant, Fichte, and Hegel. That reorientation marks the second aspect of Green's importance in the development of political thought, for out of it there emerged a distinctive political philosophy which was clearly related with Millite liberalism in outlook and programme, but possessed a theoretical focus which directed attention to the neglected but crucial question of the nature of the state and the subjects' relationship to it.

II

Thomas Hill Green was born on 7 April 1836 in Birkin, Yorkshire.[4] He was educated at home by his father, the Rev. Valentine Green, until he went to Rugby School in 1850. Green entered Balliol College, Oxford, in 1855. His undergraduate experiences were crucial; his tutor, the redoubtable Benjamin Jowett, not only encouraged the previously indolent though able youth to gain a first-class degree, but he also introduced Green to a heady mixture of Greek and German philosophy which was to sustain him for the rest of his life. The importance of this period for Green is shown by the appearance in his undergraduate essays of the major themes of his mature philosophy.

Green remained at Oxford after taking his degree, first as a tutor and Fellow of Balliol (1860), then as Whyte's Professor of Moral Philosophy (1878) until his death in 1882 a few days short of his forty-sixth birthday. His influence was felt in many areas of the life of the University, the city, and the country. He was the first layman to be appointed a tutor, one of the first to make philosophical teaching and writing their sole profession, and was among those who were instrumental in reforming the philosophical curriculum to extend beyond Plato and Aristotle.[5] His influence on the undergraduates was considerable, both because of his inspiring qualities as a teacher, but also because of the qualities of his personality and his example. Although he wrote a great deal, the bulk of his writings, including virtually all his political works, were published posthumously; they enjoyed a circulation that would be the envy of many modern philosophers and a source of gratitude for their publishers.[6]

Green married in 1871, and became a householder in Oxford. He had been active in Liberal Party politics since the mid-1860s, and in

1876 he was elected to the Oxford town council as the first don to serve as a representative of the citizens rather than of the University. His philosophy of citizenship was expressed in two major areas of public activity during his adult life. The first was education: he served as an assistant commissioner on the Taunton Commission on Secondary Education, 1865–6, was a member of the Oxford School Board, and played a major part in the foundation of the Oxford School for Boys. He was prominent in the university extension movement and (with Mrs Green) in the opening of university education to women at Oxford and elsewhere.[7] The second was temperance: he was a vice-president of the United Kingdom Alliance, and held office in several temperance organisations in Oxford.[8]

III

At the core of Green's social and political philosophy is a characteristically Idealist argument about the role of subject and object in knowledge, an argument that was specifically directed against the sceptical impasse produced by empiricist attempts to reduce the sensuous world and the minds which comprehend it to a series of primitive elements.[9] Things could only be known, Green argued, if they were relational, and could only be known by a subject who synthesised relationships. Moreover, if a claim about the world is true, it remains so whether or not it is known by any human consciousness. In order to explain this, Green postulated the existence of an 'eternal consciousness' which originally forged these relationships and possessed a knowledge of them which was independent of time and space. This eternal consciousness was the source and form of the consciousness whose progressive replication in individuals was the condition of their knowledge of the world and of right conduct.[10] The eternal consciousness was, in other words, increasingly objectified in the lives of individuals and was the essential condition of their lives as human beings. As such, it brought about the recognition of a 'better self' whose complete realisation was the goal of conduct; 'the objectification' of the eternal consciousness in 'the perfect art of living' was the true end of moral action.[11] But Green insisted that the pursuit of perfection did not merely require individuals to act in particular ways, but that they did so *in order to* perfect their characters.[12]

Green uses this epistemological argument as giving philosophical support to his religious views; his other names for the eternal consciousness are 'divine mind' and 'God'. His theology is based on the central importance of Christ incarnate, the union of God with man, and the reflection of God's purposes in human life and thought through the gradual unfolding of the Holy Spirit.[13] The basis of Christianity was not the historical authenticity of the account of the life of Christ contained in the gospels, but faith: 'we walk by faith, not by sight' (2 Cor. v:7) became Green's epitaph. Jesus thus became the symbolic representation of God's incarnation in the world of human affairs, and sin was a manifestation of an 'incompleteness' which was being continually eroded as humanity progressed along the path by which men came to realise God's consciousness in their minds and actions.

Richter has ascribed Green's influence among his Oxford contemporaries to his capacity to offer an escape from the spiritual uncertainties common in the second half of the nineteenth century. A prevailing 'crisis of conscience', induced in part by a growing disenchantment with the intellectual foundations of Christianity, in part by the apparent failure of Christian theology to grapple with the enormity of suffering and injustice, 'brought Green to perceive a great reservoir of energy and fervour [which] might be diverted to secular altruism from a crumbling faith focussed upon the next world'.[14] But although Richter identifies this 'energy and fervour' with evangelical Christianity, Green's form of 'immanentist incarnationalism'[15] eschewed the concern with the atonement central to evangelical theology. While the latter doctrine concentrated on the appeasement of God by the unique sacrifice of the sinless Christ for sinning mankind, Green maintained that crucifixion represented a '"death unto sin", in which we ideally partake, while at the same time, by the new consciousness of God's mind towards us which it gives, ... enables us gradually to actualise this ideal death unto sin as a new spiritual walk'.[16] This doctrine placed the emphasis squarely on men's efforts to embark upon the 'new spiritual walk', efforts which depended less on the detail and accuracy of the New Testament than on the willingness of men to reflect upon their own nature and to strive for their own perfection. The desire for reconciliation with God lay at the root of the search for perfection in both its practical and cognitive forms; it extended beyond the sphere of religion and ethics and embraced even those forms of scientific activity which seemed to question the very existence of the spiritual. 'The human spirit is one and indivisible, and the desire to know what nature is and means is as inseparable from it as the consciousness of God and the longing for reconciliation with him.'[17]

Green's theological views provide some of the clearest guides to the nature of his relationship with earlier German writers. His intellec-

tual biography and writings provide much evidence that his imma-
nentism and his conception of the universal potentialities of
Christianity independent of the veracity of accounts of an historical
Jesus owed a great deal to the work of such post-Hegelians as Baur
and other members of the Tübingen school of biblical criticism.[18]
There are also parallels between Green's theology and aspects of
Hegel's philosophical conception of Christianity, particularly with
respect to the institutional embodiment of an immanent God. Nevertheless, caution is needed in dealing with the relationship between
Green and Germans other than Kant, partly because of the fragmentary nature of the evidence (particularly in the case of Hegel), but
also because there are non-German contenders with equally plausible
claims to have influenced Green in these directions.[19] S. T. Coleridge and F. D. Maurice were both early favourites of Green, and
both expounded a form of Platonic immanentist incarnationalism
that must have at least prepared the way for Green's sympathetic
reception of German theology.[20] In any case, even if Green did succeed in capturing Hegel for unambiguously religious purposes, as the
conventional wisdom suggests, then his work must not be seen
merely as an anglicised version of Hegel's philosophy but as successfully overcoming the mid-century view that it had theologically suspect implications.[21]

IV

Green's ethics are firmly within the tradition which upholds the pri-
macy of self-realisation and, in this respect, his position has a great
deal in common with that of J. S. Mill. Green spoke warmly of Mill's
conception of human nature, but maintained that he provided a more
satisfactory basis for such a position than the equivocating hedonism
he attributed to Mill.[22] To act out of a desire for pleasure would,
Green maintained, be to act for a natural, as opposed to a moral,
object. Things are not desired because they produce pleasure, but
because we regard them as good. The pleasure a thing produces
'depends on its goodness'; 'so far as it [pleasure] is a necessary incident of any good [it] presupposes desire and results from its satisfaction'.[23] Goodness itself rests upon a conception of the self which can
be better, which more nearly approaches the perfection which is
God's, than the existing self, and thus cannot be mere sensation or
feeling. The potentialities of the self are not developed for the sake
of any pleasure this may bring, or indeed for the sake of any morally
significant goal except that of self-perfection, the perfection of the

self through the conscious efforts of the individual concerned. 'The actions which *ought* to be done . . . are actions expressive of a good will . . .'[24]

But, Green argued, the conception of the self as the good to be realised and the pursuit of this good, can only take place within a social context:

Only through society is any one enabled to give that effect to the idea of himself as an object of his actions, to the idea of a possible better state of himself, without which the idea would remain like that of space to a man who had not the senses either of sight or touch.[25]

Thus without recognition by others and of others by him, a man could have no conception of himself or his perfection. But once this mutual recognition has occurred, the individual becomes aware that his perfection is intimately related to the perfection of those upon whom he is dependent for recognition as a person. The goals which individuals pursue in seeking perfection are shared with others, and are enriched by universal attainment. The good, Green argued, must be a *common* good, and it must be non-competitive in that its attainment by some does not limit but contributes to its attainment by everyone in that society.[26]

This idea of the common good is absolutely central to Green's theory. It provides the basis on which he discusses the social and political structures and conditions necessary to the realisation of human potentialities, and the extent to which political authority could be used to facilitate the pursuit of self-perfection. It thus has a crucial role in Green's attempts to specify the rights it is proper for individuals to claim and the duty of the state to uphold, and hence in his theory of the nature and limits of the moral obligation owed to political authority. But although the social and political context has an essential role in bringing about the moral development of the individuals within it, Green always insisted that the focal point of that development was the individual rather than the social group: 'our ultimate standard of worth is an ideal of personal worth'. Collectivities have no moral existence independent of the lives of the individuals of which they are constituted: 'To speak of any progress or improvement or development of a nation or society or mankind, except as relative to some greater worth of persons, is to use words without meaning.'[27]

Green argues that the essential social dimension to individual self-realisation means that the individual must regard social institutions and practices (political organisation, customs, mores, law) as collective efforts after a common good. They are the result of the need to secure and maintain the conditions within which individuals can pursue their self-realisation in their own ways, and of the need to harmonise the ways in which they do so. As such, these institutions and practices need to be acknowledged by the individual as deserving his allegiance and consideration as essential to his own self-realisation – provided they continue to act as means to the common good and not as impediments to it.[28] Social institutions and practices cannot *make* men moral, for that requires a certain motive for acting rather than mere action itself; indeed, nor should they, for this very reason, curtail spheres of moral action by intruding a coercive apparatus in areas of life where the harm produced by wrong action is outweighed by moral benefits.[29] They do, however, have an indirect role in the 'moralisation' of the individual because they restrain people from acting from mere inclination, but they do so by appearing as an *external* authority which will impose sanctions in the event of non-compliance.[30] Green regards this imposition upon the individual's ability to act as leading to the understanding that he does have interests in common with others, and to 'a conception (under whatever name) of something that universally should be, of something absolutely desirable, of a single end or object of life'.[31] The individual may not have a very clear or articulated idea of this 'end or object of life', but he knows that there must be one, and that social institutions and conventional morality are at least means to it; hence he obeys out of conviction rather than conforms out of fear of sanctions. A few may achieve the next stage of reflective morality, 'the growth of a personal interest in the realisation of an idea of what should be, in doing what is believed to contribute to the absolutely desirable, or to human perfection, because it is believed to do so'.[32] This person obeys out of a sense of self-imposed duty towards the moral ideal; he is now truly free and autonomous since reason determines the will directly, not externally as in mere conformity to conventional morality, but as the motive for self-originated and self-determined action.

There are elements in Green's account of the progressive development of self-consciousness, of the dependence of consciousness on mutual recognition, and of the importance of social and political institutions, which are reminiscent of parts of Hegel's arguments.[33] We should be aware, however, that these merely constitute parallels rather than established connections, and that on at least one crucial point, the centrality of personality, Green is far closer to Fichte than to Hegel.[34]

In stressing considerations of personal worth, and in seeing this as

something that ultimately had to come from within individuals rather
than being forced on them by others, Green was expressing a view
which had close affinities with traditional liberal concerns with individual well-being and autonomy. The theological form of Green's
statement, however, gave it a distinctive character which relates
neither to Fichte nor to liberal social humanism. When Green wrote
of individuals as objectifying an 'eternal consciousness', and of a
'divine unity' being realised in 'the perfect art of living', he implied
that while the perfection of persons was the goal of political activity
and the starting point of political philosophy, individuality was ultimately important for religious reasons. Green's consideration of individuals and their perfection was not the result of a concern with the
defence of individuals as such, because his conception of well-being
was structured by a metaphysical, and hence religious, notion of perfection rather than by a concern with the preservation of individual
autonomy. The claim that individuals were morally significant,
because it was in them that the divine mind unfolded, also appears in
early nineteenth-century Platonists such as Coleridge and Maurice,
and beyond them in the Cambridge Platonists of the seventeenth
century. These Platonic aspects of Green's thought distinguish his
position clearly from that of the secular liberal social humanists.[35]

V

Green's ethical theory gave rise to a conception of politics which was
similar to, although not identical with, the form of liberalism associated with John Stuart Mill.[36] A concern with self-development, with
the realisation of human potentialities, necessitated an approach to
politics which placed a premium on the free action necessary for that
development. The social, political and historical significance of
Green's political philosophy has received considerable attention in
the scholarly literature, but what is often overlooked is the extent to
which Green's work marked an attempt to revive a form of formal
political philosophy which dealt with the nature of the state and the
rationale for obedience to it, and hence generated specific goals for
state action. From the perspective of formal political philosophy, it is
significant that the writers Green considered in the *Lectures* –
Hobbes, Locke, Spinoza and Rousseau – all discussed (although in
Green's view, could not adequately account for) the nature of the
state and the grounds for obedience to it, and that the one nineteenth-
century writer who attracted his critical attention, John Austin, had
side-stepped these issues through the use of an essentially empty

concept of sovereignty which had gained widespread acceptance in contemporary political theorising.[37] While accepting Austin's description of the sovereign as the possessor of supreme coercive power,[38] Green refused to treat it as exhaustive, and argued that the habitual obedience accorded the sovereign depended, to a significant extent, on a more or less conscious appreciation of the role the state played in facilitating and encouraging the pursuit of goals which were not peculiar to state-like entities but lay at the heart of all social interaction. It followed therefore that a description of the state in terms of its possession of supreme coercive capacities was inadequate *even as a description*. It also deprived statements about political obligation of any moral force, for this depended on the necessity for the state as an agent in the process of human perfection, a process which preceded the state (and could in fact be traced to the requirements of human consciousness) but was facilitated by it. Thus Green claimed that it made no sense to equate 'I am under an obligation to . . .' with 'I am forced to . . .'.[39] In his view, the question of obligation was crucial, since only if one understood the grounds of what both he and Austin acknowledged to be 'habitual obedience' could one arrive at a theory of the morally justifiable state in terms of the rationale for endowing a determinate person or persons with supreme coercive power.[40]

Green described Austin's account of sovereignty as 'abstract' because it ignored the rationale underlying the fact of habitual obedience by failing to treat the sovereign as part of a wider network of social institutions that lacked supreme coercive power. Sovereignty could only be understood in relation to the sum of institutions that made up the modern state because the basis of the sovereign's capacity to command was precisely the same as that upon which all social institutions rested. It was grounded on

a common desire for certain ends . . . to which the observance of law or established usage contributes, and in most cases implies no conscious reference on the part of those whom it influences to any coercive power at all.[41]

The citizen thus had a moral obligation to obey because the sovereign's decrees contributed to the welfare of the entire community and thus assisted the self-realisation of all.[42] An understanding of sovereignty was therefore only possible from a consideration of the true nature of the state.

The state could best be understood as the culmination of a process through which rights had been refined and extended to facilitate the fullest possible degree of self-development. Austin had regarded rights as created by the commands of the sovereign, and so thought that any obligation to recognise rights was quite independent of the nature of the right, or of the subject's perception of the value of the right. Green, by contrast, understood rights as historical phenomena that were embodied in an increasingly wide range of social institutions reflecting men's growing recognition of the conditions under which moral action was possible.[43] Institutions could only promote morality indirectly, by maintaining the conditions in which moral action was possible. They did so by maintaining rights, not as the 'arbitrary creatures of law' but as the result of 'a recognition by members of a society of powers in each other contributory to a common good'.[44] Rights rested on a 'consciousness of common interest on the part of members of a society'; hence, Green claimed, it made no sense to talk of 'natural rights' if by this was meant rights which existed independently of social attachment and recognition. Moreover, Green argued that there was a significant range of rights which 'do not come into being with the state, but arise out of social relations that may exist where the state is not . . .'[45]

One of the important features of Green's theory of rights was that their recognition contributed to the moral development of *everyone* in that society. This was clearly so in the case of the person acknowledged as having the right, but it was no less true for those who recognised it. Thus when Green discussed a particular right such as that to property, he not only stressed the positive relationship between the possession of such a right and moral development, but he also criticised those who seemed unprepared to facilitate the universalisation of an effective form of possession, on the grounds that by failing to recognise adequately the claims of others, they exhibited a flawed moral character.[46]

Green's attempt to found a theory of rights on some other basis than the sovereign's power did not mean that coercion played no part in the maintenance of rights. It did mean, however, that Green minimised this particular facet of the sovereign's role. Indeed, the less the role of the sovereign's coercive powers in the affairs of a society, the more morally developed would be the character of that society and its citizens. Furthermore, Green's attempt to divorce the essence of rights from power meant that the use or threat of force in social life had to be justified in terms of the purposes that social life helped to foster. Thus from Green's point of view, Austin's command conception of rights was unsatisfactory because rights and duties were emptied of any specific content: a right was a right merely because the sovereign declared it to be so. Green argued, however, that rights could not be understood as merely representing the will of the sovereign; they were a function of man's existence as a social being, and reflected an interest in the pursuit of the common good that had its source in the conditions of human consciousness, and hence existed in forms of community prior to the state. These earlier forms are in fact 'presupposed' by the state; they embody a 'rational principle', 'the power of conceiving a good consisting in the more perfect being of the individual and of those in whom he is interested'.[47] This 'rational principle' found increasingly complete embodiment in social institutions, the most highly developed of which is the state. But the appropriateness of institutionalised forms of social rationality depends on the extent to which they actually reflect the conscious or unconscious aspirations of the people. As Green argued in his lectures on the English revolution, attempts to establish institutions and practices that ran ahead of popular conceptions were bound to fail: the tragedies of Oliver Cromwell and Sir Henry Vane were a direct consequence of their attempt to rationalise English life at a time when neither the opinions of the population nor the level of intellectualised consciousness were ready to accept a radical restructuring of political, religious, or social life.[48]

The same theme recurs in Green's discussion of the conditions under which the subject could justifiably disobey the sovereign. He linked the character of sovereign power, the empirical reasons for obedience, and the subject's obligation to obey the sovereign to the type of social order that the sovereign existed to maintain. The capacity to command had to be explained in terms of 'the function which it [the sovereign] serves in maintaining those conditions of freedom which are the conditions of the moral life'.[49] This stipulation has important implications for Green's view of the duties the subject owed to the sovereign and the duties of the state towards the subjects. On the one hand, he argued that disobedience was justifiable, even in a democracy, provided that all legitimate avenues had been explored, that the populace could come to understand the disobedients' arguments, and that their actions seemed less likely to inhibit the pursuit of the common good than continued allegiance to and compliance with the commands of a sovereign whose performance of his functions was very imperfect.[50] On the other hand, however, Green was able to claim that the sovereign itself was under an obligation to further the common good to the greatest extent possible given the particular circumstances of the time.[51]

By relating sovereignty to the character of the state, Green was able to provide a basis for a positive conception of the state's role without abandoning the concern with individual freedom which lay at the heart of his conception of moral development. If the exercise of sovereign power was seen (as by Austin) in terms of the arbitrary will of the sovereign being forced on the subject, then presumably it was better for the subject if the sovereign did as little as possible. By arguing that the relationship between subject and sovereign was not purely coercive but depended upon the connection between the existence of political institutions and the 'impalpable congeries of the hopes and fears of a people, bound together by common interests and sympathy',[52] Green could claim that an increase in state activity in some circumstances did not necessarily impinge on the freedom of the subjects, and may in fact enhance it. The popular election of governments extended the positive relationship between the exercise of political power by the state and the awareness of individuals that there was a common good which constituted the rationale of state power. Green maintained that popular participation in decision-making was desirable since it strengthened the connection between obedience and freedom in a morally significant way, and because it acknowledged that all were capable of self-realisation and hence ought to participate in deciding the conditions under which they could pursue their own perfections.

Because Green provided a generalised description of the state which included a rationale for obedience to it, he was able to provide a framework for considering the grounds of resistance to political authority, and to consider the extent to which differing constitutional arrangements strengthened the state by facilitating the attainment of the goals through which it gained its moral status. The character of these goals, and particularly the fact that their attainment depended on their being pursued by individuals in a quest for universal perfection, provided an agenda for detailed state action which was imperative rather than permissive.[53] Green stressed, however, that the detailed formulation of programmes of state action must take account of the particular circumstances of a given community, and especially of the capacity of its members to embrace the opportunities which state action opened up.[54] Much of what Green says in the *Lectures* and elsewhere is premised upon his assessment of the potentialities for self-realisation in late nineteenth-century British society, but these immediate and, in a sense, contingent aspects of his writings should not be allowed to obscure his wider significance as a reviver and exponent of a mode of political philosophy which takes the state as its primary focus, and which was notably absent from the mainstream of nineteenth-century British political thought.

1

Lectures on the Principles of Political Obligation *

====

A. THE GROUNDS OF POLITICAL OBLIGATION

1. *a*I have entitled the subject of the course 'political obligation'. I mean that term to include both the obligation of the subject towards the sovereign, of the citizen towards the state, and the obligations of individuals to each other as enforced by a political superior.*a* My purpose is to consider the moral function or object served by law, or by the system of rights and obligations which the state enforces, and in so doing to discover the true ground or justification for obedience to law. My plan will be (1) to state in outline what I consider the true function of law to be, *b*which is*b* at the same time the true ground of our moral duty to obey *c*it (moral duty I always distinguish from legal obligation);*c* (2) to examine the chief doctrines of political obligation that have been current in modern Europe, and by criticising them to bring out more clearly the main points of *d*the*d* truer doctrine; (3) to consider in detail the chief rights and obligations enforced in civilised states, inquiring what is their justification, and what is the ground for respecting them, on the principle stated.

2. In previous lectures[1] I have explained what I understand moral goodness to be, and how it is possible that there should be such a thing; in other words, what are the conditions on the part of reason and will which are implied in our being able to conceive moral goodness as an object to be aimed at, and to give some partial reality to the conception. *a*I shall not go over the ground already traversed, but start from the point at which we there arrived.*a*

The highest moral goodness we found was an attribute of character so far as it issued in acts done for the sake of their goodness, not for the sake of any pleasure or any satisfaction of *b*desire*b* which they bring to the agent. But it is impossible that an action should be done for the sake of its goodness, unless it has been previously contemplated as good for some other reason than that which consists in its being done for the sake of its goodness. It must have been done, or conceived as possible to be done, and *have been accounted good,*

13

irrespectively of its being done from this which we ultimately come to regard as the highest motive. In other words, a prior morality, founded upon interests which are other than the pure interest in being good, and governed by rules of conduct relative to a standard of goodness other than that which makes it depend on this interest, is the condition of there coming to ^{c}be the morality of a character^c governed by interest in an ideal of goodness. Otherwise this ideal would be an empty one; it would be impossible to say what the good actions were, that were to be done for the sake of their goodness; and the interest in ^{d}it^d impossible, since it would be an interest without an object.

3. When, however, morality of the latter kind has come to be recognised as the highest, the only true, morality, the prior morality needs to be criticised from the point of view thus gained. Those interests, other than the interest in being good, which form the motives on the part of the individual on which it rests, will not indeed be rejected as of no moral value; for no one can suppose that without them, or except as regulating them, the pure interest in being good could determine conduct at all. But they will be estimated according to their value as leading up to, or as capable of becoming elements in, a character in which this interest is the governing principle. Again, those rules of conduct, according to which the terms right and wrong, good and bad, are commonly applied, and which, as was just now said, are relative to a ^{a}standard which is certainly^a not founded on the conception of good as consisting in the character described, are not indeed to be rejected; for without them there would be nothing to define the duties which the highest character is prepared to do for their own sake, but have to be revised according to a method which inquires into their rationale or justification, as conditions of approximation to the highest ^{b}character, in the sense explained^b.

4. The criticism of moral interests – of the general motives which determine moral conduct and regulate such moral approbation and disapprobation as is not based on a strict theory of moral ^{a}good – from the point of view stated may be called by the term a 'theory of the^a moral sentiments'. The criticism of recognised rules of conduct will fall under two heads according as these rules are embodied in 'positive law' (law of which the observance is enforced on the individual by a political superior) or only form part of the 'law of opinion' – part of what the individual feels to be expected of him by some person or persons to whose expectations he ought to conform.[2]

5. Moral interests are so greatly dependent on generally recognised rules of conduct that the criticism of the latter should come first. The law of opinion, again, in so many ways presupposes a social fabric

supported by 'positive' law, that we can only fairly take account of it when we have considered the moral value and justifiability of the fabric so supported. I propose therefore to begin our inquiry into the detail of goodness – into the particular kinds of conduct which the man wishing to do good for the sake of its goodness is entitled to count good – by considering what is of permanent moral value in the institutions of civil life, as established in Europe; in what way they have contributed and contribute to the possibility of morality in the higher sense of the term, and are justified, or have a moral claim upon our loyal conformity, in consequence.

6. The condition of a moral life is the possession of will and reason.[3] Will is the capacity in a man of being determined to action by the idea of a possible satisfaction of himself. An act of will is an action so determined. A state of will is the capacity as determined by the particular objects in which the man seeks self-satisfaction; which becomes a character in so far as the self-satisfaction is habitually sought in objects of a particular kind. Practical reason is the capacity in a man of conceiving the perfection of his nature as an object to be attained by action. All moral ideas have their origin in reason, i.e. in the idea of a possible self-perfection to be attained by the moral agent. This does not mean that the moral agent in every stage of his progress could state this idea to himself in an abstract form, any more than in every stage in the acquisition of knowledge about nature a man can state to himself in an abstract form the conception of the unity of nature which yet throughout conditions the acquisition of his knowledge. Ideas do not first come into existence, or begin to operate, upon the formation of an abstract expression for them. This expression is only arrived at upon analysis of a concrete experience which they have rendered possible. Thus we only learn to express the idea of self-perfection in that abstract form upon analysis of an experience of self-improvement which we have gone through ourselves, and which must have been gone through by those with whom the possession of language and an organisation of life (however elementary) connect us; but the same analysis shows that the idea must have been at work to make such experience possible. In this idea all particular moral ideas – all ideas of particular forms of conduct as *a*estimable*a* – originate, though an *b*abstract*b* expression for the latter is arrived at much sooner than such an expression for the idea in which they originate. They arise as the individual's conception of the society on the well-being of which his own depends, and of the constituents of that well-being, becomes wider and fuller; and they are embodied in the laws, institutions, and social expectation, which make conventional

^cmorality. This growth of conventional morality forms the 'moral progress of mankind'. But it must be remembered that a merely conventional morality is not a true morality; that it becomes so only^c in so far as upon habits disciplined by conformity to conventional morality there supervenes an intelligent interest in some of the objects contributory to human perfection, which that conventional morality subserves and in so far as that interest becomes the dominant interest of the character.

7. The value then of the institutions of civil life lies in their operation as giving reality to these ^acapacities, as^a enabling them to be really ^bexercised. The way in which they thus operate is what now has to be exhibited. In their^b general effect, apart from particular aberrations, they render it possible for a man to be freely determined by the idea of a possible satisfaction of himself instead of being driven this way and that by external ^cforces – thus giving^c reality to the capacity called will: and they enable him to realise his reason, i.e. his idea of self-perfection, by acting as a member of a social organisation in which each contributes to the better-being of all the rest.[4] So far as they do in fact thus operate they are morally justified, and may be said to correspond to the 'law of nature', the *jus naturæ*, according to the only sense in which that phrase can be intelligibly used.

8. There has been much controversy as to what the *jus naturæ* (*Naturrecht*) really is, or whether there is such a thing at all. The controversy, when it comes to be dealt with in English, is further embarrassed by the fact that we have no one term to represent the full meaning of *jus* or *Recht*, as a system of correlative rights and obligations, actually enforced or that should be enforced by law. The essential questions are: (1) whether we are entitled to distinguish the rights and obligations which are anywhere actually enforced by law from rights and obligations which really exist though not enforced; and (2), if we are entitled to do so, what is to be our criterion of rights and obligations which are really valid, in distinction from those that are actually enforced.

9. No one would seriously maintain that the system of rights and obligations, as it is anywhere enforced by law – the *jus* or *Recht* of any nation – is all that it ought to be. Even Hobbes holds that a law, though it cannot be unjust, may be pernicious.[5] But there has been much objection to the admission of *natural* rights and obligations. At any rate the phrase is liable to misinterpretation. It may be taken to imply that rights and obligations can exist in a 'state of nature' – a state in which every individual is free to do as he likes; that legal rights and obligations derive their authority from a voluntary act by

which individuals contracted themselves out of this state; and that the individual retains from the state of nature certain rights with which no legal obligations ought to conflict. Such a doctrine is generally admitted untenable; but it does not follow from this that there is not a true and important sense in which natural rights and obligations exist – the same sense as that in which ^aduties exist,^a though unfulfilled. There is a system of rights and obligations which *should be* maintained by law, whether it is so or not, and which may properly be called '*natural*', not in the sense in which the term 'natural' would imply that such a system ever did exist or could exist independently of force exercised by society over individuals, but 'natural' because necessary to the end which it is the vocation of ^bhuman society^b to realise.

10. The *jus naturæ*, thus understood, is at once distinguished from the sphere of moral duty, and relative to it. It is distinguished from it because admitting of enforcement by law. Moral duties do not admit of being so enforced. The question sometimes put, whether moral duties *should be* enforced by law, is really an unmeaning one, for they simply *cannot* be enforced. They are duties to act, it is true, and an act can be enforced: but duties to act *from certain dispositions and with certain motives*, and these cannot be enforced.⁶ Nay, the enforcement of the outward act, of which the moral character depends on a certain motive and disposition, may often contribute to render that motive and disposition impossible; and from this fact arises a limitation to the proper province of law in enforcing acts, which will have to be further considered below. When *obligations* then are spoken of in this connection, as part of the *jus naturæ* correlative to rights, they must always be understood not as moral duties, not as relative to states of will, but as relative to outward acts, of which the performance or omission can and should be enforced. There is a moral duty to discharge such obligations, and to do so in a certain spirit, but the obligation ^aas such, as^a that with which law has to do or ^bmay properly have^b to do, is relative to an outward act merely, and does not amount to a moral duty. There is a moral duty in regard to obligations, but there can be no obligation in regard to moral duties. Thus the *jus naturæ* – the system of rights and obligations, as it should become no less than as it actually is maintained – is distinct from morality in the proper sense. But it is relative to it. This is implied in saying that there is a moral duty in regard to actual obligations, as well as in speaking of the system of rights and obligations as it *should* become. If such language is justifiable, there must be a moral ground both for conforming to, and for seeking to develop ^cor^c

improve established ^{d}*Recht*; which^d can only lie in the moral end
served by ^{e}it.^{e}

11. Thus we begin the ethical criticism of law with two principles:
– that nothing but external acts can be matter of 'obligation' (in the restricted sense); and that, in regard to that which *can* be made matter
of obligation, the question what *should* be made matter of obligation
– the question how far rights and obligations, actually established by
law, correspond to the true *jus naturæ* – must be considered with
reference to the moral end, as serving which alone law and the obligations imposed by it have their value.^{7}

12. Before proceeding, some remarks have to be made as to what is
implied in these principles. (*a*) Does the law, or is it possible that it
should, confine its view to external acts? What exactly is meant by an
external act? In the case of obligations which I am legally punishable
for disregarding, the law, in deciding whether punishment is or is not
due, takes account of much beside the external act; and this implies
that much beside external action is involved in legal obligation. In the
case where the person or property of another is damaged by me, the
law does not inquire merely whether the act of damage was done, and
done by means of my bodily members, but whether it was done intentionally; and if not done with the direct intention of inflicting the
damage, whether the damage arose in a manner that might have been
foreseen out of something which I did intend to do: whether, again, if
it was done quite accidentally the accident was due to culpable negligence. This however does not show that the law can enforce or prevent anything but external action, but only that it is *action* which it
seeks to enforce or prevent, for without intention there is no action.
We talk indeed of a man acting against his will, but if this means
acting against intention it is what it is impossible to do. What I call an
act done against my will is either (1) an act done by someone else
using my body through superior force, as a means, ^{a}e.g. if another
uses my hand to pull the trigger of a gun by which someone is shot: in
which case there is an act, but it is not mine; or (2)^a a natural event in
which my limbs are affected in a certain way which causes certain results to another person, e.g. if the rolling of a ship throws me against
another person who is thus thrown into the water, ^{b}in which case
there is no act at all; or (3)^b an act which I do under the influence of
some strong inducement, e.g. fear of death, but which is contrary to
some strong wish. In this case the act is mine, but mine because I
intend it; because it is not against my will as = intention. In saying
then that the proper, because the only possible, function of law is to
enforce performance of or abstinence from external *actions*, it is

implied that its function is to produce or prevent certain intentions, for without intention on the part of someone there is no act.

13. But if act necessarily includes intention, what is the nature of the restriction implied in calling it external? An *external* action is a determination of will as exhibited in certain motions of the bodily members which produce certain effects in the material world; *not* a determination of the will as arising from certain motives and a certain disposition. All that the law can do is to enjoin or forbid determinations of will as exhibited in such motions, &c. It does indeed present a motive, for it enforces its injunctions and prohibitions primarily by fear – by its threat of certain consequences if its commands are disobeyed. This enforcement is not an exercise of physical force in the strict sense, for in this sense no force can produce an action since it cannot produce a determination of will; and the only way in which the law or its administrators employ such force is not in the production but in the prevention of action (as when a criminal is locked up or the police prevent mischievous persons from assaulting us or breaking into our houses). But though, in enforcing its commands by threats, the law is presenting a motive, and thus, according to our distinction, affecting action on its inner side, it does this solely for the sake of the external act. It does not regard the relation of the act to the motive fear as of any intrinsic importance. If the action is performed without this motive ever coming into play under the influence of what the moralist counts higher motives, the purpose of the law is equally satisfied. Indeed, it is always understood that its purpose is most thoroughly served when the threat of pains and penalties has ceased to be necessary, and the obligations correlative to the "rights" of individuals and of societies are fulfilled from other motives. Its business is to maintain certain conditions of life—to see that certain actions are done which are necessary to the maintenance of those conditions, others omitted which would interfere with them. It has nothing to do with the motive of the actions or omissions, on which, however, the moral value of them depends.

14. It appears, then, that legal obligations – obligations which can possibly form the subject of positive law – can only be obligations to do or abstain from certain acts, not duties of acting from certain motives, or with a certain disposition. It is not a question whether the law *should* or *should not* oblige to anything but performance of outward acts. It simply *cannot* oblige to anything else, because the only means at its command for obtaining the fulfilment of obligations are (1) threats of pain, and offers of reward, by means of which it is possible indeed to secure the general performance of certain acts, but

not their performance from the motive even of fear of the pain threatened or hope of the reward offered, much less from any higher
motive; (2) the employment of physical force, (*a*) in restraining men
disposed to violate obligations, (*b*) in forcibly applying the labour or
the property of those who violate obligations to make good the
breach, so far as is possible; (as, e.g., when the magistrate forestalls
part of a man's wages to provide for a wife whom he has deserted, or
when the property of a debtor is seized for the benefit of his creditors.)

15. Only outward acts, then, *can* be matter of legal obligation; but
what sort of outward acts *should* be matter of legal obligation? The
answer to this question arises out of the above consideration of the
means which law employs to obtain fulfilment of obligations, combined with the view of law as relative to a moral end, i.e. the formation of a society of persons acting from a certain disposition, from
interest in the society as such. Those *ª*acts should*ª* be matter of legal
injunction or prohibition of which the performance or omission, irrespectively of the motive from which it proceeds, is so necessary to the
existence of a society in which the moral end stated can be realised
that it is better for them to be done or omitted from that unworthy
motive which consists in fear or hope of legal consequences than not
to be done at all.

16. We distinguish, then, the system of rights actually maintained
and obligations actually enforced by legal sanctions (*Recht* or *jus*)
from the system of relations and obligations which *should be* maintained by such sanctions (*Naturrecht*); and we hold that those actions
or omissions should be made obligations which, when made obligations, serve a certain moral end; that this end is the ground or justification or rationale of legal obligation; and that thus we obtain a
general rule, of both positive and negative application, in regard to
the proper matter or content of legal obligation. For since the end
consists in action proceeding from a certain disposition, and since
action done from apprehension of legal consequences does not proceed from that disposition, no action should be enjoined or prohibited by law of which the injunction or prohibition interferes with
actions proceeding from that disposition, and every action should be
so enjoined of which the performance is found to produce conditions
favourable to action proceeding from that disposition, and of which
the legal injunction does not interfere with such action.

17. Does this general rule give any real guidance in the difficulties
which practically arise in regard to the province of law – as to what
should be required by law, and what left to the inclination of indi-

viduals? What cases are there or have there been of enactments which on this principle we can pronounce wrong? Have attempts ever been made by law to enforce acts as virtuous which lose their virtue when done under fear of legal penalties? It would be difficult, no doubt, to find instances of attempts to enforce by law actions of which we should say that the value lies in the disposition from which they are done – actions, e.g. of disinterested kindness – because the clear conception of virtue as depending not on outward results but on dispositions is but slowly arrived at, and has never been reflected in law. But without any strictly moral object at all, laws have been made which check the development of the moral disposition. This has been done (*a*) by legal requirements of religious observance and profession of belief, which have tended to vitiate the religious source of morality; (*b*) by prohibitions and restraints, unnecessary, or which have ceased to be necessary, for maintaining the social conditions of the moral life, and which interfere with the growth of self-reliance, with the formation of a manly conscience and sense of moral dignity – in short, with the moral autonomy which is the condition of the highest goodness; (*c*) by legal institutions which take away the occasion for the exercise of certain moral virtues (e.g. the Poor-law, which takes away the occasion for the exercise of parental forethought, filial reverence, and neighbourly kindness).[8]

18. Laws of this kind have often been objected to on the strength of a one-sided view of the function of Law; the view, viz., that its only business is to prevent interference with the liberty of the individual.[9] And this view has gained undue favour on account of the real reforms to which it has led. The laws which it has helped to get rid of were really mischievous, but mischievous for further reasons than those conceived of by the supporters of this theory. Having done its work, the theory now tends to become obstructive, because in fact advancing civilisation brings with it more and more interference with the liberty of the individual *to do as he likes*, and this theory affords a reason for resisting all positive reforms – all reforms which involve an action of the state in the way of promoting conditions favourable to moral life. It is one thing to say that the state in promoting these conditions must take care not to defeat its true end by narrowing the region within which the spontaneity and disinterestedness of true morality can have play; another thing to say that it has no moral end to serve at all, and that it goes beyond its province when it seeks to do more than secure the individual from violent interference by other individuals. The true ground of objection to 'paternal government' is not that it violates the '*laissez faire*' principle and conceives that its

office is to make people good, to promote morality, but that it *"rests
on a misconception of"* morality. The real function of government
being to maintain conditions of life in which morality shall be possible, and morality consisting in the disinterested performance of self-
imposed duties, 'paternal government' does its best to make it
impossible by narrowing the room for the self-imposition of duties
and for the play of disinterested motives.

19. The question before us, then, is: in what ways and how far do
the main obligations enforced and rights maintained by law in all civilised societies contribute to the moral end described – to establish
those conditions of life in which a true, i.e. a disinterested or unselfish, morality shall be possible? The answer to this question will be a
theory of the *jus naturæ*; i.e. it will explain how far positive law is
what it should be, and what is the ground of the duty to obey it; in
other words, of political obligation. There are two things from which
such a theory must be distinguished.

It is not an inquiry into the process by which actual law came to be
what it is; nor is it an inquiry how far actual law corresponds to and is
derived from the exercise of certain original or natural rights. It is not
the former, because the process by which the law of any nation and
the law in which civilised nations agree has come to be what it is, has
not been determined by reference to that end to which we hold that
law ought to be directed and by reference to which we criticise it.
That is to say, the process has not been determined by any such conscious reference on the part of the agents in the process. No doubt, a
desire for social good as distinct from private pleasure, for what is
good on the whole as distinct from what is good for the moment, has
been a necessary condition of it, but (1), as an agent in the development of law, this has not reached the form of a conception of moral
good according to that definition of it by which the value of law is to
be estimated; and (2) in bringing law to its present state it has been
indistinguishably blended with purely selfish passions and with the
simple struggle for existence.

20. A true theory of *jus naturæ*, a rationale of law or ideal of what it
should be, is not to be had by inquiring how far actual law corresponds to, and is derived from, the exercise of certain original or
natural rights, if that is taken to mean that we know, or can ascertain,
what rights are natural on grounds distinct from those on which we
determine what laws are justifiable, and that then we can proceed to
ascertain what laws are justifiable by deduction from such rights.
'Natural rights', so far as there are such things, are themselves relative to the moral end to which perfect law is relative. A law is not good

because it enforces 'natural rights', but because it contributes to the *ªrealisationª* of a certain end. We only discover what rights are natural by considering what powers must be secured to a man in order to the attainment of this end. These powers a perfect law will secure to their full extent. Thus the consideration of what rights are 'natural' (in the only legitimate sense) and the consideration what laws are justifiable form one and the same process, each presupposing a conception of the moral vocation of *ᵇmen.ᵇ*

21. The doctrine here asserted, that all rights are relative to moral ends or duties, must not be confused with the ordinary statement that every right implies a duty, or that rights and duties are correlative. This of course is true in the sense that possession of a right by any person both implies an obligation on the part of someone else, and is conditional upon the recognition of certain obligations on the part of the person possessing it. But what is meant is something different, viz. that the claim or right of the individual to have certain powers secured to him by society, and the counter-claim of society to exercise certain powers over the individual, alike rest on the fact that these powers are necessary to the fulfilment of *ªhisª* vocation as a moral being, to an effectual self-devotion to the work of developing the perfect character in himself and others.

22. This, however, is not the ground on which the claim in question has generally been asserted. Apart from the utilitarian theory, which first began to be applied politically by Hume,[10] the ordinary way of justifying the civil rights of individuals, i.e. the powers secured to them by law as against each other, as well as the rights of the state against individuals, i.e. the powers which, with the general approval of society, it exercises against them, has been to deduce them from certain supposed prior rights, called natural rights. In the exercise of these natural rights, it has been supposed, men with a view to their general interest established political society. From that establishment is derived both the system of rights and obligations maintained by law as between man and man, and the right of the state to the submission of its subjects. If the question then is raised, why I ought to respect the legal rights of my neighbours, to pay taxes, or have my children vaccinated, serve in the army if the state requires it, and generally submit to the law, the answer according to this theory will be that if I fail to do so I shall directly or indirectly be violating the natural rights of other men; directly in those cases where the legal rights of my neighbours are also natural rights, as they very well may be (e.g. rights of liberty or personal safety); indirectly where this is not the case, because, although the rights of the state itself are not

natural and many rights exercised by individuals would not only not
be secured but would not exist at all but for legal enactment, yet the
state itself results from a covenant which originally in the exercise of
their natural rights men made with each other, and to which all born
under the state and sharing the advantages derived from it must be
considered parties. There is a natural right, therefore, on the part of
each member of a state to have this compact observed, with a corresponding obligation to observe it; and this natural right of all is violated by any individual who refuses to obey the law of the state or to
respect the rights, not in themselves natural, which the state confers
on individuals.

23. This, on the whole, was the form in which the ground of political obligation, the justification of established rights, was presented
throughout the seventeenth century, and in the eighteenth till the rise
of the 'utilitarian' theory of obligation. Special adaptations of it were
made by Hobbes and others. In Hobbes, perhaps (of whom more
later), may be found an effort to fit an anticipation of the utilitarian
theory of political obligation into the received theory which traced
political obligation, by means of the supposition of a primitive contract, to an origin in natural right. But in him as much as anyone the
language and framework of the theory of compact is retained, even if
an alien doctrine may be read between the lines. Of the utilitarian
theory of political obligation more shall be said later.[11] It may be presented in a form in which it would scarcely be distinguishable from
the doctrine just now stated,[12] the doctrine, viz., that the ground of
political obligation, the reason why certain powers should be recognised as belonging to the state and certain other powers as secured by
the state to individuals, lies in the fact that these powers are necessary
to the fulfilment of man's vocation as a moral being, to an effectual
self-devotion to the work of developing the perfect character in himself and others. Utilitarianism proper, however, recognises no vocation of man but the attainment of pleasure and avoidance of pain.[13]
The only reason why civil rights *should be* respected – the only justification of them – according to it, would be that more pleasure is
attained or pain avoided by the general respect for them; the ground
of our consciousness that we ought to respect them, in other words
their ultimate sanction, is the fear of what the consequences would be
if we did not. This theory and that which I deem true have one negative point in common. They do not seek the ground of actual rights in
a prior natural right, but in an end to which the maintenance of the
rights contributes. They avoid the mistake of identifying the inquiry
into the ultimate justifiability of actual rights with the question

whether there is a prior right to the possession of them. The right to the possession of them, if properly so called, would not be a mere power, but a power recognised by a society as one which *should* exist. This recognition of a power, in some way or other, as that which should be, is always necessary to render it a right. Therefore when we had shown that the rights exercised in political society were derived from prior 'natural' rights, a question would still remain as to the ground of those natural rights. We should have to ask why certain powers were recognised as powers which *should* be exercised, and thus became these natural rights.

24. Thus, though it may be possible and useful to show how the more seemingly artificial rights are derived from rights more simple and elementary, how the rights established by law in a political society are derived from rights that may be called natural, not in the sense of being prior to society but in the sense of being prior to the existence of a society governed by written law or a recognised sovereign, still such derivation is no justification of them. It is no answer to the question why they *should be* respected; because this question remains to be asked in regard to the most primitive rights themselves. Political or civil rights, then, are not to be explained by derivation from natural rights, but in regard to both political and natural rights, in any sense in which there can be truly said to be natural rights, the question has to be asked, how it is that certain powers are recognised by men in their intercourse with each other as powers that *should be* exercised, or of which the possible exercise *should be* secured.

25. I have tried to show in lectures on morals[14] that the conception expressed by the 'should be' is not identical with the conception of a right possessed by some man or men, but one from which the latter conception is derived. It is, or implies on the part of whoever is capable of it, the conception of an ideal, unattained condition of himself, as an absolute end. Without this conception the recognition of a power as a right would be impossible. A power on the part of anyone is so recognised by others, as one which should be exercised, when these others regard it as in some way a means to that ideal good of themselves which they alike conceive: and the possessor of the power comes to regard it as a right through consciousness of its being thus recognised as contributory to a good in which he too is interested. No one therefore can have a right except (1) as a member of a society, and (2) of a society in which some common good is recognised by the members of the society as their own ideal good, as that which *should be* for each of them. The capacity for being determined by a good so

recognised is what constitutes personality in the ethical sense; and for this reason there is truth in saying that only among persons, in the ethical sense, can there come to be rights; (which is quite compatible with the fact that the logical disentanglement of the conception of rights precedes that of the conception of the legal person; and that the conception of the moral person, in its abstract and logical form, is not arrived at till after that of the legal person).

Conversely, everyone capable of being determined by the conception of a common good as his own ideal good, as that which unconditionally should be (of being in that sense an end to himself), in other words, every moral person, is capable of rights; i.e. of bearing his part in a society in which the free exercise of his powers is secured to each member through the recognition by each of the others as entitled to the same freedom with himself. To say that he is capable of rights, is to say that he *ought* to have them, in that sense of '*ought*' in which it expresses the relation of man to an end conceived as absolutely good, to an end which, whether desired or no, is conceived as intrinsically desirable. The moral capacity implies a consciousness on the part of the subject of the capacity that its realisation is an end desirable in itself, and rights are the condition of realising it. Only through the possession of rights can the power of the individual freely to make a common good his own have reality given to it. Rights are what may be called the negative realisation of this power. That is, they realise it in the sense of providing for its free exercise, of securing the treatment of one man by another as equally free with himself, but they do not realise it positively, because their possession does not imply that in any active way the individual makes a common good his own. The possession of them, however, is the condition of this positive realisation of the moral capacity, and they ought to be possessed because this end (in the sense explained) *ought to be* attained.

26. Hence on the part of every person ('*person*' in the moral sense explained) the claim, more or less articulate and reflected on, to rights on his own part is co-ordinate with his recognition of rights on the part of others. The capacity to conceive a common good as one's own and to regulate the exercise of one's powers by reference to a good which others recognise, carries with it the consciousness that powers *should be* so exercised; which means that there *should be* rights, that powers should be regulated by mutual recognition. There ought to be rights, because the moral personality – the capacity on the part of an individual for making a common good his own – ought to be developed; and it is developed through rights; i.e. through the recognition by members of a society of powers in each other contri-

butory to a common good and the regulation of those powers by that recognition.

27. In saying that only among 'persons' can there come to be rights, and that every 'person' should have rights, I have been careful to explain that I use 'person' in the moral, not merely in the legal, sense. In dealing, then, with such phrases as *'jura personarum'* and 'personal rights', we must keep in view the difference between the legal and ethical sense of the proposition that all rights are personal, or subsist as between persons. In the legal sense, so far as it is true – and it is so only if 'person' is used in the sense of Roman law – it is an identical proposition. A person means a subject of rights and nothing more. Legal personality is derived from the possession of right, not *vice versa*. Like other identical propositions, its use is to bring out and emphasise in the predicate what is included in the understood connotation of the subject; to remind us that when we speak of rights we imply the existence of parties, in English phraseology, capable of suing and being sued. In the ethical sense, it means that rights are derived from the possession of personality as = a rational will (or the capacity which man possesses of being determined to action by the conception of such a perfection of his being as involves the perfection of a society in which he lives), in the sense (*a*) that only among beings possessed of rational will can there come to be rights, (*b*) that they fulfil their idea, or are justifiable, or such rights as should be rights, only as contributing to realisation of rational will. It is important to bear this distinction in mind in order that the proposition in its ethical sense, which can stand on its own merits, may not derive apparent confirmation from a juristic truism.

28. The moral idea of personality is constantly tending to affect the legal conception of the relation between rights and persons. Thus the *jura personarum*, which properly = either rights arising out of 'status', or rights which not only (like all rights) reside in someone having a legal status and are available against others having a legal status, but are exercised over, or in respect of, someone possessed of such status (e.g. a wife or *ᵃa free servant)ᵃ* come to be understood as rights derived from the human personality or belonging to man as man. It is with some such meaning that English writers on law speak of rights to life and liberty as personal rights. The expression might seem pleonastic, since no right can exist except as belonging to a person in the legal sense. They do not use the phrase either pleonastically or in the sense of the Roman lawyers' *jura personarum* above, but in the sense that these rights are immediately derived from, or necessarily attach to, the human personality in whatever that personality

is supposed to consist. There is no doubt, however, that historically the conception of the moral person, in any abstract form, is not
arrived at till after that of the legal person has been thus disentangled
and formulated; and further that the abstract conception of the legal
person, as the sustainer of rights, is not arrived at till long after rights
have been actually recognised and established. But the disentanglement or abstract formulation of the conception of moral personality is
quite a different thing from the action of the consciousness in which
personality consists.

29. The capacity, then, on the part of the individual of conceiving a
good as the same for himself and others, and of being determined to
action by that conception, is the foundation of rights; and rights are
the condition of that capacity being realised. No right is justifiable or
should be a right except on the ground that directly or indirectly it
serves this purpose. Conversely every power should be a right, i.e.
society should secure to the individual every power, that is necessary
for realising this capacity. Claims to such powers as are directly
necessary to a man's acting as a moral person at all – acting under the
conception of a good as the same for self and others – may be called in
a special sense personal rights (though they will include more than
Stephen includes under that designation);[15] they may also be called,
if we avoid misconceptions connected with these terms, 'innate' or
'natural' rights. They are thus distinguished from others which are
(1) only indirectly necessary to the end stated, or (2) are so only
under special conditions of society; as well as from claims which rest
merely on legal enactment and might cease to be enforced without
any violation of the *jus naturæ*.

30. The objection to calling them 'innate' or 'natural', when once it
is admitted on the one side that rights are not arbitrary creations of
law or custom but that there are certain powers which ought to be
secured as rights, on the other hand that there are no rights antecedent to society, none that men brought with them into a society
which they 'contracted' to form, is mainly one of words. They are
'innate' or 'natural' in the same sense in which according to Aristotle
the state is natural – not in the sense that they actually exist when a
man is born and that they have actually existed as long as the human
race – but that they arise out of, and are necessary for the fulfilment
of, a moral capacity without which a man would not be a man.[16]
There cannot be 'innate' rights in any other sense than that in which
there are innate duties, of which, however, much less has been heard.
Because a group of beings are capable each of conceiving an absolute
good of himself and of conceiving it to be good for himself as identical

with, and because identical with, the good of the rest of the group, there arises for each a consciousness that the common good should be the object of action, i.e. a duty, and a claim in each to a power of action that shall be at once secured and regulated by consciousness of a common good on the part of the rest, i.e. a right. There is no ground for saying that the right arises out of a primary human capacity, and is thus 'innate' which does not apply equally to the duty.

31. The dissociation of *a*"innate"*a* rights from 'innate' duties has gone along with the delusion that such rights existed apart from society. Men were supposed to have existed in a state of nature, which was not a state of society, but in which certain rights attached to them as individuals, and then to have formed societies by contract or covenant. Society having been formed, certain other rights arose through positive enactment; but none of these, it was held, could interfere with the natural rights which belonged to men antecedently to the social contract or survived it.

Such a theory can only be stated by an application to an imaginary state of things, prior to the formation of societies as regulated by custom or law, of terms that have no meaning except in relation to such societies. 'Natural right', as = right in a state of nature which is not a state of society, is a contradiction. There can be no right without a consciousness of common interest on the part of members of a society. Without this there might be certain powers on the part of individuals, but no recognition of these powers by others as powers of which they allow the exercise, nor any claim to such recognition, and without this recognition or claim to recognition there can be no right.

B. SPINOZA

32. Spinoza is aware of this. In the *Tractatus Politicus*, he says 'By the right of nature, then, I mean the actual laws or rules of nature in accordance with which all things come to be; that is, the actual power of nature . . . Hence everything a man does in accordance with the laws of his nature, he does by the sovereign right of nature, and he has as much right against other things in nature as he has power and strength' (II.4).[1] If only, seeing that the *jus naturæ* [law of naure] was mere *potentia* [power], he had denied that it was *jus* at all, he would have been on the right track. Instead of that, however, he treats it as properly *jus*, and consistently with this regards all *jus* as mere *potentia*: nor is any *jus humanum* [human law] according to him, guided by or the product of reason. It arises, in the modern phrase, out of the 'struggle for existence'. As Spinoza says ' . . . men

are led more by blind desire than by reason; and so their natural
power, or natural right, must not be defined in terms of reason, but
must be held to cover every possible appetite by which they are determined to act, and by which they try to preserve themselves' (II.5).
The *jus civile* [civil law] is simply the result of the conflict of natural
powers, which = natural rights, which arises from the effort of every
man to gratify his passions and 'preserve his own being'. Man is
simply a *pars naturæ* [part of nature], the most crafty of the animals.
'In so far as men are tormented by anger, envy, or any passion involving hatred, they are divided and at odds with one another; and are the
more to be feared because they are more powerful, more cunning and
astute, than other creatures. But men are by nature subject to these
passions in the highest degree ... so men are by nature
enemies' (II.14). Universal hostility means universal fear, and fear
means weakness. It follows that in the state of nature there is nothing
fit to be called *potentia* or consequently *jus*;

I therefore conclude that the right of nature peculiar to human beings can
scarcely be conceived save where men hold rights as a body, and thus have
the power to defend their possession of territories which they can inhabit and
cultivate, to protect themselves, to repel all force, and to live in accordance
with the common judgement of all. For (by section 13 of this Chapter) the
more men there be that unite in this way, the more right they collectively possess; ... (II.15).

The collective body, i.e., has more *jus in naturam* [right in nature],
i.e. *potentiam*, than any individual could have singly (II.13). In the
advantage of this increased *jus in naturam* the individual shares. On
the other hand,

Where men hold rights as a body, and are all guided as if by one mind, then,
of course, (by Section 13 of this Chapter) each of them has the less right the
more the rest together exceed him in power; that is, his only real right against
other things in nature is what the corporate right allows him. In other matters he must carry out every command laid upon him by the common decision; or (by Section 4 of this Chapter) be compelled to do so by right
(II.16).

This *jus* by which the individual's actions are now to be regulated, is
still simply *potentia*. 'This corporate right, which is defined by the
power of a people, is generally called sovereignty...' (II.17). It is
not to be considered anything different from *jus naturæ*. It is simply
the *naturalis potentia* of a certain number of men combined; 'of a
people which is guided as if by one mind' (III.2).

Thus in the *status civilis* [civil state] the *jus naturæ* of the individual in one sense disappears, in another does not. It disappears in the sense that the individual member of the state has no mind to act or power to act against the mind of the state. Anyone who had such a mind or power would not be a member of the state. He would be an enemy against whose *potentia* the state must measure its own. On the other hand, *in statu civili*, just as much as *in statu naturali*, 'man acts in accordance with the laws of his own nature and pursues his own advantage' (III.3). He exercises his *naturalis potentia* for some natural end of satisfying his wants and preserving his life as he did or would do outside the *status civilis*. Only *in status civilis* these motives on the part of individuals so far coincide as to form the 'one mind' (II.16) which directs the 'power of the people' (II.17).

According to this view, any member of a state will have just so much *jus*, i.e. *potentia*, against other members as the state allows him. If he can exercise any *jus* or *potentia* against another 'on his own judgement' (III.3), he is so far not a member of the state and the state is so far imperfect. If he could exercise any *jus* or *potentia* against the state itself, there would be no state, or, which is the same, the state would not be *sui juris* [autonomous].

33. Is there then no limit to the *jus* which the state may exercise? With Spinoza this is equivalent to the question, is there no limit to the *potentia* which it can exercise? As to this, he suggests three considerations.

(1) Its power is weakened by any action against right reason, because this must weaken the 'union of minds' on which it is founded. '... [T]he right of a commonwealth is determined by the power of a people guided as if by one mind; but this union of minds is quite inconceivable unless the commonwealth does its best to achieve those conditions which sound reason declares to be for the good of all men' (III.7). And it is a contradiction to say that the state has a right to weaken its own power.

(2) The 'right' or 'power' of the state depends on its power of affecting the hopes and fears of individual citizens. 'Subjects are under the control of the commonwealth, and not possessed of their own right, only in so far as they fear its power or its threats, or in so far as they love the political order (by Section 10 of the previous Chapter). It follows that all actions which no one can be induced to do by rewards or threats fall outside the right of the commonwealth' (III.8). Whatever cannot be achieved by rewards and threats is beyond the power and therefore beyond the 'right' of the state. Examples are given in the same section.[2]

(3) '... commands which arouse the indignation of a great number of subjects hardly fall within the right of the common-wealth.' Severities of a certain kind lead to conspiracies against the state, and thus weaken it; '... what is true of each citizen, or of each man in the state of nature, is true of a commonwealth also; the greater cause for fear it has, the less is it possessed of its own right' (III.9).

Just so far then as there are certain things which the state cannot do, or by doing which it lessens its power, so far there are things which it has no 'right' to do.

34. Spinoza proceeds to consider the relation of states or sovereign powers to each other. Here the principle is simple. They are to each other as individuals in the state of nature, except that they will not be subject to the same weaknesses.

For since (by Section 2 of this Chapter) the right of the sovereign is simply the right of nature itself, two states are in the same relation to one another as two men in the condition of nature; with this exception, that a common-wealth can guard itself against being subjugated by another, as a man in the state of nature cannot do. For, of course, a man is overcome by sleep every day, is often afflicted by disease of body or mind, and is finally prostrated by old age; in addition, he is subject to other troubles against which a common-wealth can make itself secure (III.11).

In other words '... two commonwealths are enemies by nature. For men in the state of nature are enemies ...; and so all who retain the right of nature, and are not united in a single commonwealth, remain enemies' (III.13). 'Rights to make war' are simply the powers of any one state to attack or defend itself against another. 'Rights to maintain peaceful relations' (III.13), on the other hand, do not appertain to any single state, but arise out of the agreement of two at least. They last as long as the agreement, the *foedus*, lasts; and this lasts as long as the fear or hope, which led to its being made, continues to be shared by the states which made it (III.14). As soon as this ceases to be the case, the agreement is necessarily at an end, '[and a state] cannot be accused of treachery or perfidy because it breaks faith as soon as its reason for fear or hope is removed. For in this respect each contract-ing party was on precisely the same footing; if it could be the first to free itself from fear it would gain possession of its own right, and would use it as its own judgement dictated' (III.14).

35. It would seem to follow from the above that a state can do no wrong, in the sense that there are no rights that it can violate. The same principle is applicable to it as to the individual; '... there is no sin in the state of nature; or rather, ... if anyone sins, it is against

himself, and not against others . . . [the law of nature] forbids absolutely nothing that is within human power' (II.18). A state is to any other state, and to its subjects, as one individual against another *in statu naturali*. A wrong, a *peccatum*, consists in a violation by individuals of the *commune decretum* [common decree]. There can be no *peccare* on the part of the *commune decretum* itself. But

I do not assert that everything which I say is done in the best way. It is one thing to cultivate a field by right, and another to cultivate it in the best way; it is one thing, I say, to defend and preserve oneself, to give judgement and so on by right, another to defend and preserve oneself in the best way, and to give the best judgement. In consequence, it is one thing to rule and have charge of public affairs by right, another to rule and direct public affairs in the best way. So now that I have dealt with the right of commonwealths in general, it is time for me to discuss their best condition. (V.1)

Hence a further consideration 'of the best condition of commonwealths' (V.1). This is guided by reference to the '*finis status civilis* [purpose of the political order]', which is '*pax vitaeque securitas*' ['peace and security of life'; V.2]. Accordingly that is the best government under which men live in harmony and of which the rights are kept inviolate. Where this is not the case the fault lies with the government, not with any 'wickedness of its subjects. For citizens are not born, but made. Besides, man's natural passions are not the same everywhere . . .' (V.2).

The end is not fully attained where men are merely kept in order by fear. Such a state of things is not peace but merely absence of war. 'For peace is not absence of war, but a virtue based on strength of mind [*animi fortitudine*];[3] since . . . obedience is the steadfast will to do what the general decree of the commonwealth requires' (V.4).

The 'peace', then, which it is the end of the state to obtain, consists in rational virtue; in a common mind, governed by desire on the part of each individual for perfection of being in himself and others. The harmony of life, too, which is another way of expressing its object, is to be understood in an equally high sense. The life spoken of is one 'characterised primarily by reason, the true virtue and life of the mind' (V.5).

The *imperium* [sovereignty] which is to contribute to this end must clearly be one 'established by a free people, and not . . . a tyranny acquired over a people by the right of war' (V.6). Between the two forms of *imperium* there may be no essential difference in respect of the *jus* which belongs to each, but there is the greatest in respect of the ends which they serve as well as in the means by which they have to be maintained' (V.6).

36. This conclusion of Spinoza's doctrine of the state does not seem really consistent with the beginning. *At the outset,* no motives are recognised in men but such as render them *natura hostes* [natural enemies]. From the operation of these motives the state is supposed to result. Each individual finds that the war of all against all is weakness for all. Consequently the desire on the part of each to strengthen himself, which is a form of the universal effort 'to preserve his own being' (II.5), leads to combination, it being discovered that 'nothing is more useful to man than man' (*Ethic*, IV.18, Schol.). But we are expressly told that the civil state does not bring with it other motives than those operative *in statu naturali*. 'The fact is that man acts in accordance with the laws of his own nature and pursues his own advantage in both the natural and the political order' (III.3). But then it appears that there supervenes or may supervene on such motives '. . . the steadfast will to do what the general decree of the commonwealth requires' (V.4), and that not of a kind which seeks to carry out the *commune decretum* as a means of escaping pain or obtaining pleasure, for it is said to arise from the *animi fortitudo* which rests on reason ('related to the mind in so far as it thinks' – *Ethic*, III.59, Schol.) and includes *generositas* defined as above. It is also said that the true object of *imperium* is '*vitam concorditer tanigere*' ['living in harmony'] or '*vitam colere*' ['improving life'] in a sense of *vita* in which it is 'characterised primarily by reason' (V.5). And as the *imperium* established for this end is one which is 'established by a free people' (V.6), it seems[4] to be implied that there is a desire for such an end on the part of the people. It is not explained how such desires should arise out of the conflict of *naturales potentiæ* or out of the impulses which render men *natura hostes*. On the other hand, if the elements of them already exist in the impulses which lead to the formation of the *status civilis*, the reasons for saying that men are *natura hostes* disappear, and we get a different view of *jus* whether *naturale* or *civile* from that which identifies it simply with *potentia*. Some power of conceiving and being interested in a good *as common*, some identification of the *esse* of others with *suum esse* which every man, as Spinoza says, seeks to preserve and promote, must be supposed in those who form the most primitive social combinations if these are to issue in a state directed to such ends and maintained by such a 'steadfast will'[5] as Spinoza describes. And it is the interest of men in a common good, the desire on the part of each which he thinks of others as sharing, for a good which he conceives to be equally good

for them, that transforms mere *potentia* into what may fitly be called *jus*, i.e. a power claiming recognition as exercised or capable of being exercised for the common good.

37. If this qualification of *potentia* which alone renders it *jus* had been apprehended by Spinoza, he would have been entitled to speak of a *jus naturale* [natural law] as preceding the *jus civile*, i.e. of claims to the recognition of powers and the actual customary recognition of such, as exercised for a common good, preceding the establishment of any regular institutions or general laws for securing their exercise. As it is, the term *jus naturale* is with him really unmeaning. If it means no more than *potentia*, why call it *jus*?

Jus might have a meaning distinct from that of *potentia* in the sense of a power which a certain *imperium* enables one man to exercise as against another. This is what Spinoza understands by *jus civile*. But there is no need to qualify it as *civile*, unless *jus* may be employed with some other qualification and with a distinctive meaning. But the *jus naturale*, as he understands it, has no meaning other than that of *potentia*, and his theory as it stands would have been more clearly expressed if instead of *jus naturale* and *jus civile* he had spoken of *potentia* and *jus*, explaining that the latter was a power on the part of one man against others, maintained by means of an *imperium* which itself results from a combination of 'powers'. He himself in one passage shows a consciousness of the impropriety of speaking of *jus* except with reference to a community; '... the right of nature peculiar to human beings can scarcely be conceived save where men hold rights as a body, and thus have the power to defend their possession of territories which they can inhabit and cultivate, to protect themselves, to repel all force, and to live in accordance with the common judgement of all' (II.15). He takes no notice, however, of any forms of community more primitive than that of the state.[6] The division into the *status naturalis* and the *status civilis* he seems to treat as exhaustive, and the *status naturalis* he regards, after the manner of his time, as one of pure individualism, of simple detachment of man from man, or of detachment only modified by conflict. Such a *status naturalis* lacks both the natural and the rational principles of social development – the natural principle, i.e. the interest in others arising primarily from family ties, and the rational principle, i.e. the power of conceiving a good consisting in the more perfect being of the individual and of those in whom he is interested. No process could be *a*traced from it to*a* the *status civilis*. The two *status* stand over against each other with an impassable gulf between. 'Citizens are not born but made' (V.2). They are so made, he seems to

hold, by the action of the *imperium* upon them. But how is the
imperium to be made? Men must first be, if not *civiles*, yet something
very different from what they are in the *status naturalis*, between
which and the *status civilis* Spinoza recognises no middle term,
before any *imperium* which could render them *civiles* could be
possible.

38. The cardinal error of Spinoza's *Politics* is the admission of the
possibility of a right in the individual apart from life in society, apart
from the recognition by members of a society of a correlative claim
upon and duty to each other, as all interested in one and the same
good. The error was the error of his time, but with Spinoza it was
confirmed by his rejection of final causes. The true conception of
'right' depends on the conception of the individual as being what he
really is in virtue of a function which he has to fulfil relatively to a certain end, that end being the common well being of a society. A 'right'
is an ideal attribute ('ideal' in the sense of not being sensibly verifiable, not reducible to any perceivable fact or facts) which the individual possesses so far as this function is in some measure freely
fulfilled by him – i.e. fulfilled with reference to or for the sake of the
end – and so far as the ability to fulfil it is secured to him through its
being recognised by the society as properly belonging to him. The essence of right lies in its being not simply a power producing sensible
effects, but a power relative to an insensible function and belonging
to individuals only in so far as each recognises that function in himself
and others. It is not in so far as I can do this or that that I have a right
to do this or that, but so far as I recognise myself and am recognised
by others as able to do this or that for the sake of a common good, or
so far as in the consciousness of myself and others I have a function
relative to this end. Spinoza, however, objects to regard anything as
determined by relation to a final cause. He was not disposed therefore
to regard individuals as being what they are in virtue of functions
relative to the life of society, still less as being what they are in virtue
of the recognition by each of such functions in himself and others. He
looked upon man, like everything else in nature, as determined by
material and efficient causes, and as himself a material and efficient
cause. But as such he has no 'rights' or 'duties' but only 'powers'.

39. It was because Plato and Aristotle conceived the life of the *polis*
[state][7] so clearly as the *telos* [end] of the individual, relation to
which makes him what he is – the relation in the case of the *politēs*
[citizen] proper being a conscious or recognised relation – that they
laid the foundation for all true theory of 'rights'. It is true that they
have not even a word for 'rights'. The claims which in modern times

have been advanced on behalf of the individual against the state under the designation 'natural rights' are most alien from their way of thinking. But in saying that the *polis* was a 'natural' institution and that man was *phusei politikos* [political by nature] Aristotle, according to the sense which he attached to *polis*, was asserting the doctrine of 'natural rights' in the only sense in which it is true. He regards the state (*polis*) as a society of which the life is maintained by what its members do for the sake of maintaining it – by functions consciously fulfilled with reference to that end, which in that sense imposes duties – and from which at the same time its members derive the ability, through education and protection, to fulfil their several functions, which in that sense confers rights. It is thus that the *politēs metechei tou archein kai tou archesthai* [the citizen participates both in ruling and in being ruled].[8] Man, being *phusei politēs* [by nature a citizen] – being already in respect of capacities and tendencies a member of such a society, existing only in *koinōniai* [associations] which contain its elements – has 'naturally' the correlative duties and rights which the state imposes and confers. Practically it is only the Greek man that Aristotle regards as *phusei politēs*, but the Greek conception of citizenship once established was applicable to all men capable of a common interest.[9] This way of conceiving the case, however, depends on the 'teleological' view of man and the forms of society in which he is found to live, i.e. on the view of men as being what they are in virtue of insensible functions and of certain forms of *^a*life as determined*^a* by relation to more perfect forms which they have the capacity or tendency to become.

40. Spinoza, like Bacon, found the assumption of ends which things were meant to fulfil in the way of accurate inquiry into what things are (materially) and do. He held Plato and Aristotle cheap as compared with Democritus and Epicurus (Letter LVI).[10] Accordingly he considers the individual apart from his vocation as a member of society, the state apart from its office as enabling the individual to fulfil that vocation. Each so considered is merely a vehicle of so much power (natural force). On the other hand, he recognises a difference between a higher and lower, a better and worse, state of *^acivil^a* society, and a possibility of seeking the better state because it is understood to be better. And this is to admit the possibility of the course of human affairs being affected by the *conception* of a final cause. It is characteristic of Spinoza that while he never departs from the principle 'man is simply a *pars naturæ*' (II.5), he ascribes to him the faculty of understanding the order of nature, and of conforming to it or obeying it in a new way on account of that understanding. In

other words, he recognised the distinction called by Kant the distinction between determination according to law and determination according to the consciousness of law;[11] though in his desire to assert the necessity of each kind of determination he tends to disguise the distinction and to ignore the fact that, if rational determination or the determination by a conception of a law is a part of nature, it is so in quite a different sense from determination merely according to laws of nature. As he puts it, the clear understanding that we are parts of nature, and of our position in the universe of things, will yield a new character. We shall only then desire what is ordained for us and shall find rest in the truth, in the knowledge of what is necessary. This he regards as the highest state of the individual, and the desire to attain it he evidently considers the supreme motive by which the individual should be governed. The analogue in political life to this highest state of the individual is the direction of the *imperium* by a '*libera multitudo*' ['free people'] to the attainment of '*pax vitaeque securitas*' (V.2), in the high sense which he attaches to those words in *Tractatus Politicus*, ch. V.[12]

41. The conclusion then is that Spinoza did really, though not explicitly, believe in a final cause determining human life. That is to say, he held that the conception of an end consisting in the greater perfection of life on the part of the individual and the community might, and to some extent did, determine the life of the individual and the community. He would have said no doubt that this end, like every good, existed only in our consciousness; that it was 'nothing positive in things considered in themselves' (*Ethic*, IV, Preface), but an existence of the end in human consciousness, determining human action, is a sufficiently real existence, without being 'positive in things'. But he made the mistake of ignoring the more confused and mixed forms in which the conception of this end operates; of recognising it only in the forms of the philosophic 'love of God', or in the wisdom of the exceptional citizen, whom alone he would admit are guided by reason. And in particular he failed to notice that it is the consciousness of such an end to which his powers may be directed that constitutes the individual's claim to exercise them as rights, just as it is the recognition of them by a society as capable of such direction which renders them actually rights; in short that, just as according to him nothing is good or evil but thinking makes it so, so it is only thinking that makes a might a right – a certain conception of the might as relative to a social good on the part at once of the person or persons exercising it and of a society which it affects.

C. HOBBES

42. All the more fruitful elements in Spinoza's political doctrine are
lacking in Hobbes', but the principle of the two theories is very much
the same. Each begins with the supposition of an existence of human
individuals, unaffected by society, and each struggling for existence
against the rest so that men are *natura hostes* [natural enemies]. Each
conceives *jus naturale* [natural law] as = *potentia naturalis* [natural
power]. But Spinoza carries out this conception much more consistently. He does not consider that the natural right, which is might,
ceases to exist or becomes anything else when a multitude combine
their natural rights or mights in an *imperium* [sovereignty]. If the ostensible *imperium* comes into collision with the powers of individuals, single or combined, among those who have hitherto been
subject to it and proves the weaker, it *ipso facto* ceases to be an
imperium. Not having superior power, it no longer has superior right
to the *subditi* [subjects]. It is on this principle, as we have seen, that
he deals with the question of limitations to the right of a sovereign. Its
rights are limited because its powers are so. Exercised in certain ways
and directions they defeat themselves. Thus as he puts it in Letter L
(where he points out his difference from Hobbes), '. . . the Supreme
Power in a State has no more right over a subject than is proportionate to the power by which it is superior to the subject'.[1] Hobbes on the
other hand supposes his sovereign power to have an absolute right to
the submission of all its subjects, singly or collectively, irrespectively
of the question of its actual power against them. This right he considers it to derive from a convenant by which individuals, weary of
the state of war, have agreed to devolve their *personæ*, in the language
of Roman law, upon some individual or collection of individuals
which is henceforward to represent them, and to be considered as
acting with their combined powers. This covenant being in the
nature of the case irrevocable, the sovereign derives from it an inde-
feasible right to direct the actions of all members of the society over
which it is sovereign.

43. The doctrine may be found in *Leviathan*, Part II, chapter 17.[2]
In order

to erect such a common power, as may be able to defend them from the invasion of foreigners, and the injuries of one another, [men] confer all their
power and strength upon one man, or upon one assembly of men, [i.e.]
appoint one man, or assembly of men, to bear their person . . . This is more
than consent, or concord; it is a real unity of them all, in one and the same

person, made by covenant of every man with every man, in such manner, as if every man should say to every man, *I authorise, and give up my right of governing myself, to this man, or to this assembly of men, on this condition, that thou give up thy right to him, and authorise all his actions in like manner.* This done, the multitude so united in one person is called a COMMON-WEALTH, in Latin CIVITAS ... which, to define it, is *one person, of whose acts a great multitude, by mutual covenant one with another, have made themselves every one the author, to the end he may use the strength and means of them all, as he shall think expedient, for their peace and common defence.* And he that carrieth this person, is called SOVEREIGN, and said to have *sovereign power*; and every one besides, his SUBJECT.

44. In order to understand the form in which the doctrine is stated, we have to bear in mind the sense in which *persona* is used by the Roman lawyers, as = either a complex of rights, or the subject (or possessor) of those rights, whether a single individual or a corporate body. In this sense of the word, a man's person is separable from his individual existence as a man. '*Unus homo sustinet plures personae*' ['Each man has many *personas*']. A magistrate, e.g. would be one thing in respect of what he is in himself, another thing in respect of his *persona* or complex of rights belonging to him as a magistrate, and so too a monarch. On the same principle, a man remaining a man as before, might devolve his *persona*, the complex of his rights, on another. A son, when by the death of his father according to Roman law he was delivered from *patria potestas* [fatherly authority] and became in turn head of a family, acquired a *persona* which he had not before – the *persona* which had previously belonged to the father. Again, to take a modern instance, the fellows of a college, as a corporation, form one *persona*, but each of them would bear other 'persons', if, e.g., they happened to be magistrates, or simply in respect of their rights as citizens. Thus 'one person' above = one sustainer of rights; while in the second passage, 'carrieth this person', it rather = the rights sustained.

45. Hobbes expressly states that the sovereign 'person' may be an *assembly of men*, but the natural associations of the term, when the sovereign is spoken of as a person, favour the development of a monarchical doctrine of sovereignty.

Sovereign power is attained either: by acquisition or institution. By acquisition, when a man makes his children and their children, or a conqueror his enemies, to submit under fear of death; by institution, when men agree among themselves to submit to some man or assembly 'on confidence to be protected by him against all others'.[3] Hobbes speaks as if these were two ways by which a commonwealth and a sovereign defined as above could be brought into existence, but clearly a sovereign by acquisition is not a sovereign in the sense explained. He does not 'carry a person . . . of whose acts a great multitude by *mutual covenant one with another, have made themselves every one the author, to the end he may use the strength and means of them all, as he shall think expedient, for their peace and common defence.'*[4] And what Hobbes describes in the sequel (ch. 18) are, as he expressly says, *rights of sovereigns by institution*; but he seems tacitly to assume that every sovereign may claim the same, though he could hardly have supposed that the existing sovereignties were in their origin other than sovereignties by *acquisition*.

> A *commonwealth* is said to be *instituted*, when a *multitude* of men do agree and *covenant, every one with every one*, that to whatsoever *man* or *assembly of men*, shall be given by the major part the *right* to *present* the person of them all, . . . every one, as well he that *voted for it*, as he that *voted against it*, shall *authorise* all the actions and judgments of that man or assembly of men, in the same manner as if they were his own, to the end to live peaceably amongst themselves, and be protected against other men.[5]

Here a distinction is drawn between the covenant of all with all to be bound by the act *of the majority* in appointing a sovereign, and that act of appointment itself which is not a covenant of all with all. The natural conclusion would be that it was no violation of the covenant if the majority afterwards transferred the sovereign power to other hands. But in the sequel Hobbes expressly makes out such a transference to be a violation of the original compact. This is an instance of his desire to vindicate the absolute right of a *de facto* monarch.[6]

46. Throughout these statements we are moving in a region of fiction from which Spinoza keeps clear. Not only is the supposition of the devolution of wills or powers on a sovereign by a covenant historically a fiction (about that no more need be said); the notion of an *ᵃobligation as distinct from a compulsion to observeᵃ* this covenant is inconsistent with the supposition that there is no right other than power prior to the act by which the sovereign power is established. If there is no such right antecedent to the establishment of the sovereign power, neither can there be any after its establishment except in the sense of a power on the part of individuals which the sovereign enables them to exercise. This power, or *jus civile*, cannot itself belong to the sovereign, who enables individuals to exercise it. The only right which can belong to the sovereign is the *jus naturale*,[7] consisting in the superiority of his power, and this right must be measured by the inability of the subjects to resist. If they *can* resist,

the right has disappeared. In a successful resistance, then, to an ostensibly sovereign power, there can on the given supposition be no wrong done to that power. To say that there is, would be a contradiction in terms. Is such resistance, then, a violation of the *jus civile* as between the several subject citizens? In the absence of a sovereign power, no doubt, the *jus civile* (according to the view in question, which makes it depend on the existence of an *imperium*) would cease to exist. But then a successful resistance would simply show that there was no longer such a sovereign power. It would not itself be a violation of *jus civile*, but simply a proof that the conditions of *jus civile* were no longer present. It might at the same time be a step to re-establishing them if, besides being a proof that the old *imperium* no longer exists, it implied such a combination of powers as suffices to establish a new one.

47. No obligation, then, as distinct from compulsion, to submit to an ostensibly sovereign power can consistently be founded on a theory according to which *right* either = simple power, or only differs from it, in the form of *jus civile*, through being a power which an *imperium* enables individuals to exercise as against each other. Hobbes could not, indeed, have made out his doctrine (of *ª*the obligatoriness of absolute*ª* submission to the sovereign) with any plausibility if he had stated with the explicitness of Spinoza that *jus naturale = naturalis potentia.* That it is so is implied in the account of the state of things preceding the establishment of sovereignty as one of *bellum omnium contra omnes* [war of all against all][8] for where there is no recognition of a common good, there can be no right in any other sense than power. But where there are no rights but natural powers, no obligatory covenant can be made. In order, however, to get a sovereignty, to which there is a perpetual obligation of submission, Hobbes has to suppose a covenant of all with all, preceding the establishment of sovereignty, and to the observance of which, therefore, there cannot be an obligation in the sense that the sovereign punishes for the non-observance (the obligation corresponding to *jus civile* in Spinoza's sense), but which no one can ever be entitled to break. As the obligatoriness of this covenant, then, cannot be derived from the sovereignty which is established through it, Hobbes has to ascribe it to a 'law of nature' which enjoins '*that men perform their covenants made*'.[9] Yet in the immediate sequel of this passage he says expressly, 'the nature of justice consisteth in keeping of valid covenants, but the validity of covenants begins not but with the constitution of a civil power, sufficient to compel men to keep them; and then it is also that propriety begins'. On this principle the covenant

by which a civil power is for the first time constituted cannot be a valid covenant. The men making it are not in a position to make a valid covenant at all. The 'law of nature', to which alone Hobbes can appeal according to his principles, as the source of the obligatoriness of the covenant of all with all, he defines as a 'precept or general rule, found out by reason, by which a man is forbidden to do that, which is destructive of his life, or taketh away the means of preserving the same; and to omit that, by which he thinketh it may be best preserved'.[10] When a law of nature, however, is said to command or forbid, we must not understand those terms in that sense which, according to Hobbes, could only be derived from the establishment of an *imperium*. This 'law of nature', therefore, is merely an expression in a general form of the instinct by which, as Spinoza says, every living creature 'seeks to preserve his own being',[11] as guided by a calculation of consequences (for no meaning but this can be given to 'reason' according to Hobbes).[12] The prohibition, then, by this law of nature of a breach of that covenant of all with all, by which a sovereign power is supposed to be established, can properly mean nothing more than that it is everyone's interest to adhere to it. This however could only be a conditional prohibition – conditional, in particular, on the way in which the sovereign power is exercised. Hobbes tries to show that it must always be for the advantage of all to obey it, because not to do so is to return to the state of universal war, but a successful resistance to it must be *ipso facto* an establishment of a new combined power which prevents the *bellum omnium contra omnes* from returning. At any rate an obligation to submit to established *imperium* measured by the self-interest of each in doing so, is quite a different thing from the obligation which Hobbes describes in terms only appropriate (according to his own showing) to contracts between individuals enforced by a sovereign power.

48. It would seem that Hobbes' desire to prove all resistance to established sovereignty unjustifiable leads him to combine inconsistent doctrines. He adopts the notion that men are *natura hostes*, that *jus naturale* = mere power, because it illustrates the benefit to man's estate derived from the establishment of a supreme power and the effects of the subversion of such power once established, which he assumes to be equivalent to a return to a state of nature. But this notion does not justify the view that a rebellion, which is strong enough to succeed, is wrong. For this purpose he has to resort to the representation of the sovereign as having a right, distinct from power, founded on a conract of all with all, by which sovereignty is established. This representation is quite alien to Spinoza, with whom

sovereignty arises, it is true, when 'many are united',[13] but in the sense of combining their powers, not of contracting. But after all, the fiction of this contract will not serve the purpose which Hobbes wants it to serve. The sovereignty established by the contract can only have a *natural* right to be maintained inviolate, for all other right presupposes it and cannot be presupposed by it. If this natural right means mere power, then upon a successful rebellion it disappears. If it means anything else, it must mean that there are natural rights of men other than their mere power, which are violated by its subversion. But if there are such rights, there must equally be a possibility of collision between the sovereign power and these natural rights, which would justify a resistance to it.

49. It may be asked whether it is worth while to examine the internal consistency of a theory which turns upon what is admitted to be historically a fiction – the supposition of a contract of all with all. There are fictions and fictions however. The supposition that *ªsome eventª* took place which as a matter of history did not take place may be a way of conveying an essentially true conception of some moral relation of man. The great objection to the representation of the right of a sovereign power over subjects, and the rights of individuals which are enforced by this *imperium*, as having arisen out of a contract of all with all, is that it conveys a false notion of rights. It is not merely that the possibility of such a contract being made presupposes just that state of things – a *régime* of recognised and enforced obligations – which it is assumed to account for. Since those who contract must already have rights, the representation of society with its obligations as formed by contract implies that individuals have certain rights, independently of society and of their functions as members of a society, which they bring with them to the transaction. But such rights abstracted from social function and recognition could only be powers or (according to Hobbes' definition) liberties to use powers, which comes to the same; i.e. they *ᵇwould not beᵇ* rights at all; and from no combination or devolution of them could any right in the proper sense, anything more than a combined power, arise.

50. *ªSpinoza's then is the only logical development of that separation of right from social duty which is implied in the doctrine of 'social contract'.ª* Happily the doctrine has not been logically developed by those whose way of thinking has been affected by it. The reduction of political right—the right of the state over its subjects – to superior power, has not been popularly accepted, though the general conception of *national* right seems pretty much to identify it with power. Among the enlightened, indeed, there has of late appeared a

tendency to adopt a theory very *like Spinoza's,* without the higher elements which we noticed in Spinoza; to consider all right as a power attained in that 'struggle for existence' to which human 'progress' is reduced. But for one person, who, as a matter of speculation, considers the right of society over him to be a disguised might, there are thousands who, as a matter of practice, regard their own right as independent of that correlation to duty without which it is merely a might. The popular effect of the notion that the individual brings with him into society certain rights which he does not derive from society – which are other than claims to fulfil freely (i.e. for their own sake) certain functions towards society – is seen in the inveterate irreverence of the individual towards the state in the assumption that he has rights against society irrespectively of his fulfilment of any duties to society, that all powers that be are restraints upon his natural freedom which he may rightly defy as far as he safely can.

D. LOCKE

51. It was chiefly Rousseau who gave that cast to the doctrine of the origin of political obligation in contract in which it best lends itself to the assertion of rights apart from duties on the part of individuals, in opposition to the counter-fallacy which claims rights for the state irrespectively of its fulfilment of its function as securing the rights of individuals. It is probably true that the *Contrat Social* had great effect on the founders of American independence – an effect which appears in the terms of the Declaration of Independence and in preambles to the constitutions of some of the original American states.[1] But the essential ideas of Rousseau are to be found in Locke's *Second Treatise of Government*, which was probably well known in America for half a century before Rousseau was heard of.[2] Locke again constantly appeals to Hooker's first book on *Ecclesiastical Polity*,[3] and Grotius[4] argues in exactly the same strain.

Hooker, Grotius, Hobbes, Locke, and Rousseau only differ in their application of the same conception; viz. that men live first in a state of nature, subject to a law of nature, also called the law of reason; that in this state they are in some sense free and equal; that 'finding many inconveniences'[5] in it they covenant with each other to establish a government – a covenant which they are bound by the 'law of nature' to observe – and that out of this covenant the obligation of submission to the 'powers that be' arises. Spinoza alone takes a different line: he does not question the state of nature or the origin of government in a combination of men who find the state of nature 'inconvenient'; but he regards this combination as one of powers directed to a common end and constituting superior force, not as a covenant which men are bound by the law of nature to observe.

52. The common doctrine is so full of ambiguities that it readily lends itself to opposite applications. In the first place 'state of nature' may be understood in most different senses. The one idea common to all the writers who suppose such a state to have preceded that of civil society is a negative one. It was a state which was *not* one of political society, one in which there was no civil government; i.e. no supreme power, exercised by a single person or plurality of persons, which could compel obedience on the part of all members of a society and was recognised as entitled to do so by them all, or by a sufficient number of them to secure general obedience. But was it one of society at all? Was it one in which men had no dealings with each other except in the way of one struggling to make another serve his will and to get for himself what the the other had, or was it one in which there were ties of personal affection and common interest, and recognised obligations, between man and man? Evidently among those who spoke of a state of nature there were very various and wavering conceptions on this point. They are apt to make an absolute opposition between the state of nature and the political state, and to represent men as having suddenly contracted themselves out of one into the other. Yet evidently the contract would have been impossible unless society in a form very like that distinctively called political had been in existence beforehand. If political society is to be supposed to have originated in a pact at all, the difference between it and the preceding state of nature cannot with any plausibility be held to have been much more than a difference between a society regulated by written law and officers with defined power and one regulated by customs and tacitly recognised authority.

53. Again, it was held that in a state of nature men were 'free and equal'. This is maintained by Hobbes as much as by the founders of American independence. But if freedom is to be understood in the sense in which most of these writers seem to understand it, as a power of executing, of giving effect to, one's will, the amount of freedom possessed in a state of nature, if that was a state of detachment and collision between individuals, must have been very small. Men must have been constantly thwarting each other and (in the absence of that *jus in naturam* [right in nature], as Spinoza calls it, which combination gives) thwarted by powers of nature. In such a state those only could be free, in the sense supposed, who were *not* equal to the rest, who in virtue of superior power could use the rest. But whether we

suppose an even balance of weaknesses, in subjection to the crushing forces of nature, or a dominion of few over many by means of superior strength, in such a state of nature no general pact would be possible. No equality in freedom is possible except for members of a society of whom each recognises a good of the whole which is also his own, and to which the free cooperation of all is necessary. But if such society is supposed in the state of nature – and otherwise the 'pact' establishing political society would be impossible – it is already in principle the same as political society.

54. It is not always certain whether the writers in question considered men to be actually free and equal in the state of nature, or only so according to the 'law of nature', which might or might not be observed. (Hobbes represents the freedom and equality in the state of nature as actual, and this state as being for that reason *bellum omnium contra omnes* [a war of all against all].)[6] They all, however, implicitly assume a *consciousness* of the law of nature in the state of nature. It is thus not a law of nature in the sense in which we commonly use the term. It is not a law according to which the agents subject to it act necessarily but without consciousness of the law. It is a law of which the agent subject to it has a consciousness, but one according to which he may or may not act; i.e. one according to which he *ought* to act. It is from it that the *obligation* of submission to civil government, according to all these writers, is derived. But in regard to such a law, two questions have to be asked: firstly, how can the consciousness of obligation arise without recognition by the individual of claims on the part of others – social claims in some form or other – which may be opposed to his momentary inclinations? and secondly, given a society of men capable of such a consciousness of obligation, constituting a law according to which the members of the society are free and equal, in what does it differ from a political society? If these questions had been fairly considered, it must have been seen that the distinction between a political society and a state of nature, governed by such a law of nature, was untenable; that a state of things out of which political society could have arisen by compact must have been one in which the individual regarded himself as a member of a society which has claims on him and on which he has claims, and that such society is already in principle a political society. But the ambiguity attending the conception of the 'law of nature' prevented them from being considered. When the writers in question spoke of a law of nature, to which men in the state of nature were subject, they did not make it clear to themselves that this law, as understood by them, could not exist at all without there being some recognition or consciousness of it

on the part of those subject to it. The designation of it as 'law of nature' or 'law of God' helped to disguise the fact that there was no imponent of it, in the sense in which a law is imposed on individuals by a political superior. In the absence of such an imponent, unless it is either a uniformity in the relations of natural events or an irresistible force – and it is not represented in either of these ways in juristic writings – it can only mean a recognition of obligation arising in the consciousness of the individual from his relations to society. But this not being clearly realised, it was possible to represent the 'law of nature' as antecedent to the laws imposed by a political superior, without its being observed that this implied the antecedence of a condition of things in which the result supposed to be obtained through the formation of political society – the establishment, viz. of reciprocal claims to freedom and equality on the part of members of a society – already existed.

55. In fact, the condition of society in which it could properly be said to be governed by a law of nature, i.e. by an obligation of which there is no imponent but the consciousness of man, an obligation of which the breach is not punished by a political superior, is not antecedent to political society but one which it gradually tends to produce. It is the radical fault of the theory which finds the origin of political society in compact that it has to reverse the true process. To account for the possibility of the compact of all with all it has to assume a society subject to a law of nature, prescribing the freedom and equality of all. But a society governed by such a law as a law of nature, i.e. with no imponent but man's consciousness, would have been one from which political society would have been a decline – one in which there could have been no motive to the establishment of civil government. Thus this theory must needs be false to itself in one of two ways. Either it is false to the conception of a 'law of nature', with its prescription of freedom and equality as governing the state of things prior to the compact by which political society is established, only introducing the law of nature as the ground of the obligatoriness of that compact but treating the state of nature as one of universal war in which no reciprocal claims of any sort were recognised (so Hobbes); or just so far as it realises the conception of a society governed by a law of nature, as equivalent to that spontaneous recognition by each of the claims of all others, without which the covenant of all with all is in fact unaccountable, it does away with any appearance of necessity for the transition from the state of nature to that of political society and tends to represent the latter as a decline from the former. This result is seen in Rousseau;[7] but to a great

extent Rousseau had been anticipated by Locke. The broad differences between Locke and Hobbes in their development of a common doctrine, are (1) that Locke denies that the state of nature is a state of war, and (2) that Locke distinguishes the act by which political society is established from that by which the government, legislative and executive, is established, *and consequently the* dissolution of the (political) society from the dissolution of the government (§ 211).

56. '*The State of Nature, and the State of War* ... are as far distant, as a State of Peace, Good Will, Mutual Assistance, and Preservation, and a State of Enmity, Malice, Violence, and Mutual Destruction are one from another. Men living together according to reason, without a common Superior on Earth, with Authority to judge between them, is *properly the State of Nature*. But force, or a declared design of force upon the Person of another, where there is no common Superior on Earth to appeal to for relief, *is the State of War...*' (§ 19). In the state of nature, however, when the state of war has once begun, there is not the same means of terminating it as in civil society.

The *right* of war may belong to a man, 'though he be in Society and a fellow Subject' (§ 19), when his person or property is in such immediate danger that it is impossible to appeal for relief to the common superior. 'But when the actual force is over, the *State of War ceases* between those that are in Society ... because then there lies open the remedy of appeal for the past injury, and to prevent future harm...' (§ 20). In the state of nature, when the state of war has once begun it continues until the aggressor offers peace and reparation. The state of war, though not proper to the state of nature, is a frequent incident of it, and to avoid it 'is one great *reason of Mens* putting themselves into Society...' (§ 21). The state of nature is not one that is altogether over and done with. 'All *Princes* and Rulers of *Independent* Governments all through the World, are in a State of Nature...' (§ 14). The members of one state in dealing with those of another are in a state of nature, and the law of nature alone binds them, 'For Truth and keeping of Faith belongs to Men, as men, and not as Members of Society' (§ 14). '[A]ll Men are naturally in that State, and remain so, till by their own Consents they make themselves Members of some Politick Society...' (§ 15).

57. The antithesis, as put above, between the state of nature and the state of war can only be maintaned on the supposition that the 'law of nature' is observed in a state of nature. Locke does not explicitly state that this is the case. If it were so, it would not appear how the

state of war should arise in the state of nature. But he evidently thought of the state of nature as one in which men recognised the law of nature, though without fully observing it. He quotes with approval from Hooker language which implies that not only is the state of nature a state of equality, but that in it there is such consciousness of equality with each other on the part of men that they recognise the principle 'do as you would be done by'.[8] With Hobbes, in the supposed state of nature the 'law of nature' is emphatically not observed, and hence it is a state of war. As has been pointed out above, a 'law of nature' in the sense in which these writers use the term, as a law *which obliges* but yet has no imponent in the shape of a sovereign power, as Locke says (§ 136), 'is no where to be found but in the minds of Men'; it can only have its being in the consciousness of those subject to it. If therefore we are to suppose a state of nature in which such a law of nature exists, it is more consistent to conceive it in Locke's way than in Hobbes'; more consistent to conceive it as one in which men recognise duties to each other than as a *bellum omnium contra omnes*.

58. *"From his conception*[a] of what men are in the state of nature, and of the ends for which they found political societies, Locke derives certain necessary limitations of what the supreme power in a commonwealth may rightfully do. The prime business of the political society, once formed, is to establish the legislative power. This is 'sacred and unalterable in the hands where the Community have once placed it' (§ 134); 'unalterable', i.e., as we gather from the sequel, by anything short of an act of the community which originally placed it in these hands. But as men in a state of nature have no 'Arbitrary Power' (§ 8) over each other (which must mean that according to the 'law of nature' they have no such power), so they cannot transfer any such power to the community nor it to the legislature. No legislature can have the right to destroy, enslave or designedly impoverish the subjects. And as no legislature can be entitled to do anything which the individual in the state of nature would not by the law of nature be entitled to do, so its great business is to declare the law of nature in general terms and administer it by known authorised judges. The state of nature, Locke seems to think, would have done very well, but for the inconvenience of every man being judge in his own case of what the law of nature requires. It is to remedy this inconvenience by establishing (1) a settled law, received by common consent, (2) a known and indifferent judge, (3) a power to enforce the decisions of such a judge, that political society is formed (§ 87).

Hence a legislature violates the 'trust that is put in them by the Society' unless it observes the following rules: (1) to govern by established promulgated laws, not to be varied to suit particular interests; (2) these laws are to be designed only for the good of the people; (3) it must not raise taxes but by consent of the people through themselves or deputies; (4) it 'neither must *nor can transfer the Power of making Laws* to any Body else, or place it anywhere but where the People have' (§ 142).

59. Thus 'the Legislative being only a Fiduciary Power to act for certain ends, there remains still in the People a Supream Power to remove or alter the Legislative . . .' (§ 149). Subject to this ultimate 'sovereignty' (a term which Locke does not use) of the people, the legislative is necessarily the supreme power, to which the executive is subordinate. An appearance to the contrary can only arise in cases where (as in England) the supreme executive power is held by a person who has also *a share* in the legislative. Such a person 'in a very tolerable sense may also be called Supream . . .' (§ 151). It is not, however, to him as supreme legislator (which he is not, but only a participator in supreme legislation) but to him as supreme executor of the law that oaths of allegiance are taken. It is only as executing the law that he can claim obedience (§ 151), his executive power being, like the power of the legislative, 'a Fiduciary Trust, placed in him' (§ 156) to enforce obedience to law and that only.

This distinction of the supreme power of the people from that *ª*of the supreme legislative and the*ª* supreme executive, corresponding to a distinction between the act of transferring individual powers to a society and the subsequent act by which that society establishes a particular form of government, enables Locke to distinguish what Hobbes had confounded, dissolution of government and dissolution of political society.

60. He gets rid of Hobbes' notion, that because the 'covenant of all with all', by which a *ª*government*ª* is established, is irrevocable, therefore the government once established is unalterable.[9] He conceives the original pact merely as an agreement to form a civil society, which must indeed have a government, but not necessarily always the same government. The pact is a transfer by individuals of their natural rights to a society, and can only be cancelled through the dissolution of the society by foreign conquest. The delegation by the society of legislative and executive powers to a person or persons is a different matter. The society always retains the right, according to Locke, of resuming the powers thus delegated, and must exercise the right in the event either of the legislative being altered, placed in different hands from those originally intended, of a collision between its executive and legislative officers, or of a breach between different

branches of the legislature (when as in England there are such different branches), or when legislative and executive or either of them 'act contrary to their trust'. He thus in effect vindicates the right of revolution, ascribing to a 'sovereign people' the attributes which Hobbes assigned to a 'person', single or corporate, on which the people forming a society were supposed by an irrevocable act to have devolved their powers. In other words, he considered the whole civil society in all cases to have the rights which Hobbes would only have allowed it to possess where the government was not a monarchy or aristocracy but a democracy; i.e. where the supreme 'person' on to which all devolve their several *personæ* is an 'assembly of all that will come together'.[10] As such a democracy did not then exist in Europe, any more than it does now, except in some Swiss cantons, the practical difference between the two views was very great. Both Locke and Hobbes wrote with a present political object in view, Hobbes wishing to condemn the Rebellion, Locke to justify the Revolution. For practical purposes, Locke's doctrine is much the better; but if Hobbes' translation of the irrevocability of the covenant of all with all into the illegitimacy of resistance to an established government in effect entitles any tyrant[11] to do as he likes, on the other hand, it is impossible upon Locke's theory to pronounce when resistance to a *de facto* government is legitimate or otherwise. It would be legitimate according to him when it is an act of the 'sovereign people' (not that Locke uses the phrase), superseding a government which has been false to its trust. But this admitted, all sorts of question arise as to the means of ascertaining what is and what is not an act of the 'sovereign people'.

61. The rapid success of the Revolution without popular disorder prevented *a*these questions*a* from becoming of importance, but in the presence of such sectarian enthusiasm as existed in Hobbes' time they would have become dangerous. *b*Locke's theory*b* would not any more than that of Hobbes justify resistance to the powers that be on the part of any body of men short of the civil society acting as a whole, i.e. by a majority. The sectaries of the time of the Rebellion, in pleading a natural or divine right to resist the orders of the government, would have been as much condemned by Locke's theory as by Hobbes'.[12] But who can say when any popular action by which established powers, legislative or executive, are resisted or altered is an act of the 'sovereign people', of the civil society acting as a whole or no? Where government is democratic, in Hobbes' sense, i.e. vested in an assembly of all who will come together, the act of the 'sovereign people' is unmistakeable. It is the act of the majority of such an assembly. But in such a case the difficulty cannot arise. There can be no withdrawal

by the sovereign people of power from its legislative or executive representatives, since it has no such representatives. In any other case it would seem impossible to say whether any resistance to or deposition of an established legislative or executive is the act of the majority of the society or no. Any sectary or revolutionary may plead that he has the 'sovereign people' on his side. If he fails, it is not certain that he has them not on his side; for it may be that, though he has the majority of the society on his side, yet the society has allowed the growth within it of a power which prevents it from giving effect to its will. On the other hand, if the revolution succeeds, it is not certain that it had the majority on its side when it began, though the majority may have come to acquiesce in its result. In short, on Locke's principle that any particular government derives its authority from an act of the society, and the society by a like act may recall the authority, how can we ever be entitled to say that such an act has been exercised?

62. It is true that there is no greater difficulty about supposing it to be exercised in the dissolution than in the establishment of a government – indeed not so much – but the act of first establishing a government is thrown back into an indefinite past. It may easily be taken for granted without inquiry into the conditions of its possibility. On the other hand, as the act of legitimately dissolving a government or superseding one by another has to be imagined as taking place in the present, the inquiry into the conditions of its possibility cannot well be avoided. If we have once assumed with Hobbes and Locke that the authority of government is derived from a covenant of all with all – either directly or mediately by a subsequent act in which the covenanted society delegates its powers to a representative or representatives – it will follow that a like act is required to cancel it, and the difficulties of conceiving such an act under the conditions of the present are so great, that Hobbes' view of *ª*the original act by which any Government was established as irrevocable*ª* has much to say for itself. If the authority of any government – its claim on our obedience – is held to be derived not from an original, or from any, covenant but from the function which it serves in maintaining those conditions of freedom which are conditions of the moral life, then no act of the people in revocation of a prior act need be reckoned necessary to justify its dissolution. If it ceases to serve this function, it loses its claim on our obedience. It is a *parekbaois* [corruption]. (Here again the Greek theory, deriving the authority of government not from consent but from the end it serves, is sounder than the modern.) Whether or no any particular government has on this ground lost its claim and may be rightly resisted is a question, no doubt, difficult for the individual

to answer with certainty. In the long run, however, it seems generally if not always to answer itself. A government no longer serving the function described – which, it must be remembered, is variously served according to circumstances – brings forces into play which are fatal to it. But if it is difficult upon this theory for the individual to ascertain, as a matter of speculation, under any particular circumstances whether resistance to an established government is justified or no, at any rate upon this theory such a justification of resistance is possible. Upon Locke's theory, the condition necessary to justify it – viz. an act of the whole people governed – is one which, anywhere except in a Swiss canton, would be impossible to fulfil. For practical purposes Locke comes to a right result by ignoring this impossibility. Having supposed the reality of one impossible event – the establishment of government by compact or by act of a society founded on compact – he cancels this error in the result by supposing the possibility of another transaction equally impossible – viz. the collective act of a people dissolving its government.

63. It is evident from the *a*chapter on dissolution of government*a* [XIX] that he did not seriously contemplate the conditions under which such an act could be exercised. What he was really concerned about was to dispute 'the right divine of kings to govern wrong'[13] on the part of a legislative as much as on the part of an executive power; to maintain the principle that government is only justified by being for the good of the people, and to point out the difference between holding that some government is necessarily for the good of the people and holding that any particular government is for their good – a difference which Hobbes had ignored. In order to do this, starting with the supposition of an actual deed on the part of a community establishing a government, he had to suppose a reserved right on the part of the community by a like deed to dissolve it. But in the only particular case in which he contemplates a loss by the legislature of representative character he does not suggest the establishment of another by an act of the whole people. He saw that the English Parliament in his time could not claim to be such as it could be supposed that the covenanting community originally intended it to be. *b*See the notable passage in § 157:

... it often*b* comes to pass, that in Governments, where part of the Legislative consists of *Representatives* chosen by the People, that in tract of time this *Representation* becomes very *unequal* and disproportionate to the reasons it was first established upon... [T]he bare Name of a Town, of which there remains not so much as the ruines, where scarce so much Housing as a Sheep-coat; or more Inhabitants than a Shepherd is to be found, sends *as many Representatives* to the grand Assembly of Law-makers, as a whole County numerous in People, and powerful in riches. This Strangers stand amazed at, and everyone must confess needs a remedy. Though most think it hard to find one, because the Constitution of the Legislative being the original and supream act of the Society, antecedent to all positive Laws in it, and depending wholly on the People, no inferiour Power can alter it. And therefore the *People* when the *Legislative* is once Constituted, *having* in such a Government as we have been speaking of, *no Power* to act as long as the Government stands; this inconvenience is thought incapable of a remedy.

The only remedy which he suggests is not an act of the sovereign people, but an exercise of prerogative on the part of the executive, in the way of redistributing representation, which would be justified by *'salus populi suprema est lex'* ['the good of the people is the highest law'].[14]

E. ROUSSEAU

64. That 'sovereignty of the people', which Locke looks upon as held in reserve after its original exercise in the establishment of government, only to be asserted in the event of a legislature proving false to its trust, Rousseau supposes to be in constant exercise. Previous writers had thought of the political society or commonwealth, upon its formation by compact, as instituting a sovereign. They differed chiefly on the point whether the society afterwards had or had not a right of displacing an established sovereign. Rousseau does not think of the society, *civitas* or commonwealth, as thus instituting a sovereign, but as itself in the act of its formation becoming a sovereign and ever after continuing so.

65. In his conception of a state of nature, Rousseau does not differ from Locke.[1] He conceives the motive for passing out of it, however, somewhat differently and more after the manner of Spinoza. With Locke the motive is chiefly a sense of the desirability of having an impartial judge, and efficient enforcement, of the law of nature. According to Rousseau, *a*the social pact*a* takes place when men find the hindrances to their preservation in a state of nature too strong for the forces which each individual can bring to bear against them. This recalls Spinoza's view of the *jus in naturam* [right in nature] as acquired by a combination of the forces of individuals in civil society.

66. The 'problem of which the social contract is a solution' Rousseau states thus: 'To find a form of association which protects with the whole common force the person and property of each associate, and in virtue of which everyone, while uniting himself to all, only obeys

himself and remains as free as before' (*Contrat Social*, I, vi).[2] The terms of the contract which solves this problem Rousseau states thus: 'Each of us throws into the common stock his person and all his faculties under the supreme direction of the general will; and we accept each member as an *"indivisible"* part of the whole.' There results from this act of association, in place of the several persons of the several contracting parties, a 'collective moral body, composed of as many members as there are voices in the assembly, which body receives from this act its unity, its common self, its life, and its will . . .' It is called by its members a *state* when it is passive, a *sovereign* when it is active, a *power* when compared with similar bodies. The associates are called collectively a *people*, severally *citizens* as sharing in the sovereign authority, *subjects* as submitted to the laws of the state (I, vi). Each of them is under an obligation in two relations, 'as a member of the sovereign body towards the individuals, and as a member of the state towards the sovereign'. All the subjects can by a public vote be placed under a particular obligation towards the sovereign, but the sovereign cannot thus incur an obligation towards itself. It cannot impose any law upon itself which it cannot cancel. Nor is there need to restrict its powers in the interest of the subjects. For the sovereign body, being formed only of the individuals which constitute it, can have no interest contrary to theirs. 'From the mere fact of its existence, it is always all that it ought to be' (since, from the very fact of its institution, all merely private interests are lost in it). On the other hand, the will of the individual (his particular interest as founded upon his particular desires) may very well conflict with that general will which constitutes the sovereign. Hence the social pact necessarily involves a tacit agreement, that anyone refusing to conform to the general will shall be forced to do so by the whole body politic; in other words,'shall be forced to be free', since the universal conformity to the general will is the guarantee to each individual of freedom from dependence on any other person or persons (I, vii).

67. The result to the individual may be stated thus. He exchanges the natural liberty to do and get what he can – a liberty limited by his relative strength – for a liberty at once limited and secured by the general will; he exchanges the mere possession of such things as he can get – a possession which is the effect of force – for a property founded on a positive title, on the guarantee of society. At the same time he becomes a moral agent. Justice instead of instinct becomes the guide of his actions. For the moral slavery to appetite he substitutes the moral freedom which consists in obedience to a self-imposed law.

Now for the first time it can be said that there is anything which he *ought* to do, as distinguished from that which he is *forced* to do (I, viii).

68. Such language makes it clear that the sovereignty of which Rousseau discusses the origin and attributes, is something essentially different from the supreme coercive power which previous writers on the *'jus civile'* ['civil law'] had in view. A contemporary of Hobbes had said that

> 'there's on earth a yet auguster thing,
> Veiled though it be, than Parliament and King.'[3]

It is to this 'auguster thing', not to such supreme power as English lawyers held to be vested in 'Parliament and King', that Rousseau's account of the sovereign is really applicable. What he says of it is what Plato or Aristotle might have said of the *theios nous* [divine intelligence], which is the source of the laws and discipline of the ideal polity, and what a follower of Kant might say of the 'pure practical reason', which renders the individual obedient to a law of which he regards himself, in virtue of his reason, as the author, and causes him to treat humanity equally in the person of others and in his own always as an end, never merely as a means.[4] But all the while Rousseau himself thinks that he is treating of the sovereign in the ordinary *ª*sense – of*ª* some power of which it could be reasonably asked how it was established in the part where it resides, when and by whom and in what way it is exercised. *ᵇ*His reader*ᵇ* more or less familiar with the legal conception of sovereignty, but not at all with that of practical reason or of a 'general will' – a common ego, which wills nothing but what is for the common good – is pretty sure to retain the idea of supreme coercive power as the attribute of sovereignty, and to ignore the attribute of pure disinterestedness, which, according to Rousseau, must characterise every act that can be ascribed to the sovereign.

69. The practical result is a vague exaltation of the prerogatives of the sovereign people, without any corresponding limitation of the conditions under which an act is to be deemed that of the sovereign people. The justifiability of laws and acts of government, and of the rights which these confer, comes to be sought simply in the fact that the people wills them, not in the fact that they represent a true *volonté générale* [general will], an impartial and disinterested will for the common good. Thus the question of what really needs to be enacted by the state in order to secure the condition under which a good life is possible, is lost sight of in the quest for majorities; and as the will of the people in any other sense than the measure of what the

people will tolerate is really unascertainable in the great nations of Europe, the way is prepared for the sophistries of modern political management, for manipulating electoral bodies, for influencing elected bodies, and procuring plebiscites.

70. The incompatibility between the ideal attributes which Rousseau ascribes to the sovereign and any power that can actually be exercised by any man or body of men becomes clearer as we proceed. He expressly distinguishes 'sovereignty' from 'power', and on the ground of this distinction holds that it cannot be alienated, represented, or divided. 'Sovereignty being simply the exercise of the general will can never be alienated, and the sovereign, who is only a collective being, can only be represented by himself. Power can be transmitted, but not will' (II, i). In order to the possibility of a representation of the general will, there must be a permanent accord between it and the individual will or wills of the person or persons representing it. But such *permanent* accord is impossible (*Ib.*). Again, a general will is from the nature of the case indivisible. It is commonly held to be divided, not, indeed, in respect of its source, but in respect of the objects to which its acts are directed, e.g. into legislative and executive powers; into rights of taxation, of war, of justice, etc. But this supposed division of sovereign powers or rights implies that 'what are only emanations from the sovereign authority are taken to be parts of it' (II, ii). The only exercise of sovereign power, properly so called, is in legislation, and there is no proper act of legislation except when the whole people comes to a decision with reference to the whole people. Then the matter decided on is as general as the will which decides on it; and this is what constitutes a law (II, vi). By this consideration several questions are answered. Whose office is it to make laws? It is that of the general will, which can neither be alienated nor represented. Is the prince above the law? The answer is, He is a member of the state, and cannot be so. Can the law be unjust? No one can be unjust to himself: therefore not the whole people to the whole people. How can we be free and yet subject to the laws? The laws are the register of our own will (II, vi).

Laws, in short, are properly those general 'conditions of civil association' which the associates impose on themselves. Where either of the specified conditions is lacking, where either it is not the universal will from which an ordinance proceeds or it is not the whole people to which it relates, it is not a law but a decree, not an act of sovereignty but of magistracy (II, vi).

71. This leads to a consideration of the nature and institution of magistracy or government (III, i). The government is never the same

as the sovereign. The two are distinguished by their functions, that of the one being legislative, that of the other executive. Even where the people itself governs, its acts of government must be distinguished from its acts of sovereignty, the former having a particular, the latter a general, reference. Government is the exercise according to law of the executive power, and the 'prince' or 'magistrate' is the man or body of men charged with this administration; 'a body intermediary between the subjects and the sovereign, charged with the execution of the laws, and with the maintenance of civil and political freedom' (*Ib.*). Where all or most of the citizens are magistrates, or charged with the supreme functions of government, we have a democracy; where a few, an aristocracy; where one is so charged, a monarchy (III, iii). The differences depend, not as Hobbes and others had supposed, on the quarter where the sovereignty resides – for it must always reside in the whole body of people – but on that in which government resides. The idea of government is that the dominant will of the prince should be the general will or law, that it should be simply the public force by which that general will is brought to bear on individuals or against other states, serving the same purpose in the state as the union of soul and body in the individual (III, i); and this idea is most likely to be satisfied under a democracy. There, the general will (if there *is* a general will, which the democracy is no guarantee for there being, according to Rousseau's distinction between the *volonté générale* and *volonté de tous* [will of all], of which more hereafter) cannot fail to coincide with the dominant will of the government. The prevalence of particular interests may prevent there being a will at all of the kind which Rousseau would count general or truly sovereign, but they cannot be more prevalent in the magistracy, constituted by the whole people, than in the same people acting in the way of legislation. In a democracy, therefore, the will of the sovereign, so far as there is a sovereign in the proper sense, necessarily finds expression in the will of the magistracy. On the other hand, though under either of the other forms of government there is danger of collision between sovereign and government, yet the force of the government is greater than in a democracy. It is greatest when the government is a monarchy because under all other forms there is more or less discrepancy between the individual wills of the several persons composing the government, as directed to the particular good of each, and the corporate will of the government of which the object is its own efficiency, and under a monarchy this source of weakness is avoided (III, ii). As there is more need of force in the government in proportion to the number of subjects whose particular

wills it has to control, it follows that monarchy is best suited to the
largest, democracy to the smallest states (III, iii).

72. As to the institution of government, Rousseau maintains
strenuously that it is not established by contract. 'There is only one
contract in the state, viz. that of the original association; and this
excludes every other. No other public contract can be imagined
which would not be a violation of the first' (III, xvi). Even when
government is vested in an hereditary body, monarchic or aristocratic, this is merely a provisional arrangement, made and liable to be
reversed by the sovereign, whose officers the governors are. The act
by which government is established is twofold, consisting first of the
passing of a law by the sovereign, to the effect that there shall be a
government; secondly, of an act in execution of this law, by which
the governors – the 'magistrates' – are appointed. But it may be
asked, How can the latter act, being one not of sovereignty but of
magistracy (for it has a particular reference in the designation of the
governors), be performed when as yet there is no government? The
answer is that the people resolves itself from a sovereign body into a
body of magistrates, as the English Parliament resolves itself constantly from a legislative body into a committee. In other words, by a
simple act of the general will a democracy is for the time established,
which then proceeds either to retain the government in its own
hands, or place it in those of an *a*officer or officers according*a* to the
form in which the sovereign has decided to establish the government
(III, xvii). Acts similar to that by which the government was originally constituted need to be periodically repeated in order to prevent
the government from usurping the function of the sovereign, i.e. the
function of legislation. (Could this usurpation occur under a democracy?) In order that the sovereignty may not fall into abeyance, it
must be exercised, and it can only be exercised in assemblies of the
whole people. These must be held periodically, and at their opening
two questions ought to be submitted; one, whether it pleases the sovereign to maintain the present form of government; the other,
whether it pleases the people to leave the administration in the hands
of those at present charged with it (III, xviii). Such assemblies are entitled to revise and repeal all previously enacted laws. A law not so
repealed the sovereign must be taken tacitly to confirm, and it retains
its authority. But as the true sovereign is not any law but the general
will, no law, even the most fundamental, can be exempt from liability
to repeal. Even the social pact itself might legitimately be dissolved,
by agreement of all the citizens assembled (III, xviii). (Whether *unanimity* is necessary for the purpose is not specified.) Without such

assemblies there can be no exercise of the general will (which, as before stated, cannot be represented), and consequently no freedom. 'The English people, e.g., is quite mistaken in thinking itself free. It is only free while the election of members of Parliament is going on. As soon as they are elected, it is in bondage, it is nothing. In the short moments of its freedom it makes such a bad use of it that it well deserves to lose it' (III, xv).

73. It appears from the above that, according to Rousseau, the general will, which is the true sovereign, can only be exercised in assemblies of the whole people. On the other hand, he does not hold that an act of such an assembly is necessarily an act of the general will. After telling us that the 'general will is always right, and always tends to the public good,' he adds, 'but it does not follow that the deliberations of the people have always the same rectitude... There is often a great difference between the will of all and the general will. The latter only looks to the common interest; the other looks to private interests, and is only a sum of the wills of individuals' (II, iii). Again (II, iv), 'that which generalises the will is not so much the number of voices as the common interest which unites them'. He holds apparently that in the assembly of the whole people, if they had sufficient information, and if no minor combinations of particular interests were formed within the entire body, the difference between the wills of individuals would neutralise each other, and the vote of the whole body would express the true general will. But in fact in all assemblies there is at least a liability to lack of information and to the formation of cliques; and hence it cannot be held that the vote of the assembly necessarily expresses the 'general will'. Rousseau, however, does not go so far as to say that unless the law is actually such as contributes to the common good, it is not an expression of the general will. The general will, according to him, always aims at or wills the common good, but is liable to be mistaken as to the means of attaining it. 'It is always right, but the judgment which guides it is not always enlightened... Individuals see the good which they reject; the public wills the good which it does not see' (II, vi). Hence the need of a guide in the shape of a great lawgiver. Apparently, however, the possible lack of enlightenment on the part of the 'general will' does not, in Rousseau's view, prevent its decisions from being for the public good. In discussing the 'limits of the sovereign power' he maintains that there can be no conflict between it and the natural right of the individual, because, 'although it is only that part of his power, his goods, his freedom, of which the use is important to the community, that the individual transfers to the sovereign by the

social pact, yet the sovereign alone can be judge of the importance'; and the sovereign 'cannot lay on the subjects any constraint which is not for the good of the community'. 'Under the law of reason' (which is thus identified with the general will) 'nothing is done without a cause, any more than under the law of nature' (II, iv).

74. But though even an unenlightened 'general will' is the general will still, and (as we are left to infer) cannot in its decisions do otherwise than promote the public good, Rousseau distinctly contemplates the possibility of the 'general will' being so overpowered by particular interests that it finds no expression in the votes of a popular assembly, though the assembly be really one of a whole people, and the vote of the majority is duly taken (IV, i). In such cases it is not that the 'general will' is 'annihilated or corrupted; it is always constant, unalterable, and pure'. Even in the individual whose vote is governed by his private interest the 'general will' is not extinct, nor is he unaware either of what the public good requires or of the fact that what is for the public good is also for his own. But his share in the public evil to which he knows that his vote will contribute, seems nothing by the side of the special private good which he hopes to gain. By his vote, in short, he does not answer the question, Is so and so for the advantage of the state? but, Is it for the advantage of this particular man or party (IV, i)?

75. The test of the dominance of the general will in assemblies of the people is an approach to unanimity. 'Long debates, discussions, tumult, indicate the ascendency of particular interests and the decline of the state' (IV, ii). Rousseau, however, does not venture to say that absolute unanimity in the assembly is necessary to an expression of the general will, or to give a law a claim upon the obedience of the subjects. This would have been to render effectual legislation impossible. Upon the theory, however, of the foundation of legitimate sovereignty in consent – the theory that the natural right of the individual is violated unless he is himself a joint imponent of the law which he is called to obey – it is not easy to see what rightful claim there can be to the submission of a minority. Rousseau so far recognises the difficulty that he requires unanimity in the original compact (IV, ii). If among those who are parties to it there are others who oppose it, the result is simply that the latter are not included in it. 'They are strangers among the citizens.' But this does not explain how they are to be *rightfully* controlled, on the principle that the only rightful control is founded on consent; or, if they are not controlled, what is the value of the 'social compact'. How can the objects of the pact be attained while those who are bound by it have these 'strangers' living among them who are not bound by it, and who, not being

bound by it, cannot be rightfully controlled? The difficulty must recur with each generation of the descendants of those who were parties to the original pact. The parties to the pact, it is true, have no right to resist the general will, because the pact is *ex hypothesi* to the effect that each individual, in all things of common concern, will take the general will for his own. The true form, therefore, of the question upon which each party to the pact should consider himself to be voting in the assembly is, as Rousseau puts it, not 'Is the proposed measure what I wish for, or what I approve, or no?' but 'Is it in conformity with the general will?' If, having voted upon this question, he finds himself in a minority, he is bound to suppose that he is mistaken in his views of the general will, and to accept the decision of the majority as the general will which, by the pact, he is bound to obey. So far all is consistent; though how the individual is to be answered if he pleads that the vote of the assembly has been too much biassed by particular interest to be an expression of the 'general will', and that therefore it is not binding on him, does not appear.

76. But after the first generation of those who were parties to the supposed original compact, what is to settle whether anyone is a party to it or no? Rousseau faces the question, but his only answer is that 'when once the state is instituted, consent is implied in residence; to dwell on the territory is to submit to the sovereignty' (IV, ii).[5] This answer, however, will scarcely stand examination. Rousseau himself does not consider that residence in the same region with the original parties to the pact renders those so resident also parties to it. Why should it do so, when the pact has descended to a later generation? It may be argued of course that everyone residing in a settled society, which secures him in his rights of person and property, has the benefit of the society from the mere fact of his residence in it, and is therefore morally bound to accept its laws. But this is to abandon the doctrine of obligation being founded on consent. Residence in a territory governed by a certain sovereign can only be taken to imply consent to the rule of that sovereign, if there is any real possibility of relinquishing it, and this there can scarcely ever be.

77. Rousseau certainly carried out the attempt to reconcile submission to government with the existence of natural rights antecedent to the institution of government, by the hypothesis of a foundation of government in consent, more consistently than any other writer; and his result shows the hopelessness of the attempt. To the consistency of his theory he sacrifices every claim to right on the part of any state except one in which the whole body of citizens directly legislates, i.e. on the part of nearly all states then or now existing; and finally he can

only justify the control of the minority by the majority in any state
whatever by a subterfuge. It does not follow, however, because the
doctrine of natural rights and the consequent conception of government as founded on compact are untenable, that there is no truth in
the conception of the state or sovereign as representing a 'general
will', and as authorised or entitled to obedience on that account. It is
this conception, as the permanently valuable thing in Rousseau, that
we have now further to consider.

78. The first remark upon it which suggests itself is that, as Rousseau puts the matter, there may be an independent political society in
which there is no sovereign power at all, or in which, at any rate, it is
not exercised. The sovereign is the 'general will'. But the general will
can only be exercised through the assembly of a whole people. The
necessary conditions of its exercise, then, in Rousseau's time, were
only fulfilled in the Swiss cantons and (perhaps) in the United Provinces.[6] In England they were fulfilled in a way during the time of a
general election. But even where these conditions were fulfilled, it
did not follow that the 'general will' was put in force. It might be overpowered, as in the Roman *comitia*, by particular interests. Is it then
to be understood that, according to Rousseau, either there could be
independent states without any sovereignty in actual exercise, or that the
European 'states' of his time, and equally the great states of the present
day – for in none of these is there any more exercise of the general
will than in the England of his time – are not properly states at all?

79. We may try to answer this question by distinguishing sovereign
de facto from sovereign *de jure*, and saying that what Rousseau meant
was that the 'general will', as defined by him and as "exercised" under
the conditions which he prescribes, was the only sovereign *de jure*,
but that he would have recognised in the ordinary states of his time a
sovereign *de facto*; that in the same way, when he describes the institution of government as arising out of a twofold act consequent on the
original pact – an act in which the sovereign people first decides that
there shall be a government and then, not as a sovereign people, but
as a democratic magistracy, decides in what hands the government
shall be placed – he does not conceive himself to be describing what
has actually taken place, but what is necessary to give a government a
moral title to obedience. Whether Rousseau himself had this distinction in view is not always clear. At the outset he states his object thus:
'Man is born free, and everywhere he is in fetters. How has this
change come about? I do not know. What can render it legitimate?
That is a question which I deem myself able to answer' (I, i). The
answer is the account of the establishment of a sovereign by social

pact. It might be inferred from this that he considered himself in the sequel to be delineating transactions to the actual occurrence of which he did not commit himself, but which, if they did occur, would constitute a duty as distinct from a physical necessity of submission on the part of subjects to a sovereign, and to which some equivalent must be supposed, in the shape of a tacit present convention on the part of the members of a state if their submission is to be matter of duty as distinct from physical necessity, or is to be *ᵇ*claimed*ᵇ* as a matter of right by the ostensible sovereign. This, however, would merely be an *inference* as to his meaning. His actual procedure is to describe transactions, by which the sovereignty of the 'general will' was established, and by which it in turn established a government, as if they had actually taken place. Nor is he content with supposing a tacit consent of the people as rendering subjection legitimate. The people whose submission to law is to be 'legitimate' must actually take part in sovereign legislative assemblies. It is very rarely that he uses language which implies the possibility of a *sovereign* power otherwise constituted. He does indeed speak[7] of the possibility of a prince – in the special meaning of the term, as representing the head of the executive – usurping sovereignty, and speaks of the sovereignty thus usurped as existing *de facto*, not *de jure*; but in no other connection (so far as I have observed) does he speak of anything short of the *volonté générale* exercised through the vote of an assembled people as sovereign at all. And the whole drift of his doctrine is to show that no sovereign, otherwise constituted, had any claim on obedience. There was no state in Europe at his time in which his doctrine would not have justified rebellion, and even under existing representative systems the conditions are not fulfilled which according to him are necessary to give laws that claim on our obedience which arises from their being an expression of the general will. The only system under which these conditions could be fulfilled would be one of federated self-governing communes, small enough to allow each member an active share in the legislation of the commune. It is probably the influence of Rousseau that has made such a system the ideal of political enthusiasts in France.

F. SOVEREIGNTY AND THE GENERAL WILL

Rousseau and Austin

80. The questions then arise (1) whether there is any truth in Rousseau's conception of sovereignty as founded upon a *volonté générale* in

its application to actual sovereignty. Does anything like such a
sovereignty exist in the societies properly called political? (2) Is there
any truth in speaking of a sovereignty *de jure* founded upon the *volonté générale*? (3) If there is, are we to hold with Rousseau that
this 'will' can only be exercised through the votes of a sovereign
people?

81. (1) The first question is one which, if we take our notions of
sovereignty from such writers as Austin,[1] we shall be at first disposed
decidedly to negative. Austin is considered a master of precise definition. We may begin, therefore, by looking to his definition of
sovereignty and the terms connected with it. His general definition of
law runs as follows: 'A law, in the most general and comprehensive
acceptation in which the term, in its literal meaning, is employed,
may be said to be a rule laid down for the guidance of an intelligent
being by an intelligent being having power over him.'[2] These rules
are of two kinds: *"laws of God, and Human law."* We are only concerned with the *"latter. Human laws are"* again distinguished into two
classes, according as they are or are not established by political
superiors. 'Of the laws or rules set by men to men, some are established by *political* superiors, sovereign and subject; by persons exercising supreme and subordinate *government*, in independent nations,
or independent political societies . . . the aggregate of the rules established by political superiors, is frequently styled *positive* law . . .' (I,
88–9). This is distinguished from 'positive morality'. Laws are further explained as a species of commands. A command is 'a signifi-
cation of desire', distinguished by the fact that 'the party to whom it is
directed is liable to evil from the other, in case he does comply not
with the desire' (I, 91). This liability to evil forms the sanction of the
command. Where it 'obliges *generally* to acts or forbearances of a
class, a command is a law or rule' (I, 95).

Every positive law, or every law simply and strictly so called, is set by a sovereign person, or a sovereign body of persons, to a member or members of the
independent political society wherein that person or body is sovereign or
supreme. Or (changing the expression) it is set by a monarch, or sovereign
number, to a person or persons in a state of subjection to its author. Even
though it sprung directly from another fountain or source, it *is* a positive law,
or a law strictly so called, by the institution of that present sovereign in the
character of political superior. Or (borrowing the language of Hobbes) 'the
legislator is he, not by whose authority the law was first made, but by whose
authority it continues to be a law'. (I, 225–6)

The notions of sovereignty and independent political society may be expressed concisely thus. If a *determinate* human superior, *not* in a habit of obedience to a like superior, receive *habitual* obedience from the *bulk* of a given society, that determinate superior is sovereign in that society, and the society (including the superior) is a society political and independent. (I, 226)

In order that a given society may form a society political and independent, the two distinguishing marks which I have mentioned above must unite. The *generality* of the given society must be in a *habit* of obedience to a *determinate* and *common* superior; whilst that determinate person, or determinate body of persons, must *not* be habitually obedient to a determinate person or body. It is the union of that positive, with this negative mark, which renders that certain superior sovereign or supreme, and which renders that given society (including that certain superior) a society political and independent. (I, 227)

82. It may be remarked in passing that, according to the above, while every law implies a sovereign, from whom directly or indirectly (through a subordinate political superior) it proceeds, it is not necessary to a sovereign that his commands should take the form of laws, as opposed to 'occasional or particular commands' (I, 95). A superior might signify his desires only in the form of such particular and occasional commands, and yet there might be a habit of obedience to him, and he might not be habitually obedient to any other person or body; in which case he would be a 'sovereign'.

83. Austin's doctrine seems diametrically opposed to one which finds the sovereign in a *volonté générale*, because (a) it only recognises sovereignty in a determinate person or persons, and (b) it considers the essence of sovereignty to lie in the power, on the part of such determinate person or persons, to put compulsion without limit on subjects, to make them do exactly as it pleases.[3] The *volonté générale*, on the other hand, it would seem, cannot be identified with the will of any determinate person or persons; it can, indeed, according to Rousseau, only be expressed by a vote of the whole body of subject citizens, but when you have got them together there is no certainty that their vote does express it; and it does not – at any rate necessarily – command any power of compulsion, much less unlimited power. Rousseau expressly contemplates the possibility of the executive power conflicting with and overbearing the 'general will'. Indeed according to his view it was the ordinary state of things, and though this view may be exaggerated, no one could maintain that the 'general will', in any intelligible sense of the words, had always unlimited force at its command.

84. The two views thus seem mutually exclusive, but perhaps it may be by taking each as complementary to the other that we shall gain the truest view of sovereignty, as it actually exists. In those states of society, in which obedience is habitually rendered by the bulk of society to some determinate superior, single or corporate, who in turn is independent of any other superior, the obedience is so rendered because this determinate superior is regarded as expressing or embodying what may properly be called the general will, and is virtually conditional *upon the superior being so* regarded. It is by no means an unlimited power of compulsion that the superior exercises, but one dependent in the long run, or dependent for the purpose of insuring an *habitual* obedience, upon conformity to certain convictions on the part of the subjects as to what is for their general interest. As Maine says (*Early History of Institutions* [Lecture XII], p. 359), 'The vast mass of influences, which we may call for shortness moral, perpetually shapes, limits, or forbids the actual direction of the forces of society by its Sovereign.' Thus, quite apart from any belief in the right of revolution, from the view that the people in any state are entitled to an ultimate sovereignty, or are sovereign *de jure*, and may withdraw either legislative or executive power from the hands in which it has been placed in the event of its being misused, it may fairly be held that the ostensible sovereign – the determinate person or persons to whom we can point and say that with him or them lies the ultimate power of exacting habitual obedience from the people – is only able to exercise this power in virtue of an assent on the part of the people, nor is this assent reducible to the fear of the sovereign felt by each individual. It is rather a common desire for certain ends – specially the *'pax vitaeque securitas'* ['peace and security of life']⁴ – to which the observance of law or established usage contributes, and in most cases implies no conscious reference on the part of those whom it influences to any supreme coercive power at all. Thus when it has been ascertained in regard to any people that there is some determinate person or persons to whom in the last resort they pay habitual obedience, we may call this person or persons sovereign if we please, but we must not ascribe to him or them the real power which governs the actions and forbearances of the people, even those actions and forbearances (only a very small part) which are prescribed by the sovereign. This power is a much more complex and less determinate, *or rather less* easily determinable, thing; but a sense of possessing common interests, a desire for common objects on the part of the people, is always the condition of its existence. Let this sense or desire – which may properly be called general will – cease to operate,

or let it come into general conflict with the sovereign's commands, and the habitual obedience will cease also.

85. If, then, those who adopt the Austinian definition of a sovereign mean no more than that in a thoroughly developed state there must be some determinate person or persons, with whom in the last resort lies the recognised power of imposing laws and enforcing their observance, over whom no legal control can be exercised, and that even in the most thorough democracy, where laws are passed in the assembly of the whole people, it is still with determinate persons, viz. a majority of those who meet in the assembly, that this power resides, they are doubtless right. So far they only need to be reminded that the thoroughly developed state, as characterised by the existence of such definite sovereignty, is even among civilised people but imperfectly established. It *a*is only perfectly*a* established (1) where customary or 'common' or 'judge-made' law, which does not proceed from any determinate person or persons, is either superseded by *b*express*b* enactments that do proceed from such person or persons, or (as in England) is so frequently trenched upon by statute law that it may fairly be said only to survive upon sufferance, or to be itself virtually enacted by the sovereign legislature; and (2) where no question of right can be raised between local legislatures or authorities and the legislature claiming to be supreme (as in America before the war of secession, and as might perhaps be found to be the case in Germany now, if on certain educational and ecclesiastical matters the Imperial legislature came to be at issue with the local legislatures). But though the organisation of the state, even in civilised and independent nations, is not everywhere complete, it no doubt involves the residence *c*with a determinate person or persons, or*c* a body or bodies, of supreme – i.e. legally uncontrolled – power to make and enforce laws. The term 'sovereign' having acquired this definite meaning, Rousseau was misleading his readers when he ascribed sovereignty to the 'general will'. He could only be understood as meaning, and in fact understood himself to mean, that there was no legitimate sovereign except in the most thorough democracy, as just described.

86. But the Austinians, having found their sovereign, are apt to regard it as a much more important institution than, if it is to be identified with a determinate person or persons, it really is; they are apt to suppose that the sovereign, with the coercive power (i.e. the power of operating on the fears of the subjects) which it exercises, is the real determinant of the habitual obedience of the people – at any rate of their habitual obedience in respect of those acts and forbearances which are prescribed by law.[5] But, as we have seen, this

is not the case. It then needs to be pointed out that if the sovereign power is to be understood in this fuller, less abstract sense – if we mean by it the 'real determinant of the habitual obedience of the people', we must look for its sources much more widely and deeply than the 'analytical jurists' do; that it can no longer be said to reside in a determinate person or persons, but in that impalpable congeries of the hopes and fears of a people bound together by common interests and sympathy, which we call the general will.

87. It may be objected that this view of the 'general will', as that on which habitual obedience to the sovereign really depends, is at best only applicable to 'self-governing' communities, not to those under a despotic sovereign. The answer is that it is applicable in all forms of society where a sovereign in the sense above defined (as a determinate person or persons with whom in the last resort lies the recognised power of imposing laws and enforcing their observance) really exists, but that there are many where there cannot fairly be said to be any such sovereign at all; in other words, that in all organised communities the power which practically commands the habitual obedience of the people in respect of those acts and forbearances which are enjoined by law or authoritative custom, is one dependent on the general will of the community, but this power is often not sovereign in the sense in which the ruler of an independent state is sovereign. It may very well be that there is at the same time another power merely coercive – a power really operating on people simply through their fears – to which obedience is rendered and which is not in turn representative of a general will; but where this is the case we shall find that such power is only in contact with the people, so to speak, at one or two points; that their actions and forbearances, as determined by law and custom, are in the main independent of it; that it cannot in any proper sense be said to be a sovereign power over them; at any rate, not in the sense in which we speak of King, Lords, and Commons as sovereign in England.

88. Maine has pointed out (*Early History of Institutions*, Lecture XIII [p. 384]) that the great despotic empires of ancient times, excluding the Roman, of which more shall be said directly, and modern empires in the East, were in the main tax-collecting institutions. They exercise coercive force over their subjects of the most violent kind for certain purposes, at certain times, but they do not impose laws as distinct from 'occasional or particular commands', nor do they judicially administer or enforce a customary law. In a certain sense the subjects render them habitual obedience, i.e. they habitually submit when the agents of the empire descend on them for taxes

and recruits, but in the general tenor of their lives their actions and forbearances are regulated by authorities with which the empire never interferes – with which probably it could not interfere without destroying itself. These authorities can scarcely be said to reside in a determinate person or persons at all, but, so far as they do so, they reside *ª*mixedly*ª* in priests, or exponents of customary religion, in heads of families acting within the family, and in some village-council acting beyond the limits of the family. Whether in such a state of things we are to consider that there is a sovereign power at all, and, if so, where it is to be considered to reside, are chiefly questions of words. If complete uncontrolledness by a stronger power is essential to sovereignty, the local authorities just spoken of are not sovereign. The conquering despot could descend on them and sweep them away, leaving anarchy in their place, and he does *ᵇ*compel them to be put in exercise for*ᵇ* a particular purpose, that of raising tribute or sometimes recruits. On the other hand, these authorities, which represent a general will of the communities, form the power which determines such actions and forbearances of the individual as do not proceed from natural inclination. The military ruler, indeed, is sovereign in the sense of possessing irresistible coercive power, but in fact this power is only exercised within narrow limits, and not at all in any legislative or judicial way. If exercised beyond these limits and in conflict with customary law, the result would be a general anarchy. The truest way of expressing the state of the case is to say that, taking the term 'sovereign' in the sense which we naturally associate with it and in which it is used by modern European writers on sovereignty, there is under such conditions no sovereign, but that the practical regulation of life, except during intervals of military violence and anarchy, rests with authorites representing the general will, though these are to a certain extent interfered with by an alien force.

89. The same account is applicable to most cases of foreign dominion over a people with any organised common life of their own. The foreign power is not sovereign in the sense of being a maker or maintainer of laws. Law-making, under such conditions, there is properly none. The subject people inherits laws, written or unwritten, and maintains them for itself, a certain shelter from violence being afforded by the foreign power. Such, in the main, was the condition of North Italy, for instance, under Austrian domination.[6] Where this is the case, the removal of the coercive power of the foreigner need not involve anarchy, or any violation of established rights (such as Hobbes supposes to follow necessarily from the deposition

of an actual sovereign). The social order does not depend on the foreign dominion and may survive it. The question whether in any particular case it actually can do so must depend on the possibility of preventing further foreign aggression, and on the question whether there is enough national unity in the subject people to prevent them from breaking up into hostile communities when the foreign dominion is removed.

90. It is otherwise where the foreign power is really a law-making and maintaining one, and is sovereign in that proper sense, as was the Roman Empire. But just so far as the Roman Empire was of this sovereign, i.e. law-making and maintaining, character, it derived its permanence, its hold on the 'habitual obedience' of its subjects, from the support of the 'general will'. As the empire superseded customary or written laws of conquered countries, it conferred rights of Roman citizenship, a much more perfect system of protection in action and acquisition than the conquered people had generally possessed before. Hence, while nothing could be further removed from what Rousseau would have counted liberty than the life of the citizens of the Roman Empire, for they had nothing to do with making the laws which they obeyed, yet *probably no political system was ever more* firmly grounded on the good-will of the subjects, none in the maintenance of which the subjects felt a stronger interest. The British power in India exercises a middle function between that of the Roman Empire and that of the mere tax-collecting and recruit-raising empire with which the Roman Empire has just been contrasted. It presents itself to the subject people in the first place as a tax-collector. It leaves the customary law of the people mostly untouched. But if only to a very small extent a law-making power, it is emphatically a law-maintaining one. It regulates the whole judicial administration of the country, but applies its power generally only to enforce the customary law which it finds in existence. For this reason an 'habitual obedience' may fairly be said to be rendered by the Indian people to the English government, in a sense in which it could not be said to be rendered to a merely tax-collecting military power; but the habitual obedience is so rendered only because the English government presents itself to the people, not merely as a tax-collector, but as the maintainer of a customary law, which, on the whole, is the expression of the 'general will'. The same is true in principle of those independent states which are despotically governed, in which, i.e., the ultimate legislative power does not reside, wholly or in part, with an assembly representing the people, or with the people themselves; e.g. Russia. It is not the absolute coercive power of the Czar which

determines the habitual obedience of the people. This coercive power, if put to the test as a *coercive* power, would probably be found very far from absolute. *b*This*b* habitual obedience is determined by a system of law, chiefly customary, which the administration controlled by the Czar enforces against individuals but which corresponds to the general sense of what is equitable and necessary. If a despotic government comes into anything like habitual conflict with the unwritten law which represents the general will, its dissolution is beginning.

91. The answer, then, to the question whether there is any truth in Rousseau's conception of sovereignty as founded upon a *volonté générale*, in its application to actual sovereignty, must depend on what we mean by 'sovereign'. The essential thing in political society is a power which guarantees men rights, i.e. a certain freedom of action and acquisition conditionally upon their allowing a like freedom in others. It is but stating the same condition otherwise to speak of a power which *a*guarantees the members of the society these*a* rights, this freedom of action and acquisition, impartially or according to a general *b*rule*b* or law. What is the lowest form in which a society is fit to be called political, is hard to say. The political society is more complete as the freedom guaranteed is more complete, both in respect of the persons enjoying it and of the range of possible action and acquisition over which it extends.[7] A family or a nomad horde could not be called a political society, on account of the narrow range of the *c*freedoms which*c* they severally guarantee. The nomad horde might indeed be quite as numerous as a Greek state or as the sovereign canton of Geneva in Rousseau's time; but in the horde the range within which reciprocal freedom of action and acquisition is guaranteed to the individuals is exceedingly small. It is the power of guaranteeing rights, defined as above, which the old writers on sovereignty and civil government supposed to be established by covenant of all with all, translating the common interest which men have in the maintenance of such a power into an imaginary historical act by which they instituted it. It was this power that they had chiefly in view when they spoke of sovereignty.

92. It is to be observed, however, that the power may very well exist and serve its purpose where it is not sovereign in the sense of being exempt from any liability of being interfered with by a stronger coercive power, such as that of a tax-collecting military ruler. The occasional interference of the military ruler is so far a drawback to the efficiency with which freedom of action and acquisition is guaranteed, but does not nullify the general maintenance of rights. On the

other hand, when the power by which rights are guaranteed is sovereign (as it is desirable that it should be) in the special sense of being maintained by a person or persons, wielding coercive force not liable to control by any other human force, it is not this coercive force that is the important thing about it, or that determines the habitual obedience essential to the real maintenance of rights. That which determines this habitual obedience is a power residing in the common will and reason of men, i.e. in the will and reason of men as determined by social relations, as interested in each other as acting together for common ends. It is a power which this 'universal' rational will exercises over the inclinations of the individual, and which only needs exceptionally to be backed by coercive force.

93. Thus, though it may be misleading to speak of the general will as anywhere either actually or properly sovereign, because the term 'sovereign' is best kept to the ordinary usage in which it signifies a determinate person or persons charged with the supreme coercive function of the state, and the general will does not admit of being vested in a person or persons, yet it is true that the institutions of political society – those by which equal rights are guaranteed to members of such a society – are an expression of, and are maintained by, a general will. The sovereign should be regarded, not in abstraction as the wielder of coercive force, but in connection with the whole complex of institutions of political society. It is as their sustainer, and thus as the agent of the general will, that the sovereign power must be presented to the minds of the people if it is to command habitual loyal obedience; and obedience will scarcely be habitual unless it is loyal, not forced. If once the coercive power, which must always be an incident of sovereignty, becomes the characteristic thing about it in its relation to the people governed, this must indicate one of two things; either that the general interest in the maintenance of equal rights has lost its hold on the people, or that the sovereign no longer adequately fulfils its function of maintaining such rights, and thus has lost the support derived from the general sense of interest in supporting it. It may be doubted whether the former is ever really the case; but whatever explanation of the case may be the true one, it is certain that when the idea of coercive force is that predominantly associated with the law-imposing and enforcing power, then either a disruption of the state or a change in the *ª*sources of sovereignty must*ª* sooner or later take place. In judging, however, whether this is the case, we must not be misled by words. In England, e.g., from the way in which many people speak of 'government', we might suppose that it was looked on mainly as the wielder of coercive force, but it would be a mistake on

that account to suppose that English people commonly regard the laws of the country as so much coercion, instead of as an institution in the maintenance of which they are interested. When they speak [b]dys-logistically[b] of 'government', they are not thinking of the general system of law but of a central administrative agency which they think interferes mischievously with local and customary administration.

94. It is more true to say that law, as the system of rules by which rights are maintained, is the expression of a general will than that the general will is the sovereign. The sovereign, being a person or persons by whom in the last resort laws are imposed and enforced in the long run and on the whole, is an agent of the general will – contributes to realise that will. Particular laws may, no doubt, be imposed and enforced by the sovereign, which conflict with the general will – not in the sense that if all the subject people could be got together to vote upon them, a majority would vote against them; that might be or might not be – but in the sense that they tend to thwart those powers of action, acquisition, and self-development on the part of the members of the society, which there is always a general desire to extend though the desire may not be enlightened as to the best means to the end, and which it is the business of law to sustain and extend. The extent to which laws of this kind may be intruded into the general *corpus juris* [body of law] without social disruption it is impossible to specify. Probably there has never been a civilised state in which they bore more than a very small proportion to the amount of law which there was the strongest general interest in maintaining. But, so far as they go, they always tend to lessen the 'habitual obedience' of the people, and thus to make the sovereign cease to be sovereign. The hope must be that this will result in the transfer of sovereignty to other hands before a 'social disruption' ensues; before the general system of law has been so far perverted as to lose its hold on the people. Of the possibility of a change in sovereignty without any detraction from the law-abiding habits of the people, France has lately given a conspicuous example. Here, however it must be remembered that a temporary foreign conquest made the transition easier.[8]

95. (2) After what has been said, we need not dwell long on the [a]question of the tenability of the distinction between sovereignty *de facto* and sovereignty *de jure*.[a] It is a distinction which can only be maintained so long as either 'sovereign' is not used in a determinate sense, or by '*jus*' is understood something else than law or right established by law. If by 'sovereign' we understand something short of a person or persons holding the supreme law-making and law-

enforcing power, e.g. an English king who is often called sovereign, we might say that sovereignty was exercised '*de facto*' but not '*de jure*' when the power of such a 'sovereign' was in conflict with, or was not sanctioned by, the law as declared and enforced by the really supreme power. Thus an English king, so far as he affected to control the army or raise money without the co-operation of Parliament, might be said to be sovereign '*de facto*' but not '*de jure*'; only, however, on the supposition that the supreme law-making and law-enforcing power does not belong to him, and thus that he is called 'sovereign' in other than the strict sense. If he were sovereign in the full sense '*de facto*', he could not fail to be so '*de jure*', i.e. legally. In such a state of things, if the antagonism between King and Parliament continued for any length of time, it would have to be admitted that there was no 'sovereign' [b]as =[b] supreme law-making and law-enforcing power; that sovereignty in this sense was in abeyance, and that anarchy prevailed. Or the same thing might be explained by saying that sovereignty still resided '*de jure*' with the King and Parliament, though not '*de facto*' exercised by them – but if we use such language, we must bear in mind that we are qualifying 'sovereignty' by an epithet which neutralises its meaning as actually supreme power. If, however, the king succeeded in establishing such a power on a permanent footing, he would have become sovereign in the full sense, and there would be no ground for saying, as before, that he was not sovereign *de jure*; for the qualifications '*de jure*' and 'not *de jure*', in that sense in which they might be applied to a power which is not supreme, are equally inapplicable to the power of making and enforcing law which is supreme. The monarch's newly established supremacy may be in conflict with laws that were previously in force, but he has only to abolish those laws in order to render it legal. If, then, it is still to be said to be not *de jure*, it must be because '*jus*' is used for something else than law or right established by law; viz. either for 'natural right' as not merely = natural power, or for certain claims which the members of the subject community have come to recognise as inherent in the community and in themselves as members of it – claims regarded as the foundation of law, not as founded upon it, and with which the commands of the sovereign conflict. But even according to this meaning of '*jus*', a sovereign in the strict Austinian sense, that is not so *de jure*, is in the long run an impossibility. 'Habitual obedience' cannot be secured in the face of such claims.

96. But whether or no in any qualified sense of '*sovereign*' or '*jus*', a sovereign that is not so '*de jure*' is possible, once understand by 'sovereign' the determinate person or persons with whom the ultimate

law-imposing and law-enforcing power resides, and by '*jus*' law, it is then obviously a contradiction to speak of a sovereign '*de jure*' as distinguished from one '*de facto*'. The power of the ultimate imponent of law cannot be derived from or limited by law. The sovereign may no doubt by a legislative act of its own lay down rules as to the mode in which its power shall be exercised, but if it is sovereign in the sense supposed it must always be open to it to alter these rules. There can be no illegality in its doing so. In short, in whatever sense '*jus*' is derived from the sovereign, in that sense no sovereign can hold his power '*de jure*'. So Spinoza held that '*imperium*' was '*de jure*' indeed, but '*de jure naturali*' ('*jus naturale*' = natural power), which is the same as '*de jure divino*'; only powers exercised in subordination to '*imperium*' are '*de jure civili*'. So Hobbes said that there could be no unjust law.[9] A law was not a law unless enacted by a sovereign, and the just being that to which the sovereign obliges, the sovereign could not enact the unjust, though it might enact the inequitable and the pernicious – the 'inequitable' presumably meaning that which conflicts with a 'law of nature', the 'pernicious' that which tends to weaken individuals or society. Rousseau retains the same notion of the impeccability of the sovereign, but on different grounds. Every act of the sovereign is according to him *de jure*, not because all right is derived from a supreme coercive power and the sovereign is that power, but because the sovereign is the general will which is necessarily a will for the good of all.[10] The enactment of the sovereign could as little, on this view, be 'inequitable' or 'pernicious' as it could be 'unjust'. But this view necessitates a distinction between the sovereign, thus conceived, and the actually supreme power of making and enforcing law as it exists anywhere but in what Rousseau considered a perfect state. Rousseau indeed generally avoids calling this actually supreme power 'sovereign,' though he cannot, as we have seen, altogether avoid it; and since, whatever he liked to call it, the existence of such a power in forms which according to him prevented its equivalence to the general will was almost everywhere a fact, his readers would naturally come to think of the actually supreme power as sovereign *de facto*, in distinction from something else which was sovereign *de jure*. And further, under the influence of Rousseau's view that the only organ of the general will was an assembly of the whole people, they would naturally regard such an assembly as sovereign *de jure*, and any other power actually supreme as merely sovereign *de facto*. This opposition, however, really arises out of a confusion in the usage of the term 'sovereign' – out of inability on the one side to hold fast the identification of sovereign with 'general will', on the other, to keep it simply to the sense of supreme law-making and law-enforcing power. If 'sovereign' = 'general will', the distinction of *de facto* and *de jure* is inapplicable to it. A certain desire either is or is not the general will. A certain interest is or is not an interest in the common good. There is no sense in saying that such desire or interest is general will *de jure* but not *de facto*, or *vice versa*. On the other hand, if 'sovereign' = supreme law-making and law-enforcing power, the distinction is equally inapplicable to it. If any person or persons have this power at all, they cannot be said to have it merely *de facto* while others have it *de jure*.

97. It may be urged with much truth that the actual possession of such power by a determinate person or persons is rather a convenient hypothesis of writers on jurisprudence than an actual fact; and, as we have seen, the actual condition of things at certain times in certain states may conveniently be expressed by saying that there was a sovereign *de facto* that was not so *de jure*, or *vice versa*, but only on the supposition that 'sovereign' is not taken necessarily in the full sense of a supreme law-making and enforcing power. In a state of things that can be so described, however, there is no 'sovereignty' at all in the sense of an actually supreme power of making and enforcing law resident in a determinate person or persons. Sovereignty in this sense can only exist *de facto*; and when it so exists, it is obvious that no other can in the same sense exist *de jure*. It may be denied indeed in particular cases that an actually supreme power of making and enforcing law is exercised *de jure*, in a sense of that phrase already explained [§ 95]. Reasons were given for doubting whether a power could really maintain its sovereign attributes if conflicting with *jus*, in the same sense thus explained. But supposing that it could, the fact that it was not exercised *de jure* would not entitle us to say that any other person or persons were sovereign *de jure*, without altering the meaning of 'sovereign'. If any one has supreme power *de facto*, that which any one else has cannot be supreme power. The qualification of a power as held not *de facto* but *de jure* is one which destroys its character as supreme, i.e. as sovereign in the sense before us.

98. It is only through trying to combine under the term 'sovereign' the notions of the 'general will' and of supreme power that we are led to speak of the people as sovereign *de jure*, if not *de facto*. There would be no harm indeed in speaking of the 'general will' as sovereign, if the natural association of 'sovereign' with supreme coercive power could be got rid of; but as this cannot be, when once we have pronounced the general will 'sovereign', we are pretty sure to identify the general will with a vote of the majority of citizens. A majority of

citizens *can* be conceived as exercising a supreme coercive power, but a 'general will' in the sense of an unselfish interest in the common good which in various degrees actuates men in their dealings with each other cannot be so conceived. Thus for the sovereignty, in an impalpable and unnatural sense, of the 'general will' we get a sovereignty, in the natural and demonstrable sense, of the multitude. But as the multitude is not everywhere supreme, the assertion of its sovereignty has to be put in the form that it is sovereign *de jure*. The truth which underlies this proposition is that an interest in common good is the ground of political society, in the sense that without it no body of people would recognise any authority as having a claim on their common obedience. It is so far as a government represents to them a common good that the subjects are conscious that they ought to obey it, i.e. that obedience to it is a means to an end desirable in itself or absolutely. This truth is latent in Rousseau's doctrine of the sovereignty of the 'general will', but he confounds with it the proposition that no government has a claim on obedience but that which originates in a vote passed by the people themselves who are called on to obey (a vote which must be unanimous in the case of the original compact, carried by a majority in subsequent cases).

99. This latter doctrine arises out of the delusion of natural right. The individual, it is thought, having a right, not derived from society, to do as he likes, can only forego that right by an act to which he is a party. Therefore he has a right to disregard a law unless it is passed by an assembly of which he has been a member and by the decision of which he has expressly or tacitly agreed to be bound. Clearly, however, such a natural right of the individual would be violated *a*under the most popular sovereignty*a* no less than under one purely monarchical, if he happened to object to the decision of the majority; for to say, as Rousseau says, that he has virtually agreed, by the mere fact of residence in a certain territory, to be bound by votes of the majority of those occupying that territory,[11] is a mere trick to save appearances. But in truth there is no such natural right to do as one likes irrespectively of society. It is on the relation to a society – to other men recognising a common good – that the individual's rights depend, as much as the gravity of a body depends on relations to other bodies. A right is a power claimed and recognised as contributory to a common good. A right against society, in distinction from a right to be treated as a member of society, is a contradiction in terms. No one therefore has a right to resist a law or ordinance of government, on the ground that it requires him to do what he does not like, and that he has not agreed to submit to the authority from which it

proceeds: and if no one *b*person, no number of persons.*b* If the common interest requires it, no right can be alleged against it. Neither can its enactment by popular vote enhance, nor the absence of such vote diminish, its right to be obeyed. Rousseau himself well says that the proper question for each citizen to ask himself in regard to any proposal before the assembly is not, Do I like or approve it? but, Is it according to the general will? which is only another way of asking, Is it according to the general interest? It is only as the organ of this general interest that the popular vote can endow any law with the right to be obeyed; and Rousseau himself, if he could have freed himself from the presuppositions of natural right, might have admitted that, as the popular vote is by no means necessarily an organ of the general interest, so the decree of a monarch or of an aristocratic assembly, under certain conditions, might be such an organ.

100. But, it may be asked, Must not the individual judge for himself whether a law is for the common good? and if he decides that it is not, is he not entitled to resist it? Otherwise, not only will laws passed in the interest of individuals or classes and against public good, have a claim to our absolute and permanent submission, but a government systematically carried on for the benefit of a few against the many can never be rightfully resisted. To the first part of this question we must of course answer '*yes*', without qualification. The degree to which the individual judges for himself of the relation between the common good and the laws which cross the path of his ordinary life, is the measure of his intelligent, as distinguished from a merely instinctive, recognition of rights in others and in the state; and on this recognition again depends his practical understanding of the difference between mere powers and rights as *a*exercised*a* by himself. Supposing then the individual to have decided that some 'command of a political superior' is not for the common good, how ought he to act in regard to it? In a country like ours, with a popular government and settled methods of enacting and repealing laws, the answer of common sense is simple and sufficient. He should do all he can by legal methods to get the command cancelled, but till it is cancelled he should conform to it.[12] The common good must suffer more from resistance to a law or to the ordinance of a legal authority than from the individual's conformity to a particular law or ordinance that is bad, until its repeal can be obtained. It is thus the social duty of the individual to conform, and he can have no right, as we have seen, that is against his social duty; no right to anything or to do anything, that is not involved in the *ability* to do his duty.

101. But difficulties arise when either (1) it is a case of disputed

sovereignty, and in consequence the legal authority of the supposed command is doubtful; or (2) the government is so conducted that there are no legal means of obtaining the repeal of a law; or (3) when the whole system of law and government is so perverted by private interests hostile to the public that there has ceased to be any common interest in maintaining it; or (4) – a more *a*frequent*a* case – when the authority from which the objectionable command proceeds is so easily separable from that on which *b*the general maintenance*b* of social order and the fabric of settled rights depends, that it can be resisted without serious detriment to this order and fabric. In such cases,[13] may there not be a right of resistance based on a 'higher law' than the command of the ostensible sovereign?

102. (1) As to cases where the legal authority of the supposed command is doubtful. In modern states the definition of sovereignty – the determination of the person or persons with whom the supreme power of making and enforcing law legally resides – has only been arrived at by a slow process. The European monarchies have mostly arisen out of the gradual conversion of feudal superiority into sovereignty in the strict sense. Great states such as Germany and Italy have been formed by the combination of independent or semi-dependent states. In England the unity of the state goes back much further than anywhere else, but in England it was but gradually that the residence of sovereignty jointly in King, Lords, and Commons came to be practically established, and it is still founded merely on a customary law. In the United States, with a written constitution, it required all Austin's subtlety to detect where sovereignty lay, and he places it where probably no ordinary citizen of the United States had ever thought of it as residing, viz. 'in the states' governments *as forming one aggregate body*: meaning by a state's government, not its ordinary legislature, but the body of citizens which appoints its ordinary legislature, and which, the union apart, is properly sovereign ... therein.' He bases this view on the provision in the constitution, according to which amendments to it are only valid '*when ratified by the legislature in three-fourths of the several states, or by convention in three-fourths thereof*'. (I, p. 268n)[14] But no ordinary citizen of the United States probably ever thought of sovereignty except as residing either in the government of his state or in the federal government consisting of Congress and President, or sometimes in one way, sometimes in the other. In other countries, e.g. France, where since Louis XIV the quarter in which sovereignty resides has at any given time been easily assignable, there have since the revolution been such frequent changes in the ostensible sovereign that there might almost at any

time have been a case for doubting whether the ostensible sovereign
had such command over the habitual obedience of the people as to be
a sovereign in that sense in which there is a social duty to obey the
sovereign, as the representative of the common interest in social
order; whether some prior sovereignty was not really still in force.
For these various reasons there have been occasions in the history of
all modern states at which men, or bodies of men, without the conscious assertion of any right not founded upon law, might naturally
deem themselves entitled to resist an authority which on its part
claimed a right – a legally established power – to enforce obedience,
and turned out actually to possess the power of doing so.

103. In such cases the truest retrospective account to be given of
the matter will often be that at the time there was ^anothing amounting
to a right^a on either side. A right is a power of which the exercise by
the individual or by some body of men is recognised by a society
either as itself directly essential to a common good or as conferred by
an authority of which the maintenance is recognised as so essential.
But in cases of the kind described the ^bauthorities^b, appealed to on
each side as justifying respectively compulsion and resistance, often
do not command a sufficiently general recognition of their being
necessary to the common good to enable them to confer rights of compulsion or resistance. One or other of them may be coming to do so,
or ceasing to do so, but rights, though on the one hand they are eternal or at least coeval with human society, on the other hand take time
to form themselves in this or that particular subject and to transfer
themselves from one subject to another (just as one may hold reason
to be eternal, and yet hold that it takes time for this or that being to
become rational). Hence in periods of conflict between local or customary, and imperial or written, law, between the constituent powers
of a sovereignty, such as King and Parliament in England, of which
the relation to each other has not become accurately defined, between
a ^cfallen^c and a rising sovereign in a period of revolution, between federal and state authorities in a composite state, the facts are best represented by saying that for a time there may be no right on either side
in the conflict, and that it is impossible to determine precisely the
stage at which there comes to be such a right on the one side as
implies a definite resistance to right on the other. This of course is not
to be taken to mean that in such periods rights in general are at an
end. It is merely that right is in suspense on the particular point at
issue between the conflicting powers. As we have seen, the general
fabric of rights in any society does not depend on the existence of a
definite and ascertained sovereignty, in the restricted sense of the

words; on the determination of a person or persons in whom supreme power resides, but on the control of the conduct of men according to certain regular principles by a society recognising common interests; and though such control may be more or less weakened during periods of conflict of the kind supposed, it never ceases.

104. It does not follow, however, because there may often not be strictly a right on either side in such periods of conflict that there is not a good and an evil, a better and a worse, on one side or the other. Of this we can only judge by reference to the end, whatever it be, in which we conceive the good of man to consist. There may be clear ground for saying, in regard to any conflict, that one side rather than the other *ought to have* been taken, not because those on one side were, those on the other were not, entitled to say that they had a right to act as they did, but because the common good of a nation or mankind was clearly promoted by one line of action, not by the other. E.g. in the American war of secession, though it would be difficult to say that a man had not as much a right to fight for his seceding states as for the Union, yet as the special interest of the seceding state was that of maintaining slavery, there was reason for holding that the side of the Union, not that of the seceding states, was the one which ought to be taken. On the other hand, it does not follow that in a struggle for sovereignty the good of man is more served by one of the competing powers than by the other. Good may come out of the conflict without one power contributing more to it than the other. There may thus be as little ground retrospectively for saying that one side or the other *ought* to have been taken, as that men had a right to take one and not the other. At the same time, as regards the individual, there is no reason for doubting that the better the motive which determines him to take this side or that – the more he is actuated in doing so by some unselfish desire for human good, the more free he is from egotism, and that conceit or opinionatedness which is a form of egotism – the more good he will do whichever side he adopts.

105. It is in such cases as we have been considering that the distinction between sovereign *de facto* and sovereign *de jure* arises. It has a natural meaning in the mouths of those who, in resisting some coercive power that claims their obedience, can point to another determinate authority to which they not only consider obedience due, but to which such obedience in some considerable measure is actually rendered – a meaning which it has not when all that can be opposed to sovereign *de facto* is either a 'general will', or the mere name of a fallen dynasty exercising no control over men in their dealings with each other. But where this opposition can be used with a natural

meaning, it is a truer account of the matter (as we have seen) to say
that sovereignty is in abeyance. The existence of competing powers,
each affecting to control men in the same region of outward action,
and each having partisans who regard it alone as entitled to exercise
such control, implies that there is not that unity of supreme control
over the outward actions of men which constitutes sovereignty and is
necessary to the complete organisation of a state. The state has either
not reached complete organisation, or is for the time disorganised –
the disorganisation being more or less serious according to the degree
to which the everyday rights of men (their ordinary freedom of action
and acquisition) are interfered with by this want of unity in the
supreme control.

106. In such a state of things, the citizen has no rule of *right* (in the
strict sense of the word) to guide him. He is pretty sure to think that
one or other of the competing powers has a right to his obedience
because, being himself interested (not necessarily *selfishly*
interested) in its support, he does not take account of its lacking that
general recognition as a power necessary to the common good which
is requisite in order to give it a right. But we looking back may see
that there was no such right. Was there then nothing to direct him
either way? Simply, I should answer, the general rule of looking to
the moral good of mankind, to which a necessary means is the organisation of the state, which again requires unity of supreme control, in
the common interest, over the outward actions of men. The citizen
ought to have resisted or obeyed either of the competing authorities
according as by doing so he contributed most to the organisation of
the state in the sense explained. It must be admitted that without
more knowledge and foresight than the individual can be expected to
possess, this rule, if he had recognised it, could have afforded him no
sure guidance; but this is only to say that there are times of political
difficulty in which the line of conduct adopted may have the most important effect, but in which it is very hard to know what is the proper
line to take. On the other side must be set the consideration that the
man who brings with him the character most free from egotism to the
decision even of those questions of conduct, as to which established
rules of right and wrong are of no avail, is most sure on the whole to
take the line which yields the best results.

107. We come next to the question of the possible duty of resistance in cases where no law, acknowledged or half-acknowledged,
written or customary, can be appealed to against a command (general
or *a*particular) that seems contrary*a* to public good; where no
counter-sovereignty, in the natural sense of the words, can be alleged

against that of the imponent of the law; and where at the same time, from the people having no share, direct or indirect, in the government, there is no means of obtaining a repeal of the law by legal means. I say the *duty* of resistance because, from the point of view adopted, there can be no *right* *b*unless there is a *duty* of resistance, since there can be no *right* unless on the ground*b* that it is for common good, and if so there is a duty. In writings of the seventeenth and eighteenth centuries, starting with the assumption of natural rights, the question was never put on its proper footing. It was not asked, When for the sake of the common good the citizen ought to resist the sovereign? but, What sort of injury to person or property gave him a natural right to resist? Now there is sense in inquiring upon what sort and amount of provocation from government individuals inevitably will resist – how in Spinoza's language that *indignatio* [indignation] is excited which leads them *in unum conspirare* [to conspire together][15] – but there is none in asking what gives them a right to resist, unless we suppose a wrong done to society in their persons; and then it becomes a question not of right merely but of duty, whether the wrong done is such as to demand resistance. Now when the question is thus put, no one presumably would deny that under certain conditions there might be a duty of resistance to sovereign power.

108. It is important, however, that instead of discussing the *right of a majority* to resist we should discuss the duty of resistance as equally possible for a minority and a majority. There can be no right of a *majority* of citizens, as such, to resist a *sovereign*. If, by law, written or customary, the majority of citizens possess or share in the sovereign power, then any conflict that may arise between it and any power cannot be a conflict between it and the sovereign. The majority may have a right to resist such a power, but it will not be a right to resist a *sovereign*. If, on the other hand, the majority of citizens have no share by law or custom in the supreme law-making and enforcing power, they never can have a right, simply as a majority, to resist that power. In such a case, there may arise a social duty to resist, and the exercise of men's powers in fulfilment of that duty may be sustained by such a general recognition of its being for the public good, as to become a right; but the resistance may be a duty before a majority of the citizens approve it and does not necessarily become a duty when a majority of them do approve it; while that general recognition of its exercise as being for the common good, through which the power of resistance becomes a right, must be something more habitual and sustained and *a*penetrating*a* than any vote of a majority can convey. Incidentally, however, the consideration of the attitude of the mass of

the people in regard to a contemplated resistance to established government must always be most important in determining the question whether the resistance should be made. It should be made, indeed, if at all, not because the majority approve it, but because it is for the public good, but account must be taken of the state of mind of the majority in considering whether it is for the public good or no. The presumption must generally be that resistance to a government is not for the public good when made on grounds which the mass of the people cannot appreciate; and it must be on the presence of a strong and intelligent popular sentiment in favour of resistance that the chance of avoiding anarchy, of replacing the existing government by another effectual for its purpose, must chiefly depend. On the other hand, it is under the worst governments that the public spirit is most crushed; and thus in extreme cases there may be a duty of resistance in the public interest, though there is no hope of the resistance finding efficient popular support. (An instance is the Mazzinian outbreaks in Italy.)[16] Its repeated renewal and repeated failure may afford the only prospect of ultimately arousing the public spirit which is necessary for the maintenance of a government in the public interest. And just as there may thus be a duty of resistance on the part of a hopeless minority, so on the other side resistance even to a monarchic or oligarchic government is not justified by the fact that a majority, perhaps in some temporary fit of irritation or impatience, is ready to support it, if, as may very well be, the objects for which government subsists – the general freedom of action and acquisition and self-development – are likely to suffer from an overthrow of the government in the popular interest.

109. No precise rule, therefore, can be laid down as to the conditions under which resistance to a despotic government becomes a duty. But the general questions which the good citizen should ask himself in contemplating such resistance will be, (*a*) What prospect is there of resistance to the sovereign power leading to a modification of its character or an improvement in its exercise without its subversion? (*b*) If it is overthrown, is the temper of the people such – are the influences on which the general maintenance of social order and the fabric of recognised rights depend so far separable from it – that its overthrow will not mean anarchy? (*c*) If its overthrow does lead to anarchy, is the whole system of law and government so perverted by private interests hostile to the public, that there has ceased to be any common interest in maintaining it?

110. Such questions are so little likely to be impartially considered at a time when resistance to a despotic government is in contem-

plation, and, however impartially considered, are so intrinsically difficult to answer, that it may seem absurd to dwell on them. No doubt
revolutionists do and must to a great extent 'go it blind.' Such beneficent revolutions as there have been could not have been if they did
not. But in most of those questions of right and wrong in conduct,
which have to be settled by consideration of the probable effects of
the conduct, the estimate of effects which regulates our approval or
disapproval 'upon a retrospective survey', and according to which we
say that an act should or should not have been done, is not one which
we could expect the agent himself to have made. The effort to make it
would have paralysed his power of action.

111. In the simple cases of moral duty, where there is no real doubt
as to the effects of this or that action and danger arises from interested
self-sophistication, we can best decide for ourselves whether we
ought to act in this way or that by asking whether it is what is good in
us – a disinterested or unselfish motive – that moves us to act in this
way or that; and in judging of the actions of others, where the issues
and circumstances are simple, the moral question – the question of
'ought' or 'ought not' – is often best put in the form, How far was the
action such as could represent a good character? That indeed is the
form in which the question should always be put, when the nature of
the case admits it; *a*since, as argued in lectures on the moral criterion,
it*a* is only in its relation to character that action is in the full sense
good or *b*bad, the object of moral approval and disapproval.[17] But*b*
where the probable effects of a certain line of action are at the time of
taking it very obscure, we cannot be sure that relatively the best
character will lead a man to take the line which turns out best in the
result, or that because a line of action has turned out well in result,
the character of the man who adopted it was good. This being so, in
judging of the act retrospectively, we have to estimate it by the result
simply, in abstraction from the character of the agent. Thus in looking back upon a revolutionary outbreak we can only judge whether it
was vindicated by the result. If in the light of the result it appears that
the conditions were not present under which it would have furthered
rather than interfered with the true objects of government, we judge
that it should not have been made; if otherwise, we approve it – judge
that the persons concerned in it were doing their duty in acting as
they did. But whether they were really in the full sense of the term
doing their duty in acting as they did in a case when the outbreak was
successful, or not doing it in a case where it failed, is what we simply
cannot tell; for this depends on the state of character which their
action represented, and that is beyond our ken.[18]

112. Such is the necessary imperfection under which all historical judgments labour – though historians are not apt to recognise it and would be thought much more dull if they did. They would have fewer readers if they confined themselves to the analysis of situations, which may be correctly made, and omitted judgments on the morality of individuals for which, in the proper sense, the data can never be forthcoming. We scarcely have them for ourselves – except that we know that we are none of us what we should be – still less for our intimate acquaintances; not at all for men whom we only know through history, past or present. In regard to them, we can only fall back on the generalisation, that the best man – the man most disinterestedly devoted to the perfecting of humanity, in some form or other, in his own person or that of others – is *ᵃmost*ᵃ likely to act in a way that is good as measured by its results, those results again being estimated with reference to an ideal of character, that this is so even under circumstances of political *ᵇcomplication; that appearances*ᵇ to the contrary, appearances of harm done from good motives, may be met by the considerations, (1) that there is often much egotism, in what calls itself conscientiousness, and that the 'conscientious' motives which lead to mischievous acts may not be in the highest sense disinterested; (2) that to what we call the consequences of an action many influences contribute besides the action which we call the cause, and if evil seems to clog the consequences of action pure in motive, this may be due to other influences connected with motives less worthy, *ᶜand that*ᶜ the consequences which in the rough we call bad might have been worse but for the intervention of the purely-motived action; (3) that the beneficent results are often put to the credit of the actions of selfish men when they should rather be credited to influences more remote and complex, without which those actions would have been impossible or had no good effect, and which have arisen out of unselfish activities. We see the evil in a course of events and lay the blame on someone who should have acted differently, and whom perhaps we take as an instance of how good men cause mischief ; but we do not see the greater evil which would otherwise have ensued.

In regard to the questions stated above as those which the good citizen should *ᵈask*ᵈ himself in contemplation of a possible rebellion, though they are questions to which it is impossible for a citizen in the heat of a revolutionary crisis to give a sufficient answer, and which in fact can only be answered after the event, yet they represent objects which the good citizen will set before himself at such times; and in proportion to the amount of good citizenship, as measured by interest in ᵉthese ᵉ objects (interest in making the best of existing institutions, in maintaining social order and the general fabric of ᶠrights, the interest ᶠ which leads to a *bona fide* estimate of the value of the existing government in its relation to public good) will be the good result of the political movement.

G. WILL, NOT FORCE, IS THE BASIS OF THE STATE

113. Looking back on the political theories we have discussed, we may see that they all start with putting the question to be dealt with in the same way, and that their errors are very much due to the way in which they put it. They make no inquiry into the development of society and of man through society. They take no account of other forms of community than that regulated by a supreme coercive power, either in the way of investigating their historical origin and connection, or of considering the ideas and states of mind which they imply or which render them possible. They leave out of sight the process by which men have been clothed with rights and duties, and with senses of right and duty, which are neither natural nor derived from a sovereign power. They look only to the supreme coercive power on the one side and to individuals, to whom natural rights are ascribed, on the other, and ask what is the nature and origin of the right of that supreme coercive power as against these natural rights of individuals. The question so put can only be answered by some device for representing the individuals governed as consenting parties to the exercise of government over them. This they no doubt are so long as the government is exercised in a way corresponding to their several wishes, but so long as this is the case, there is no interference with their 'natural liberty' to do as they like. It is only when this liberty is interfered with that any occasion arises for an explanation of the compatibility of the sovereign's right with the natural right of the individual; and it is just then that the explanation by the supposition that the right of the sovereign is founded on consent, fails. But the need of the fictitious explanation arises from a wrong way of putting the question – the power which regulates our conduct in political society is conceived in too abstract a way on the one side, and on the other are set over against it, as the subjects which it controls, individuals invested with all the moral attributes and rights of humanity. But in truth it is only as members of a society, as recognising common interests and objects, that individuals come to have these attributes and rights, and the power, which in a political society they have to obey, is derived from the development and systematisation of those insti-

tutions for the regulation of a common life without which they would have no rights at all.

114. To ask why I am to submit to the power of the state, is to ask why I am to allow my life to be regulated by that complex of institutions without which I literally should not have a life to *call my own*, nor should be able to ask for a justification of what I am called on to do. For that I may have a life which I can call my own, I must not only be conscious of myself and of ends which I present to myself as mine; I must be able to reckon on a certain freedom of action and acquisition for the attainment of those ends, and this can only be secured through common recognition of this freedom on the part of each other by members of a society, as being for a common good. Without this, the very consciousness of having ends of his own and a life which he can direct in a certain *a*way – of*a* which he can make something – would remain dormant in a man. It is true that slaves have been found to have this consciousness in high development; but a slave even at his lowest has been partly made what he is by an ancestral life which was not one of slavery pure and simple – a life in which certain elementary rights were secured to the members of a society through their recognition of a common interest. He retains certain spiritual aptitudes from that state of family or tribal freedom. This perhaps is all that could be said of most of the slaves on plantations in modern times, but the slavery of the ancient world, being mainly founded on captivity in war, was compatible with a considerable amount of civilisation on the part of the slaves at the time when their slavery began. A Jewish slave, e.g., would carry with him into slavery a thoroughly developed conception of right and law. Slavery, moreover, implies the establishment of some regular system of rights in the slave-owning society. The slave, especially the domestic slave, has the signs and effects of this system all about him. Hence such elementary consciousness of rights – of powers that are his own to make the best of – as the born slave may inherit from an ancestral life of freedom, finds a stimulus to its inward development, though no opportunity for outward exercise, in the habits and ideas of civilised life with which a common language enables the slave to become conversant, and which through the sympathy implied in a common language he to some extent makes his own. Thus the appearance in slaves of the conception that *b*self mastery is properly theirs,*b* does not conflict with the proposition that only so far as a certain freedom of action and acquisition is secured to a body of men through their recognition of the exercise of that freedom by each other as being for the common good, is there an actualisation of the individual's conscious-

ness of having life and ends of his own. The exercise, manifestation, expression of this consciousness through a freedom secured in the way described is necessary to its real existence, just as language of some sort is necessary to the real existence of thought, and bodily movement to that of the soul.

115. The demand, again, for a justification of what one is called on by authority to do presupposes some standard of right, recognised as equally valid for and by the person making the demand and others who form a society with him, and such a recognised standard in turn implies institutions for the regulation of men's dealings with each other, institutions of which the relation to the consciousness of right may be compared, as above, to that of language to thought. It cannot be said that the most elementary consciousness of right is prior to them, or they to it. They are the expression in which it becomes real.[1] As conflicting with the momentary inclinations of the individual, these institutions are a power which he obeys unwillingly; which he *has to*, or is *made to*, obey. But it is only through them that the consciousness takes shape and form which expresses itself in the question, 'Why should I thus be constrained? By what right is my natural right to do as I like overborne?'

116. The doctrine that the rights of government are founded on the consent of the governed is a confused way of stating the truth that the institutions by which man is moralised – by which he comes to do what he sees that he must as distinct from what he would like – express a conception of a common good; that through them that conception takes form and reality; and that it is in turn through its presence in the individual that they have a constraining power over him – a power which is not that of mere fear, still less a physical compulsion, but which leads him to do what he is not inclined to because there is a law that he should.

Rousseau, it will be remembered, speaks of the 'social pact' not merely as the foundation of sovereignty or civil government, but as the foundation of morality.[2] Through it man becomes a moral agent; for slavery to appetite he substitutes freedom of subjection to self-imposed law. If he had seen at the same time that rights do not begin till duties begin, and that if there was no morality prior to the pact there could not be rights, he might have been saved from the error which the notion of there being natural rights introduces into his theory. But though he does not seem himself to have been aware of the full bearing of his own conception, the conception itself is essentially true. Setting aside the fictitious representation of an original covenant as having given birth to that common 'ego' or general will, without which no such covenant would have been possible, and of obligations arising out of it, as out of a bargain made between one man and another, it remains true that only through a recognition by certain men of a common interest, and through the expression of that recognition in certain regulations of their dealings with each other, could morality originate, or any meaning be gained for such terms as 'ought' and 'right' and their equivalents.

117. Morality, in the first instance, is the observance of such regulations, and though a higher morality – the morality of the character governed by 'disinterested motives', i.e. by interest in some form of human perfection – comes to differentiate itself from this primitive morality consisting in the observance of rules established for a common good, yet this 'outward' morality is the presupposition of the 'higher'.[3] Morality and political subjection thus have a common source – '*political* subjection' being distinguished from that of a slave, as a subjection which secures rights to the subject. That common source is the rational recognition by certain human beings – it may be merely by children of the same parent – of a common well-being which *is* their well-being, and which they conceive as their well-being whether at any moment any one of them is inclined to it or no, and the embodiment of that recognition in rules by which the inclinations of the individuals are restrained, and a *ᵃcorrespondingᵃ* freedom of action for the attainment of well-being on the whole is secured.

118. From this common source morality and political subjection in all its forms always retain two elements in common – one consisting in antagonism to some inclination, the other consisting in the consciousness that the antagonism to inclination is founded on reason or on the conception of some adequate good. It is the antagonism to inclination involved in the moral life, as alone we know it, that makes it proper to speak analogically of moral 'laws' and 'imperatives'. It must be remembered, however, that such language *is* analogical, and that there is an essential difference between laws in the strictest sense – laws which are indeed not adequately described as general commands of a political superior, sanctioned by liability to pains which that superior can inflict, but in which a command so sanctioned is an essential element – and the laws of conscience, of which it is the peculiar dignity that they have no external imponent and no sanction consisting in fear of bodily evil. The relation of constraint, in the one case between the man and the externally imposed law, in the other between some particular desire of the man and his consciousness of something absolutely desirable, we naturally represent in English, when we reflect on it, by the common term 'must'. 'I must connect

with the main-drainage', says the householder to himself, reflecting on an edict of the Local Board. 'I must try to get A.B. to leave off drinking', he says to himself, reflecting on a troublesome moral duty of benevolence to his neighbour. And if the 'must' in the former case represents in part the knowledge that compulsion may be put on the man who neglects to do what he 'must', which is no part of its meaning in the second, on the other hand the consciousness that the constraint is for a common good, which wholly constitutes the power over inclination in the second case, must always be an element in that obedience which is properly called obedience to law, or civil or political obedience. Simple fear can never constitute such obedience. To represent it as the basis of civil subjection is to confound the citizen with the slave, and to represent the motive which is needed for the restraint of those in whom the civil sense is lacking and for an occasional reinforcement of the law abiding principle in others, as if it were the normal influence in habits of life of which the essential value lies in their being independent of it. How far in any particular act of conformity to law the fear of penalties may be operative, it is impossible to say. What is certain is that a habit of subjection founded upon such fear could not be a basis of political or free society; *to which* it is necessary, not indeed that everyone subject to the laws should take part in voting them, still less that he should consent to their application to himself, but that it should represent an idea of common good, which each member of the society can make his own so far as he is rational, or capable of the conception of common good, however much particular passions may lead him to ignore it and thus necessitate the use of force to prevent him from doing that which, so far as influenced by the conception of common good, he would willingly abstain from.

119. Whether the legislative and administrative agencies of society can be kept in the main free from bias by private interests and true to the idea of common good without popular control – whether again, if they can, that 'civil sense', that appreciation of common good, on the part of the subjects, which is as necessary to free or political society as the direction of law to the maintenance of common good, can be kept alive without active participation of the people in legislative functions, is a question of circumstances which perhaps does not admit of unqualified answer. The views of those who looked mainly to the highest development of political life in a single small society[4] have to be modified if the object sought for is the extension of political life to the largest number of people. The size of modern states renders necessary the substitution of a representative system for one in which

the citizens shared directly in legislation, and this so far tends to weaken the active interest of the citizens in the commonwealth, though the evil may partly be counteracted by giving increased importance to municipal or communal administration. In some states, from the want of homogeneity or facilities of communication, a representative legislature is scarcely possible. In others, where it exists, a great amount of power, virtually exempt from popular control, has to be left with what Rousseau would have called the 'prince or magistrate'.[5] In all this there is a lowering of civil vitality as compared with that of the ancient, and perhaps of some exceptionally developed modern, commonwealths. But perhaps this is a temporary loss that we have to bear as the price of having recognised the claim to citizenship as the claim of all men. Certainly all political ideals, which require active and direct participation by the citizens in the functions of the sovereign state, fail us as soon as we try to conceive their realisation on the wide area even of civilised mankind. It is easy to conceive a better system than that of the great states of modern Europe, with their national jealousies, rival armies and hostile tariffs, but the condition of any better state of things would seem to be the recognition of some single constraining power, which would be even more remote from the active co-operation of the individual citizen than is the sovereign power of the great states at present.[6]

120. These considerations may remind us how far removed from any foundation in their own will the requirements of the modern state must seem to be to most of those who have to submit to them. It is true that the necessity which the state lays upon the individual is for the most part one to which he is so accustomed that he no longer kicks against it; but what is it, we may ask, but an external necessity, which he no more lays on himself than he does the weight of the atmosphere or the pressure of summer heat and winter frosts, that compels the ordinary citizen to pay rates and taxes, to serve in the army, to abstain from walking over the squire's fields or snaring his hares, or fishing in preserved streams, to pay rent, or respect those artificial rights of property which only the possessors of them have any obvious interest in maintaining, or even (if he is one of the 'proletariate') to keep his hands off the superfluous wealth of his neighbour, when he has none of his own to lose?[7] Granted that there are good reasons of social expediency for maintaining institutions which thus compel the individual to actions and forbearances that are none of his willing, is it not abusing words to speak of them as founded on a conception of general good? A conception does not float in the air. It must be somebody's conception. Whose conception, then, of general good.is it that

these institutions represent? Not that of most of the people who conform to them, for they do so because they are made to, or have come
to do so habitually from having been long *a*made to (in the sense of
being frightened of the consequences of not conforming – not of consequences which follow*a* from not conforming in the ordinary course
of nature, but of consequences which the state inflicts, artificial consequences.)[8] But when a man is said to obey an authority from interest
in a common good, some other good is meant than that which consists
in escaping the punishment which the authority would inflict on disobedience. *b*Is the conception of common good alleged, then, a conception*b* of it on the part of those who founded or maintain the
institutions in question? But is it not certain that private interests
have been the main agents in establishing, and are still in maintaining, at any rate all the more artificial rights of property? Have not our
modern states again, in nearly every case, been founded on conquest,
and are not the actual institutions of government in great measure the
direct result of such conquest, or, where revolutions have intervened,
of violence which has been as little governed by any conception
of general good?[9] Supposing that philosophers can find exquisite
reasons for considering the institutions and requirements which have
resulted from all this self-seeking and violence to be contributory to
the common good of those who have to submit to them, is it not trifling to speak of them as founded on or representing a conception of
this good, when no such conception has influenced those who established, maintain, or submit to them? And is it not seriously *c*misleading to speak of an obedience to the requirements of the state, when
these requirements have so largely arisen out of force directed by selfish motives and when the motive to the obedience is determined by
fear, as*c* having a common source with the morality of which it is
admitted that the essence is to be disinterested and spontaneous.

121. If we would meet these objections fairly, certain admissions
must be made. That idea of a common good which the state fulfils has
never been the sole influence actuating those who have been agents in
the historical process by which states have come to be formed; and
even so far as it has actuated them, it has been only as conceived in
some very imperfect form that it has done so. This is equally true of
those who contribute to the formation and maintenance of states
rather as agents, and of those who do so rather as patients. No one
could pretend that even the most thoughtful and dispassionate publicist[10] is capable of the idea of the good served by the state to which he
belongs, in all its fulness. He apprehends it only in some of its bearings, but it *is as a common good* that he apprehends it, i.e. not as a

good for himself or for this man or that more than another, but for all
members equally in virtue of their relation to each other and their
common nature. "The idea of the common good served by the state
on the part of the ordinary citizen, is*ᵃ* much more limited in content.
Very likely he does not think of it at all in connection with anything
that the term 'state' represents to him. But he has a clear understanding of certain interests and rights common to himself with his neighbours – if only such as consist in getting his wages paid at the end of
the week, in getting his money's worth at the shop, in the inviolability
of his own person and *ᵇ*his wife's.*ᵇ* Habitually and instinctively, i.e.
without asking the reason why, he regards the claim which in these
respects he makes for himself as conditional upon his recognising a
like claim in others, and thus as in the proper sense a right – a claim of
which the essence lies in its being common to himself with others.
Without this instinctive recognition he is one of the 'dangerous
classes', virtually outlawed by himself. With it, though he has no
reverence for the 'state' under that name, no sense of an interest
shared with others in maintaining it, he has the needful elementary
conception of a common good maintained by law. It is the fault of the
state if this conception fails to make him a loyal subject, if not an intelligent patriot. It is a sign that the state is not a true state – that it is not
fulfilling its primary function of maintaining law equally in the interest of all, but is being administered in the interest of classes;
whence it follows that the obedience which, if not rendered willingly,
the state compels the citizen to render, is not one that he feels any
spontaneous interest in rendering, because it does not present itself to
him as the condition of the maintenance of those rights and interests,
common to himself with his neighbours, which he understands.

122. But even if the law which regulates private relations and its
administration are so equally applied to all, that all who are capable of
a common interest are prompted by that interest to conform to the
law, the result is still only the loyal subject as distinct from the intelligent patriot, i.e. as distinct from the man who so appreciates the good
which in common with others he derives from the state – from the
nation organised in the form of a self-governing community to which
he belongs – as to have a passion for serving it – whether in the way of
defending it from external attack or developing it from within. The
citizens of the Roman Empire were loyal subjects; the admirable
maintenance of private rights made them that; but they were not
intelligent patriots, and chiefly because they were not, the empire
fell. That active interest in the service of the state, which makes
patriotism in the better sense, can hardly arise while the individual's

relation to the state is that of a passive recipient of protection in the exercise of his rights of person and property. While this is the case, he will give the state no thanks for the protection which he will *a*not specially associate with it,*a* and will only be conscious of it when it descends upon him with some unusual demand for service or payment, and then he will be conscious of it in the way of resentment. If he is to have a higher feeling of political duty, he must take part in the work of the state. He must have a share, direct or indirect, by himself acting as a member or by voting for the members of supreme or provincial assemblies, in making and maintaining the laws which he obeys. Only thus will he learn to regard the work of the state as a whole, and to transfer to the whole the interest which otherwise his particular experience would lead him to feel only in that part of its work that goes to the maintenance of his own and his neighbour's rights.

123. And even then his patriotism will hardly be the *passion* which it needs to be, unless his judgement of what he owes to the state is quickened by a feeling of which the *patria*, the fatherland, the seat of one's home, is the natural object and of which the state becomes the object only so far as it is an organisation of a people to whom the individual feels himself bound by ties analogous to those which bind him to his family – ties derived from a common dwelling-place with its associations, from common memories, traditions and customs, and from the common ways of feeling and thinking which a common language and still more a common literature embodies. Such an organisation of an homogeneous people the modern state in most cases is (the two Austrian states being the most conspicuous exceptions),[11] and such the Roman state emphatically was not.

124. But, it will be said, we are here again falling back on our unproved assumption that the state is an institution for the promotion of a common good. This granted, it is not difficult to make out that in most men at any rate there is a sufficient interest in some form of social well-being, sufficient understanding of the community between their own well-being and *a*their neighbours', to*a* make them loyal to such an institution. But the question is, whether the promotion of a common good, at any rate in any sense appreciable by the multitude, is any necessary characteristic of a state. It is admitted that the outward visible sign of a state is the presence of a supreme or independent coercive power, to which habitual obedience is rendered by a certain multitude of people, and that this power may often be exercised in a manner apparently detrimental to general well-being. It may be the case, as we have tried to show that it is, that a power

which is in the main so exercised and is generally felt to be so, is not
likely long to maintain its supremacy, but this does not show that a
state cannot exist without promotion of the common good of its subjects or that (in any intelligible sense) the promotion of such good belongs to the idea of a state. A *short-lived* state is not therefore not a
state, and if it were, it is rather the active interference with the subjects' well-being, than a failure to promote it, that is fatal to the long
life of a state. How, finally, can the state be said to exist for the sake of
an end, or to fulfil an idea, the contemplation of which, it is admitted,
has had little to do with the actions which have had most to do with
bringing states into existence?

125. The last question is a crucial one, which must be met at the
outset. It must be noticed that the ordinary conception of organisation, as we apply it in the interpretation of nature, implies that
agents may be instrumental in the attainment of an end or the fulfilment of an idea of which there is no consciousness on the part of the
organic agents themselves. If it is true on the one hand that the interpretation of nature by the supposition of ends external to it, with
reference to which its processes are directed, has been discarded, and
that its rejection has been the condition of growth in an exact knowledge of nature, on the other hand the recognition of ends immanent
in nature, of ideas realised within it, is the basis of a scientific explanation of life.[12] The phænomena of life are not 'ideal', in the sense in
which the ideal is opposed to that which is sensibly verifiable, but
they are related to the processes of material change which are their
conditions, as ideas or ideal ends which those processes contribute to
realise, because while they determine the processes – while the processes would not be what they are but for relation to them – yet they
are *not* those processes – *not* identical with any one or number of
them, or all of them together. Life does not reside in any of the organs
of life or in any or all of the processes of material change through
which these pass. Analyse or combine these as you will, you do not
detect it as the result of the analysis or combination. It is a function or
end which they realise according to a plan or idea which determines
their existence before they exist and survives their disappearance. If
it were held, then, that the state were an organised community in the
same sense in which a living body is, of which the members at once
^acontribute to^a the function called life and are made what they are by
that function, according to an idea of which there is no consciousness
on their part, we should only be following the analogy of the established method of interpreting nature.

126. The objection to such a view would be that it represents the

state as a purely natural, not at all as a moral, organism. Moral agency is not merely agency by which an end is attained, or an idea realised or a function fulfilled, but agency determined by an idea on the part of the agent, by his conception of an end or function; and the state would be brought into being and sustained by merely natural, as opposed to moral, agency unless there were a consciousness of ends – and of ends the same in principle with that served by the state itself – on the part of those by whom it is brought into being and sustained. I say 'ends the same in principle with that served by the state itself', because if the state arose out of the action of men determined indeed by the consciousness of ends, but ends wholly heterogeneous to that realised by the state, it would not be a moral institution, would not stand in any moral relation to men. Now among the influences that have operated in the formation of states, a large part, it must be admitted, are simply natural. Such are influences of climate, of distribution of mountain and plain, land and water, etc., of all physical demarcations and means of communication. But these, it is clear, are only organic to the formation of states so far as, so to speak, they take a character, which does not belong to them as merely natural, from agencies distinctively human.

127. 'Human, if you like,' it may be replied, 'but not moral, if a moral agency implies any reference to a social or human good – to a good which the *ᵃindividual in any measure desiresᵃ* because it is good for others, or for mankind, as well as himself. In the earth-hunger of conquering hordes, in the passions of military despots, in the pride of avarice or vindictiveness which moved such men as Louis XI or Henry VIII to over-ride the semi-anarchy of feudalism with a real sovereignty, what is there of reference to such good? Yet if we suppose the influence of such motives as these, together with the natural influences just spoken of, to be erased from the history of the formation of states, its distinguishing features are gone.'

128. The selfish motives described must not, any more than the natural influences, be regarded in abstraction if we would understand their true place in the formation of states. The pure desire for social good does not indeed operate in human affairs unalloyed by egotistic motives, but on the other hand what we call egotistic motives do not act without direction from an involuntary reference to social good – 'involuntary' in the sense that it is so much a matter of course that the individual does not distinguish it from his ordinary state of mind. The most conspicuous modern instance of a man who was instrumental in working great and in some ways beneficial changes in the political order of Europe, from what we should be apt to call the most

purely selfish motives, is Napoleon. Without pretending to analyse these motives precisely, we may say that a leading one was the passion for glory; but if there is to be truth in the statement that this passion governed Napoleon, it must be qualified by the farther statement that the passion was itself governed by social influences, operative on him, from which it derived its particular direction.[13] With all his egotism, his individuality was so far governed by the action of the national spirit in and upon him that he could only glorify himself in the greatness of France; and though the national spirit expressed itself in an effort after greatness which was in many ways of a mischievous and delusive kind, yet it again had so much of what may be called the spirit of humanity in it that it required satisfaction in the belief that it was serving mankind. Hence the aggrandisement of France, in which Napoleon's passion for glory satisfied itself, had to take at least the semblance of a deliverance of oppressed peoples, and in taking the semblance to a great extent performed the reality; at any rate in western Germany and northern Italy, wherever the *Code Napoléon* was introduced.

129. It is thus that actions of men whom in themselves we reckon bad are 'overruled' for good. There is nothing mysterious or unintelligible in such 'overruling.' There is nothing in the effect which we ascribe to the 'overruling', any more than in any effect belonging to the ordinary course of nature which there was not in the cause as it really was and as we should see it to be if we fully understood it. The appearance to the contrary arises from our taking too partial and abstract a view of the cause. We look at the action e.g. of Napoleon with reference merely to the selfishness of his motives. We forget how far his motives, in respect of their concrete reality – in respect of the actual nature of the ends pursued as distinct from the particular relation in which those ends stood to his personality – were made for him by influences with which his selfishness had nothing to do. It was not his selfishness that made France a nation or presented to him continuously an end consisting in the national aggrandisement of France, or at particular periods such ends as the expulsion of the Austrians from Italy, the establishment of a centralised political order in France on the basis of social equality, the promulgation of the civil code, the maintenance of the French system along the Rhine.[14] His selfishness gave a particular character to his pursuit of these ends, and (so far as it did so) did so for evil. Finally it led him into a train of action altogether mischievous. But at each stage of his career, if we would understand what his particular agency really was, we must take account of his ends in their full character, as determined

by influences with which his passion for glory no doubt co-operated, but which did not originate with it or with him, and in some measure represented the struggle of mankind towards perfection.

130. And not only must we thus correct our too abstract views of the particular agency of such a man as Napoleon. If we would understand the apparent results of his action we must bear in mind how much besides his particular agency has really gone to produce them, so far as they were good, how much of unnoticed effort on the part of men obscure because unselfish, how much of silent process in the general heart of man. Napoleon was called the 'armed soldier of revolution'[15] and it was in that character that he rendered what service he did to men; but the revolution was not the making of him or his likes. Cæsar again we have learnt to regard as a benefactor of mankind, but it was not Cæsar that made the Roman law through which chiefly or solely the Roman Empire became a blessing. The idiosyncrasy, then, of the men who have been most conspicuous in the production of great changes in the condition of mankind, though it has been an essential element in their production, has been so only so far as it has been overborne by influences and directed to ends, which were indeed not external to the men in question – which on the contrary helped to make them inwardly and spiritually what they really were – but which formed no part of their distinguishing idiosyncrasy. If that idiosyncrasy was conspicuously selfish, it was still not through their selfishness that such men contributed to mould the institutions by which nations have been civilised and developed, but through their fitness to act as organs of impulses and ideas which had previously gained a hold on some society of men, and for the realisation of which the means and conditions had been preparing quite apart from the action of those who became the most noticeable instruments of their realisation.

131. The assertion, then, that an idea of social good is represented by or realised in the formation of states, is not to be met by pointing to the selfishness and bad passions of men who have been instrumental in forming them, if there is reason to think that the influences, under direction of which these passions became thus instrumental, are due to the action of such an idea. And when we speak thus, we do not refer to any action of the idea otherwise than in the consciousness of men. It may be legitimate, as we have seen, to consider ideas as existing and acting otherwise, and perhaps, on thinking the matter out, we should find ourselves compelled to regard the idea of social good as a communication to the human consciousness – a consciousness developing itself in time – from an eternally complete consciousness. But here we are considering it as a source of the moral action of men, and

therefore necessarily as having its seat in their consciousness, and the proposition advanced is that such an idea is a determining element in the consciousness of the most selfish men who have been instrumental in the formation or maintenance of states; that only through its influence in directing and controlling their actions could they be so instrumental; and that, though its active presence in their consciousness is due to the institutions, the organisation of life, under which they are born and bred, the existence of these institutions is in turn due to the action, under other conditions, of the same idea in the minds of men.

132. It is the necessity of a supreme coercive power to the existence of a state that gives plausibility to the view that the action of merely selfish passions may lead to the formation of states. They have been motive causes, it would seem, in the processes by which this '*imperium*' has been established; as, e.g., the acquisition of military power by a tribal chieftain, the conquest of one tribe by another, the supersession of the independent prerogatives of families by a tyrant which was the condition antecedent of the formation of states in the ancient world, the supersession of feudal prerogatives by the royal authority which served the same purpose in modern Europe. It is not, however, supreme coercive power, simply as such, but supreme coercive power, exercised in a certain way and for certain ends, that makes a state; viz. exercised according to law, written or customary, and for the maintenance of rights. The abstract consideration of sovereignty has led to these qualifications being overlooked. Sovereignty = supreme coercive power, indeed, but such power as exercised in and over a state,[16] which means with the qualifications specified: but the mischief of beginning with an inquiry into sovereignty, before the idea of a State has been investigated, is that it leads us to adopt this abstract notion of sovereignty as merely supreme coercive power, and then, when we come to think of the state as distinguished by sovereignty, makes us suppose that supreme coercive power is all that is essential to a state, forgetting that it is rather the state that makes the sovereign than the sovereign that makes the state. Supposing one man had been master of all the slaves in one of the states of the American Union, there would have been a multitude of men under one supreme coercive power, but the slaves and the master would have formed no state, because there would have been no (recognised) rights of slave against slave enforced by the master, nor would dealings between master and slaves have been regulated by any *a*law, and in consequence the multitude consisting of slaves and master would not have been a state. The*a* fact that sover-

eign power, as implied in the fact of its supremacy, can alter any laws, is apt to make us overlook the necessity of conformity to law on the part of the sovereign, if he is to be sovereign of *a state*. A power that altered laws otherwise than according to law, according to a constitution, written or unwritten, would be incompatible with the existence of a state, which is a body of persons, recognised by each other as having rights, and possessing certain institutions for the maintenance of those rights. The office of the sovereign, as an institution of such a society, is to protect those rights from invasion, either from without, from foreign nations, or from within, from members of the society who cease to behave as such. Its supremacy is the society's independence of such attacks from without or within. It is an agency of the society, or the society itself acting for this end. If the power, existing for this end, is used on the whole otherwise than in conformity either with a formal constitution or with customs which virtually serve the purpose of a constitution, it is no longer an institution for the maintenance of rights and ceases to be the agent of a state. We only count Russia a state by a sort of courtesy on the supposition that the power of the Czar, though subject to no constitutional control is so far exercised in accordance with a recognised tradition of what the public good requires as to be on the whole a sustainer of rights.

It is true that just as in a state, all law being derived from the sovereign, there is a sense in which the sovereign is not bound by any law, so there is a sense in which all rights are derived from the sovereign and no power which the sovereign refuses to allow can be a right;[17] but it is only in the sense that, the sovereign being the state acting in a certain capacity, and the state being an institution for the more complete and harmonious maintenance of the rights of its members, a power, claimed as a right, but which the state or sovereign refuses to allow, cannot be really compatible with the general system of rights. In other words, it is true only on supposition that a state is made a state by the function which it fulfils of maintaining the rights of its members as a whole or a system, in such a way that none gains at the expense of another (no one has any power guaranteed to him through another's being deprived of that power). Thus the state, or the sovereign as a characteristic institution of the state, does not create rights, but gives fuller reality to rights already existing. It secures and extends the exercise of powers, which men, influenced in dealing with each other by an idea of common good, had recognised in each other as being capable of direction to that common good, and had already in a certain measure secured to each other in consequence of that recognition. It is not a state unless it does so.

133. It may be said that this is an arbitrary restriction of the term 'state'. If any other word, indeed, can be found to express the same thing, by all means let it be used instead. But some word is wanted for the purpose, because as a matter of fact societies of men, already possessing rights, and whose dealings with each other have been regulated by customs conformable to those rights, but not existing in the form to which the term 'state' has just been applied – i.e. not having a systematic law in which the rights recognised *a*are expressed and harmonised,*a* and which is enforced by a power strong enough at once to protect a society against disturbance within and aggression from without – have come to take on that form. A word is needed to express that form of society, both according to the idea of it which has been operative in the minds of the members of the societies which have undergone the change described, an idea only gradually taking shape as the change proceeded, and according to the more explicit and distinct idea of it which we form in reflecting on the process. The word 'state' is the one naturally used for the purpose. The exact degree to which the process must have been carried before the term 'state' can be applied to the people in which it has gone on cannot be precisely determined, but as a matter of fact we never apply it except in cases where it has gone some way, and we are justified in speaking of the state according to its idea as the society in which it is completed.

134. It is a mistake then to think of the state as an aggregation of individuals under a sovereign – equally so whether we suppose the individuals as such, or apart from what they derive from society, to possess natural rights, or suppose them to depend on the sovereign for the possession of rights. A state presupposes other forms of community, with the rights that arise out of them, and only exists as sustaining, securing, and completing them. In order to make a state there must have been families of which the members recognised rights in each other (recognised in each other powers capable of direction by reference to a common good); there must further have been intercourse between families, or between tribes that have grown out of families, of which each in the same sense recognised rights in the other. The recognition of a right being very short of its definition, the admission of a right in each other by two parties, whether individuals, families, or tribes, being very different from agreement as to what the right consists in – what it is a right to do or acquire – the rights recognised need definition and reconciliation in a general law. When such a general law has been arrived at, regulating the position of members of a family towards each other and the dealings of fam-

ilies or tribes with each other; when it is voluntarily recognised by a community of families or tribes, and maintained by a power strong enough at once to enforce it within the community and to defend the integrity of the community against attacks from without, then the elementary state has been formed.

135. That, however, is the beginning, not the end, of the state. When once it has come into being, new rights arise *ᵃin it and further purposes are served by it. New rights arise in it (1) throughᵃ* the claim for recognition on the part of families and tribes living on the same territory with those which in community form the state but living at first in some relation of subjection to them. A common humanity, of which language is the expression, necessarily leads to recognition of some good as common to these families with those which form the state. This is in principle the recognition of rights on their part; and the consequent embodiment of this recognition in the law of the state is their admission as members of it (Instances of this process are found in the states of Greece and the early history of Rome.) (2) The same thing may happen in regard to external communities ('external' territorially), whether these have been already formed into states or no. It may happen through conquest of one by another, through their submission to a common conqueror, as under the Roman empire, or through voluntary combination (as with the Swiss cantons and the United States of America). However the combination may arise, it results in new rights as between the combined communities within the system of a single state. (3) The extended intercourse between individuals, which formation of the state renders possible, leads to new complications in their dealings with each other, and with it to new forms of right, especially in regard to property – rights as far removed from any obvious foundation on the *suum cuique* principle as that of a college to the great tithes of a parish for which it does nothing.[18] (4) The administration of the state gives rise to rights; to the establishment of powers necessary for its administration. (5) New situations of life may arise out of the extended dealings of man with man which the state renders possible, e.g. through crowding of population in certain localities, which make new modes of protecting the people a matter virtually of right. And, as new rights arise in the state once formed, so further purposes are served. It leads to a development and moralisation of man beyond the stage which they must have reached before it could be possible.

136. On this I shall dwell more next term. What I am now concerned to point out is that, however necessary a factor force may have been in the process by which states have been formed and trans-

formed, it has only been such a factor as co-operating with those ideas without which rights could not exist. I say 'could not *exist*', not 'could not be recognised', because rights are made by recognition. There is no right but thinking makes it so – none that is not derived from some idea that men have about each other. Nothing is more real than a right, yet its existence is purely ideal, if by 'ideal' is meant that which is not dependent on anything material but has its being solely in consciousness. It is to these ideal realities that force is subordinate in the creation and development of states. The force of conquest from without, the force exercised within communities by such agents as the early Greek Tyrants or the royal suppressors of feudalism in modern Europe, has only contributed to the formation of states in so far as its effects have taken a character which did not belong to them as effects of force through their operation in a moral world, in which rights already existed, resting on the recognition by men of each other as determined, or capable of being determined, by the conception of a common good. It is not indeed true that only a state can produce a state, though modern history might seem to favour that notion. As a matter of fact the formation of modern states through feudalism out of an earlier tribal system has been dependent on ideas *a*derived from, if not on institutions actually handed down from, the Roman state; and*a* the improvement and development of the state system which has taken place since the French Revolution has been through agencies which all presuppose and are determined by the previous existence of states. But the Greek states, so far as we know, were a first institution of the kind, not a result of propagation from previously existing states. But the action, which brought them into being, was only effectual for its purpose because the idea of right, though only in the form of family or tribal right, was already in *b*in operation. Next*b* term I hope further to pursue the subject of the functions of the State: to consider the rationale of the rights which it maintains or should maintain, and its further office (if it turns out to have such an office) in the moralization of man beyond the enforcement of rights. This will lead us on to the consideration of 'social virtues'.

H. HAS THE CITIZEN RIGHTS AGAINST THE STATE?

137. I propose to pursue the inquiry, begun *a*last term*a*, into the nature and functions of the state. *b*Last term*b* we were chiefly occupied with criticism. We have seen that no true conception of the rights of individuals against each other or against the state, or of the

rights of the state over individuals, can be arrived at, while we look upon the state merely as an aggregation of individuals under a sovereign power that is able to compel their obedience, and consider this power of compelling a general obedience to be the characteristic thing in a state. So long as this view is retained, no satisfactory answer can be given to the question, by what right the sovereign compels the obedience of individuals. It can only be met either by some device for representing the individuals as so consenting to the exercise of sovereign power over them that it is no violation of their individual rights, or by representing the rights of individuals as derived from the sovereign and thus as having no existence against it. But it is obviously very often against the will of individuals that sovereign power is exercised over them; indeed if it were not so, its characteristic as a power of compulsion would be lost; it would not be a sovereign power; and the fact that the *majority* of a given multitude may consent to its exercise over an unconsenting minority is no justification for its exercise over that minority, if its justification is founded on consent; the representation that the minority virtually consents to be bound by the will of the majority being an obvious fiction. On the other hand, the theory that all right is derived from a sovereign, that it is a power of which the sovereign secures the exercise to the individual, and that therefore there can be no right against that sovereign, conflicts with the primary demands of human consciousness. It implies the identification of 'I ought' with 'I am forced to'. Reducing the 'right' of the sovereign simply to a power, it makes it unintelligible that this power should yet ᶜrepresent itself, and claim obedience to itself, as a right.ᶜ No such theory indeed admits of consistent statement. To say (with Hobbes) that a law may be inequitable or pernicious, though it cannot be unjust,[1] is to admit a criticism of laws, a distinction between those enactments of the sovereign which are what they should be and those which are not. And this is to recognise the individual's demand for a justification of the laws which he obeys; to admit in effect that there is some rule of right, of which the individual is conscious and to which law ought to conform.

138. It is equally impossible, then, to hold that the right of the sovereign power in a state over its members is dependent on their consent, and, on the other hand, that these members have no rights except such as are constituted and conferred upon them by the sovereign. The sovereign, and the state itself as distinguished by the existence of a sovereign power, presupposes rights and is an institution for their maintenance. But these rights do not belong to individuals as they might be in a state of nature, or as they might be if each acted

irrespectively of others. They belong to them as members of a society in which each recognises the other as an originator of action in the same sense in which he is conscious of being so himself (as an 'ego' – as himself the object which determines the action), and thus regards the free exercise of his own powers as dependent upon his allowing an equally free exercise of his powers to every other member of the society. There is no harm in saying that they belong to individuals as such, if we understand what we mean by 'individual', and if we mean by 'individual' a self-determining subject conscious of itself as one among other such subjects, and of its relation to them as making it what it is; for then there is no opposition between the attachment of rights to the individuals as such and their derivation from society. They attach to the individual, but only as a member of a society of free agents, as recognising himself and recognised by others to be such a member, as doing and done by accordingly. A right, then, to act unsocially – to act otherwise than as belonging to a society of which each member keeps the exercise of his powers within the limits necessary to the like exercise by all the other members – is a contradiction. No one can say that, unless he has consented to such a limitation of his powers, he has a right to resist it. The fact of his not consenting would be an extinction of all right on his part.

139. The state then presupposes rights, and *rights of individuals*. It is a form which society takes in order to maintain them. But rights have no being except in a society of men recognising each other as *isoi kai homoioi* [equals]. They are constituted by that mutual recognition. In analysing the nature of any right, we may conveniently look at it on two sides, and consider it as on the one hand a claim of the individual, arising out of his rational nature, to the free exercise of some [a]faculty[a]; on the other, as a concession of that claim by society, [b]a power given to the individual of putting the claim in force by society.[b] But we must be on our guard against supposing that these distinguishable sides have any really separate existence. It is only a man's consciousness of having an object in common with others, a well-being which is consciously his in being theirs and theirs in being his – only the fact that they are recognised by him and he by them as having this object – that gives him the claim described. There can be no reciprocal claim on the part of a man and an animal each to exercise his powers unimpeded by the other, because there is no consciousness common to them. But a claim founded on such a common consciousness is already a claim conceded; already a claim to which reality is given by social recognition, and thus implicitly a right.

140. It is in this sense that a slave has 'natural rights'. They are

'natural' in the sense of being independent of, and in conflict with, the laws of the state in which he lives, but they are not independent of social relations. They arise out of the fact that there is a consciousness of objects common to the slave with those among whom he lives – whether other slaves or the family of his owner – and that this consciousness constitutes at once a claim on the part of each of those who share it to exercise a free activity conditionally upon his allowing a like activity in the others, and a recognition of this claim by the others, through which it is realised. The slave thus derives from his social relations a real right which the law of the state refuses to admit. The law cannot prevent him from acting and being treated, within certain limits, as a member of a society of persons freely seeking a common ªgood. And as that capabilityª of living in a certain limited community with a certain limited number of human beings, which the slave cannot be prevented from exhibiting, is in principle a capability of living in a community with any other human beings, supposing the necessary training to be allowed; and as every such capability constitutes a right, we are entitled to say that the slave has a right to citizenship – to a recognised equality of freedom with any and every one with whom he has to do – and that in refusing him not only citizenship but the means of training his capability of citizenship, the state is violating a right, founded on that common human consciousness which is evinced both by language which the slave speaks and by actual social relations subsisting between him and others. And on the same principle upon which a state is violating natural rights in maintaining slavery, it does the same in using force, except under necessity of self-defence, against members of another community. Membership of any community is so far in principle membership of all communities as to constitute a right to be treated as a freeman by all other men, to be exempt from subjection to force except for prevention of force.

141. A man may thus have rights as a member of a family or of human society in any other form without being a member of a state at all – rights which remain rights though any particular state or all states refuse to recognise them; and a member of a state, on the ground of that capability of living as a freeman among freemen which is implied in his being a member of a state, has rights as against all other states and their members. These latter rights are in fact during peace recognised by all civilised states. It is the object of 'private international law' to reduce them to a system. But though it follows from this that the state does not create rights, it may be still true to say that the members of a state derive their rights from the state and

have no rights against it. We have already seen that a right against society, as such, is an impossibility; that every right is derived from some social relation; that a right against any group of associated men depends on association, as *isos kai homoios* [an equal], with them and with some other men. Now for the member of a state to say that his rights are derived from his social relations, and to say that they are derived from his position as member of a state, are the same thing. The state is for him the complex of those social relations out of which rights arise, so far as those rights have come to be regulated and harmonised according to a general law, which is recognised by a certain multitude of persons, and which there is sufficient power to secure against violation from without and from within. The other forms of community which precede and are independent of the formation of the state do not continue to exist outside it, nor yet are they superseded by it. They are carried on into it. They become its organic members, supporting its life and in turn maintained by it in a new harmony with each other. Thus the citizen's rights, e.g. as husband or head of a family or a holder of property, though such rights, arising out of other social relations than that of citizen to citizen, existed when as yet there was no state, are yet to the citizen derived from the state – from that more highly developed form of society in which the association of the family and that of possessors who respect each other's possessions are included as in a fuller whole; which secures to the citizen his family rights and his rights as a holder of property, but under conditions and limitations which membership of the fuller whole – the reconciliation of rights arising out of one sort of social capability with those arising out of another – renders necessary. Nor can the citizen have any right against the state, in the sense of a right to act otherwise than as a member *a*of the state. For a citizen this is as much a contradiction as the right of a man to act otherwise than as a member of some society; the state*a* being for its members the society of societies – the society in which all their claims upon each other are mutually adjusted.

142. But what exactly is meant by the citizen's acting 'as a member of his state'? What does the assertion that he can have no right to act otherwise than as a member of his state amount to? Does it mean that he has no right to disobey the law of the state to which he belongs, whatever that law may be? that he is not entitled to exercise his powers in any way that the law forbids and to refuse to exercise them in any way that it commands? This question was virtually dealt with last term in considering the justifiability of resistance to an ostensible sovereign.[2] The only unqualified answer that can be given to it is one

that may seem too general to be of much practical use, viz. that so far as the laws anywhere or at any time in force fulfil the idea of a state, there can be no right to disobey them; or, that there can be no right to disobey the law of the state except in the interest of the state; i.e. for the purpose of making the state in respect of its actual laws more completely correspond to what it is in tendency or idea, viz. the reconciler and sustainer of the rights that arise out of the social relations of men. On this principle there can be no right to disobey or evade any particular law on the ground that it interferes with any freedom of action, any right of managing his children or 'doing what he will with his own', which but for that law the individual would possess. Any power which has been allowed to the individual up to a certain time, he is apt to regard as permanently his right. It has, indeed, been *so far* his right if the exercise of that power has been allowed with any reference to social good but it does not, as he is apt to think, remain his right when a law has been enacted that interferes with it. A man, e.g., has been allowed to drive at any pace he likes through the streets, to build houses without any reference to sanitary conditions, to keep his children at home or send them to work 'analphabetic', to buy or sell alcoholic drinks at his pleasure. If laws are passed interfering with any or all of these powers, he says that his rights are being violated. But he only possessed these powers *as rights* through membership of a society which secured them to him, and of which the only permanent bond consists in the reference to the well-being of its members as a whole. It has been the social recognition grounded on that reference that has rendered certain of his powers rights. If upon new conditions arising, or upon elements of social good being taken account of which had been overlooked before, or upon persons being taken into the reckoning as capable of participating in the social well-being who had previously been treated merely as means to its attainment[3] – if in any of these ways or otherwise the reference to social well-being suggests the necessity of some further regulation of the individual's liberty to do as he pleases, he can plead no right against this regulation, for every right that he has possessed has been dependent on that social judgment of its compatibility with general well-being which in respect to the liberties in question is now reversed.

143. 'Is then the general judgment as to the requirements of social well-being so absolutely authoritative that no individual right can exist against it? What if according to this judgment the institution of slavery is so necessary that citizens are prohibited by law from teaching slaves to read and from harbouring runaways? or if according to it

the maintenance of a certain form of worship is so necessary that no other worship can be allowed and no opinion expressed antagonistic to it? Has the individual no rights against enactments founded on such accepted views of social well-being?'[4] We may answer: A right against society as such, a right to act without reference to the needs or good of society, is an impossibility, since every right depends on some social relation, and a right against any group of associated men depends on association upon some footing of equality with them or with some other men. We saw how the right of the slave really rested on this basis – on a social capacity shown in the footing on which he actually lives with other men. On this principle it would follow, if we regard the state as the sustainer and harmoniser of social relations, that the individual can have no right against the state; that its law must be to him of absolute authority. But in fact, as actual states at best fulfil but partially their ideal function, we cannot apply this rule to practice. The general principle that the citizen must never act otherwise than as a citizen does not carry with it an obligation under all conditions to conform to the law of his state, since those laws may be inconsistent with the true end of the state as the sustainer and har- moniser of social relations. The assertion by the citizen of any right, however, which the state does not recognise must be founded on a ref- erence to an *acknowledged* social good. The fact that the individual would like to exercise the power claimed as a right does not render the exercise of it a right, nor does the fact that he has been hitherto allowed to exercise it render it a right, if social requirements have newly arisen under changed conditions, or have newly come to be recognised, with which its exercise is incompatible. The reason that the assertion of an illegal right must be founded on reference to *ac- knowledged* social good is that, as we have seen, no exercise of a power, however abstractedly desirable for the promotion of human good it might be, can be claimed as a right unless there is some common consciousness of utility shared by the person making the claim and those on whom it is made.[5] It is not a question whether or no it ought to be claimed as a right; it simply can *not* be except on this condition. It would have been impossible, e.g., in an ancient state, where the symbol of social union was some local worship, for a mono- theistic reformer to claim a right to attempt the subversion of that worship. If a duty to do so had suggested itself, consciousness of the duty could never have expressed itself in the form of a claim of right, in the absence of any possible sense of a public interest in the *ᵃreligious revolutionᵃ* to which the claim could be addressed. Thus just as it is not the exercise of every power, properly claimable as a right, that is a right in the full or explicit sense of being legally established, so it is not every power, of which the exercise would be desirable in an ideal state of things, that is properly claimable as a right. The condition of its being so claimable is that its exercise should be contributory to some social good which the public conscience is capable of appreciating – not necessarily one which in the existing prevalence of private interests can obtain due acknowledgment, but still one of which men in their actions and language show themselves to be aware.

144. *a*Applying these considerations to the question whether a citizen of a state which forbade education of slaves could claim a right on these points above the law,*a* we may answer, he has no rights against them founded on any right to do as he likes. Whatever counter-rights he has must be founded on a relation to social well-being, and that a relation of which his fellow-citizens are aware. He must be able to point to some public interest, generally recognised as such, which is involved in the exercise of the power claimed by him as a right; to show that it is not the general well-being, even as conceived by his fellow-citizens, but some special interest of a class that is concerned in preventing the exercise of the power claimed. In regard to the right of teaching or harbouring the slave, he must appeal to the actual capacity of the slave for community with other men as evinced in the manner described above, to the recognition of this capacity as shown by the actual behaviour of the citizens in many respects towards the slave, on the addition to social well-being that results from the realisation of this capacity in all who possess it through rights being legally guaranteed to them. In this way he must show that the reference to social well-being, on which is founded the recognition of powers as rights, if fairly and thoroughly carried out, leads to the exercise of powers in favour of the slave, in the manner described, not to prohibition of that exercise as the supposed law prohibits it. The response which in so doing he elicits from the conscience of fellow-citizens shows that in talking of the slave as 'a man and a brother' he is exercising what is implicitly his right, though it is a right which has not become explicit through legal enactments. This response supplies the factor of social recognition which, as we have seen, is necessary in order to render the exercise of any power a right. To have an implicit right, however, to exercise a power which the law disallows is not the same thing as having a right to exercise that right. The right may be claimed without the power being actually exercised so long as the law prohibits its exercise. The question, therefore, would arise whether the citizen was doing his duty as such – acting as a member of the

state – if he not merely did what he could for repeal of the law prohibiting the instruction of a slave or the assistance of runaways, but himself in defiance of the law instructed and assisted them. As a general rule, no doubt, even bad laws – laws representing the interests of classes or individuals as opposed to those of the community – should be obeyed. There can be no right to disobey them, even while their repeal is urged on the ground that they violate rights, because the public interest, on which all rights are founded, is more concerned in the general obedience to law than in the exercise of those powers by individuals or classes which the objectionable laws unfairly withhold. The maintenance of [b]a prohibitory duty upon import[b] of certain articles in the interest of certain manufacturers would be no justification for smuggling these articles. The smuggler acts for his private gain, as does the man who buys of him, and no violation of the law for the private gain of the violator, however unfair the law violated, can justify itself by reference to a recognised public good, or be vindicated as a right. On the other hand, there may be cases in which the public interest – not merely according to some remote philosopher's view of it but according to conceptions which the people are able to assimilate – is best served by a violation of some actual law.[6] It is so in regard to slavery when the public conscience has come to recognise a capacity for right (for exercising powers under control of a reference to general well-being) in a body of men to whom legal rights have hitherto been refused, but when some powerful class in its own interest resists alteration of the law. In such a case a violation of the law on behalf of the slave is not only not a violation in the interest of the violator; the general sense of right on which general observance of law depends being represented by it, there is no danger of its making a breach in the law-abiding habits of the people.

145. But this, it will be said, is to assume a condition of things in which the real difficulty of the question disappears. What is to be done when no recognition of the implicit rights of the slave can be elicited from the public conscience; when the legal prohibitions described are supported by the only conceptions of general good of which the body of citizens is capable? Has the citizen still a right to disregard these legal prohibitions? Is the assertion of such a right compatible with the doctrine that social recognition of any mode of action as contributory to the common good is necessary to constitute a right so to act, and that no member of a state can have a right to act otherwise than according to that position? The question, be it observed, is not as to the right of the slave, but as to the right of the citizen to treat the slave as having rights in a state of which the law

forbids his being so treated. The claim of the slave to be free, his right *implicit* to have rights *explicit*, i.e. to membership of a society of which each member is treated by the rest as entitled to seek his own good in his own way on supposition that he so seeks it as not to interfere with the like freedom of quest on the part of others, rests, as we have seen, on the fact that the slave is determined by conceptions of a good common to himself with others, as shown by the actual social relations in which he lives. No state law can neutralise this right. The state may refuse him family rights and rights of property, but it cannot help his living as a member of a family – acting and being treated as a father, husband, son, or brother – and therefore cannot extinguish the rights which are necessarily involved in his so acting and being so treated. Nor can it prevent him from appropriating things and from associating with others on the understanding that they respect each other's appropriations, and thus possessing and exercising rights of property. He has thus rights which the state neither gives nor can take away, and they amount to or constitute a right to freedom in the sense explained. The state, under which the slave is a slave, refusing to recognise this right, he is not limited in its exercise by membership of the state. He has a right to assert his right to such membership in any way compatible with that susceptibility to the claims of human fellowship on which the right rests. Other men have claims upon him, *"conditioning"* his rights, but the state, as such, which refuses to recognise his rights, has no claim on him. The obligation to observe the law, because it is the law, does not exist for him.

146. It is otherwise with the citizen. The slave has a claim upon him to be treated in a certain way, the claim which is properly described as that of a common humanity. But the state which forbids him so to treat the slave has also a claim upon him, a claim which embodies many of the claims that arise out of a common humanity in a form that reconciles them with each other. Now it may be argued that the claim of the state is only absolutely paramount on supposition that in its commands and prohibitions it takes account of *all* the claims that arise out of human fellowship; that its authority over the individual is in principle the authority of those claims, taken as a whole; that if, as in the case supposed, its ordinances conflict with those claims as possessed by a certain class of persons, their authority, which is essentially a conditional or derived authority, disappears; that a disregard of them in the interest of the claims which they disregard is really conformity to the requirements of the state according to its true end or idea, since it interferes with none of the claims or interests which the state has its value in maintaining or protecting,

but, on the contrary, forces on the attention of members of the state claims which they hitherto disregarded; and that if the conscience of the citizens is so far mastered by the special private interests which the institution of slavery breeds that it cannot be brought to recognise action on the slave's behalf as contributory to a common good, yet there is no ground under such conditions for considering a man's fellow-citizens to be the sole organs of the recognition which is needed to render his power of action a right; that the needful recognition is at any rate forthcoming from the slaves and from all those acquainted with the action in whom the idea of a good common to each man with others operates freely.[7]

147. This may be truly urged, but it does not therefore follow that the duty of befriending the slave is necessarily paramount to the duty of obeying the law which forbids his being befriended: and if it is possible for the latter duty to be paramount, it will follow, on the principle that there is no right to violate a duty, that under certain conditions the right of helping the slave may be cancelled by the duty of obeying the prohibitory law. It would be so if the violation of law in the interest of the slave were liable to result in *a*general anarchy – in the destruction of the state, not merely*a* in the sense of the dissolution of this or that form of civil combination, but of the disappearance of conditions under which any civil combination is possible; for such a destruction of the state would mean a general loss of freedom – a general substitution of force for mutual good-will in men's dealings with each other – that would outweigh the evil of any slavery under such limitations and regulations as an organised state imposes on it.

I. PRIVATE RIGHTS. THE RIGHT TO LIFE AND LIBERTY

148. *a*In order then to understand the nature of the state,*a* we must understand the nature of those rights which do not come into being with it but arise out of social relations that may exist where a state is not; it being the first, though not the only, office of the state to maintain those rights. They depend for their existence, indeed, on society – a society of men who recognise each other as *isoi kai homoioi* [equals], as capable of a common well-being – but not on society's having assumed the form of a state. They may therefore be treated as claims of the individual without reference to the form of the society which concedes or recognises them, and on whose recognition, as we have seen, their nature as rights depends. Only it must be borne in mind that the form in which these claims are admitted and acted on

by men in their dealings with each other varies with the form of society – that the actual form, e.g., in which the individual's right of property is admitted under a patriarchal *régime* is very different from that in which it is admitted in a state – and that though the principle of each right is throughout the same, it is a principle which only comes to be fully recognised and acted on when the state has not only been formed, but fully developed according to its idea.

149. The rights which may be treated as independent of the state in the sense explained are of course those which are commonly distinguished as *private*, in opposition to *public* rights. '[I]f rights be analysed, they will be found to consist of several kinds. For first they are such as regard a man's own person; secondly, such as regard his dominion over the external and sensible things by which he is surrounded; thirdly, such as regard his private relations, as a member of a family; fourthly, such as regard his social state or condition, as a member of the community; the first of which classes may be designated as *personal rights*, the second, as *rights of property*, the third, as *rights in private relations*, and the fourth, as *public rights*.'[1]

150. An objection might fairly be made to distinguishing one class of rights as *personal*, on the ground that all rights are so – not merely in the legal sense of 'person', according to which the proposition is a truism, since every right implies a person as its subject, but in the moral sense, since all rights depend on that capacity in the individual for being determined by a conception of well-being, as an object at once for himself and for others, which constitutes personality in the moral sense. By personal rights in the above classification are meant rights of life and liberty – i.e. of preserving one's body from the violence of other men, and of using it as an instrument only of one's own will – if of another's, still only through one's own. The reason why these come to be spoken of as 'personal' is probably the same with the reason why we talk of a man's 'person' in the sense simply of his body. They may, however, be reckoned in a special sense personal even by those who consider all rights personal because the person's possession of a body and its exclusive determination by his own will is the condition of his exercising any other rights – indeed, of all manifestation of personality. Prevent a man from possessing property (in the ordinary sense), and his personality may still remain. Prevent him (if it were possible) from using his body to express a will, and the will itself could not become a reality; he would not be really a person.

151. If there are such things as rights at all, then, there must be a right to life and liberty, or, to put it more properly, to free life. No distinction can be made between the right to life and the right to

liberty, for there can be no right to mere life – no right to life on the
part of a being that has not also the right to *ª*direct*ª* the life according
to the motions of its own will. What is the foundation of this right?
The answer is, capacity on the part of the subject for membership of a
society – for determination of the will, and through it of the bodily organisation, by the conception of a well-being as common to self with
others. This capacity is the *foundation* of the right, or the right *potentially*, which becomes *actual* through recognition of the capacity by a
society, and through the power which the society in consequence
secures to the individual of acting according to the capacity. In principle, or intrinsically, or in respect of that which it has it in itself to
become, the right is one that belongs to every man in virtue of his
human nature (of the qualities which render him capable of any fellowship with any other men), and is a right as between him and *ᵇ*all*ᵇ*
men; because, as we have seen, the qualities which enable him to act
as a member of any one society having the general well-being of its
members for its object (as distinct from any special object requiring
special talent for its accomplishment) form a capacity for membership of any other such society. But actually, or as recognised, it only
gradually becomes a right of a man, as man, and against all men.

152. At first it is only a right of the man as a member of some one
particular society, and a right as between him and the other members
of that society, the society being naturally a family or tribe. Then, as
several such societies come to recognise, in some limited way, a
common well-being and thus to associate on settled terms, it comes to
be a right not merely between the members of any one of the societies
but between members of the several families or tribes in their dealings with each other – not, however, as men, but only as belonging to
this or that particular family. This is the state of things in which, if
one man is damaged or killed, compensation is made according to the
terms of some customary law by the family or tribe of the offender to
that of the man damaged or killed, the compensation varying according to the rank of the family. Upon this system – generally through
some fusion of family demarcations and privileges, whether through
pressure upward of a population hitherto inferior, or through a level-
ling effected by some external power – there supervenes one in which
the relation between citizen and citizen, as such, is substituted for
that between family and family, as such. This substitution is one of
the essential processes in the formation of the state. It is compatible,
however, with the closest limitation of the privileges of citizenship
and implies no acknowledgment in man as man of the right to free life
ascribed to the citizen as citizen. In the ancient world, the companion

of citizenship is everywhere slavery, and it was only actual citizenship, not any such capacity for becoming a citizen as might naturally be held to be implied in civil birth, that was considered to give a right to live; for the exposure of children was everywhere practised (and with the approval of the philosophers), a practice in strong contrast with the principle of modern law that even a child in the womb has a right to live.[2]

153. The influences commonly pointed out as instrumental in bringing about the recognition of rights in the man, as independent of particular citizenship, are: (1) adjudication by Roman prætors of questions at issue between citizens and those who were not so, which led to the formation of the system of 'equity', independent of the old civil law and tending gradually to be substituted for it. The existence of such a system, however, presupposes the recognition of rights so far independent of citizenship in a particular state as to obtain between citizens of different states. (2) The doctrine of a 'law of nature', applicable to dealings of all men, popularised by the Stoics. (3) The Christian conception of the universal redemption of a brotherhood, of which all could become members through a mental act within the power of all.[3]

154. The admission of a right to free life on the part of every man, as man, does in fact logically imply the conception of all men as forming one society in which each individual has some service to render, one organism in which each has a function to fulfil. There can be no claim on society, such as constitutes a right, except in respect of a capacity freely (i.e. under determination by conception of the good) to contribute to its good. If the claim is made on behalf of any and every human being, it must be a claim on human society as a whole, and there must be a possible common good of human society as a whole, conceivable as independent of the special conditions of particular societies, to render such a claim possible. We often find, however, that men assimilate a practical idea in respect of one of its implications without doing so in respect of the rest. Thus the idea of the individual's right to free life has been strongly laid hold of in Christendom in what may be called an abstract or negative way, but little notice has been taken of what it involves. Slavery is everywhere condemned. It is established that no one has a right to prevent the individual from determining the conditions of his own life. We treat life as sacred even in the human embryo, and even in hopeless idiots and lunatics recognise a right to live – a recognition which can only be rationally explained on either or both of two grounds: (1) that we do not consider either their lives or the society which a man may freely

serve to be limited to this earth, and thus ascribe to them a right to live on the strength of a social capacity which under other conditions may become what it is not here; or (2) that the distinction between curable and incurable, between complete and incomplete, social incapacity is so indefinite that we cannot in any case safely assume it to be such as to extinguish the right to live. Or perhaps it may be argued that even in cases where the incapacity is ascertainably incurable, the patient has still a social function (as undoubtedly those who are incurably ill in other ways have) – a passive function as the object of affectionate ministrations arising out of family instincts and memories – and that the right to have life protected corresponds to this passive social function. The fact, however, that we have almost to cast about in certain cases for an explanation of the established belief in the sacredness of human life shows how deeply rooted that belief is unless where some counter-belief interferes with it.[4]

155. On the other hand, it is equally noticeable that there are counter-beliefs which, under conditions, do neutralise it, and that certain other beliefs, which form its proper complement, have very slight hold on the mind of modern Christendom. It is taken for granted that the exigencies of the state in war, whether the war be necessary or not for saving the state from dissolution, absolutely neutralise the right to live. We are little influenced by the idea of the universal brotherhood of men – of mankind as forming one society with a common good, of which the conception may determine the action of its members. In international dealings we are apt to suppose that it can have no place at all. Yet, as has been pointed out, it is the proper correlative of the admission of a right to free life as belonging to man in virtue simply of his human nature. And though this right can only be grounded on the capacity, which belongs to the human nature, for freely fulfilling some function in the social organism, we do very little to give reality to the capacity or to enable it to realise itself. We content ourselves with enacting that no man shall be used by other men as a means against his will, but we leave it to be pretty much a matter of chance whether or no he shall be qualified to fulfil any social function – to contribute anything to the common good – and to do so freely (i.e. under the conception of a common good). The only reason why a man should not be used by other men simply as a means to their ends is that he should use himself as a means to an end which is really his and theirs at once. But while we say that he shall not be used as a means, we often leave him without the chance of using himself for any social end at all.

156. Four questions then arise[5]: (1) With what right do the necess-

ities of war override the individual's right of life? (2) In what relation do the rights of states to act for their own interest stand to that right of human society, as such, of which the existence is implied in the possession of right by the individual as a member of that society, irrespectively of the laws of particular states? (3) On what principle is it to be assumed that the individual by a certain conduct of his own forfeits the right of free life, so that the state (at any rate for a time) is entitled to subject him to force – to treat him as an animal or a thing? Is this forfeiture ever so absolute and final that the state is justified in taking away his life? (4) What is the nature and extent of the individual's claim to be enabled to realise that capacity for contributing to a social good, which is the foundation of his right to free life?

K. THE RIGHT OF THE STATE OVER THE INDIVIDUAL IN WAR

157. It may be admitted that to describe war as 'multitudinous murder' is a figure of speech.[1] The essence of murder does not lie in the fact that one man takes away the life of another, but that he does this to 'gain his private ends' and with 'malice' against the person killed. I am not here speaking of the legal definition of murder, but of murder as a term of moral reprobation, in which sense it must be used by those who speak of war as 'multitudinous murder'. They cannot mean murder in the legal sense, because in that sense only 'unlawful killing', which killing in war is not, is murder. When I speak of 'malice', therefore, I am not using 'malice' in the legal sense. In that sense 'malice' is understood to be the attribute of every 'wrongful act done intentionally without just or lawful excuse',[2] and is ascribed to acts (such as killing an officer of justice, knowing him to be such, while resisting him in a riot) in which there is no ill-will of the kind which we suppose in murder, when we apply the term in its natural sense as one of moral disapprobation. Of murder in the moral sense the characteristics are those stated, and these are not present in the case of a soldier who kills one on the other side in battle. He has no ill-will to that particular person or to any particular person. He incurs an equal risk with the person whom he kills, and incurs that risk not for the sake of killing him. His object in undergoing it is not private to himself but a service (or what he supposes to be a service) to his country – a good which is his own, no doubt (that is implied in his desiring it), but which he presents to himself as common to him with others. Indeed, those who might speak of war as 'multitudinous murder' would not look upon the soldier as a murderer. If reminded

that there cannot be a murder without a murderer, and pressed to say who, when a bloody battle takes place, the murderer or murderers are, they would probably point to the authors of the war. It may be questioned, by the way, whether there has ever been a war of which the origination could be truly said to rest with a definite person or persons, in the same way in which the origination of an act which would be called murder in the ordinary sense rests with a particular person. No doubt there have been wars for which certain assignable individuals were specially blameable – wars which they specially helped to bring about or had special means of preventing – and the more the wickedness of such persons is kept in mind the better; but even in these cases the cause of the war can scarcely be held to be gathered up within the will of any individual, or the combined will of certain individuals, in the same way as is the cause of murder or other punishable acts. When A.B. is murdered, the sole cause lies in some definite volition of C.D. or others, however that volition may have been caused. ᵀ ·ᵤ when a war 'breaks out', though it is not to be considered, as we are too apt to consider it, a natural calamity which could not be prevented, it would be hard to maintain that the sole cause lies in some definite volition on the part of some assignable person or persons, even of those who are most to blame. Passing over this point, however, if the acts of killing in war are not murders (in the *moral* sense, the *legal* being out of the question) because they lack those characteristics on the part of the agent's state of mind which are necessary to constitute a murder, the persons who cause those acts to be committed, if such persons can be pointed out, are not the authors of murder, multitudinous or other. They would only be so if the characteristic of 'malice', which is absent on the part of the immediate agent of the act, were present on their part as its ultimate agents. But this is not the case. However selfish their motives, they cannot fairly be construed into ill-will towards the persons who happened to be killed in the war; and therefore, whatever wickedness the persons responsible for the war are guilty of, they are not guilty of 'murder' in any natural sense of the term, nor is there any murder in the case at all.

158. It does not follow from this, however, that war is ever other than a great wrong, as a violation on a multitudinous scale of the individual's right to life. Whether it is so or not must be discussed on other grounds. If there is such a thing as a right to life, on the part of the individual man as such, is there any reason to doubt that this right is violated in the case of every man killed in war? It is not to the purpose to allege that in order to a violation of right there must be not

only a suffering of some kind on the part of the subject of a right but an intentional act causing it on the part of a human agent. There is of course no violation of right when a man is killed by a wild beast or a stroke of lightning, because there is no right as between a man and a beast or between a man and natural force. But the deaths in a battle are caused distinctly by human *agency, agent and patient being alike members of the human society, between whom the relation of right subsists, and intentional* agency. The individual soldier may not have any very distinct intention when he fires his rifle except to obey orders, but the commanders of the army and the statesmen who send it into the field intend the death of as many men as may be necessary for their purpose. It is true they do not intend the death of this or that particular person, but no more did the Irishman who fired into a body of police guarding the Fenian prisoners.[3] It might fairly be held that this circumstance exempted the Irishman from the special moral guilt of murder, though according to our law it did not exempt him from the legal guilt expressed by that term; but no one would argue that it made the act other than a violation of the right to life on the part of the policeman killed. No more can the *absence, on the part of those who cause men to be killed in battle, of* an intention to kill this or that specific person, save their act from being a violation of the right to life.

159. Is there then any condition on the part of the persons killed that saves the act from having this character? It may be urged that when the war is conducted according to usages that obtain between civilised nations (not when it is a village-burning war like that between English and Afghans)[4] the persons killed are voluntary combatants, and *oudeis adikeitai ekōn* [no one does wrong willingly].[5] Soldiers, it may be said, are in the position of men who voluntarily undertake a dangerous employment. If some of them are killed, this is not more a violation of the human right to life than is the death of men who have engaged to work in a dangerous coal-pit. To this it must be answered that if soldiers did in fact voluntarily incur the special risk of death incidental to their calling, it would not follow that the right to life was not violated in their being killed. It is not a right which it rests with a man to retain or give up at his pleasure. It is not the less a wrong that a man should be a slave because he has sold himself into slavery. The individual's right to live is but the other side of the right which society has in his living. The individual can no more voluntarily rid himself of it than he can of the social capacity, the human nature, on which it is founded. Thus, however ready men may be for high wages to work in a dangerous pit, a wrong is held to

be done if they are killed in it. If provisions which might have made it safe have been neglected, someone is held responsible. If nothing could make it safe, the working of the pit would not be allowed. The reason for not more generally applying the power of the state to prevent voluntary noxious employments, is not that there is no wrong in the death of the individual through the incidents of an employment which he has voluntarily undertaken, but that the wrong is more effectually prevented by training and trusting individuals to protect themselves than by the state protecting them.[6] Thus the waste of life in war would not be the less a wrong – not the less a violation of the right, which subsists between all members of society, and which none can alienate, that each should have his life respected by society – if it were the fact that those whose lives are wasted voluntarily incurred the risk of losing them. But it can scarcely be held to be the fact. Not only is it impossible, even when war is conducted on the most civilised methods, to prevent great incidental loss of life (to say nothing of other injury) among non-combatants; the waste of the life of the combatants is one which the power of the state compels. This is equally true whether the army is raised by voluntary enlistment or by conscription. It is obviously so in the case of conscription, but under a system of voluntary enlistment, though the individual soldier cannot say that he in particular has been compelled by the government to risk his life, it is still the case that the state compels the risk of a certain number of lives. It decrees that an army of such a size shall be raised, though if it can get the men by voluntary hiring it does not exercise compulsion on the men of a particular age, and it sends the army into the field. Its compulsive agency causes the death of the soldiers killed, not any voluntary action on the part of the soldiers themselves. The action of the soldiers no doubt contributes to the result, for if they all refused to fight there would be no killing, but it is an action put in motion and directed by the power of the state, which is compulsive in the sense that it operates on the individual in the last resort through fear of death.

160. We have then in war a destruction of human life inflicted on the sufferers intentionally by voluntary human agency. It is true, as we saw, that it is not easy to say in any case by whose agency in particular. We may say indeed that it is by the agency of the state, but what exactly does that mean? The 'state' here must = the sovereign power in the state, but it is always difficult to say by whom that power is wielded, and if we could in any case specify its present holders, the further question will arise whether their course of action has not been shaped for them by previous holders of power.[7] But however widely

distributed the agency may be which causes the destruction of life in war, it is still intentional human agency. The destruction is not the work of accident or of nature. If then it is to be other than a wrong, because a violation of the right to mutual protection of life involved in membership of human society, it can only be because there is exercised in war some right that is paramount to this. It may be argued that this is the case; that there is no right to the preservation of life at the cost of losing the necessary conditions of 'living well'; that war is in some cases the only means of maintaining these conditions, and that where this is so, the wrong of causing the destruction of physical life disappears in the paramount right of preserving the conditions under which alone moral life is possible.

161. This argument, however, seems to be only available for shifting the quarter in which we might be at first disposed to lay the blame of the wrong involved in war, not for changing the character of that wrong. It goes to show that the wrong involved in the death of certain soldiers does not necessarily lie with the government which sends those soldiers into the field, because this may be the only means by which that government can prevent more serious wrong; it does not show that there is no wrong in their death. If the integrity of any state can only be maintained at the cost of war, and if that state is more than what many so-called states have been – more than an aggregation of individuals or communities under one ruling power – if it so far fulfils the idea of a state, that its maintenance is necessary to the free development of the people belonging to it; then by the authorities or people of that state no wrong is done by the destruction of life which war involves, except so far as they are responsible for the state of things which renders the maintenance of the integrity of the state impossible by other means. But how does it come about that the integrity of such a state is endangered? Not by accident or by forces of nature, but by intentional human agency in some form or other, however complicated; and with that agency lies the wrong-doing. To determine it (as we might be able to do if a horde of barbarians broke in on a civilised state, compelling it to resort to war for its defence) is a matter of small importance: what *is* important to bear in mind (being one of those obvious truths out of which we may allow ourselves to be sophisticated) is that the destruction of life in war is always wrong-doing, whoever be the wrong-doer, and that in the wars, most strictly defensive of political freedom, the wrong-doing is only removed from the defenders of political freedom to be transferred elsewhere. If it is difficult in any case to say precisely where, that is only a reason for more general self-reproach [a]– as the

preachers would say – for a more humbling sense^a of complicity in that radical (but conquerable because moral) evil of mankind which renders such a means of maintaining political freedom necessary. The language, indeed, which we hear from the pulpit about war being a punishment for the sins of mankind, is perfectly true, but it needs to be accompanied by the reminder that this punishment of sin is simply a consequence of the sin and itself a further sin, brought about by the action of the sinner, not an external infliction brought about by agencies to which man is not a party.

162. In fact, however, if most wars had been wars for the maintenance or acquisition of political freedom, the difficulty of fixing the blame of them, or at any rate of freeing one of the parties in each case from blame, would be much less than it really is. Of the European wars of the last four hundred years, how many could be fairly said to have been wars in which either or any of the parties were fighting for this end? Perhaps the wars in which the Dutch Republics defended themselves against Spain and against Louis XIV, and that in which Germany shook off the dominion of Napoleon. Perhaps the more recent struggles of Italy and Hungary against Austrian government.[8] Perhaps in the first outset of the war of 1792 the French may be fairly held to have been defending institutions necessary for the development of social freedom and equality. In this war, however, the issue very soon ceased to be one between the defenders of such institutions on the one side, and their assailants on the other, and in most modern wars the issue has not been of this kind at all. The wars have arisen primarily out of the rival ambition of kings and dynasties for territorial aggrandisement, with national antipathies and ecclesiastical ambitions, and the passions arising out of religious partisanship, as complicating influences. As nations have come more and more to distinguish and solidify themselves, and a national consciousness has come definitely to be formed in each, the rival ambitions of nations have tended more and more first to support, then perhaps to supersede, the ambitions of dynasties as causes of war. The delusion has been practically dominant that the gain of one nation must mean the loss of another. Hence national jealousies in regard to colonial extensions, hostile tariffs and the effort of each nation to exclude others from its markets. The explosion of this idea in the region of political economy has had little effect in weakening its hold on men's minds. The people of one nation still hear with jealousy of another nation's advance in commerce, as if it meant some decay of their own. And if the commercial jealousy of nations is very slow in disappearing, their vanity, their desire apart from trade each to become or to seem

stronger than the other, has very much increased. A hundred and fifty years ago national vanity could scarcely be said to be an influence in politics. The people under one ruler were not homogeneous enough, had not enough of a corporate consciousness, to develop a national vanity. Now (under the name of patriotism) it has become a more serious disturber of peace than dynastic ambition. Where the latter is dangerous, it is because it has national vanity to work upon.

163. Our conclusion then is that the destruction of life in war (to say nothing of other evils incidental to it with which we are not here concerned) is always wrong-doing, with whomsoever the guilt of the wrong-doing may lie; that only those parties to a war are exempt from a share in the guilt who can truly plead that to them war is the only means of maintaining the social conditions of the moral development of man, and that there have been very few cases in which this plea could be truly made. In saying this it is not forgotten either that many virtues are called into exercise by war, or that wars have been a means by which the movement of mankind, which there is reason for con- sidering a progress to higher good, has been carried on. These facts do not make the wrong-doing involved in war any less so. If nothing is to be accounted wrong-doing through which final good is wrought, we must give up either the idea of there being such a thing as wrong- doing, or the idea of there being such a thing as final good. If final good results from the world of our experience, it results from pro- cesses in which wrong-doing is an inseparable element. Wrong-doing is voluntary action, either (in the deeper moral sense) proceeding from a will uninfluenced by the desire to be good on the part of the agent (which may be taken to include action tending to produce such action) or (in the sense contemplated by the *jus naturæ* [law of nature]) it is action that interferes with the conditions necessary to the free-play and development of a ᵃgood willᵃ on the part of others. It may be that, according to the divine scheme of the world, such wrong-doing is an element in a process by which men gradually approximate more nearly to good (in the sense of a good will). We cannot think of God as a moral being without supposing this to be the case. But this makes no difference to wrong-doing in those relations in which it *is* wrong-doing, and with which alone we are concerned, viz. in relation to the will of human agents and to the results which those agents can foresee and intend to produce. If an action, so far as any results go which the agent can have in view or over which he has control, interferes with conditions necessary to the free-play and de- velopment of a good will on the part of others, it is not the less wrong- doing because, through some agency which is not his, the effects

which he intended and which rendered it wrong-doing, come to contribute to an ulterior good. Nor, if it issues from bad will (in the sense explained), is it less wrong (in the moral sense) because this will is itself, in the view of some higher being, contributory to a moral good which is not, in whole or part, within the view of the agent. If then war is wrong-doing in both the above senses (as it is always – at any rate on the part of those with whom the ultimate responsibility for it lies), it does not cease to be so on account of any good resulting from it in a scheme of providence.

164. 'But,' it may be asked, 'are we justified in saying that it is always wrong-doing on the part of those with whom the ultimate responsibility lies? It is admitted that certain virtues may be evoked by war; that it may have results contributory to the moral progress of mankind; may not the eliciting of these virtues, the production of these results, be contemplated by the originators of war, and does not the origination of war, so far as influenced by such motives, cease to be wrong-doing? It must be admitted that Cæsar's wars in Gaul were unprovoked wars of conquest, but their effect was the establishment of Roman civilisation with its equal law over a great part of western Europe in such a way that it was never wholly swept away, and that a permanent influence in the progress of the European polity can be traced to it. May he not be credited with having had, however indefinitely, such an effect as this in view? Even if his wish to extend Roman civilisation was secondary to a plan for raising an army by which he might master the Republic, is he to have no credit for the beneficent results which are admitted to have ensued from the success of that plan? May not a similar justification be urged for English wars in India? If, again, the establishment of the civil unity of Germany, and the liberation of Christian populations in Turkey, are admitted to have been gains to mankind, is not that a justification of such persons concerned in the origination of the wars that brought about those results as can be supposed to have been influenced by a desire for them?'[9]

165. These objections might be to the purpose if we were attempting the task (generally, if not always, an impossible one) of determining the moral desert, good or ill, of those who have been concerned in bringing this or that war about. Their tendency merely is to distribute the blame of the wrong-doing involved in war, to show how widely ramified is the agency in that wrong-doing, not to affect its character as wrong-doing. If the only way of civilising Gaul was to kill all the people whom Cæsar's wars caused to be killed, and if the desire for civilising it was a prevailing motive in Cæsar's mind, so

much the better for Cæsar but so much the worse for the other unassignable and innumerable human agents who brought it about that such an object could only be attained in such a way. We are not, indeed, entitled to say that it could have been brought about in any other way. It is true to say (if we know what we are about in saying it) that nothing which happens in the world could have happened otherwise than it has. The question for us is whether that condition of things which rendered e.g. Cæsar's Gallic wars, with the violation of human rights which they involved – the interference in the case of innumerable persons with the conditions under which man can be helpful to man, physical life being the first of these – the *sine qua non* in the promotion of ulterior human welfare, was or was not the work of human agency. If it was – and there is no doubt that it was, for to what merely natural agency could the necessity be ascribed? – then in that ordinary sense of the word 'could' in which it expresses our responsibility for our actions, men *could* have brought about the good result without the evil means. They could have done so *if they had been better*. It was owing to human wickedness – if less on Cæsar's part, then so much the more on the part of innumerable others – that the wrong-doing of those wars was the appropriate means to this ulterior good. So in regard to the other cases instanced. It is idle to speculate on other means by which the permanent pacification of India, or unification of Germany, or liberation of Christians in European Turkey might have been *a*brought about than those by which each result respectively has been brought about;*a* but it is important to bear in mind that the innumerable wrong acts involved in achieving them – acts wrong because violations of the rights of those directly affected by them – did not cease to be wrong acts because under the given condition of things the results specified would not have been obtained without them. This given condition of things was not like that (e.g.) which compels the castaways from a shipwreck, so many days from shore and with only so much provision in their boat, to draw lots which shall be thrown overboard. It was a condition of things which human wickedness, through traceable and untraceable channels, brought about. If the individual promoters of wars, which through the medium of multitudinous wrong-doing have yielded good to mankind, have been really influenced by desire for any such good – and much scepticism is justified in regard to such a supposition – then so much less of the guilt of the wrong-doing has been theirs. No nation, at any rate, that has taken part in such wars can fairly take credit for having been governed by such a motive. It has been either a passive instrument in the hands of its rulers or has been animated by less worthy motives, very mixed but of which perhaps a diffused desire for excitement has been the most innocent. On what reasonable ground can Englishmen or Germans or Russians claim that their several nations took part in the wars by which India was pacified, Germany unified, Bulgaria liberated, under the dominant influence of a desire for human good? Rather, if the action of a national conscience in such matters is possible at all, they should take shame for their share in that general human selfishness which rendered certain conditions of human development only attainable by such means.

166. Reverting then to the questions which arose out of the assertion of a right to free life on the part of the individual man as such (§156), it appears that the first must be answered in the negative. No state of war can make the destruction of man's life by man other than a wrong, though the wrong is not always chargeable upon all the parties to a war. The second question is virtually answered by what has been said about the first. In regard to the state according to its idea the question could not arise, for according to its idea the state is an institution in which all rights are harmoniously maintained, in which all the capacities that give rise to rights have free play given to them. No action in its own interest of a state that fulfilled this idea could conflict with any true interest or right of general society, of the men not subject to its law taken as a whole. There is no such thing as an inevitable conflict between states. There is nothing in the nature of the state that, given a multiplicity of states, should make the gain of the one the loss of the other. The more perfectly each one of them attains its proper object of giving free scope to the capacities of all persons living on a certain range of territory, the easier it is for others to do so; and in proportion as they all do so the danger of conflict disappears.

167. On the other hand, the imperfect realisation of civil equality in the full sense of the term in certain states is in greater or less degree a source of danger to all. The presence in states either of a prerogatived class or of a body of people who, whether by open denial of civil rights or by restrictive laws, are thwarted in the free development of their capacities, or of an ecclesiastical organisation which disputes the authority of the state on matters of right and thus prevents the perfect civil fusion of its members with other citizens,[10] always breeds an imagination of there being some competition of interests between states. The privileged class involuntarily believes and spreads the belief that the interest of the state lies in some extension without, not in an improvement of organisation within. A suffering class attracts sym-

pathy from without and invites interference with the state which contains it; and that state responds not by healing the sore but by *^a*defending what*^a* it conceives to be its special interests, but which are only special on account of its bad *^b*organisation, against aggression.*^b* Or perhaps the suffering population overflows into another state, as the Irish into America, and there becomes a source not only of internal difficulty but of hostile feeling between it and the state where the suffering population still survives. People, again, who *^c*take their direction in matters which the state treats as belonging to itself*^c* from an ecclesiastical power external to the state under which they live, are necessarily in certain relations alien to that state, and may at any time prove a source of apparently conflicting interests between it and some other state which under the influence of the hostile ecclesiastical power espouses their cause. Remove from European states, as they are and have been during the last hundred years, the occasions of conflict, the sources of apparently competing interests, which arise in one or other of the ways mentioned – either from the mistaken view of state interests which a privileged class inevitably takes or from the presence in them of oppressed populations, or from what we improperly call the antagonism of religious confessions – and there would not be or have been anything to disturb the peace between them. And this is to say that the source of war between states lies in their incomplete fulfilment of their function; in the fact that there is some defect in the maintenance or reconciliation of rights among their subjects.[11]

168. This is equally true in regard to those causes of conflict which are loosely called 'religious'. These do not arise out of any differences between the convictions of different people in regard to the nature of God or their relations to Him, or the right way of worshipping Him, but either out of some aggression upon the religious freedom of certain people, made or allowed by the powers of the state, which thus puts these people in the position of an alien or unenfranchised class, or else out of an aggression on the rights of the state by some corporation calling itself spiritual but really claiming sovereignty over men's actions in the same relations in which the state claims to determine them. There would be nothing tending to international disturbance in the fact that bodies of people who worship God in the Catholic manner live in a state where the majority worship in the Greek or Protestant manner and alongside of another state where the majority is Catholic but for one or other or both of these circumstances, viz. if the Catholic worship and teaching is interfered with by the Protestant or Greek state, and that Catholics are liable to a direction by a power which claims to regulate men's transactions with each other by a law

of its own, and which may see fit (e.g.) to forbid the Catholic subjects
in the Greek or Protestant state from being married, or having their
parents buried, or their children taught the necessary *acts,* in the
manner which the state directs. This reciprocal invasion of right – the
invasion of the rights of the state by the church on one side, and on
the other the restriction placed by the sovereign upon the subject's
freedom, not of conscience (for that is impossible), but of expressing
his conscience in word and act – has sometimes caused a state of
things in which certain of the subjects of a state have been better
affected to another state than to their own, and in such a case there is
an element of natural hostility between the states. An obvious
instance to give of this relation between states would have been that
between Russia and Turkey, if Turkey could be considered to have
been constituted as a state at all.[12] Perhaps a better instance would be
the position of Ireland in the past – its disaffection to England and
gravitation, first to France, then to the United States, caused chiefly
by Protestant penal laws which in turn were at least provoked by the
aggressive attitude of the church towards the English state.[13] Whenever a like invasion of rights still takes place, e.g. in the treatment of
the Catholic subjects of Russia in Poland, in the ultramontane movement of resistance to certain requirements of the state among the
Catholic subjects of Germany,[14] it tends to international conflict.
And what is now a somewhat remote tendency has in the past been a
formidable stimulant to war.

169. It is nothing then in the necessary organisation of the state,
but rather some defect of that organisation in relation to its proper
function of maintaining and reconciling rights, of giving scope to capacities, that leads to a conflict of apparent interests between one
state and another. The wrong, therefore, which results to human
society from conflicts between states cannot be condoned on the
ground that it is a necessary incident of the existence of states. The
wrong cannot be held to be lost in a higher right, which attaches to
the maintenance of the state as the institution through which alone
the freedom of man is realised. It is not the state, as such, but this or
that particular state, which by no means fulfils its purpose, and might
perhaps be swept away and superseded by another with advantage to
the ends for which the true state exists, that needs to defend its
interests by action injurious to those outside it. Hence there is no
ground for holding that a state is justified in doing whatever its
interests seem to require, irrespectively of effects on other men. If
those effects are bad, involving either a direct violation of personal
rights or obstruction to the moral development of society anywhere

in the world, then there is no *ultimate* justification for the political action that gives rise to them. The question can only be (as we have seen generally in regard to the wrong-doing of war) where in particular the blame lies. Whether there is any justification for a particular state which in defence of its interests inflicts an injury on some portion of mankind (e.g., the Germans in holding Metz,[15] on the supposition that their tenure of such a thoroughly French town necessarily thwarts in many ways the healthy activity of the inhabitants, or the English in carrying fire and sword in Afghanistan for the sake of acquiring a scientific frontier;[16]) must depend (1) on the nature of the interests thus defended, (2) on the impossibility of otherwise defending them, (3) on the question how they came to be endangered. If they are interests of which the maintenance is essential to those ends as a means to which the state has its value, if the state which defends them has not itself been a joint-cause of their being endangered, and if they cannot be defended except at the cost of injury to some portion of mankind, then the state which defends them is clear of the guilt of that injury. But the guilt is removed from it only to lie somewhere else, however wide its distribution may be. It may be doubted, however, whether the second question could ever be answered altogether in favour of a state which finds it necessary to protect its interests at the cost of inflicting an injury on mankind.

170. It will be said, perhaps, that these formal arguments in proof of the wrong-doing involved in war, and of the unjustifiability of the policy which nations constantly adopt in defence of their apparent interests, carry very little conviction; that a state is not an abstract complex of institutions for maintenance of rights, but a nation, a people, possessing such institutions; that the nation has its passions which inevitably lead it to judge all questions of international right from its own point of view, and to consider its apparent national interests as justifying anything; that if it were otherwise, if the cosmopolitan point of view could be adopted by nations, patriotism would be at an end: that whether this be desirable or no, such an extinction of national passions is impossible; that while they continue, wars are as inevitable between nations as they would be between individuals, if individuals were living in what philosophers have imagined to be the state of nature, without recognition of a common superior; that nations in short are in the position of men judging their own causes, which it is admitted that no one can do impartially;[17] and that this state of things cannot be altered without the establishment of a common constraining power, which would mean the extinction of the life of independent states – a result as

undesirable as it is unattainable. Projects of perpetual peace, to be logical, must be projects of all-embracing empire.[18]

171. There is some cogency in language of this kind. It is true that when we speak of a state as a living agency, we mean, not an institution or complex of institutions, but a nation organised in a certain way; and that members of the nation in their corporate or associated action are animated by certain passions, arising out of their association, which, though not egoistic relatively to the individual subjects of them (for they are motives to self-sacrifice), may, in their influence on the dealings of one nation with another, have an effect analogous to that which egoistic passions, properly so called, have upon the dealings of individuals with each other. On the other hand, it must be remembered that the national passion, which in any good sense is simply the public spirit of the good citizen, may take and every day is taking, directions which lead to no collision between one nation and another; (or, to say the same thing negatively, that it is utterly false to speak as if the desire for one's own nation to show more military strength than others were the only or the right form of patriotism); and that though a nation, with national feeling of its own, must everywhere underlie a state, properly so called, yet still, just so far as the perfect organisation of rights within each nation, which entitles it to be called a state, is attained, the occasions of conflict between nations disappear; and again, that by the same process, just so far as it is satisfactorily carried out, an organ of expression and action is established for each nation in dealing with other nations, which is not really liable to be influenced by the same egoistic passions in dealing with the government of another nation as embroil individuals with each other. The love of mankind, no doubt, needs to be particularised in order to have any power over life and action. Just as there can be no true friendship except towards this or that individual, so there can be no true public spirit which is not localised in some way. The man whose desire to serve his kind is not centred primarily in some home, radiating from it to a commune, a municipality, and a nation, presumably has no effectual desire to serve his kind at all. But there is no reason why this localised or nationalised philanthropy should take the form of a jealousy of other nations or a desire to fight them, personally or by proxy. Those in whom it is strongest are every day expressing it in good works which benefit their fellow-citizens without interfering with the men of other nations. Those who from time to time talk of the need of a great war to bring unselfish impulses into play give us reason to suspect that they are too selfish themselves to recognise the unselfish activity that is going on all round them. Till all the methods

have been exhausted by which nature can be brought into the service of man, till society is so organised that everyone's capacities have free scope for their development, there is no need to resort to war for a field in which patriotism may display itself.

172. And in fact, just so far as states are thoroughly formed, the diversion of patriotism into the military channel tends to come to an end. It is a survival from a condition of things in which, as yet, the state, in the full sense, was not; in the sense, namely, that in each territory controlled by a single independent government the rights of all persons, as founded on their capacities for contributing to a common good, are equally established by one system of law. If each separately governed territory were inhabited by a people so organised within itself, there would be nothing to lead to the association of the public spirit of the good citizen with military aggressiveness – an association which belongs properly not to the *politeia* [constitutional state], but to the *dynasteia* [arbitrary oligarchy]. The Greek states, however complete might be the equality of their citizens among themselves, were all *dynasteiai* in relation to some subject populations, and, as such, jealous of each other. The Peloponnesian war was eminently a war of rival *dynasteia*. And those habits and institutions and modes of feeling in Europe of the present day, which tend to international conflict, are either survivals from the *dynasteiai* of the past, or arise out of the very incomplete manner in which as yet, over most of Europe the *politeia* has superseded the *dynasteia*. Patriotism, in that special military sense in which it is distinguished from public spirit, is not the temper of the citizen dealing with fellow-citizens, or with men who are themselves citizens of their several states, but that of the follower of the feudal chief, or of the member of a privileged class conscious of a power, resting ultimately on force, over an inferior population, or of a nation holding empire over other nations.

173. Standing armies, again, though existing on a larger scale now than ever before, are not products of the *civilisation* of Europe, but of the predominance over that civilisation of the old *dynasteiai*. The influences which have given rise to and keep up those armies essentially belong to a state of things in which mankind – even European mankind – is not yet thoroughly organised into political life. Roughly summarised, they are these: (1) The temporary confiscation by Napoleon to his own account of the products of the French Revolution, which thus, though founded on a true idea of a citizenship in which not the few only, but all men, should partake, for the time issued in a *dynasteia* over the countries which most directly felt the effects of the revolution. (2) The consequent revival in dynastic

forms, under the influence of antagonism to France, of national life in Germany.[19] (3) The aspiration after national unity elsewhere in Europe – a movement which must precede the organisation of states on a sound basis, and for the time readily yields itself to direction by a *dynasteia*. (4) The existence over all the Slavonic side of Europe of populations which are only just beginning to make any approach to political life – the life of the *politeia*, or *civitas* – and still offer a tempting field to the ambition of rival *dynasteiai*, Austrian, Russian, and Turkish (which, indeed, are by no means to be put on a level, but are alike as not resting on a basis of citizenship). (5) The tenure of a great Indian empire by England, which not only gives it a military character which would not belong to it simply as a state, but brings it into outward relations with the *dynasteiai* just spoken of. This is no doubt a very incomplete account of the influences which have combined to 'turn Europe into a great camp' (a very exaggerated expression), but it may serve to show what a fuller account would show more clearly, that the military system of Europe is no necessary incident of the relations between independent states, but arises from the fact that the organisation of state-life, even with those peoples that have been brought under its influence at all, is still so incomplete.

174. The more complete it becomes, the more the motives and occasions of international conflict tend to disappear, while the bonds of unity become stronger. The latter is the case, if for no other reason, yet for this; that the better organisation of the state means freer scope to the individual (not necessarily to do as he likes, e.g. in the buying and selling of alcohol, but in such development of activity as is good on the whole). This again means freer intercourse between members of one state and those of another, and in particular more freedom of trade. All restrictions on freedom of wholesome trade are really based on special class interests, and must disappear with the realisation of that idea of individual right, founded on the capacity of every man for free contribution to social good, which is the true idea of the state. And as trade between members of different states becomes freer and more full, the sense of common interests between them, which war would infringe, becomes stronger.[20] The bond of peace thus established is sometimes depreciated as a selfish one, but it need be no more selfish than that which keeps the peace between members of the same state, who have no acquaintance with each other. In one case as in the other it may be said that the individual tries to prevent a breach of the peace because he knows that he has more to gain than to lose by it. In the latter case, however, this account of the matter would be, to say the least, insufficient. The good citizen observes the law in letter

and in spirit, not from any fear of consequences to himself if he did not, but from an idea of the mutual respect by men for each other's rights as that which should be, which has become habitual with him and regulates his conduct without his asking any questions about it. There was a time, however, when this idea only thus acted spontaneously in regulating a man's action towards his family or immediate neighbours or friends. Considerations of interest were the medium through which a wider range of persons came to be brought within its range. And thus, although considerations of an identity of interests, arising out of trade, may be the occasion of men's recognising in men of other nations those rights which war violates, there is no reason why upon that occasion and through the familiarity which trade brings about an idea of justice, as a relation which *should* subsist between all mankind as well as between members of the same state, may not come to act on men's minds as independently of all calculation of their several interests as does the idea which regulates the conduct of the good citizen.

175. If the *"restraining"* or impelling power of the idea of what is due from members of different nations to each other is weak, it must be observed on the other hand that the individual members of a nation have no such apparent interest in their government's dealing unfairly with another nation as one individual may have in getting the advantage of another. Thus, so far as this idea comes to form part of the habit of men's minds, there ceases to be anything in the passions of the people which a government represents to stimulate the government to that unfairness in dealing with another government to which an individual might be moved by self-seeking passions in dealing with another individual, in the absence of an impartial authority having power over both. If at the same time the several governments are purely representative of the several peoples, as they should become with the due organisation of the state, and thus have no dynastic interests of their own in embroiling one nation with another, there seems to be no reason why they should not arrive at a passionless impartiality in dealing with each other, which would be beyond the reach of the individual in defending his own cause against another. At any rate, if no government can ever get rid of some bias in its own favour, there remains the possibility of mediation in cases of dispute by disinterested governments. With the abatement of national jealousies and the removal of those more deeply-seated causes of war which, as we have seen, are connected with the deficient organisation of states, the dream of an international court with authority resting on the consent of independent states may come to be realised. Such a

result may be very remote, but it is important to bear in mind that there is nothing in the intrinsic nature of a system of independent states incompatible with it, but that on the contrary every advance in the organisation of mankind into states in the sense explained is a step towards it.

L. THE RIGHT OF THE STATE TO PUNISH

176. We come now to the third of the questions raised [§156] in regard to the individual's right to free life – the question under what conditions that right may be forfeited; the question, in other words, of the state's right of punishment. The right (power secured by social recognition) of free life in every man rests on the assumed capacity in every man of free action contributory to social good ('free' in the sense of determined by the idea of a common good. Animals may and do contribute to the good of man, but not thus 'freely'[1]). This right on the part of associated men implies the right on their part to prevent such action as interferes with the possibility of free action contributory to social good. This constitutes the right of punishment – the right so far to use force upon a person (treat him as an animal or a thing) as may be necessary to save others from this interference.[2]

177. Under what conditions a person needs to be thus dealt with – what particular actions on his part constitute such an interference – is a question which can only be answered when we have considered what powers in particular need to be secured to individuals or to officials in order to the possibility of free action of the kind described. Every such power is a right of which the violation – if intended as a violation of a right – requires a punishment, of which the kind and amount must depend on the relative importance of the right and of the extent to which its general exercise is threatened. Thus every theory of rights in detail must be followed by, or indeed implies, a corresponding theory of punishment in detail – a theory which considers what particular acts are punishable, and how they should be punished. The latter cannot precede the former. All that can be done here is further to consider what general rules of punishment are implied in the principle on which we hold all right of punishment to rest, and how far in the actual practice of punishment that principle has been realised.

178. It is commonly asked whether punishment according to its proper nature is retributive or preventive or reformatory.[3] The true answer is that it is and should be all three. The statement, however, that the punishment of the criminal by the state is retributive, though

true in a sense that will be explained directly, yet so readily lends itself to a misunderstanding, that it is perhaps best avoided. It is not true in the sense that in legal punishment as it should be there survives any element of private vengeance, of the desire on the part of the individual who has received a hurt from another to inflict an equivalent hurt in return. It is true that the beginning of punishment by the state first appears in the form of a regulation of private vengeance, but it is not therefore to be supposed that punishment by the state is in any way a continuation of private vengeance. It is the essence of the former to suppress and supersede the latter, but it only does so gradually, just as rights *in actuality* are only formed gradually. Private vengeance belongs to the state of things in which rights are not as yet actualised in the sense that the powers which it is for the social good that a man should be allowed to exercise, are not yet secured to him by society. In proportion as they are actualised, the exercise of private vengeance must cease. A *right* of private vengeance is an impossibility; for just so far as the vengeance is private, the individual in executing it is exercising a power not derived from society nor regulated by reference to *a*social good,*a* and such a power is not a right. Hence the view commonly taken by writers of the seventeenth and eighteenth centuries, implies an entire misconception of the nature of a right,[4] the view, viz., that there first existed rights of self-defence and self-vindication on the part of individuals in a state of nature and that these came to be devolved on a power representing all individuals, so that the state's right of using force against those men who use or threaten force against other men, is merely the sum or equivalent of the private rights which individuals would severally possess if there were no public equivalent for them. It is to suppose that to have been a right which in truth, under the supposed conditions, would merely have been animal impulse and power and public right (which is a pleonasm, for all right is public) to have resulted from the combination of these animal impulses and powers – to suppose that from a state of things in which '*homo homini lupus*' ['man is no man, but a wolf, to a stranger'], by mere combination of wolfish impulses there could result the state of things in which '*homo homini deus*' ['man is but a god to a stranger'].[5]

179. In a state of things in which private vengeance for hurt inflicted was the universal practice, there could be no rights at all. In the most primitive society in which rights can exist, it must at least within the limits of the family be suppressed by that authority of the family or its head which first constitutes rights. In such a society it is only on the members of another family that a man may retaliate at

pleasure a wrong done to him, and then the vengeance is not strictly
speaking taken by individual upon individual, though individuals
may be severally the agent and patient of it, but by family upon
family.[6] Just because there is as yet no idea of a state independent of
ties of birth, much less of a universal society from relation to which a
man derives rights, there is no idea of rights attaching to him as a citizen or as a man but only as a member of a family. That social right,
which is at once a right of society over the individual, and a right
which society communicates and secures the individual, appears so
far only as a control exercised by the family over its members in their
dealings with each other, as an authorisation which it gives them in
prosecuting their quarrels with members of another family, and at
the same time to a certain extent as a limitation on the manner in
which feuds between families may be carried on – a limitation
generally dependent on some religious authority equally recognised
by the families at feud.

180. From this state of things it is a long step to the *régime* of law in
a duly constituted state. Under it the arm of the state alone is the
organ through which force may be exercised on the individual; the individual is prohibited from averting violence by violence, except so
far as is necessary for the immediate protection of life, and altogether
from avenging wrong done to him, on the understanding that the
society, of which he is an organ and from which he derives his rights,
being injured in every injury to him, duly protects him against
injury, and when it fails to prevent such injury from being done,
inflicts such punishment on the offender as is necessary for future
protection. But the process from the one state of things to the other,
though a long one, consists in the further development of that social
right[7] which properly speaking was the only right the individual ever
had, and from the first, or ever since a permanent family tie existed,
was present as a qualifying and restraining element in the exercise of
private vengeance so far as that exercise partook at all in the nature of
a right. The process is not a continuance of private vengeance under
altered forms, but a gradual suppression of it by the fuller realisation
of the higher principle which all along controlled it.

181. But it will be asked, how upon this view of the nature of
punishment as inflicted by the state it can be considered retributory.
If no private vengeance – no vengeance of the injured individual – is
involved in punishment, there can be no vengeance in it at all. The
conception of vengeance is quite inappropriate to the action of society
or the state on the criminal. The state cannot be supposed capable of
vindictive passion. Nor, if the essence of crime is a wrong done to

society, does it admit of retaliation upon the person committing it. A hurt done to an individual can be requited by the infliction of a like hurt upon the person who has done it; but no equivalent of wrong done to society can be paid back to the doer of it.

182. It is true that there is such a thing as a national desire for revenge[8] (France and Germany): and, if a state = a nation organised in a certain way, why should it not be 'capable of vindictive passion'? No doubt there is a unity of feeling among the members of a nation which makes them feel any loss of strength, real or apparent, sustained by the nation in its corporate character, as a hurt or disgrace to themselves, which they instinctively desire to revenge. The corporate feeling is so strong that individuals feel themselves severally hurt in the supposed hurt of the nation. But when it is said that a crime is an offence against the state, it is not meant that the body of persons forming the nation feel any hurt in the sense in which the person robbed or wounded does – such a hurt as excites a natural desire for revenge. What is meant is that there is a violation of a system of rights which the nation has, no doubt, an interest in maintaining, but a purely social interest, quite different from the egoistic interest of the individual of which the desire for vengeance is a form. A nation is capable of vindictive feeling, but not so a nation as acting through the medium of a settled, impartial, general law for the maintenance of rights, and that is what we mean when we talk of the state as that against which crimes are committed and which punishes them.

183. It is true that when a crime of a certain sort, e.g. a cold-blooded murder, has been committed, a popular sympathy with the sufferer is excited, which expresses itself in the wish to 'serve out' the murderer. This has some *ᵃresemblance toᵃ* the desire for personal revenge, but is really *ᵇquiteᵇ* different, because not egoistic. Indignation against wrong done to another has nothing in common with desire to revenge a wrong done to oneself. It borrows the language of private revenge, just as the love of God borrows the language of sensuous affection. Such indignation is inseparable from the interest in social well-being, and along with it is the chief agent in the establishment and maintenance of legal punishment. Law indeed is necessarily general while indignation is particular in its reference; and accordingly the treatment of any particular crime, so far as determined by law, cannot correspond with the indignation which the crime excites, but the law merely determines the general category under which the crime falls, and fixes certain limits to the punishment that may be inflicted under that category. Within those limits

discretion is left to the judge as to the sentence that he passes, and his sentence is in part influenced by the sort of indignation which, in the given state of public sentiment, the crime is calculated to excite; though generally much more by his opinion as to the amount of terror required for the prevention of prevalent crime. Now what is it in punishment that this indignation demands? If not the sole foundation of public punishment, it is yet inseparable from that public interest on which the system of rights, with the corresponding system of punishments protective of rights, depends. In whatever sense then this indignation demands retribution in punishment, in that sense retribution would seem to be a necessary element in punishment. It demands retribution in the sense of demanding that the criminal should have his due, should be dealt with according to his deserts, should be punished justly.

184. This is quite a different thing from an equivalence between the amount of suffering inflicted by the criminal and that which he sustains in punishment. The amount of suffering which is caused by any crime is really as incalculable as that which the criminal endures in punishment, whatever the punishment. It is only in the case of death for murder that there is any appearance of equivalence between the two sufferings, and in this case the appearance is quite superficial. The suffering involved in death depends almost entirely on the circumstances, which are absolutely different in the case of the murdered man and in that of the man executed for murder. When a man is imprisoned with hard labour for robbery there is not even an appearance of equivalence of suffering between the crime and the punishment. In what then does the justice of a punishment, or its correspondence with the criminal's deserts consist? It will not do to say that these terms merely represent the result of an association of ideas between a crime and the penalty which we are accustomed to see inflicted on it; that society has come to attach certain penalties to certain actions as a result of the experience (1) of suffering and loss caused by those acts, and (2) of the kind of suffering of which the expectation will deter men from doing them; and that these penalties having become customary, the onlookers and the criminal himself, when one of them is inflicted, feel that he has got what was to be expected, and call it his due or desert or a just punishment. If this were the true account of the matter, there would be nothing to explain the difference between the emotion excited by the spectacle of a just punishment inflicted or the demand that it should be inflicted, on the one side, and on the other that excited by the sight of physical suffering following according to the usual course of things upon a physical

combination of circumstances or the expectation that such suffering will follow. If it is said that the difference is explained by the fact that in one case both the antecedent (the criminal act) and the consequent represent voluntary human agency, while in the other they do not, we reply, Just so, but for that reason the conception of a punishment as just differs wholly from any conception of it that could result either from its being customary or from the infliction of such punishment having been commonly found a means for protecting us against hurt.

185. The idea of punishment implies on the side of the person punished at once a capacity for determination by conception of a common or public good, or in other words a practical understanding of the nature of rights as founded on relations to such public good, and an actual violation of a right or omission to fulfil an obligation, the right or obligation being one of which the agent might have been aware and the violation or omission one which he might have prevented. On the side of the authority punishing, it implies equally a conception of right founded on relation to public good, and one which, unlike that on the part of the criminal, is realised in act; a conception of which the punitive act, as founded on a consideration of what is necessary for the maintenance of rights, is the logical expression. A punishment is unjust if either element is absent; if either the act punished is not a violation of known rights or omission to fulfil known obligations of a kind which the agent might have prevented, or the punishment is one that is not required for the maintenance of rights, or (which comes to the same thing) if the ostensible rights for the maintenance of which the punishment is required are not real rights – not liberties of action or acquisition which there is any real public interest in maintaining.

186. When the specified conditions of just punishment are fulfilled, the person punished himself recognises it as just, as his due or desert, and it is so recognised by the onlooker who thinks himself into the situation.[9] The criminal, being susceptible to the idea of public good, and through it of rights, though this idea has not been strong enough to regulate his actions, sees in the punishment its natural expression. He sees that the punishment is his own act returning on himself, in the sense that it is the necessary outcome of his act in a society governed by the conception of rights – a conception which he appreciates and to which he does involuntary reverence.

It is the outcome of his act or his act returning upon himself in a different way from that in which a man's act returns on himself when, having misused his body, he is visited according to physical necessity by painful consequences. The cause of the suffering which the act entails in the one case is the relation of the act to a society governed by the conception of rights, in the other it is not. For that reason, the painful consequence of the act to the doer in the one case is, in the other is not, properly a punishment. We do indeed commonly speak of the painful consequences of imprudent or immoral acts (immoral as distinct from illegal) as a punishment of them, but this is either metaphorically or because we think of the course of the world as regulated by a divine sovereign, whom we conceive as a maintainer of rights like the sovereign of a state. We may think of it as divinely regulated, and so regulated with a view to the realisation of moral good, but we shall still not be warranted in speaking of the sufferings which follow in the course of nature upon certain kinds of conduct as punishments, according to the distinctive sense in which crime is punished, unless we suppose the maintenance of rights to be the object of the moral ^{a}government^a of the world – which is to put the cart before the horse for, as we have seen, rights are relative to morality, not morality to rights (the ground on which certain liberties of action and acquisition should be guaranteed as rights being that they are conditions of the moral perfection of society).[10]

While there would be reason, then, as against those who say that the punishment of crime is *merely* preventive, in saying that it is also retributive, if the needed correction of the 'merely preventive' doctrine could not be more accurately stated, it would seem that the truth can be more accurately stated by the proposition that punishment is not justified unless it is just, and that it is not just unless the act punished is an intentional violation of real right or neglect of real obligation which the agent could have avoided – i.e. unless the agent knowingly and by intentional act interferes with some freedom of action or acquisition which there is a public interest in maintaining – and unless the future maintenance of rights requires that the criminal be dealt with as he is in the punishment.[11]

187. It is clear, however, that this requirement that punishment of crime should be just may be covered by the statement that in its proper nature it is preventive if the nature of that which is to be prevented by it is sufficiently defined. Its proper function is in the interest of rights that are ^{a}genuine^a (in the sense explained), to prevent actions of the kind described by associating in the mind of every possible doer of them a certain terror with the contemplation of the act – such terror as is necessary on the whole to protect the rights threatened by such action. The whipping of an ill-behaved dog is preventive, but not preventive in the sense in which the punishment of crime is so because (1) the dog's ill conduct is not an intentional viola-

tion of a right or neglect of a known obligation, the dog having no conception of right or obligation, and (2) for the same reason the whipping does not lead to the association of terror in the minds of other dogs with the violation of rights and neglect of obligations. To shoot men down who resist a successful *coup d'état* may be effectually preventive of further resistance to the government established by the *coup d'état*, but it does not satisfy the true idea of punishment because the terror produced by the massacre is not necessary for the protection of genuine rights – rights founded on public interest. To hang men for sheep-stealing, again, does not satisfy the idea; because, though it is a genuine right that sheep-stealing violates, in a society where there was any decent reconciliation of rights no such terror as is caused by the punishment of death would be required for protection of the right. It is because the theory that punishment is 'merely preventive' favours the notion that the repetition of any action which any sufficient body of men find inconvenient may justifiably be prevented by any sort of terror that may be convenient for the purpose, that it requires to be guarded by substituting for the qualifying '*merely*' a statement of what it is which the justifiable punishment prevents and why it prevents it.

188. But does our theory, after all has been said about the wrongness of punishment that is not just, afford any standard for the apportionment of just punishment, any criterion of the amount of interference with a criminal's personal rights that is appropriate to his crime, except such as is afforded by a prevalent impression among men as to what is necessary for their security? Can we construe it so as to afford such a criterion without at the same time condemning a great deal of punishment which yet society could be never brought to dispense with? Does it really admit of being applied at all in the presence of the admitted impossibility of ascertaining the degree of moral guilt of criminals (as depending on their state of character or habitual motives)? How, according to it, can we justify punishments inflicted in the case of '*culpable* negligence', e.g. when an engine-driver by careless driving, for which we think very little the worse of him, is the occasion of a bad accident, and is heavily punished in consequence?

189. It is true that there can be no *a priori* criterion of just punishment, except of an abstract and negative kind. We may say that no punishment is just, unless the rights which it serves to protect are powers on the part of individuals or corporations of which the general maintenance is necessary to the well-being of society on the whole and unless the terror which the punishment is calculated to inspire is necessary for their maintenance. For a positive and *ª*detailed*ª*

criterion of just punishment we must wait till a system of rights has been established in which the claims of all men, as founded on their capacities for contributing to social well-being, are perfectly harmonised, and till experience has shown the degree and kind of terror with which men must be affected in order to the suppression of the anti-social tendencies which might lead to the violation of such a system of rights. And this is perhaps equivalent to saying that no complete criterion of just punishment can be arrived at till punishment is no longer necessary, for the state of things supposed could scarcely be realised without bringing with it an extinction of the tendencies which state-punishment is needed to suppress. Meanwhile there is no method of approximation to justice in punishment but that which consists in gradually making the system of established rights just, i.e. in harmonising the true claims of all men, and in discovering by experience the really efficient means of restraining tendencies to violation of rights. An intentional violation of a right must be punished, whether the right violated is one that should be a right or no, on the principle that social well-being suffers more from violation of any established right, whatever the nature of the right, than from the establishment as a right of a power which should not be so established; and it can only be punished in the way which for the time is thought most efficient by the maintainers of law for protecting the right in question by associating terror with its violation. This, however, does not alter the moral duty, on the part of the society authorising the punishment, to make its punishments just by making the system of rights which it maintains just. The justice of the punishment depends on the justice of the general system of rights – not merely on the propriety with reference to social well-being of maintaining this or that particular right which the crime punished violates, but on the question whether the social organisation in which a criminal has lived and acted is one that has given him a fair chance of not being a criminal.

190. We are apt to think that the justice of a punishment depends on some sort of equality between its magnitude and that of the crime punished, but this notion arises from a confusion of punishment as inflicted by the state for a wrong done to society with compensation to the individual for damage done him. Neither a crime nor its punishment admits of strictly quantitative measurement. It may be said, indeed, that the greater the crime the heavier should be its punishment, but this is only true if by the 'heavier punishment' is understood that with which most terror is associated in the popular imagination, and if the conception of the 'greater crime' is taken on

the one hand to exclude any estimation of the degree of moral guilt, and, on the other hand, to be determined by an estimate not only of the importance in the social system of the right violated by the crime but of the amount of terror that needs to be associated with the crime in the general apprehension in order to its prevention. But when its terms are thus understood, the statement that the greater the crime the heavier should be its punishment, becomes an identical proposition. It amounts to this – that the crime which requires most terror to be associated with it in order to its prevention should have most terror thus associated with it.

191. But why do the terms 'heavier punishment' and 'greater crime' need to be thus understood? Why should not the 'greater crime' be understood to mean the crime implying most moral wickedness, or partly this, partly the crime which violates the more important kind of right? Why should a consideration of the amount of terror that needs to be associated with it in order to its prevention enter into the determination of the 'greater crime' at all? Why again should not the 'heavier punishment' mean simply that in which the person punished actually suffers most pain? Why should it be taken to mean that with which most terror is associated upon the contemplation? In short, is not the proposition in question at once true and significant in the sense that the crime which implies most moral depravity, or violates the most important right (such as the right to life), or which does both, should be visited with the punishment that involves most pain to the sufferer?

192. The answer is: As regards heaviness of punishment, it is not in the power of the state to regulate the amount of pain which it causes to the person whom it punishes. If it could only punish justly by making this pain proportionate in each case to the depravity implied in the crime, it could not punish justly at all. The amount of pain which any kind of punishment causes to the particular person depends on his temperament and circumstances, which neither the state nor its agent, the judge, can ascertain. But if it could be ascertained, and if (which is equally impossible) the amount of depravity implied in each particular crime could be ascertained likewise, in order to make the pain of the punishment proportionate to the depravity, a different punishment would have to be inflicted in each case according to the temperament and circumstances of the criminal. There would be an end to all general rules of punishment.

193. In truth, however, the state in its capacity as the sustainer of rights – and it is in this capacity that it punishes – has nothing to do with the amount of moral depravity in the criminal, and the primary

reference in punishment, as inflicted by the state, is not to the effect
of the punishment on the person punished but to its effect on others.
The considerations determining its amount should be prospective
rather than retrospective. In the crime a right *has* been violated. No
punishment can undo what has been done, or make good the wrong to
the person who has suffered. What it can do is to make less likely the
doing of a similar wrong in other cases. Its object, therefore, is not to
cause pain to the criminal for the sake of causing it, nor *chiefly* for the
sake of preventing him, individually, from committing the crime
again, but to associate terror with the contemplation of the crime in
the mind of others who might be tempted to commit it. And this
object, unlike that of making the pain of the punishment commensu-
rate with the guilt of the criminal, is in the main attainable. The effect
of the spectacle of punishment on the onlooker is independent of any
minute inquiry into the degree to which it affects the particular criminal. The attachment of equal penalties to offences that are alike in
respect of the importance of the rights which they violate, and in
respect of the ordinary temptations to them, will on the whole lead to
the association of an equal amount of terror with the prospect of committing the like offences in the public mind. When the circumstances
indeed of two criminals guilty of offences alike in both the above
respects are very greatly and obviously different – so different as to
make the operation of the same penalty upon them very conspicuously different – then the penalty may be varied without interfering
with its terrific effect on the public mind. We will suppose, e.g., that
a fraud on the part of a respectable banker is equivalent, both in
respect of the rights which it violates and of the terror needed to prevent the recurrence of like offences, to a burglary. It will not follow
because the burglary is punished by imprisonment with hard labour
that hard labour should be inflicted on the fraudulent banker likewise. The infliction of hard labour is in everyone's apprehension so
different to the banker from what it is to the burglar, that its infliction
is not needed in order to equalise the terror which the popular imagination associates with the punishment in the two cases.

194. On the same principle may be justified the consideration of extenuating circumstances in the infliction of punishment. In fact,
whether under that name or another, they are taken account of in the
administration of criminal law among all civilised nations. 'Extenuating circumstances' is not a phrase in use among our lawyers, but in
fact consideration of them does constantly, with the approval of the
judge, convert what would otherwise have been conviction for
murder into conviction for manslaughter, and, when there has been

conviction for murder, leads to commutation of the sentence. This fact is often taken to show that the degree of moral depravity on the part of the criminal, the question of his character and motive, is and must be considered in determining the punishment due to him. In truth, however, 'extenuating circumstances' may very well make a difference in the kind of terror which needs to be associated with a crime in order to the future protection of rights, and under certain conditions the consideration of them may be sufficiently justified on this ground. Suppose a theft by a starving man,[12] or a hare shot by an angry farmer whose corn it is devouring.[13] These are crimes, but crimes under such extenuating circumstances that there is no need to associate very serious terror with them in order to the protection of essential rights of property. In the latter case the right which the farmer violates is one which perhaps might be disallowed altogether without interference with any right which society is interested in maintaining. In the former case the right violated is a primary and essential one; one which, where there are many starving people, is in fact pretty sure to be protected by the most stringent penalties. And it might be argued that on the principle stated this is as it should be – that so far from the hunger of the thief being a reason for lightening his punishment, it is a reason for increasing it, in order that the special temptation to steal when far gone in hunger may, if possible, be neutralised by a special terror associated with the commission of the crime under those conditions. But this would be a one-sided application of the principle. It is not the business of the state to protect one order of rights specially, but all rights equally. It ought not therefore to protect a certain order of rights by associating special terror with the violation of them when the special temptation to their violation itself implies a violation of right in the persons of those who are so tempted, as is the case when a general danger to property arises from the fact that many people are on the edge of starvation. The attempt to do so is at once ineffectual and diverts attention from the true way of protecting the endangered right, which is to prevent people from falling into a state of starvation. In any tolerably organised society the condition of a man, ordinarily honest and industrious, who is driven to theft by hunger, will be so abnormal that very little terror needs to be associated with the crime as so committed in order to maintain the sanctity of property in the general imagination. Suppose again a man to be killed in a quarrel arising out of his having tampered with the fidelity of his neighbour's wife. In such a case 'extenuating circumstances' may fairly be pleaded against the infliction of the extremest penalty, because the extremest terror does not need to be associated with homicide, as committed under such conditions, in order to the general protection of human life, and because the attempt so to associate it would tend, so far as successful, to weaken the general sense of the wrong – the breach of family right – involved in the act which, in the case supposed, provokes the homicide.

195. 'After all,' it may be said, 'this is a far-fetched way of explaining the admission of extenuating circumstances as modifying the punishment of crime. Why so strenuously avoid the simpler explanation, that extenuating circumstances are taken into account because they are held to modify the moral guilt of the crime? Is not their recognition a practical proof that punishment of a crime by the state represents the moral disapproval of the community? Does it not show that, however imperfectly the amount of punishment inflicted on a crime may in fact correspond to its moral wickedness, it is generally felt that it ought to do so?'

196. ^aAnswer: The^a reasons for holding that the state neither can nor should attempt to adjust the amount of punishment which it inflicts on a crime to the degree of moral depravity which the crime ^bimplies are (1).^b That the degree of moral depravity implied in any crime is unascertainable. It depends on the motive of the crime, and on this as part of the general character of the agent; on the relation in which the habitual set of his character stands to the character habitually set on the pursuit of goodness. No one can ascertain this in regard to himself. He may know that he is always far from being what he ought to be; that one particular action of his represents on the whole, with much admixture of inferior motives, the better tendency; another, with some admixture of better motives, the worse. But any question in regard to the degree of moral goodness or badness in any action of his own or of his most intimate friend is quite unanswerable. Much less can a judge or jury answer such a question in regard to an unknown criminal. We may be sure indeed that ^cevery^c ordinary crime – nay, perhaps even that of the 'disinterested rebel' – implies the operation of some motive which is morally bad – for though it is not necessarily the worst men who come into conflict with established rights, it probably never can be the best – but the degree of badness implied in such a conflict in any particular case is quite beyond our ken, and it is this degree that must be ascertained if the amount of punishment which the state inflicts is to be proportionate to the moral badness implied in the crime. (2) The notion that the state should, if it could, adjust the amount of punishment which it inflicts on a crime to the moral wickedness of the crime rests on a false view of the re-

lation of the state to morality. It implies that it is the business of the state to punish wickedness as such. But it has no such business. It cannot undertake to punish wickedness, as such, without vitiating the disinterestedness of the effort to escape wickedness and thus checking the growth of a true goodness of the heart in the attempt to promote a goodness which is merely on the surface. This, however, is not to be understood as meaning that the punishment of crime serves no moral purpose. It does serve such a purpose, and has its value in doing so, but only in the sense that the protection of rights, and the association of terror with their violation, is the condition antecedent of any general advance in moral well-being.

197. The punishment of crime, then, neither is, nor can, nor should be adjusted to the degree of moral depravity, properly so called, implied in the crime. But it does not therefore follow that it does not represent the disapproval which the community feels for the crime. On the whole, making allowance for the fact that law and judicial custom vary more slowly than popular feeling, it does represent such disapproval. And the disapproval may fitly be called moral, so far as that merely means that it is a disapproval relating to voluntary action. But it is disapproval founded on a sense of what is necessary for the protection of rights, not on a judgment *of moral good* and evil of that kind which we call conscience when it is applied to our own actions, and which is founded on an ideal of moral goodness with which we compare our inward conduct (*inward*, as representing motives and character). It is founded essentially on the outward aspect of a man's conduct, on the view of it as related to the security and freedom in action and acquisition of other members of society. It is true that this distinction between the outward and inward aspects of conduct is not present to the popular mind. It has not been recognised by those who have been the agents in establishing the existing law of crimes in civilised nations. As the state came to control the individual or family in revenging hurts, and to substitute its penalties for private vengeance, rules of punishment came to be enacted expressive of general disapproval, without any clear consciousness of what was the ground of the disapproval. But in fact it was by what have been just described as the outward consequences of conduct that a general disapproval of it was ordinarily excited. Its morality in the stricter or inward sense was not matter of general social consideration. Thus in the main it has been on the ground of its interference with the general security and freedom in action and acquisition, and in proportion to the apprehension excited by it in this respect, that conduct has been punished by the state. Thus the actual practice of

criminal law has on the whole corresponded to its true principle. So far as this principle has been departed from, it has not been because the moral badness of conduct, in the true or inward sense, has been taken account of in its treatment as a crime, for this has not been generally contemplated at all, but because 'religious' considerations have interfered. Conduct which did not call for punishment by the state as interfering with any true rights (rights that *should be* rights) has been punished as 'irreligious'. This, however, did not mean that it was punished on the ground of moral badness, properly so called. It meant that its consequences were feared either as likely to weaken the belief in some divine authority on which the established system of rights was supposed to rest, or as likely to bring evil on the community through provoking the wrath of some unseen power.

198. This account of the considerations which have regulated the punishment of crimes explains the severity with which *ª*'criminal*ª* negligence' is in some cases punished, and that severity is justified by the account given of the true principle of criminal law, the principle, viz., that crime should be punished according to the importance of the right which it violates and to the degree of terror which in a well-organised society needs to be associated with the crime in order to the protection of the right. It cannot be held that the carelessness of an engine-driver who overlooks a signal and causes a fatal accident implies more moral depravity than is implied in such negligence as all of us are constantly guilty of. Considered with reference to the state of mind of the agent, it is on a level with multitudes of actions and omissions which are not punished at all. Yet the engine-driver would be found guilty of manslaughter and sentenced to penal servitude. The justification is not to be found in distinctions between different kinds of negligence on the part of different agents but in the effect of the negligence in different cases upon the rights of others. In the case supposed, the most important of all rights, the right to life, on the part of railway passengers depends for its maintenance on the vigilance of the drivers. Any preventible failure in such vigilance requires to have sufficient terror associated with it in the mind of other engine-drivers to prevent the recurrence of a like failure in vigilance. Such punishment is just, however generally virtuous the victim of it, because necessary to the protection of rights of which the protection is necessary to social well-being; and the victim of it, in proportion to his sense of justice, which means his habit of practically recognising true rights, will recognise it as just.

199. On this principle crimes committed in drunkenness must be dealt with. Not only is *ª*all consideration of depravity*ª* of motive

specially inapplicable to them – since the motives actuating a drunken man often seem to have little connection with his habitual character; it is not always the case that a crime committed in drunkenness is even intentional. When a man in a drunken rage kills another, he no doubt intends to kill him, or at any rate to do him 'grievous bodily harm', and perhaps the association of great penal terror with such an offence may tend to restrain men from committing it even when drunk; but when a drunken mother lies on her child and smothers it, the hurt is not intentional but accidental. The drunkenness, however, is not accidental, but preventible by the influence of adequate motives. It is therefore proper to treat such a violation of right, though committed unknowingly, as a crime, and to associate terror with it in the popular imagination, in order to the protection of rights by making people more careful about getting drunk, about allowing or promoting drunkenness, and about looking after drunken people. It is unreasonable, however, to do this and at the same time to associate so little terror, as in practice we do, with the promotion of dangerous drunkenness.[14] The case of a crime committed by a drunkard is plainly distinguishable from that of a crime committed by a lunatic, for the association of penal terror with the latter would tend neither to prevent a lunatic from committing a crime nor people from becoming lunatics.

200. The principle above stated, as that according to which punishment by the state should be inflicted and regulated, also justifies a distinction between crimes and civil injuries, i.e. between breaches of right for which the state inflicts punishment without redress to the person injured, and those for which it procures or seeks to procure redress to the person injured without punishment of the person causing the injury. We are not here concerned with the history of this distinction,[15] nor with the question whether many breaches of right now among us treated as civil injuries ought not to be treated as crimes, but with the justification that exists for treating certain kinds of breach of right as cases in which the state should interfere to procure redress for the person injured, but not in the way of inflicting punishment on the injurer until he wilfully resists the order to make redress. The principle of the distinction as ordinarily laid down, viz. that civil injuries 'are violations of public or private rights, when considered in reference to the injury sustained by the individual', while crimes are 'violations of public or private rights, when considered in reference to their evil tendency as regards the community at large'[16] is misleading *because* if the well-being of the community did not suffer in the hurt done to the individual, that hurt would not be a

violation of a right in the true sense at all, nor would the community
have any ground for insisting that the hurt shall be redressed, and for
determining the mode in which it shall be redressed. A violation of
right cannot in truth be considered merely in relation to injury
sustained by an individual, for thus considered it would not be a violation of right. It may be said that the state is only concerned in procuring redress for civil injuries because if it left an individual to
procure redress in his own way, there would be no public peace. But
there are other and easier ways of preventing fighting than by procuring redress of wrongs. We prevent our dogs from fighting, not by
redressing wrongs which they sustain from each other (of wrongs as
of rights they are in the proper sense incapable), but by beating them
or tying them up. The community would not keep the peace by procuring redress for hurt or damage sustained by individuals unless it
conceived itself as having interest in the security of individuals from
hurt and damage, unless it considered the hurt done to individuals as
done to itself. The true justification for treating some breaches of
right as cases merely for redress, others as cases for punishment, is
that, in order to the general protection of rights, with some it is
necessary to associate a certain terror, with others it is not.

201. What then is the general ground of distinction between those
with which terror does, and those with which it does not, need to be
associated? Clearly it is purposeless *to seek to associate* terror with
breaches of right in the case where the breaker does not know that he
is violating a right, and is not responsible for not knowing it. No
association of terror with such a breach of right can prevent men from
similar breaches under like conditions. In any case, therefore, in
which it is, to begin with, open to dispute whether a breach of right
has been committed at all – e.g. when it is a question whether a contract has been really broken owing to some doubt as to the interpretation of the contract or its application to a particular set of
circumstances, or whether a commodity of which someone is in possession properly belongs to another – in such a case, though the judge
finally decides that there has been a breach of right, there is no
ground for treating it as a crime or punishing it. If in the course of
judicial inquiry it turns out that there has been fraud by one or other
of the parties to the litigation, a criminal prosecution, having punishment, not redress, for its object, should properly supervene upon the
civil suit, unless the consequences of the civil suit are incidentally
such as to amount to a sufficient punishment of the fraudulent party.
Again, it is purposeless to associate terror with a breach of obligation
which the person committing it knows to *be so,* but of an obligation

which he has no means of fulfilling, e.g. non-payment of an acknowl-edged debt by a man who, through no fault of his own, is without means of paying it. It is only in cases of one or other of the above kinds – cases in which the breach of right, supposing it to have been committed, has presumably arisen either from inability to prevent it or from ignorance of the existence of the right – that it can be held as an absolute rule to be no business of the state to interfere penally but only in the way of restoring, so far as possible, the broken right.

202. But there are many cases of breach of right which can neither be definitely reduced to one of the above kinds nor distinguished from them by any broad demarcation; cases in which the breaker of a right has been ignorant of it because he has not cared to know, or in which his inability to fulfil it is the result of negligence or extrava-gance. Whether these should be treated penally or no will depend partly on the seriousness of the wrong done through avoidable ignor-ance or negligence, partly on the sufficiency of the deterrent effect incidentally involved in the civil remedy. In the case e.g. of inability to pay a debt through extravagance or recklessness, it may be unnecessary and inadvisable to treat the breach of right penally, in con-sideration that it is indirectly punished by poverty and loss of repu-tation incidental to bankruptcy, and ᵃthatᵃ creditors should not look to the state to protect them from the consequences of lending on bad security. The negligence of a trustee, again, may be indirectly pun-ished by his being obliged to make good the property lost through his neglect to the utmost of his means. This may serve as a sufficiently deterrent example without the negligence being proceeded against criminally. Again, damage done to property, by negligence is in England dealt with civilly, not criminally; and it may be held that in this case the liability to civil action is a sufficient deterrent. On the other hand, negligence which, as negligence, is not really distinguish-able from the above, ᵇwhen itsᵇ consequences are more serious – e.g. that of the railway servant whose negligence results in a fatal acci-dent, that of the bank-director who allows a misleading statement of accounts to be published, fraudulently perhaps in the eye of the law, but in fact ᶜnegligently – is rightly treated criminally. Asᶜ a matter of principle, no doubt, if ᵈintentionalᵈ violation of the right of property is treated as ᵉpenalᵉ equally with the violation of the right of life, the negligent violation should be treated as penal in the one case as much as in the other. But as the consequences of an action for damages may be virtually though not ostensibly penal to the person proceeded against, it may be convenient to leave those negligences which do not, like the negligence of a railway-servant, affect the most important

rights, or do not affect rights on a very large scale as does that of a bank-director, to be dealt with by the civil process.

203. The actual distinction between crimes and civil injuries in English law is no doubt largely accidental. As the historians of law point out, the civil process, having compensation, not punishment, for its object, is the form which the interference of the community for the maintenance of rights originally takes. The community, restraining private vengeance, helps the injured person to redress, and regulates the way in which redress shall be obtained. This procedure no doubt implies the conviction that the community is concerned in the injury done to an individual, but it is only by degrees that this conviction becomes explicit, and that the community comes to treat all preventible breaches of right as offences against itself or its sovereign representative, i.e. as crimes or penal; in the language of English law, 'as breaches of the king's peace'. Those offences are first so treated which happen to excite most public alarm – most fear for general safety (hence, among others, anything thought sacrilegious). In a country like England, where no code has been drawn up on general principles, the class of injuries that are treated penally is gradually enlarged as public alarm happens to be excited in particular directions, but it is largely a matter of accident how the classification of crimes on one side and civil injuries on the other happens to stand at any particular time.[17]

204. According to the view here taken, then, there is no *direct* reference in punishment by the state, either retrospective or prospective, to moral good or evil. The state in its judicial action does not look to the moral guilt of the criminal whom it punishes, or to the promotion of moral good by means of his punishment in him or others. It looks not to virtue and vice but to rights and wrongs. It looks back to the wrong done in the crime which it punishes; not, however, in order to avenge it but in order to the consideration of the sort of terror which needs to be associated with such wrong-doing in order to the future maintenance of rights. If the character of the criminal comes into account at all, it can only be properly as an incident of this consideration. Thus punishment of crime is preventive in its object; not, however, preventive of any or every evil ^{a}or^a by any and every means, but (according to its idea or as it should be) *justly* preventive of *injustice*; preventive of interference with those powers of action and acquisition which it is for the general well-being that individuals should possess, and according to laws which allow those powers equally to all men. But in order effectually to attain its preventive object and to attain it *justly*, it should be reformatory. When the reformatory office

of punishment is insisted on, the reference may be, and from the judicial point of view must be, not to the moral good of the criminal as an ultimate end, but to his recovery from criminal habits as a means to that which is the proper and direct object of state-punishment, viz. the general protection of rights. The reformatory function of punishment is from this point of view an incident of its preventive function, as regulated by consideration of what is just to the criminal as well as to others. For the fulfilment of this latter function, the great thing, as we have seen, is by the punishment of an actual criminal to deter other possible criminals, but for the same purpose, unless the actual criminal is to be put out of the way or locked up for life, it must be desirable to reform him so that he may not be dangerous in future. Now when it is asked why he should not be put out of the way it must not be forgotten that among the rights which the state has to maintain are included rights of the criminal himself. These indeed are for the time suspended by his action in violation of rights, but founded as they are on the capacity for contributing to social good, they could only be held to be finally forfeited on the ground that this capacity was absolutely extinct.

205. This consideration limits the kind of punishment which the state may justly inflict. It ought not in punishing *unnecessarily* to sacrifice to the maintenance of rights in general what may be called the reversionary rights of the criminal – rights which, if properly treated, he might ultimately become capable of exercising for the general good. Punishment therefore either by death or by perpetual imprisonment is justifiable only on one of two grounds; either that association of the extremest terror with certain actions is under certain conditions necessary to preserve the possibility of a social life based on observance of rights, or that the crime punished affords a presumption of a permanent incapacity for rights on the part of the criminal. The first justification may be pleaded for the executions of men concerned in treasonable outbreaks, or guilty of certain breaches of discipline in war (on supposition that the war is necessary for the safety of the state and that such punishments are a necessary incident of war). Whether the capital punishment is really just in such cases must depend, not only on its necessity as an incident in defence of a certain state, but on the question whether that state itself is fulfilling its function as a sustainer of true rights. For the penalty of death for murder both justifications may be urged. It cannot be defended on any other ground, but it may be doubted whether the presumption of permanent incapacity for rights is one which in our ignorance we can ever be entitled to make. As to the other plea, the question is

whether, with a proper police system and sufficient certainty of detection and conviction, the association of this extremest terror with the murderer is necessary to the security of life. Where the death-penalty, however, is unjustifiable, so must be that of really permanent imprisonment; one as much as the other is an absolute deprivation of free social life, and of the possibilities of moral development which that life affords. The only justification for a sentence of permanent imprisonment in a case where there would be none for capital punishment would be that, though inflicted as permanent, the imprisonment might be brought to an end in the event of any sufficient proof appearing of the criminal's amendment. But such proof could only be afforded if the imprisonment were so modified as to allow the prisoner a certain amount of liberty.

206. If punishment then is to be *just*, in the sense that in its infliction due account is taken of all rights, including the suspended rights of the criminal himself, it must be, so far as public safety allows, *reformatory*. It must tend to qualify the criminal for the resumption of rights. As reformatory, however, punishment has for its *a*direct*a* object the qualification for the exercise of rights, and is only concerned with *b*true*b* moralisation of the criminal indirectly so far as it may result from the exercise of rights. But even where it cannot be reformatory in this sense, and over and above its reformatory function in cases where it has one, punishment has a moral end. Just because punishment by the state has for its direct object the maintenance of rights, it has, like every other function of the state, indirectly a moral object, because true rights according to our definition, are powers which it is for the general well-being that the individual (or association) should possess, and that well-being is essentially a moral well-being. Ultimately, therefore, the just punishment of crime is for the moral good of the community. It is also for the moral good of the criminal himself, unless – and it is a supposition which we ought not to make – he is beyond the reach of moral influences. Though not inflicted for that purpose, and though it would not the less have to be inflicted if no moral effect on the criminal could be discerned, it is morally the best thing that can happen to him. It is so, even if a true social necessity requires that he be punished with death. The fact that society is obliged so to deal with him affords the best chance of bringing home to him the anti-social nature of his act. It is true that the last utterances of murderers generally convey the impression that they consider themselves interesting persons, quite sure of going to heaven, but these are probably conventional. At any rate if the solemn infliction of punishment *c*on behalf*c* of human society, and

without any ^{d}sign^d of vindictiveness, will not breed the shame, which is the moral new birth, presumably nothing else within human reach will.

M. THE RIGHT OF THE STATE TO PROMOTE MORALITY ·

207. The right of the individual man, as such, to free ^{a}life on its negative side is constantly gaining^a more general recognition. It is the basis of the growing scrupulosity in regard to punishments which are not reformatory, which put rights finally out of the reach of a criminal instead of qualifying him for their renewed exercise. But the only rational foundation for the ascription of this right is ascription of capacity for free contribution to social ^{b}good. Is it then reasonable for us as a community to treat^b this capacity in the man whose crime has given proof of its having been overcome by anti-social tendencies, as yet giving him a title to a further chance of its development; on the other hand, to act as if it conferred no title on its possessors, before a crime has been committed, to be placed under conditions in which its realisation would be ^{c}possible? Are^c not all modern states so ^{d}acting – allowing^d their ostensible members to grow up under conditions which render the development of social capacity practically impossible? Was it no more reasonable, as in the ancient states, to deny the right to life in the human subject as such, than to admit it under conditions which prevent the realisation of the capacity that forms the ground of its admission? This brings us to the fourth of the questions that arose[1] out of the assertion of the individual's right to free life. What is the nature and extent of the individual's claim to be enabled positively to realise that capacity for freely contributing to social good which is the foundation of his right to free life?

208. In dealing with this question, it is important to bear in mind that the capacity we are considering is essentially a free or (what is the same) a moral capacity.[2] It is a capacity, not for action determined by relation to a certain end, but for action determined by a conception of the end to which it is relative. Only thus is it a foundation of rights. The action of an animal or plant may be made contributory to social good, but it is not therefore a foundation of rights on the part of an animal or plant, because they are not affected by the conception of the good to which they contribute. A right is a power (of acting for his own ends – for what he conceives to be his good) secured to an individual by the community, on the supposition that its exercise contributes to the good of the community. But the exercise of such a power cannot be so contributory unless the individual, in acting for his own

ends, is at least affected by the conception of a good as common to himself with others. The condition of making the animal contributory to human good is that we do not leave him free to determine the exercise of his powers – that we determine them for him, that we use him merely as an instrument; and this means that we do not, because we cannot, endow him with rights. We cannot endow him with rights because there is no conception of a good common to him with us which we can treat as a motive to him to do to us as he would have us do to him. It is not indeed necessary to a capacity for rights, as it is to true moral goodness, that interest in a good conceived as common to himself with others should be a man's dominant motive. It is enough if that which he presents to himself from time to time as his good, and which accordingly determines his action, is so far affected by consideration of the position in which he stands to others – of the way in which this or that possible action of his would affect them, and of what he would have to expect from them in return – as to result habitually, without force or fear of force, in action not incompatible with conditions necessary to the pursuit of a common good on the part of others. In other words, it is the presumption that a man in his general course of conduct will of his own motion have respect to the common good, which entitles him to rights at the hands of the community. The question of the moral value of the motive which may induce this respect – whether an unselfish interest in common good or the wish for personal pleasure and fear of personal pain – does not come into the account at all. An agent, indeed, who could only be induced by fear of death or bodily harm to behave conformably to the requirements of the community, would not be a subject of rights, because this influence could never be brought to bear on him so constantly, if he were free to regulate his own life, as to secure the public safety. But a man's desire for pleasure to himself and aversion from pain to himself, though dissociated from any desire for a higher object – for any object that is desired because good for others – may constitute a capacity for rights, if his imagination of pleasure and pain is so far affected by sympathy with the feeling of others about him as to make him, independently of force or fear of punishment, observant of established rights.[3] In such a case the fear of punishment may be needed to neutralise anti-social impulses under circumstances of special temptation, but by itself it could never be a sufficiently uniform motive to qualify a man, in the absence of more spontaneously social feelings, for the life of a free citizen. The qualification for such a life is a spontaneous habit of acting with reference to a common good, whether that habit be founded on an imagination of pleasures and pains or on a conception of what ought to be. In either case the habit implies at least an understanding that there is such a thing as a common good, and a regulation of egoistic hopes and fears, if not an inducing of more 'disinterested' motives, in consequence of that understanding.

209. The capacity for rights, then, being a capacity for spontaneous action regulated by a conception of a common good – either so regulated through an interest which flows directly from that conception or through hopes and fears which are affected by it through more complex channels of habit and association – is a capacity which cannot be generated – which on the contrary is neutralised – by any influences that interfere with the spontaneous action of social interests. Now any direct enforcement of the outward conduct, which ought to flow from social interests, by means of threatened penalties – and a law requiring such conduct necessarily implies penalties for disobedience to it – does interfere with the spontaneous action of those interests, and consequently checks the growth of the capacity which is the condition of the beneficial exercise of rights. For this reason the effectual action of the state, i.e. the community as acting through law, for the promotion of habits of true citizenship, seems necessarily to be confined to the removal of obstacles. Under this head, however, there may and should be included much that most states have hitherto neglected, and much that at first sight may have the appearance of an enforcement of moral duties, e.g. the requirement that parents have their children taught the elementary arts. To educate one's children is no doubt a moral duty, and it is *not* one of those duties, like that of paying debts, of which the neglect directly interferes with the rights of someone else. It might seem, therefore, to be a duty with which positive law should have nothing to do, any more than with the duty of striving after a noble life. On the other hand, the neglect of it does tend to prevent the growth of the capacity for beneficially exercising rights on the part of those whose education is neglected, and it is on this account – not as a purely moral duty on the part of a parent, but as the prevention of a hindrance to the capacity for rights on the part of children – that education should be enforced by the state. It may be objected, indeed, that in enforcing it we are departing in regard to the parents from the principle above laid down – that we are interfering with the spontaneous action of social interests, though we are doing so with a view to promoting this spontaneous action in another generation. But the answer to this objection is, that a law of compulsory education, if the preferences, ecclesiastical or other, of those parents who show any

practical sense of their responsibility are duly respected, is from the
beginning only felt as compulsion by those in whom, so far as this
social function is concerned, there is no spontaneity to be interfered
with, and that in the second generation, though the law with its penal
sanctions still continues, it is not felt as 'a law, as an enforcement of
action by penalties, at all.

210. On the same principle the freedom of contract ought probably
to be more restricted in certain directions than is at present the case.[4]
The freedom to do as they like on the part of one set of men may
involve the ultimate disqualification of many others, or of a succeeding generation, for the exercise of rights. This applies most obviously
to such kinds of contract or traffic as affect the health and housing of
the people, the growth of population relatively to the means of subsistence, and the accumulation or distribution of landed property. In
the hurry of removing those restraints on free dealing between man
and man, which have arisen partly perhaps from some confused idea
of maintaining morality, but much more from the power of class-
interests, we have been apt to take too narrow a view of the range of
persons[5] – not one generation merely but succeeding generations –
whose freedom ought to be taken into account, and of the conditions
necessary to their freedom ('freedom' here meaning their qualification for the exercise of rights). Hence the massing of population
without regard to conditions of health; unrestrained traffic in deleterious commodities; unlimited upgrowth of the class of hired
labourers in particular industries which circumstances have suddenly
stimulated, without any provision against the dangers of an impoverished proletariate in following generations. Meanwhile, under pre-
tence of allowing freedom of bequest and settlement, a system has
grown up which prevents the landlords of each generation from being
free either in the government of their families or in the disposal of
their land, and aggravates the tendency to crowd into towns, as well
as the difficulties of providing healthy house-room, by keeping land
in a few hands.[6] It would be out of place here to consider in detail the
remedies for these evils, or to discuss the question how far it is well to
trust to the initiative of the state or individuals in dealing with them.
It is enough to point out the directions in which the state may remove
obstacles to the realisation of the capacity for beneficial exercise of
rights without defeating its own object by vitiating the spontaneous
character of that capacity.

N. THE RIGHT OF THE STATE IN REGARD TO
PROPERTY

211. We have now considered the ground of the right to free life, and
what is the justification, if any, for the apparent disregard of that
right (*a*) in war, (*b*) in the infliction of punishment. We have also
dealt with the question of the general office of the state in regard to
the development of that capacity in individuals which is the foundation of the right, pointing out on the one hand the necessary limitation of its office in this respect, on the other hand the directions in
which it may remove obstacles to that development. We next have to
consider the rationale of the rights of property.

In discussions on the 'origin of property' two questions are apt to
be mixed up which, though connected, ought to be kept distinct. One
is the question how men have come to appropriate; the other the
question how the idea of right has come to be associated with their
appropriations. As the term 'property' not only implies a permanent
possession of something, or a possession which can only be given up
with the good will of the possessor, but also a possession recognised
as a right, an inquiry into the origin of property must involve both
these questions, but it is not the less important that the distinction between them should be observed. Each of them again has both its analytical and its historical side. In regard to the first question it is
important to learn all that can be learnt as to the kind of things that
were first, and afterwards at successive periods, appropriated; as to
the mode in which, and the sort of persons or societies by whom, they
were appropriated. This is an historical inquiry. But it cannot take
the place of a metaphysical or psychological analysis of the conditions
on the part of the appropriating subject implied in the fact that he
does such a thing as appropriate. So too, in regard to the second
question, it is important to investigate historically the forms in which
the *right* of men in their appropriations has been recognised; the
parties, whether individuals or societies, to whom the right has been
allowed; and the sort of objects, capable of appropriation, to which it
has been considered to extend. But neither can these inquiries help us
to understand, in the absence of a metaphysical or moral analysis,
either what is implied in the ascription of a *right* to certain appropriations, or why there *should be* a right to them.[1]

212. We have then two questions, as above stated, each requiring
two different methods of treatment. But neither have the questions
themselves, nor the different methods of dealing with them, been
duly distinguished.

It is owing to confusion between them that the right of property in things has been supposed to originate in the first occupancy of them.[2] This supposition, in truth, merely disguises the identical proposition that in order to property there must to begin with have been some appropriation. The truism that there could be no property in anything which had not been at some time and in some manner appropriated tells us nothing as to how or why property in it, as a right, came to be recognised, or why that right *should* be recognised. But owing to the confusion between the origin of appropriation and the origin of property as a right, an identical proposition as to the beginning of appropriation seemed to be an instructive statement as to the basis of the rights of property. Of late, in a revulsion from theories founded on identical propositions, 'historical' inquiries into the 'origin of property' have come into vogue.[3] The right method of dealing with the question has been taken to lie in an investigation of the earliest forms in which property has existed. But such investigation, however valuable in itself, leaves untouched the questions, (1) what it is in the nature of men that makes it possible for them, and moves them, to appropriate; (2) why it is that they conceive of themselves and each other as having a right in their appropriations; (3) on what ground is this conception treated as of moral authority – as one that should be acted on.

213. (1) Appropriation is an expression of will; of the individual's effort to give reality to a conception of his own good; of his consciousness of a possible self-satisfaction as an object to be attained. It is different from mere provision to supply a future want. Such provision appears to be made by certain animals, e.g. ants. It can scarcely be made under the influence of the imagination of pain incidental to future want derived from previous experience, for the ant lays up for the winter though it has not previously lived through the winter. It may be suggested that it does so from inherited habit, but that this habit has originally arisen from an experience of pain on the part of ants in the past. Whether this is the true account of the matter we have not, I think, – perhaps from the nature of the case, cannot have – the means of deciding. We conceal our ignorance by saying that the ant acts instinctively, which is in effect a merely negative statement, that the ant is not moved to make provision for winter either by imagination of the pain which will be felt in winter if it does not, or by *knowledge of the fact (conception* of the fact) that such pain will be felt. In fact, we know nothing of the action of the ant from the inside, or as an expression of consciousness. If we are not entitled to deny dogmatically that it expresses consciousness at all, neither are we entitled to say that it does express consciousness, still less what con-

sciousness it expresses. On the other hand we are able to interpret the acts of ourselves, and of those with whom we can communicate by means of signs to which we and they attach the same meaning, as expressions of consciousness of a certain kind, and thus by reflective analysis to assure ourselves that acts of appropriation in particular express a will of the kind stated; that they are not merely a passing employment of such materials as can be laid hands on to satisfy this or that want, present or future, felt or imagined, but reflect the consciousness of a subject which distinguishes itself from its wants; which presents itself to itself as still there and demanding satisfaction when this or that want, or any number of wants, have been satisfied; which thus not merely uses a thing to fill a want, and in so doing at once destroys the thing and for the time removes the want, but says to itself, 'this shall be mine to do as I like with, to satisfy my wants and express my ^bemotions^b as they arise'.

214. One condition of the existence of property, then, is appropriation, and that implies the conception of himself on the part of the appropriator as a permanent subject for whose use, as instruments of satisfaction and expression, he takes and fashions certain external things – certain things external to his bodily members. These things, so taken and fashioned, cease to be external as they were before. They become a sort of extension of the man's organs – the constant apparatus through which he gives reality to his ideas and wishes. But another condition must be fulfilled in order to constitute property, even of the most simple and primitive sort. This is the recognition by others of a man's appropriations as something which they will treat as his, not theirs, and the guarantee to him of his appropriations by means of that recognition. What then is the ground of the recognition? The writers of the seventeenth and eighteenth centuries, who discussed the basis of the rights of property, took it for granted, and in so doing begged the question. Grotius makes the right of property rest on contract, but clearly until there is a recognised *meum* [mine] and *tuum* [yours] there can be no contract. Contract presupposes property. The property in a particular thing may be derived from a contract through which it has been obtained in exchange for another thing or for some service rendered, but that implies that it was previously the property of another, and that the person obtaining it had a property in something else if only in the labour of his hands, which he could exchange for ^ait. 'At the same time we learn how things became subject to private ownership ... by a kind of agreement, either expressed, as by a decision, or implied, as by occupation. In fact, as soon as community ownership was abandoned, and as yet no division

had been made it is supposed that, all agreed, that whatever each one had taken possession of should be his property.' But he supposes a previous process by which things had been appropriated (§4), owing to the necessity of spending labour on them in order to satisfy desire for a more refined kind of living than could be supplied by spontaneous products of the earth. 'The reason was that men were not content to feed on the spontaneous products of the earth, to dwell in caves ... but chose a more refined mode of life; this gave rise to industry, which some applied to one thing, others to another.' The *'communis rerum'* [common ownership], thus departed from when labour came to be expended on things, Grotius had previously described (§1) as a state of things in which everyone had a right to whatever he could lay hands on. '"All things", as Justin says, "were the undivided possession of all men, as if all possessed a common inheritance." In consequence, each man could at once take whatever he wished for his own needs, and could consume whatever was capable of being consumed. The enjoyment of this universal right then served the purpose of private ownership; for whatever each had thus taken for his own needs another could not take from him except by an unjust act.' Here then a virtual right of property, though not so called, seems to be supposed in two forms previous to the establishment of what Grotius calls the right of property by contract. There is (1) a right of property in which each can 'take to his use and consume' out of the raw material supplied by nature; (2) a further right of each man in that on which he has extended labour. Grotius does not expressly call this a right, but if there is a right, as he says there is, on the part of each man to that which he is able 'to take to his use and consume', much more must there be a right to that which he has not only taken but fashioned by his labour. On the nature and rationale of this right Grotius throws no light, but it is clearly presupposed by that right of property which he supposes to be derived from contract, and must be recognised before any such contract could be possible.[4] Hobbes[a] is so far more logical that he does not derive property from contract, but treats property and 'the validity of covenants' as coordinately dependent on the existence of a sovereign power of compulsion.[5] But his account of this, as of all other forms of right, is open to the objection (before dwelt on) that if the sovereign power is merely a strongest force it cannot be a source of rights; and that if it is other than this – if it is a representative and maintainer of rights – its existence presupposes rights, which remain to be accounted for. As previously shown, Hobbes, while professing to make all rights dependent on the sovereign power, presupposes rights in his account of the institution of this power.[6] The validity of contracts 'begins not but with its constitution',[7] yet its own right is derived from an irrevocable contract of all with all in which each devolves his *persona* – the body of his rights – upon it. Without pressing his particular forms of expression unfairly against him, it is clear that he could not really succeed in thinking of rights as derived simply from supreme force; that he could not associate the idea of absolute right with the sovereign without supposing prior rights which it was made the business of the sovereign to enforce, and in particular such a recognised distinction between *meum* and *tuum* as is necessary to a covenant. Nor when we have dropped Hobbes' notion of government or law-making power, as having originated in a covenant of all with all, shall we succeed any better in deriving rights of property, any more than other rights, from law or a sovereign which makes law, unless we regard the law or sovereign as the organ or sustainer of a general social recognition of certain powers, as powers which *should be* exercised.

215. Locke treats property – fairly enough so long as only its simplest forms are in question – as derived from labour. By the same law of nature and reason by which a man has 'a *Property* in his own *Person*', 'the *Labour* of his Body, and the *Work* of his Hands . . . are properly his' too.[8] Now that the right to free life, which we have already dwelt on, carries with it a certain right to property – to a certain permanent apparatus beyond the bodily organs – for the maintenance and expression of that life, is quite true. But apart from the difficulty of tracing some kinds of property in which men are in fact held to have a right, to the labour of anyone – even of someone from whom it has been derived by inheritance or bequest (a difficulty to be considered presently) – to say that it is a 'law of nature and reason' that a man should have a property in the work of his hands is no more than saying that that on which a man has impressed his labour is recognised by others as something which *should be* his, just as he himself is recognised by them as one that should be his own master. The ground of the recognition is the same in both cases and it is Locke's merit to have pointed this out, but what the ground is he does not consider, shelving the question by appealing to a law of nature or reason.

216. The ground of the right to free life – the reason why a man is secured in the free exercise of his powers through recognition of that exercise by others as something that should be – lay, as we saw, in the conception on the part of everyone who *ᵃconcedesᵃ* the right to others and to whom it is conceded, of an identity of good for himself and

others. It is only as within a society, as a relation between its members, though the society be that of all men, that there can be such a thing as a right; and the right to free life rests on the common will of the society, in the sense that each member of the society within which the right subsists in seeking to satisfy himself contributes to satisfy the others, and that each is aware that the other does so; whence there results a common interest in the free play of the powers of all. And just as the *b*recognised*b* interest of a society constitutes for each member of it the right to free life – just as it makes each conceive of such life on the part of himself and his neighbour as what should be, and thus forms the basis of a restraining custom which secures it for each – so it constitutes the right to the instruments of such life, making each regard the possession of them by the other as for the common good, and thus through the medium first of custom, then of law, securing them to each.

217. Thus the doctrine that the foundation of the right of property lies in the will – that property is 'realised Will'[9] – is true enough if we attach a certain meaning to 'Will'; if we understand by it, not the momentary spring of any and every spontaneous action, but a constant principle, operative in all men qualified for any form of society, however frequently overborne by passing impulses, in virtue of which each seeks to give reality to the conception of a well-being which he necessarily regards as common to himself with others. A Will of this kind at once explains the effort to appropriate, and the restraint placed on each in his appropriations by a customary recognition of the interest which each has in the success of the like effort on the part of the other members of a society with which he shares a common well-being. This customary recognition, founded on a moral or rational will, requires indeed to be represented by some adequate force before it can result in a real maintenance of rights of property. The wild beast in man will not otherwise yield obedience to the rational will. And from the operation of this compulsive force, very imperfectly controlled by the moral tendencies which need its co-operation – in other words from the historical incidents of conquest and government – there result many characteristics of the institution of property, as it actually exists, which cannot be derived from the *a*spiritual*a* principle which we have assigned as its foundation. Still, without that principle it could not have come into existence, nor would it have any moral justification at all.

218. It accords with the account given of this principle that the right of property, like every other form of right, should first appear within societies founded on kinship, these being naturally the

societies within which the restraining conception of a common well-being is first operative. We are apt indeed to think of the state of things in which the members of a family or clan hold land and stock in common, as the antithesis of one in which rights of property exist. In truth it is the earliest stage of their existence, because the most primitive form of society in which the fruit of his labour is secured to the individual by the society under the influence of the conception of a common well-being. The characteristic of primitive communities is not the absence of distinction between *meum* and *tuum*, without which no society of intelligent as opposed to instinctive agents would be possible at all, but the common possession of certain materials, in particular *land*, on which labour may be expended. It is the same common interest which prevents separate appropriation of these materials and which secures the individual in the enjoyment and use of that which his labour can extract from them.

219. From the moral point of view, however, the clan-system is defective because under it the restraint imposed upon the individual by his membership of a society is not, and has not the opportunity of becoming, a self-imposed restraint – a free obedience to *a*which the individual submits, though the alternative course is left open to him, because*a* he conceives it as his true good. The area within which he can shape his own circumstances is not sufficient to allow of the opposite possibilities of right and wrong being presented to him, and thus of his learning to love right for its own sake.[10] And the other side of this moral tutelage of the individual – this withholding from him of the opportunity of being freely determined by recognition of his moral relations – is the confinement of those relations themselves, which under the clan-system have no *actual* existence except as between members of the same clan. A necessary condition at once of the growth of a free morality, i.e. a certain behaviour of men determined by an understanding of moral relations and by the value which they set on them as understood, and of the conception of those relations as relations between all men, is that free play should be given to every man's powers of appropriation. Moral freedom is not the same thing as a control over the outward circumstances and appliances of life. It is the end to which such control is a generally necessary means and which gives it its value. In order to obtain this control men must cease to be limited in their activities by the customs of the clan. The range of their appropriations must be extended – they must include more of the permanent material on which labour may be expended, and not merely the passing products of labour spent on unappropriated material – and they must be at once secured and controlled in it by the

good-will, by the sense of common interest, of a wider society, of a
society to which any and every one may belong who will observe its
conditions, and not merely those of a particular parentage; in other
words by the law, written or unwritten, of a free state.

220. It is too long a business here to attempt an account of the process by which the organisation of rights in the state has superseded
that of the clan, and at the same time the restriction of the powers of
appropriation implied in the latter has been removed. It is important
to observe, however, that this process has by no means contributed
unmixedly to the end to which, from the moral point of view, it
should have contributed. That end is at once the emancipation of the
individual from all restrictions *upon, and his provision with means
for, the free moral life.* But the actual result of the development of
rights of property in Europe, as part of its general political development, has so far been a state of things in which all indeed *may* have
property, but great numbers in fact cannot have it in that sense in
which alone it is of value, viz. as a permanent apparatus for carrying
out a plan of life, for expressing ideas of what is beautiful, or giving
effect to benevolent wishes. In the eye of the law they have rights of
appropriation, but in fact they have not the chance of providing
means for a free moral life, of developing and giving reality or expression to a good will, an interest in social well-being. A man who
possesses nothing but his powers of labour and who has to sell these
to a capitalist for bare daily maintenance,[11] might as well, in respect
of the ethical purposes which the possession of property should serve,
be denied rights of property altogether. Is the existence of so many
men in this position, and the apparent liability of many more to be
brought to it by a general fall of wages, if increase of population goes
along with decrease in the productiveness of the earth, a necessary
result of the emancipation of the individual and the free play given to
powers of appropriation? or is it an evil incident, which may yet be
remedied, of that historical process by which the development of the
rights of property has been brought about, but in which the agents
have for the most part had no moral objects in view at all?

221. Let us first be clear about the points in which the conditions of
property, as it actually exists, are at variance with property according
to its idea or as it should be. The rationale of property, as we have
seen, is that everyone should be secured by society in the power of
getting and keeping the means of realising a will, which in possibility
is a will directed to social good. Whether anyone's will is actually and
positively so directed, does not affect his claim to the power. This
power should be secured to the individual irrespectively of the use

which he actually makes of it, so long as he does not use it in a way that interferes with the exercise of like power by another, on the ground that its uncontrolled exercise is the condition of attainment by man of that free morality which is his highest good. It is not then a valid objection to the manner in which property is possessed among us, that its holders constantly use it in a way demoralising to themselves and others, any more than such misuse of any other liberties is an objection to securing men in their possession. Only then is property held in a way inconsistent with its idea, and which should, if possible, be got rid of, when the possession of property by one man interferes with the possession of property by another; when one set of men are secured in the power of getting and keeping the means of realising their will, in such a way that others are practically denied the power. In that case it may truly be said that 'property is theft'.[12] The rationale of property, in short, requires that everyone who will conform to the positive condition of possessing it, viz. labour, and the negative condition, viz. respect for it as possessed by others, should, so far as social arrangements can make him so, be a possessor of property himself – and of such propery as will at least enable him to develop a sense of responsibility, as distinct from mere property in the immediate necessaries of life.

222. But then the question arises, whether the rationale of property, as thus stated, is not inconsistent with the unchecked freedom of appropriation, or freedom of appropriation checked only by the requirement that the thing appropriated shall not have previously been appropriated by another. Is the requirement that every honest man should be a proprietor to the extent stated, compatible with any great inequalities of possession? In order to give effect to it, must we not remove those two great sources of the inequality of fortunes, (1) freedom of bequest, and the other arrangements by which the profits of the labour of several generations are accumulated on persons who do not labour at all; (2) freedom of trade, of buying in the cheapest market and selling in the dearest, by which accumulated profits of labour become suddenly multiplied in the hands of a particular proprietor? Now clearly, if an inequality of fortunes, of the kind which naturally arises from the admission of these two forms of freedom, necessarily results in the existence of a proletariate, practically excluded from such ownership as is needed to moralise a man, there would be a contradiction between our theory of the right of property and the actual consequence of admitting the right according to the theory; for the theory logically necessitates freedom both in trading and in the disposition of his property by the owner, so long as he does

not interfere with the like freedom on the part of others; and in other ways as well its realisation implies inequality.

223. Once admit as the idea of property that nature should be progressively adapted to the service of man by a process in which each, while working freely or for himself, i.e. as determined by a conception of his own good, at the same time contributes to the social good, and it will follow that property must be unequal. If we leave a man free to realise the conception of a possible well-being, it is impossible to limit the effect upon him of his desire to provide for his future well-being, as including that of the persons in whom he is interested, or the success with which at the prompting of that desire he turns resources of nature to account. Considered as representing the conquest of nature by the effort of free and variously gifted individuals, property must be unequal; and no less must it be so if considered as a means by which individuals fulfil social functions. As we may learn from Aristotle,[13] those functions are various and the means required for their fulfilment are various. The artist and man of letters require different equipment and apparatus from the tiller of land and the smith. Either then the various apparatus needed for various functions must be provided for individuals by society, which would imply a complete regulation of life, incompatible with that highest object of human attainment, a free morality; or we must trust for its provision to individual effort, which will imply inequality between the property of different persons.

224. The admission of freedom of trade follows from the same principle. It is a condition of the more complete adaptation of nature to the service of man by the free effort of individuals. 'To buy in the cheapest and sell in the dearest market' is a phrase which may no doubt be used to cover objectionable transactions, in which advantage is taken of the position of sellers who from circumstances are not properly free to make a bargain. It is so employed when the cheapness of buying arises from the presence of labourers who have no alternative but to work for 'starvation wages'. But in itself it merely describes transactions in which commodities are bought where they are of least use and sold where they are of most use. The trader who profits by the transaction is profiting by what is at the same time a contribution to social well-being.

In regard to the freedom which a man should be allowed in disposing of his property by will or gift, the question is not so simple. The same principle which forbids us to limit the degree to which a man may provide for his future, forbids us to limit the degree to which he may provide for his children, these being included in his forecast of his future. It follows that the amount which children may inherit may not rightly be limited; and in this way inequalities of property, and accumulations of it to which possessors have contributed nothing by their own labour, must arise. Of course the possessor of an estate, who has contributed nothing by his own labour to its acquisition, may yet by his labour contribute largely to the social good, and a well-organised state will in various ways elicit such labour from possessors of inherited wealth. Nor will it trust merely to encouraging the voluntary fulfilment of social functions, but will by taxation make sure of some positive return for the security which it gives to inherited wealth. But while the mere permission of inheritance, which seems implied in the permission to a man to provide unlimitedly for his future, will lead to accumulations of wealth, on the other hand, if the inheritance is to be equal among all children, and, failing children, is to pass to the next of kin, the accumulation will be checked. It is not therefore the right of inheritance, but the right of bequest, that is most likely to lead to accumulation of wealth, and that has most seriously been questioned by those who hold that universal ownership is a condition of moral well-being. Is a proprietor to be allowed to dispose of his property as he likes among his children (or, if he has none, among others), making one very rich as compared with the others, or is he to be checked by a law requiring approximately equal inheritance?

225. As to this, consider that on the same principle on which we hold that a man should be allowed to accumulate as he best can for his children, he should have discretion in distributing among his children. He should be allowed to accumulate, because in so doing he at once expresses and develops the sense of family responsibility, which naturally breeds a recognition of duties in many other directions. But if the sense of family responsibility is to have free play, the man must have due control over his family, and this he can scarcely have if all his children as a matter of necessity inherit equally, however undutiful or idle or extravagant they may be.[14] For this reason the true theory of property would seem to favour freedom of bequest, at any rate in regard to wealth generally. There may be special reasons, to be considered presently, for limiting it in regard to land. But as a general rule, the father of a family, if left to himself and not biassed by any special institutions of his country, is most likely to make that distribution among his children which is most for the public good. If family pride moves him to endow one son more largely than the rest, in order to maintain the honour of his name, family affection will keep this tendency within limits in the interest of the

other children, unless the institutions of his country favour the one tendency as against the other. And this they will do if they maintain great dignities, e.g. peerages, of which the possession of large heredi- tary wealth is virtually the condition, and if they make it easy, when the other sons have been impoverished for the sake of endowing the eldest, to maintain the former at the public expense by means of appointments in the church or state.

It must be borne in mind, further, that the freedom of bequest which is to be justified on the above principles must *not* be one which limits that freedom in a subsequent generation. It must therefore be distinguished from the power of settlement allowed by English law and constantly exercised in dealing with landed estate;[15] for this power, as exercised by the landowning head of a family in one gener- ation, prevents the succeeding head of the family from being free to make what disposition he thinks best among his children and ties up the succession to the estate to his eldest son. The practice of settle- ment in England, in short, as applied to landed estate, cancels the freedom of bequest in the case of most landowners and neutralises all the dispersive tendency of family affection, while it maintains in full force all the accumulative tendency of family pride. This, however, is no essential incident of a system in which the rights of individual ownership are fully developed, but just the contrary.

226. The question then remains, whether the full development of those rights, as including that of unlimited accumulation of wealth by the individual and of complete freedom of bequest on his part, necessarily carries with it the existence of a proletariate, nominal owners of their powers of labour, but in fact obliged to sell these on such terms that they are in fact owners of nothing beyond what is necessary from day to day for the support of life, and may at any time lose even that, so that, as regards the moral functions of property, they may be held to be not proprietors at all; or whether the existence of such a class is due to causes only accidentally connected with the development of rights of individual property.

We must bear in mind (1) that the increased wealth of one man does not naturally mean the diminished wealth of another.[16] We must not think of wealth as a given stock of commodities of which a larger share cannot fall to one without taking from the share that falls to another. The wealth of the world is constantly increasing in propor- tion as the constant production of new wealth by labour exceeds the constant consumption of what is already produced. There is no natu- ral limit to its increase except such as arises from the fact that the supply of the food necessary to sustain labour becomes more difficult as more comes to be required owing to the increase in the number of labourers, and from the possible ultimate exhaustion of the raw materials of labour in the world. Therefore in the accumulation of wealth, so far as it arises from the saving by anyone of the products of his labour, from his bequest of this capital to another who farther adds to it by saving some of the profit which the capital yields, as employed in the payment for labour or in trade either by the capitalist himself or someone to whom he lends it, and from the continuation of this process through generations, there is nothing which tends to lessen for anyone else the possibilities of ownership. On the contrary, supposing trade and labour to be free, wealth must be constantly distributed throughout the process in the shape of wages to labourers and of profits to those who mediate in the business of exchange.

227. It is true that the accumulation of capital naturally leads to the employment of large masses of hired labourers. But there is nothing in the nature of the case to keep these labourers in the condition of living from hand to mouth, to exclude them from that education of the sense of responsibility which depends on the possibility of permanent ownership. There is nothing in the fact that their labour is hired in great masses by great capitalists to prevent them from being on a small scale capitalists themselves. In their position they have not indeed the same stimulus to saving, or the same constant opening for the investment of savings, as a man who is *autourgos* [self-employed]; but their combination in work gives them every opportunity, if they have the needful education and self-discipline, for forming societies for the investment of savings. In fact, as we know, in the well-paid industries of England the better sort of labourers do become capitalists, to the extent often of owning their houses and a good deal of furniture, of having an interest in stores, and of belonging to benefit-societies through which they make provision for the future. It is not then to the accumulation of capital, but to the condition, due to antecedent circumstances unconnected with that accumulation, of the men with whom the capitalist deals and whose labour he buys on the cheapest terms, that we must ascribe the multiplication in recent times of an impoverished and reckless proletariate.[17]

228. It is difficult to summarise the influences to which is due the fact that in all the chief seats of population in Europe the labour-market is constantly thronged with men who are too badly reared and fed to be efficient labourers; who for this reason, and from the competition for employment with each other, have to sell their labour very cheap; who have thus seldom the means to save, and whose

standard of living and social expectation is so low that, if they have the
opportunity of saving, they do not use it, and keep bringing children
into the world at a rate which perpetuates the evil. It is certain, however, that these influences have no necessary connection with the
maintenance of the right of individual property and consequent unlimited accumulation of capital, though they no doubt are connected
with that régime of force and conquest by which existing governments have been established – governments which do not indeed
create the rights of individual property, any more than other rights,
but which serve to maintain them. It must always be borne in mind
that the appropriation of land by individuals has in most countries –
probably in all where it approaches completeness – been originally
effected, not by the expenditure of labour or the results of labour on
the land, but by force. The original landlords have been con-
querors.[18]

229. This has affected the condition of the industrial classes in at
least two ways: (1) When the application of accumulated capital to
any work in the way of mining or manufacture has created a demand
for labour, the supply has been forthcoming from men whose
ancestors, if not themselves, were trained in habits of serfdom – men
whose life has been one of virtually forced labour, relieved by church-
charities or the poor law (which in part took the place of these charities) – who were thus in no condition to contract freely for the sale of
their labour, and had nothing of that sense of family responsibility
which might have made them insist on having the chance of saving.
Landless countrymen, whose ancestors were serfs, are the parents of
the proletariate of great towns. (2) Rights have been allowed to landlords, incompatible with the true principle on which rights of property rest, and tending to interfere with the development of the
proprietorial capacity in others. The right to freedom in unlimited
acquisition of wealth, by means of labour and by means of the saving
and successful application of the results of labour, does not imply the
right of anyone to do as he likes with those gifts of nature, without
which there would be nothing to spend labour upon. The earth is just
as much an original natural material necessary to productive
industry, as are air, light, and water, but while the latter from the
nature of the case cannot be appropriated, the earth can be and has
been. The only justification for this appropriation, as for any other, is
that it contributes on the whole to social well-being; that the earth as
appropriated by individuals *under certain conditions* becomes more
serviceable to society as a whole, including those who are not proprietors of the soil, than if it were held in common. The justification

disappears if these conditions are not observed; and from government having been chiefly in the hands of appropriators of the soil, they have not been duly observed. Landlords have been allowed to 'do what they would with their own', as if land were merely like so much capital, admitting of indefinite extension. The capital gained by one is not taken from another, but one man cannot acquire more land without others having less; and though a growing reduction in the number of landlords is not necessarily a social evil, if it is compensated by the acquisition of other wealth on the part of those extruded from the soil, it is only not an evil if the landlord is prevented from so using his land as to make it unserviceable to the wants of men (e.g. by turning fertile land into a forest), and from taking liberties with it incompatible with the conditions of general freedom and health; e.g. by clearing out a village and leaving the people to pick up house-room as they can elsewhere – a practice common under the old poor-law, when the distinction between close and open villages grew up – or, on the other hand, by building houses in unhealthy places or of unhealthy structure, by stopping up means of communication, or forbidding the erection of dissenting chapels. In fact the restraints which the public interest requires to be placed on the use of land if individual property in it is to be allowed at all, have been pretty much ignored, while on the other hand, that full development of its resources, which individual ownership would naturally favour, has been interfered with by laws or customs which, in securing estates to certain families, have taken away the interest, and tied the hands, of the nominal owner – the tenant for life – in making the most of his property.

230. Thus the whole history of the ownership of land in Europe has been of a kind to lead to the agglomeration of a proletariate, neither holding nor seeking property, wherever a sudden demand has arisen for labour in mines or manufactures. This at any rate was the case down to the epoch of the French Revolution; and this, which brought to other countries deliverance from feudalism, left England, where feudalism had previously passed into unrestrained landlordism, almost untouched. And while those influences of feudalism and landlordism which tend to throw a shiftless population upon the centres of industry have been left unchecked, nothing till quite lately was done to give such a population a chance of bettering itself, when it had been brought together.[19] Their health, housing, and schooling were unprovided for. They were left to be freely victimised by deleterious employments, foul air, and consequent craving for deleterious drinks. When we consider all this, we shall see the unfairness of laying on capitalism or the free development of individual wealth the

blame which is really due to the arbitrary and violent manner in which rights over land have been acquired and exercised, and to the failure of the state to fulfil those functions which under a system of unlimited private ownership are necessary to maintain the conditions of a free life.

231. Whether, when those functions have been more fully recognised and executed, and when the needful control has been established in the public interest over the liberties which landlords may take in the use of their land, it would still be advisable to limit the right of bequest in regard to land, and establish a system of something like equal inheritance, is a question which cannot be answered on any absolute principle. It depends on circumstances. Probably the question should be answered differently in a country like France or Ireland, where the most important industries are connected directly with the soil, and in one like England where they are not so. The reasons must be cogent which could justify that interference with the control of the parent over his family, which seems to be implied in the limitation of the power of bequeathing land when the parent's wealth lies solely in land, and which arises, be it remembered, in a still more mischievous way from the present English practice of settling estates. But it is important to bear in mind that the question in regard to land stands on a different footing from that in regard to wealth generally, owing to the fact that land is a particular commodity limited in extent, from which alone can be derived the materials necessary to any industry whatever, on which men must find house-room if they are to find it at all, and over which they must pass in communicating with each other, however much water or even air may be used for that purpose. These are indeed not reasons for preventing private property in land or even free bequest of land, but they necessitate a ᵃsocialᵃ control over the exercise of rights of property in land, and it remains to be seen whether that control can be sufficiently established in a country where the power of great estates has not first been broken, as in France, by a law of equal inheritance.

232. To the proposal that 'unearned increment' in the value of the soil,[20] as distinct from value produced by expenditure of labour and capital, should be appropriated by the state, though fair enough in itself, the great objection is that the relation between earned and unearned increment is so complicated, that a system of appropriating the latter to the state could scarcely be established without lessening the stimulus to the individual to make the most of the land, and thus ultimately lessening its serviceableness to society.

O. THE RIGHT OF THE STATE IN REGARD TO THE FAMILY

233. In the consideration of those rights which do not arise out of the existence of the state, but which are antecedent to it (though of course implying society in some form), and which it is its office to enforce, we now come to family or household rights – also called, though not very distinctively, 'rights in private relations'[1] – of which the most important are the reciprocal rights of husband and wife, parent and child. The distinctive thing about these is that they are not merely rights of one person as against all or some other persons over some thing, or to the performance of or abstention from some action; they are rights of one person as against all other persons to require or prevent a certain behaviour on the part of another. Right to free life is a right on the part of any and every person to claim from all other persons that course of action or forbearance which is necessary to his free life. It is a right against all the world, but not a right over any particular thing or person. A right of property, on the other hand, is a right against all the world, and also *over a particular thing*; a right to claim from any and every one certain actions and forbearances in respect of a particular thing (hence called *'jus in rem'*). A right arising from contract, unlike the right of property or the right of free life, is not a right as against all the world, but a right as against a particular person or persons contracted with to claim a certain performance or forbearance. It may or may not be a right over a particular thing, but as it is not necessarily so, while it is a right against a particular person or persons in distinction from all the world, it is called *'jus in personam'* as distinct from *'in rem'*. The right of husband over wife and that of parent over children (or *vice versa*) differs from the right arising out of contract, inasmuch as it is not merely a right against the particular person contracted with, but a right against all the world. In this respect it corresponds to the right of property; but differs again from this, since it is not a right over a thing but over a person. It is a right to claim certain acts or forbearances from all other persons in respect of a particular person: or (more precisely) to claim a certain behaviour from a certain person, and at the same time to exclude all others from claiming it. Just because this kind of right is a right *over a person*, it is always reciprocal as between the person exercising it and the person over whom it is exercised. All rights are reciprocal as between the person exercising them and the person against whom they are exercised. My claim to the right of free life implies a like claim upon me on the part of those from whom I claim acts and forbearances necessary to my free life. My claim upon others in respect of the right of

property, or upon a particular person in respect of an action which he has contracted to perform, implies the recognition of a corresponding claim upon me on the part of all persons or the particular party to the contract. But the right of a husband in regard to his wife not merely implies that all those as against whom he claims the right have a like claim against him, but that the wife over whom he asserts the right has a right, though not a precisely like right, over him. The same applies to the right of a father over a son, and of a master over a servant.

234. A German[2] would express the peculiarity of the rights now under consideration by saying that, not only are persons the subjects of them, but persons are the objects of them. By the 'subject' of rights he would mean the person exercising them or to whom they belong; by 'object' that in respect of which the rights are exercised. The piece of land or goods which I own is the 'object' of the right of property, the particular action which one person contracts to perform for another is the 'object' of a right of contract; and in like manner the person from whom I have a right to claim certain behaviour, which excludes any right on the part of anyone else to claim such behaviour from him or her, is the 'object' of the right. But English writers commonly call that the *subject* of a right which the Germans would call the object. By the subject of a right of property they would not mean the person to whom the right belongs, but the thing over which, or in respect of which, the right exists. And in like manner, when a right is exercised over, or in respect of a person, such as a wife or a child, they would call that person, and not the person exercising the right, the *subject* of it. By the object of a right, on the other hand, they mean the action or forbearance which someone has a right to claim. The *object of a right* arising out of contract would be the action which the person contracting agrees to perform. The object of a connubial right would not be, as according to German usage, the person in regard to, or over, whom the right is exercised – that person would be the *subject* of the right – but either the behaviour which the person possessing the right is entitled to claim from that person, or the forbearances in respect to that person, which he is entitled to claim from others.[3] Either usage is justifiable in itself. The only matter of importance is not to confuse them. There is a convenience in expressing the peculiarity of family rights by saying, according to the sense of the terms adopted by German writers, that not only are persons *subjects of them* but persons are objects of them. It is in this sense that I shall use these terms, if at all.

235. So much for the peculiarity of family rights, as distinct from

other rights. The distinction is not merely a formal one. From the fact that these rights have persons for their *objects*, there follow important results, as will appear, in regard to the true nature of the right, to the mannner in which it should be exercised. The analytical, as distinct from the historical, questions which have to be raised with reference to family rights correspond to those raised with reference to rights of property. As we asked what in the nature of man made appropriation possible for him, so now we ask (1) what it is in the nature of man that makes him capable of family life. As we asked next how appropriations came to be so sanctioned by social recognition as to give rise to rights of property, so now we have to ask (2) how certain powers exercised by a man, certain exemptions which he enjoys from the interference of others, in his family life, come to be recognised as rights. And as we inquired further how far the actual institutions of property correspond with the idea of property as a right which for social good should be exercised, so now we have to inquire (3) into the proper adjustment of family rights, as determined by their idea; in what form these rights should be maintained; bearing in mind (*a*) that, like all rights, their value depends on their being conditions of which the general observance is necessary to a free morality, and (*b*) their distinctive character as rights of which, in the sense explained, persons are the objects.

236. (1) We saw that appropriation of that kind which, when secured by a social power, becomes property, supposes an effort on the part of the individual to give reality to a conception of his own good, as a whole or as something permanent, in distinction from the mere effort to satisfy a want as it arises.[4] The formation of family life supposes that in the conception of his own good to which a man seeks to give reality there is included a conception of the well-being of others, connected with him by sexual relations or by relations which arise out of these.[5] He must conceive of the well-being of these others as a permanent object bound up with his own, and the interest in it as thus conceived must be a motive to him over and above any succession of passing desires to obtain pleasure from, or give pleasure to, the others; otherwise there would be nothing to lead to the establishment of a household, in which the wants of the wife or wives are permanently provided for, in the management of which a more or less definite share is given to them (more definite, indeed, as approach is made to a monogamistic system, but not wholly absent anywhere where the wife is distinguished from the female), and upon which the children have a recognised claim for shelter and sustenance.[6]

237. No doubt family life as we know it is an institution of gradual

growth. It may be found in forms where it is easy to ignore the
distinction between it and the life of beasts. It is possible that the
human beings with whom it first began – beings 'human' because capable of it – may have been 'descended' from animals not capable of it,
i.e. they may have been connected with such animals by certain processes of generation. But this makes no difference in the nature of the
capacity itself, which is determined not by a past history but by its results, its functions, that of which it is a capacity.[7] As the foundation
of any family life, in the form in which we know it, implies that upon
the mere sexual impulse there has supervened on the part of the man
a permanent interest in a woman as a person with whom his own well-
being is united, and a consequent interest in the children born of her,
so in regard to every less perfect form out of which we can be entitled
to say that the family life, as we know it, has developed, we must be
also entitled to say that it expresses some interest which is in principle
identical with that described, however incompletely it has emerged
from lower influences.

238. (2) Such an interest being the basis of family relations, it is
quite intelligible that everyone actuated by the interest should recognise, and be recognised by, everyone else to whom he ascribes an interest like his own, as entitled to behave towards the objects of the
interest – towards his wife and children – in a manner from which
everyone else is excluded; that there should thus come to be rights in
family relations to a certain privacy in dealing with them; to deal with
them as his alone and not another's; claims, ratified by the general
sense of their admission being for the common good, to exercise certain powers and demand certain forbearances from others, in regard
to wife and children. It is only indeed at an advanced stage of reflection that men learn to ascribe to other men, simply as men, the
interests which they experience themselves; and hence it is at first
only within narrow societies that men secure to each other the due
privileges and privacies of family life. In others of the same kin or
tribe they can habitually imagine an interest like that of which each
feels his own family life to be the expression, and hence in them they
spontaneously respect family rights; but they cannot thus practically
think themselves into the position of a stranger, and hence towards
him they do not observe the same restraints. They do not regard the
women of another nation as sacred to the husbands and families of
that nation. But that power of making another's good one's own,
which in the more intense and individualised form is the basis of
family relations, must always at the same time exist in that more diffused form in which it serves as the basis of a society held together by

the recognition of a common good. Wherever, therefore, the family relations exist, there is sure to exist also a wider society which by its authority gives to the powers exercised in those relations the character of rights.[8] By what process the relations of husband and wife and the institution of the household may have come to be formed among descendants of a single pair, it is impossible to conceive or to discover, but in fact we find no trace in primitive history of households except as constituents of a clan recognising a common origin; and it is by the customs of the clan, founded in the conception of a common good, that those forbearances on the part of members of one household in dealing with another, which are necessary to the privacy of the several households, are secured.

239. The history of the development of family life is the history of the process (*a*) by which family rights have come to be regarded as independent of the special custom of a clan and the special laws of a state, as rights which all men and women, as such, are entitled to. This, however, characterises the history of all rights alike. It is a history farther (*b*) of the process by which the true nature of these rights has come to be recognised, as rights *over persons*; rights of which persons are the objects, and which therefore imply reciprocal claims on the part of those over whom they are exercised and of those who exercise them. The establishment of monogamy, the abolition of '*patria potestas*' ['paternal authority'] in its various forms, the 'emancipation of women' (in the proper sense of the phrase), are involved in these two processes. The principles (1) that all men and all women are entitled to marry and form households, (2) that within the household the claims of the husband and wife are throughout reciprocal, cannot be realised without carrying with them not merely monogamy, but the removal of those faulty relations between men and women which survive in countries where monogamy is established by law.

240. Under a system of polygamy, just so far as it is carried out, there must be men who are debarred from marrying. It can only exist, indeed, alongside of a slavery, which excludes masses of men from the right of forming a family. Nor does the wife, under a polygamous system, though she ostensibly marries, form a household, or become the co-ordinate head of a family, at all. The husband alone is head of the family and has authority over the children. The wife, indeed, who for the time is the favourite, may practically share the authority, but even she has no equal and assured position. The '*consortium omnis vitæ*' ['sharing of an entire life'], the '*individua vitæ consuetudo*' ['indivisible common life'], which according to the

definition in the Digest is an essential element in marriage, is not hers.[9]

And further as the polygamous husband requires a self-restraint from his wife which he does not put on himself, he is treating her unequally. He demands a continence from her which, unless she is kept in the confinement of slavery, can only rest on the attachment of a person to a person and on a personal sense of duty, and at the same time is practically ignoring the demand, which this personal attachment on her part necessarily carries with it, that he should keep himself for her as she keeps herself for him.[10] The recognition of children as having claims upon their parents reciprocal to those of the parents over them, equally involves the condemnation of polygamy. For these claims can only be duly satisfied – the responsibilities of father and mother towards the children (potentially persons) whom they have brought into the world can only be fulfilled – if father and mother jointly take part in the education of the children; if the children learn to love and obey father and mother as one authority.[11] But if there is no permanent '*consortium vitæ*' ['sharing of life'] of one husband with one wife, this joint authority over the children becomes impossible. The child, when its physical dependence on the mother is over, ceases to stand in any special relation to her. She has no recognised duties to him, or he to her. These lie between him and his father only, and just because the father's interests are divided between the children of many wives, and because these render their filial offices to the father separately, not to father and mother jointly, the true domestic training is lost.

241. Monogamy, however, may be established, and an advance so far made towards the establishment of a due reciprocity between husband and wife, as well as towards a fulfilment of the responsibilities incurred in bringing children into the world, while yet the true claims of men in respect of women, and of women in respect of men, and of children upon their parents, are far from being generally realised. Wherever slavery exists alongside of monogamy, on the one side people of the slave class are prevented from forming family ties, and on the other those who are privileged to marry, though they are confined to one wife, are constantly tempted to be false to the true monogamistic idea by the opportunity of using women as chattels to minister to their pleasures. The wife is thus no more than an institution, invested with certain dignities and privileges, for the continuation of the family; a continuation, which under pagan religions is considered necessary for the maintenance of certain ceremonies, and

to which among ourselves an importance is attached wholly unconnected with the personal affection of the man for the wife.[12] When slavery is abolished, and the title of all men and women equally to form
families is established by law, the conception of the position of the
wife necessarily rises. The *etaira* [courtesan] and *pallakē* [concu-
bine] cease at any rate to be recognised accompaniments of married
life, and the claim of the wife upon the husband's fidelity, as reciprocal to his claim upon hers, becomes established bv law.

242. Thus that marriage should only be lawful with one wife, that
it should be for life, that it should be terminable by the infidelity of
either husband or wife, are rules of *right*; not of morality, as such, but
of right. Without such rules the *rights* of the married persons are not
maintained. Those outward conditions of family life would not be
secured to them, which are necessary on the whole for the development of a free morality. Polygamy is a violation of the rights, (1) of
those who through it are indirectly excluded from regular marriage,
and thus from the moral education which results from this; (2) of the
wife, who is morally lowered by exclusion from her proper position in
the household and by being used, more or less, as the mere instrument of the husband's pleasure; (3) of the children, who lose the
chance of that full moral training which depends on the connected
action of father and mother. The terminability of marriage at the
pleasure of one of the parties to it (of its terminability at the desire of
both we will speak presently) is a violation of the rights at any rate of
the unconsenting party, on the grounds (*a*) that liability to it tends to
prevent marriage from becoming that '*individua vitæ consuetudo*'
which gives it its moral value, and (*b*) that, when the marriage is dissolved, the woman, just in proportion to her capacity for self-
devotion and the degree to which she has devoted herself to her
original husband, is debarred from forming that '*individua vitæ consuetudo*' again, and thus crippled in her moral possibilities. It is a violation of the rights of children for the same reason for which
polygamy is so.

On the other hand, that the wife should be bound indissolubly by
the marriage-tie to an unfaithful husband (or *vice versa*), is a violation of the right of wife (or husband, as the case may be), because on
the one hand the restraint which makes her liable to be used physi-
cally as the instrument of the husband's pleasures, when there is no
longer reciprocal devotion between them, is a restraint which (except
in peculiar cases) renders moral elevation impossible; and on the
other, she is prevented from forming such a true marriage as would

be, according to ordinary rules, the condition of the realisation of her moral capacities. Though the husband's right to divorce from an unfaithful wife has been much more thoroughly recognised than the wife's to divorce from an unfaithful husband, he would be in fact less seriously wronged by the inability to obtain a divorce, for it is only the second of the grounds just stated that fully applies to him. The rights of the children do not seem so plainly concerned in the dissolution of a marriage to which husband or wife has been unfaithful. In some cases the best chance for them might seem to lie in the infidelities being condoned and an outward family peace re-established. But that their rights are violated by the infidelity itself is plain. In the most definite way it detracts from their possibilities of goodness. Without any consent on their part, quite independently of any action of their own will, they are placed by it in a position which tends – though special grace may counteract it – to put the higher kinds of goodness beyond their reach.

243. These considerations suggest some further questions which may be discussed under the following heads. (1) If infidelity in marriage is a violation of rights in the manner stated, and if (as it must be) it is a wilful and knowing violation, why is it not treated as a crime, and, like other such violations of rights, punished by the state in order to the better maintenance of rights? (2) Should any other reason but the infidelity of husband or wife be allowed for the legal dissolution of the marriage tie? (3) How are the *rights* connected with marriage related to the *morality* of marriage?

(1) There is good reason why the state should not take upon itself to institute charges of adultery, but leave them to be instituted by the individuals whose rights the adultery violates. The reasons ordinarily alleged would be, (*a*) the analogy of ordinary breaches of contract, against which the state leaves it to the individual injured to set the law in motion; (*b*) the practical impossibility of preventing adultery through the action of the functionaries of the state. The analogy, however, from ordinary breaches of contract does not really hold.[13] In the first place, though marriage involves contract, though without contract there can be no marriage, yet marriage at once gives rise to right and obligations of a kind which cannot arise out of contract – in particular to obligations towards the children born of the marriage. These children, at any rate, are in no condition to seek redress – even if from the nature of the case redress could be had – for the injuries inflicted on them by a parent's adultery, as a person injured by a breach of contract can seek redress for it. Again, though the state leaves it to the individual injured by a breach of contract to institute

proceedings for redress, if the breach involves fraud, it – at any rate in certain cases – treats the fraud as a crime and punishes. Now in every breach of the marriage-contract by adultery there is that which answers to fraud in the case of ordinary breach of contract. The marriage-contract is broken knowingly and intentionally. If there were no reason to the contrary, then, it would seem that the state, though it might leave to the injured individuals the institution of proceedings against adultery, should yet treat adultery as a crime and seek to prevent it by punishment in the interest of those whose virtual rights are violated by it, though not in the way of breach of contract. But there are reasons to the contrary – reasons that arise out of the moral purposes served by the marriage-tie – which make it desirable both that it should be at the discretion of the directly injured party whether a case of adultery should be judicially dealt with at all, and that in no case should penal terror be associated with such a violation of the marriage-bond. Under ordinary conditions, it is a public injury that a violation of his rights should be condoned by the person suffering it. If the injured individual were likely to fail in the institution of proceedings for his own redress or defence, the public interest would require that the matter should be taken out of his hands. But if an injured wife or husband is willing to condone a breach of his or her rights through adultery, it is generally best that it should be condoned. That married life should be continued in spite of anything like dissoluteness on the part of husband or wife, is no doubt undesirable. The moral purposes which married life should serve cannot be served, either for the married persons themselves or for the children, under such conditions. On the other hand, the condonation of a single offence would generally be better for all concerned than an application for divorce. The line cannot be drawn at which, with a view to the higher ends which marriage should serve, divorce becomes desirable. It is therefore best that the state, while uniformly allowing the right of divorce where the marriage-bond has been broken by adultery, since otherwise the right of everyone to form a true marriage (a marriage which shall be the basis of family life) is neutralised, and taking care that procedure for divorce be cheap and easy, should leave the enforcement of the right to the discretion of individuals.[14]

244. On similar grounds, it is undesirable that adultery as such should be treated as a crime – that penal terror should be associated with it. Though rights, in the strict sense, undoubtedly arise out of marriage, though marriage has thus its strictly legal aspect, it is undesirable that this legal aspect should become prominent. It may

suffer in respect of its higher moral purposes, if the element of force
appears too strongly in the maintenance of the rights to which it gives
rise. If a husband who would otherwise be false to the marriage bond
is kept outwardly faithful to it by fear of the punishment which might
attend its breach, the right of the wife and children is indeed so far
protected, but is anything gained for those moral ends, for the sake of
which the maintenance of these rights is alone of value? The man in
whom disloyal passion is neutralised by fear of punishment will contribute little in his family life to the moral development of himself, his
wife, or his children. If he cannot be kept true by family affection and
sympathy with the social disapprobation attaching to matrimonial
infidelity – and unless it is a matter of social disapprobation no
penalties will be effectually enforced against it – he will not be kept
true in a way that is of any value to those concerned by fear of penalties. In other words, the rights that arise out of marriage are not of a
kind which can in their essence be protected by associating penal
terror with their violation, as the rights of life and property can be.
They are not rights to claim mere forbearances or to claim the performance of certain outward actions, by which a right is satisfied irrespectively of the disposition with which the act is done. They are
claims which cannot be met without a certain disposition on the part
of the person upon whom the claim rests, and that disposition cannot
be enforced. The attempt to enforce the outward behaviour in order
to satisfy the claim, which is a claim not to the outward behaviour
merely but to this in connection with a certain disposition, defeats its
own end.

245. For the protection, therefore, of the rights of married persons
and their children against infidelity, it does not appear that the law
can do more than secure facilities of divorce in the case of adultery.
This indeed is not in itself a protection against the wrong involved in
adultery, but rather a deliverance from the further wrong to the
injured husband or wife and to the children that would be involved in
the continuance of any legal claim over them on the part of the injurer. But indirectly it helps to prevent the wrong being done by
bringing social disapprobation to bear on cases of infidelity, and thus
helping to keep married persons faithful through sympathy with the
disapprobation of which they feel that they would be the objects
when they imagine themselves unfaithful. The only other effectual
way in which the state can guard against the injuries in question is by
requiring great precaution and solemnity in the contraction of marriages. This it can do by insisting on the consent of parents to the
marriage of all minors, exacting a long notice (perhaps even a prelimi-

nary notice of betrothal), and – while not preventing civil marriage – by encouraging the celebration of marriage in the presence of religious congregations and with religious rites.

246. Question (2) is one that does not admit of being answered on any absolute principle. We must bear in mind that all rights – in idea or as they should be – are relative to moral ends. The ground for securing to individuals in respect of the marriage-tie certain powers as rights, is that in a general way they are necessary to the possibility of a morally good life, either directly to the persons exercising them or to their children. The more completely marriage is a '*consortium omnis vitæ*' in the sense of a unity in all interests and for the whole of a lifetime, the more likely are the external conditions of a moral life to be fulfilled in regard both to married persons and their children. Therefore the general rule of the state in dealing with marriage should be to secure such powers as are favourable and withhold such as are not favourable to the '*consortium omnis vitæ*.' But in the application of the principle great difficulties arise. Lunacy may clearly render the '*consortium omnis vitæ*' finally impossible; but what kind and degree of lunacy? If the lunatic may possibly recover, though there is undoubtedly reason for the separation from husband or wife during lunacy, should permanent divorce be allowed? If it is allowed, and the lunatic recovers, a wrong will have been done both to him and to the children previously born of the marriage.[15] On the other hand, to reserve the connubial rights of a lunatic of whose recovery there is hope, and to restore them when he recovers, may involve the wrong of bringing further children into the world with the taint of lunacy upon them. Is cruelty to be a ground of divorce, and if so, what amount? There is a degree of persistent cruelty which renders '*consortium omnis vitæ*' impossible, but unless it is certain that cruelty has reached the point at which a restoration of any sort of family life becomes impossible, a greater wrong both to wife and children may be involved in allowing divorce than in refusing it. A husband impatient for the time of the restraint of marriage may be tempted to passing cruelty as a means of ridding himself of it, while if no such escape were open to him he might get the better of the temporary disturbing passion and settle down into a decent husband.[16] The same consideration applies still more strongly to allowing incompatibility of temper as a ground of divorce. It would be hard to deny that it might be of a degree and kind in which it so destroyed the possibility of '*consortium omnis vitæ*', that, with a view to the interests of the children, who ought in such a case to be chiefly considered, divorce implied less wrong than the maintenance of the marriage-

tie. But on the other hand, to hold out the possibility of divorce on the ground of incompatibility is just the way to generate that incompatibility. On the whole, the only conclusion seems to be that this last ground should not be allowed, and that in deciding on other grounds large discretion should be allowed to a well-constituted court.

P. RIGHTS AND VIRTUES

247. We have now considered in a perfunctory way those rights which are antecedent to the state – which are not derived from it but may exist where a state is not, and which it is the office of the state to maintain. We have inquired what it is in the nature of man that renders him capable of these rights, what are the moral ends to which the rights are relative, and in what form the rights should be realised in order to the attainment of these ends. In order to make the inquiry into rights complete, we ought to go on to examine in the same way the rights which arise out of the establishment of a state[1] – the rights connected with the several functions of government; how these functions come to be necessary, and how they may best be fulfilled with a view to those moral ends to which the functions of the state are ultimately relative. According to my project, I should then have proceeded to consider the social virtues, and the 'moral sentiments' which underlie our particular judgments as to what is good and evil in conduct. All virtues are really social; or, more properly, the distinction between social and self-regarding virtues is a false one. Every virtue is self-regarding in the sense that it is a disposition, or habit of will, directed to an end which the man presents to himself as his good; every virtue is social in the sense that unless the good to which the will is directed is one in which the well-being of society in some form or other is involved, the will is not virtuous at all.

248. The virtues are dispositions to exercise positively, in some way contributory to social good, those powers which, because admitting of being so exercised, society should secure to him, which a man has *a right* to possess, which constitute his rights. It is therefore convenient to arrange the virtues according to the division of rights. E.g. in regard to the right of all men to free life, the obligations, strictly so called, correlative to that right having been considered – *obligations* which are all of a negative nature, obligations to forbear from meddling with one's neighbour – we should proceed to consider the activities by which a society of men really free is *established*[a], or by which

some approach is made to its establishment; '*really free*', in the sense of being enabled to make the most of their capabilities. These activities will take different forms under different social conditions, but in rough outline they are those by which men in mutual helpfulness conquer and adapt nature, and overcome the influences which would make them victims of chance and accident, of brute force and animal passion. The virtuous disposition displayed in these activities may have various names applied to it according to the particular direction in which it is exerted – 'industry', 'courage', 'public spirit'. A particular aspect of it was brought into relief among the Greeks under the name of *andreia* [manliness]. The Greek philosophers already gave an extension to the meaning of this term beyond that which belonged to it in popular usage, and we might be tempted further to extend it so as to cover all the forms in which the habit of will necessary to the maintenance and furtherance of free society shows itself. The name, however, does not much matter. It is enough that there are specific modes of human activity which contribute directly to maintain a shelter for man's worthier energies against disturbance by natural forces and by the consequences of human fear and lust. The state of mind which appears in them may properly be treated as a special kind of virtue. It is true that the principle and the end of all virtues is the same. They are all determined by relation to social well-being as their final cause, and they all rest on *b*an interest which dominates the virtuous agent*b* in some form or other of that well-being; but as that interest may take different directions in different persons – as it cannot be equally developed at once in everyone – it may be said roughly that a man has one kind of virtue and not others.

249. As the kind of moral duties (in distinction from those *obligations* which are correlative to rights) which relate to the maintenance of free society and the disposition to fulfil those duties should form a special object of inquiry, so another special kind would be those which have to do with the management of property, with the acquisition and expenditure of wealth.[2] To respect the rights of property in others, to fulfil the obligations correlative to those rights, is one thing; to make a good use of property, to be justly generous and generously just in giving and receiving, is another; and that may properly be treated as a special kind of virtue which appears in the duly blended prudence, equity and generosity of the ideal man of business. Another special kind will be that which appears in family relations; where indeed that merely negative observance of *a*rights*a* which in other relations can be distinguished from the positive fulfil-

ment of moral duties, becomes unmeaning. As we have seen, there
are certain aggravations and perpetuations of wrong from which husband or wife or children can be protected by law, but the fulfilment
of the claims which arise out of the marriage-tie requires a virtuous
will in the active and positive sense – a will governed by unselfish
interests – on the part of those concerned.

250. What is called 'moral sentiment' is merely a weaker form of
that interest in social well-being which, when wrought into a man's
habits and strong enough to determine action, we call virtue. So far
as this interest is brought into play on the mere survey of action,
and serves merely to determine our approbation or disapprobation, it is called moral sentiment. The forms of moral sentiment
accordingly should be classified on *"the same"* principle as forms
of virtue, i.e. with relation to the social functions to which they
correspond.

251. For the convenience of analysis, we may treat the obligations
correlative to rights – obligations which it is the proper office of law
to enforce – apart from moral duties and from the virtues which are
tendencies to fulfil those duties. I am properly *obliged* to those
actions and forebearances which are requisite to the general freedom
necessary if each is not to interfere with the realisation of another's
will. My *duty* is to be interested positively in my neighbour's well-
being. And it is important to understand that while the enforcement
of obligations is possible, that of moral duties is impossible. But the
establishment of obligations by law or authoritative custom, and the
gradual recognition of moral duties, have not been separate processes. They have gone on together in the history of man. The
growth of the institutions by which more complete equality of rights is
gradually secured to a wider range of persons, and of those interests
in various forms of social well-being by which the will is moralised,
have been related to each other as the outer and inner side of the same
spiritual development; though at a certain stage of reflection it comes
to be discovered that the agency of force, by which the rights are
maintained, is ineffectual for eliciting the moral interests. The result
of the twofold process has been the creation of the actual content of
morality; the articulation of the indefinite consciousness that there is
something that should be – a true well-being to be aimed at other than
any pleasure or succession of pleasures – into the sentiments and
interests which form an 'enlightened conscience'. It is thus that when
the highest stage of reflective morality is reached and upon interests
in this or that mode of social good there supervenes an interest in an
ideal of goodness, that ideal has already a definite filling; and the man

who pursues Duty for Duty's sake,[3] who does good for the sake of being good or in order to realise an idea of perfection, is at no loss to say what in particular his duty is, or by what particular methods the perfection of character is to be approached.

2

Lecture on 'Liberal Legislation and Freedom of Contract'*

That a discussion on this subject is opportune will hardly be disputed by any one who noticed the line of argument by which at least two of the Liberal measures of last session[1] were opposed. To the Ground Game Act it was objected that it interfered with freedom of contract between landlord and tenant. It withdrew the sanction of law from any agreement by which the occupier of land should transfer to the owner the exclusive right of killing hares and rabbits on the land in his occupation. The Employers' Liability Act was objected to on similar grounds. It did not indeed go the length of preventing masters and workmen from contracting themselves out of its oper-ation. But it was urged that it went on the wrong principle of en-couraging the workman to look to the law for the protection which he ought to secure for himself by voluntary contract. 'The workman,' it was argued, 'should be left to take care of himself by the terms of his agreement with the employer. It is not for the state to step in and say, as by the new act it says, that when a workman is hurt in carrying out the instructions of the employer or his foreman, the employer, in the absence of a special agreement to the contrary, shall be liable for com-pensation. If the law thus takes to protecting men, whether tenant-farmers, or pitmen, or railway servants, who ought to be able to protect themselves, it tends to weaken their self-reliance, and thus, in unwisely seeking to do them good, it lowers them in the scale of moral beings.'[2]

Such is the language which was everywhere in the air last summer, and which many of us, without being convinced by it, may have found it difficult to answer. The same line of objection is equally applicable to other legislation of recent years, to our factory acts, edu-cation acts, and laws relating to public health.[3] They all, in one direc-tion or another, limit a man's power of doing what he will with what he considers his own. They all involve the legal prohibition of certain agreements between man and man, and as there is nothing to force men into these agreements, it might be argued that, supposing them to be mischievous, men would, in their own interest, gradually learn

194

to refuse them. There is other legislation which the liberal party is
likely to demand, and which is sure to be objected to on the same
ground, with what justice we shall see as we proceed. If it is proposed
to give the Irish tenant some security in his holding, to save him from
rack-renting and from the confiscation of the results of his labour in
the improvement of the soil, it will be objected that in so doing the
state goes out of its way to interfere with the contracts, possibly beneficial to both sides, which landlord and tenant would otherwise
make with each other. Leave the tenant, it will be said, to secure himself by contract. Meanwhile the demand for greater security of tenure
is growing stronger amongst our English farmers, and should it be
proposed – as it must before this parliament expires – to give legal
effect to it, the proposal will be met by the same cry, that it is an interference with the freedom of contract, unless, indeed, like Lord
Beaconsfield's Act of 1875, it undoes with one hand what it professes
to do with the other.[4]

There are two other matters with which the Liberal leaders have virtually promised to deal, and upon which they are sure to be met by an
appeal to the supposed inherent right of every man to do what he will
with his own. One is the present system of settling land, the other the
liquor traffic. The only effectual reform of the land laws is to put a
stop to those settlements or bequests by which at present a landlord
may prevent a successor from either converting any part of his land
into money or from dividing it among his children.[5] But if it is proposed to take away from the landlord this power of hampering posterity, it will be said to be an interference with his free disposal of his
property. As for the liquor traffic, it is obvious that even the present
licensing laws, ineffectual as some of us think them, interfere with the
free sale of an article in large consumption, and that with the concession of 'local option' the interference would, to say the least, be
probably carried much further.[6] I have said enough to show that the
most pressing political questions of our time are questions of which
the settlement, I do not say necessarily involves an interference with
freedom of contract, but is sure to be resisted in the sacred name of individual liberty, not only by all those who are interested in keeping
things as they are, but by others to whom freedom is dear for its own
sake, and who do not sufficiently consider the conditions of its maintenance in such a society as ours. In this respect there is a noticeable
difference between the present position of political reformers and
that in which they stood a generation ago.[7] Then they fought the fight
of reform in the name of individual freedom against class privilege.
Their opponents could not with any plausibility invoke the same

name against them. Now, in appearance – though, as I shall try to show, not in reality – the case is changed. The nature of the genuine political reformer is perhaps always the same. The passion for improving mankind, in its ultimate object, does not vary. But the immediate object of reformers, and the forms of persuasion by which they seek to advance them, vary much in different generations. To a hasty observer they might even seem contradictory, and to justify the notion that nothing better than a desire for change, selfish or perverse, is at the bottom of all reforming movements. Only those who will think a little longer about it can discern the same old cause of social good against class interests, for which, under altered names, liberals are fighting now as they were fifty years ago.

Our political history since the first reform act naturally falls into three divisions. The first, beginning with the reform of parliament, and extending to Sir R. Peel's administration, is marked by the struggle of free society against close privileged corporations. Its greatest achievement was the establishment of representative municipal governments in place of the close bodies which had previously administered the affairs of our cities and boroughs; a work which after an interval of nearly half a century we hope shortly to see extended to the rural districts. Another important work was the overhauling of the immense charities of the country, and the placing of them under something like adequate public control. And the natural complement of this was the removal of the grosser abuses in the administration of the church, the abolition of pluralities and sinecures, and the reform of cathedral chapters.[8] In all this, while there was much that contributed to the freedom of our civil life, there was nothing that could possibly be construed as an interference with the rights of the individual. No one was disturbed in doing what he would with his own. Even those who had fattened on abuses had their vested interests duly respected, for the House of Commons then as now had 'quite a passion for compensation'.[9] With the ministry of Sir R. Peel began the struggle of society against monopolies; in other words, the liberation of trade. Some years later Mr. Gladstone, in his famous budgets, was able to complete the work which his master began, and it is now some twenty years since the last vestige of protection for any class of traders or producers disappeared. The taxes on knowledge, as they were called, followed the taxes on food, and since most of us grew up there has been no exchangeable commodity in England except land – no doubt a large exception – of which the exchange has not been perfectly free.[10]

The realisation of complete freedom of contract was the special

object of this reforming work. It was to set men at liberty to dispose *as long as*
of what they had made their own that the free-trader worked. He only *he didn't*
interfered to prevent interference. He would put restraint on no man *harm*
in doing anything that did not directly check the free dealing of some *anyone else's*
one in something else. But of late reforming legislation has taken, as I *freedom*
have pointed out, a seemingly different direction. It has not at any
rate been so readily identifiable with the work of liberation. In certain
respects it has put restraints on the individual in doing what he will
with his own. And it is noticeable that this altered tendency begins, in
the main, with the more democratic parliament of 1868. It is true that
the earlier factory acts, limiting as they do by law the conditions
under which certain kinds of labour may be bought and sold, had
been passed some time before. The first approach to an effectual Factory Act dates as far back as the time of the first reform act, but it only
applied to the cotton industry, and was very imperfectly put in force.
It aimed at limiting the hours of labour for children and young persons. Gradually the limitation of hours came to be enforced, other
industries were brought under the operation of the restraining laws,
and the same protection extended to women as to young persons. But
it was only alongside of the second reform act in 1867 that an attempt
was made by Parliament to apply the same rule to every kind of factory and workshop; only later still, in the first parliament elected
partly by household suffrage, that efficient measures were taken for
enforcing the restraints which previous legislation had in principle
required.[11] Improvements and extensions in detail have since been
introduced, largely through the influence of Mr. Mundella,[12] and
now we have a system of law by which, in all our chief industries *reg of*
except the agricultural, the employment of children except as half- *the*
timers is effectually prevented, the employment of women and young *work*
persons is effectually restricted to ten hours a day, and in all places of *place*
employment health and bodily safety have all the protection which
rules can give them.

   If factory regulation had been attempted, though only in a piece-
meal way, some time before we had a democratic House of Commons, the same cannot be said of educational law. It was the
parliament elected by a more popular suffrage in 1868 that passed, as
we know, the first great education act. That act introduced compul- *edu*
sory schooling. It left the compulsion, indeed, optional with local *reform*
school-boards, but compulsion is the same in principle, is just as
much compulsion by the state, whether exercised by the central
government or delegated by that government to provincial authorities. The education act of 1870 was a wholly new departure in

English legislation, though Mr. Forster was wise enough to proceed tentatively, and leave the adoption of compulsory bye-laws to the discretion of school-boards.[13] It was so just as much as if he had attempted at once to enforce compulsory attendance through the action of the central government. The principle was established once for all that parents were not to be allowed to do as they willed with their children, if they willed either to set them to work or to let them run wild without elementary education. Freedom of contract in respect of all dealings with the labour of children was so far limited.

I need not trouble you with recalling the steps by which the principle of the act of 1870 has since been further applied and enforced.[14] It is evident that in the body of school and factory legislation which I have noticed we have a great system of interference with freedom of contract. The hirer of labour is prevented from hiring it on terms to which the person of whom he hires it could for the most part have been readily brought to agree. If children and young persons and women were not ready in many cases, either from their own wish, or under the influence of parents and husbands, to accept employment of the kind which the law prohibits, there would have been no occasion for the prohibition. It is true that adult men are not placed directly under the same restriction. The law does not forbid them from working as long hours as they please. But I need not point out here[15] that in effect the prevention of the employment of juvenile labour beyond certain hours, amounts, at least in the textile industries, to the prevention of the working of machinery beyond those hours. It thus indirectly puts a limit on the number of hours during which the manufacturer can employ his men. And if it *a*is thus only*a* accidentally, so to speak, that the hiring of men's labour is interfered with by the half-time and ten hours' system, the interference on grounds of health and safety is as direct as possible. The most mature man is prohibited by law from contracting to labour in factories, or pits, or workshops, unless certain rules for the protection of health and limb are complied *b*with. The free sale of his labour is so far interfered with. In*b* like manner he is prohibited from living in a house which the sanitary inspector pronounces unwholesome. The free sale or letting of a certain kind of commodity is thereby prevented. Here, then, is a great system of restriction, which yet hardly any impartial person wishes to see reversed; which many of us wish to see made more complete. Perhaps, however, we have never thoroughly considered the principles on which we approve it. It may be well, therefore, to spend a short time in ascertaining those principles. We shall then be on surer ground in approaching those more difficult questions of legis-

[handwritten: negative v. positive freedom]

lation which must shortly be dealt with, and of which the settlement
is sure to be resisted in the name of individual liberty.

We shall probably all agree that freedom, rightly understood, is the
greatest of blessings; that its attainment is the true end of all our
effort as citizens. But when we thus speak of freedom, we should consider carefully what we mean by it. We do not mean merely freedom
from restraint or compulsion. We do not mean merely freedom to do
as we like irrespectively of what it is that we like. We do not mean a
freedom that can be enjoyed by one man or one set of men at the cost
of a loss of freedom to others. When we speak of freedom as something to be so highly prized, we mean a positive power or capacity of
doing or enjoying something worth doing or enjoying, and that, too,
something that we do or enjoy in common with others.[16] We mean by
it a power which each man exercises through the help or security
given him by his fellow-men, and which he in turn helps to secure for
them. When we measure the progress of a society by its growth in
freedom, we measure it by the increasing development and exercise
on the whole of those powers of contributing to social good with
which we believe the members of the society to be endowed; in short,
by the greater power on the part of the citizens as a body to make the
most and best of themselves. Thus, though of course there can be no
freedom among men who act not willingly but under compulsion, yet
on the other hand the mere removal of compulsion, the mere enabling
a man to do as he likes, is in itself no contribution to true freedom.[17]
In one sense no man is so well able to do as he likes as the wandering
savage. He has no master. There is no one to say him nay. Yet we do
not count him really free, because the freedom of savagery is not
strength, but weakness. The actual powers of the ᶜnoblestᶜ savage do
not admit of comparison with those of the humblest citizen of a law-
abiding state. He is not the slave of man, but he is the slave of nature.
Of compulsion by natural necessity he has plenty of experience,
though of restraint by society none at all. Nor can he deliver himself
from that compulsion except by submitting to this restraint. So to
submit is the first step in true freedom, because the first step towards
the full exercise of the faculties with which man is endowed.[18] But we
rightly refuse to recognise the highest development on the part of an
exceptional individual or exceptional class, as an advance towards the
true freedom of man, if it is founded on a refusal of the same opportunity to other men. The powers of the human mind have probably
never attained such force and keenness, the proof of what society can
do for the individual has never been so strikingly exhibited, as among
the small groups of men who possessed civil privileges in the small re-

[handwritten margin notes: freedom; an active concept; freedom is social / social freedom; let's go over how he gets there]

[handwritten bottom: Mill's high & low pleasures]

publics of antiquity. The whole framework of our political ideas, to say nothing of our philosophy, is derived from them. But in them this extraordinary efflorescence of the privileged class was accompanied by the slavery of the multitude. That slavery was the condition on which it depended, and for that reason it was doomed to decay. There is no clearer ordinance of that supreme reason, often dark to us, which governs the course of man's affairs, than that no body of men *d*shall*d* in the long run be able to strengthen itself at the cost of others' weakness. The civilisation and freedom of the ancient world were shortlived because they were partial and exceptional.[19] If the ideal of true freedom is the maximum of power for all members of human society alike to make the best of themselves, we are right in refusing to ascribe the glory of freedom to a state in which the apparent elevation of the few is founded on the degradation of the many, and in ranking modern society, founded as it is on free industry, with all its confusion and ignorant licence and waste of effort, above the most splendid of ancient republics.

If I have given a true account of that freedom which forms the goal of social effort, we shall see that freedom of contract, freedom in all the forms of doing what one will with one's own, is valuable only as a means to an end. That end is what I call freedom in the positive sense: in other words, the liberation of the powers of all men equally for contributions to a common good. No one has a right to do what he will with his own in such a way as to contravene this end. It is only through the guarantee which society gives him that he has property at all, or, strictly speaking, any right to his possessions. This guarantee is founded on a sense of common interest. Every one has an interest in securing to every one else the free use and enjoyment and disposal of his possessions, so long as that freedom on the part of one does not interfere with a like freedom on the part of others, because such freedom contributes to that equal development of the faculties of all which is the highest good for all. This is the true and the only justification of rights of property. Rights of property, however, have been and are claimed which cannot be thus justified. We are all now agreed that men cannot rightly be the property of men. The institution of property being only justifiable as a means to the free exercise of the social capabilities of all, there can be no true right to property of a kind which debars one class of men from such free exercise altogether.[20] We condemn slavery no less when it arises out of a voluntary agreement on the part of the enslaved person. A contract by which any one agreed for a certain consideration to become the slave of another we should reckon a void contract.[21] Here, then, is a limitation upon freedom of contract which we all recognise as rightful. No contract is valid in which human persons, willingly or unwillingly, are dealt with as commodities, because such contracts of necessity defeat the end for which alone society enforces contracts at all.

Are there no other contracts which, less obviously perhaps but really, are open to the same objection? In the first place, let us consider contracts affecting labour. Labour, the economist tells us, is a commodity exchangeable like other commodities.[22] This is in a certain sense true, but it is a commodity which attaches in a peculiar manner to the person of man. Hence restrictions may need to be *justifying* placed on the sale of this commodity which would be unnecessary in *regulation* other cases, in order to prevent labour from being sold under conditions which make it impossible for the person selling it ever to become a free contributor to social good in any form. This is most *individual in relation to society* plainly the case when a man bargains to work under conditions fatal to health, *e.g.* in an unventilated factory. Every injury to the health of the individual is, so far as it goes, a public injury. It is an impediment to the general freedom; so much deduction from our power, as members of society, to make the best of ourselves. Society is, therefore, plainly within its right when it limits freedom of contract for the sale of labour, so far as is done by our laws for the sanitary regulations of factories, workshops, and mines. It is equally within its right in prohibiting the labour of women and young persons beyond certain hours. If they work beyond those hours, the result is demonstrably physical deterioration; which, as demonstrably, carries with it a lowering of the moral forces of society. For the sake of that general *justification* freedom of its members to make the best of themselves, which it is the *for work* object of civil society to secure, a prohibition should be put by law, *place regulation ↓* which is the deliberate voice of society, on all such contracts of service as in a general way yield such a result. The purchase or hire of *good of the society* unwholesome dwellings is properly forbidden on the same principle. Its application to compulsory education may not be quite so obvious, but it will appear on a little reflection. Without a command of certain *educated* elementary arts and knowledge, the individual in modern society is as *citizens* effectually crippled as by the loss of a limb or a broken constitution. *one good* He is not free to develop his faculties. With a view to securing such *for society* freedom among its members it is as certainly within the province of the state to prevent children from growing up in that kind of ignorance which practically excludes them from a free career in life, as it is within its province to require the sort of building and drainage necessary for public health.

Our modern legislation then with reference to labour, and education, and health, involving as it does manifold interference with freedom of contract, is justified on the ground that it is the business of the state, not indeed directly to promote moral goodness, for that, from the very nature of moral goodness, it cannot do, but to maintain the conditions without which a free exercise of the human faculties is impossible.[23] It does not indeed follow that it is advisable for the state to do all which it is justified in doing. We are often warned nowadays against the danger of over-legislation; or, as I heard it put in a speech of the present Home Secretary in days when he was sowing his political wild oats, of 'grandmotherly government'.[24] There may be good ground for the warning, but at any rate we should be quite clear what we mean by it. The outcry against state interference is often raised by men whose real objection is not to state interference but to centralisation, to the constant aggression of the central executive upon local authorities. As I have already pointed out, compulsion at the discretion of some elected municipal board proceeds just as much from the state as does compulsion exercised by a government office in London. No doubt, much needless friction is avoided, much is gained in the way of elasticity and adjustment to circumstances, by the independent local administration of general laws; and most of us would agree that of late there has been a dangerous tendency to override municipal discretion by the hard and fast rules of London 'departments'. But centralisation is one thing: over-legislation, or the improper exercise of the power of the state, quite another. It is one question whether of late the central government has been unduly trenching on local government, and another question whether the law of the state, either as administered by central or by provincial authorities, has been unduly interfering with the discretion of individuals. We may object most strongly to advancing centralisation, and yet wish that the law should put rather more than less restraint on those liberties of the individual which are a social nuisance. But there are some political speculators whose objection is not merely to centralisation, but to the extended action of law altogether. They think that the individual ought to be left much more to himself than has of late been the case.[25] Might not our people, they ask, have been trusted to learn in time for themselves to eschew unhealthy dwellings, to refuse dangerous and degrading employment, to get their children the schooling necessary for making their way in the world? Would they not for their own comfort, if not from more chivalrous feeling, keep their wives and daughters from overwork? Or, failing this, ought not women, like men, to learn to protect themselves? Might not all the *e*ends*e*, in short, which legislation of the kind we have been

yes, this objection is true, but it isn't realistic

discussing is intended to attain, have been attained without it; not so quickly, perhaps, but without tampering so dangerously with the independence and self-reliance of the people?

Now, we shall probably all agree that a society in which the public health was duly protected, and necessary education duly provided for, by the spontaneous action of individuals, was in a higher condition than one in which the compulsion of law was needed to secure these ends. But we must take men as we find them. Until such a condition of society is reached, it is the business *ʲof law or theʲ* state to take the best security it can for the young citizens' growing up in such health and with so much knowledge as is necessary for their real freedom. In so doing it need not at all interfere with the independence and self-reliance of those whom it requires to do what they would otherwise do for themselves. The man who, of his own right *ᵍ*feeling, would provide for the healthy housing of his family, saves*ᵍ* his wife from overwork, and sends his children to school, suffers no moral degradation from a law which, if he did not do this for himself, would seek to make him do it. Such a man does not feel the law as constraint at all. To him it is simply a powerful friend. It gives him security for that being done efficiently which, with the best wishes, he might have much trouble in getting done efficiently if left to himself. No doubt it relieves him from some of the responsibility which would otherwise fall to him as head of a family, but, if he is what we are supposing him to be, in proportion as he is relieved of responsibilites in one direction he will assume them in another.[26] The security which the state gives him for the safe housing and sufficient schooling of his family will only make him the more careful for their well-being in other respects, which he is left to look after for himself. We need have no fear, then, of such legislation having an ill effect on those who, without the law, would have seen to that being done, though probably less efficiently, which the law requires to be done. But it was not their case that the laws we are considering were especially meant to meet. It was the overworked women, the ill-housed and untaught families, for whose benefit they were intended. And the question is whether without these laws the suffering classes could have been delivered quickly or slowly from the condition they were in. Could the enlightened self-interest or benevolence of individuals, working under a system of unlimited freedom of contract, have ever brought them into a state compatible with the free development of the human faculties? No one considering the facts can have any doubt as to the answer to this question. Left to itself, or to the operation of casual benevolence, a degraded population perpetuates and increases itself. Read any of the

authorised accounts, given before royal or parliamentary com-
missions, of the state of the labourers, especially of the women and
children, as they were in our great industries before the law was first
brought to bear on them, and before freedom of contract was first
interfered with in them.[27] Ask yourself what chance there was of a
generation, born and bred under such conditions, ever contracting
itself out of them. Given a certain standard of moral and material
well-being, people may be trusted not to sell their labour, or the
labour of their children, on terms which would not allow that standard to be maintained. But with large masses of our population, until
the laws we have been considering took effect, there was no such standard. There was nothing on their part, in the way either of self-
respect or established demand for comforts, to prevent them from
working and living, or from putting their children to work and live, in
a way in which no one who is to be a healthy and free citizen can work
and live. No doubt there were many high-minded employers who did
their best for their workpeople before the days of state-interference,
but they could not prevent less scrupulous hirers of labour from
hiring it on the cheapest terms. It is true that cheap labour is in the
long run dear labour, but it is so only in the long run, and eager
traders do not think of the long run. If labour is to be had under conditions incompatible with the health or decent housing or education
of the labourer, there will always be plenty of people to buy it under
those conditions, careless of the burden in the shape of rates and taxes
which they may be laying up for posterity. Either the standard of
well-being on the part of the sellers of labour must prevent them from
selling their labour under those conditions, or the law must prevent
it. With a population such as ours was forty years ago, and still largely
is, the law must prevent it and continue the prevention for some generations, before the sellers will be in a state to prevent it for themselves.

As there is practically no danger of a reversal of our factory and
school laws, it may seem needless to dwell at such length on their justification. I do so for two reasons; partly to remind the younger generation of citizens of the great blessing which they inherited in those
laws, and of the interest which they still have in their completion and
extension; but still more in order to obtain some clear principles
for our guidance when we approach those difficult questions of the
immediate future, the questions of the land law and the liquor
law.

I pointed out just now that, though labour might be reckoned an
exchangeable commodity, it differed from all other commodities,

inasmuch as it was inseparable from the person of the labourer. Land, too, has its characteristics, which distinguish it from ordinary commodities.[28] It is from the land, or through the land, that the raw material of all wealth is obtained. It is only upon the land that we can live; only across the land that we can move from place to place. The state, therefore, in the interest of that public freedom which it is its business to maintain, cannot allow the individual to deal as he likes with his land to the same extent to which it allows him to deal as he likes with other commodities. It is an established principle, *e.g.* that the sale of land should be enforced by law when public convenience requires it. The land-owner of course gets the full value, often much more than the full value, of the land which he is compelled to sell, but of no ordinary commodity is the sale thus enforced at all. This illustrates the peculiar necessity in the public interest of putting some restraint on a man's liberty of doing what he will with his own, when it is land that he calls his own. The question is whether in the same interest further restraint does not need to be imposed on the liberty of the land-owner than is at present the case. Should not the state, which for public purposes compels the sale of land, also for public purposes prevent it from being tied up in a manner which prevents its natural distribution and keeps it in the hands of those who cannot make the most of it? At the present the greater part of the land of England is held under settlements which prevent the nominal owner from either dividing his land among his children or from selling any part of it for their benefit. It is so settled that all of it necessarily goes to the owner's eldest son. So far as any sale is allowed it must only be for the benefit of that favoured son. The evil effects of this system are twofold. In the first place it almost entirely prevents the sale of agricultural land in small quantities, and thus hinders the formation of that mainstay of social order and contentment, a class of small proprietors tilling their own land. Secondly it keeps large quantities of land in the hands of men who are too much burdened by debts or family charges to improve it. The landlord in such cases has not the money to improve, the tenant has not the security which would justify him in improving. Thus a great part of the land of England is left in a state in which, according to such eminent and impartial authorities as Lord Derby and Lord Leicester,[29] it does not yield half of what it might. Now what is the remedy for this evil? Various palliative measures have been suggested. A very elaborate one was introduced by Lord Cairns a year ago, but it fell short of the only sufficient remedy.[30] It did not propose to prevent landlords for the future from making settlements of the kind described. It left the old power of set-

tling land untouched, on the ground that to interfere with it would be
to prevent the landlord from doing what he would with his own. We
urge on the contrary that this particular power on the part of the landlord of dealing with his property, imposing, as it does, the weight of
the dead hand on posterity, is against the public interest. On the
simple and recognised principle that no man's land is his own for purposes incompatible with the public convenience, we ask that legal
sanction should be withheld for the future from settlements which
thus interfere with the distribution and improvement of land.

Such a change, though it would limit in one direction the power of
dealing with land, would extend it in other directions. It would
render English land on the whole a much more marketable commodity than it is at present. Its effect would be to restrain the owner
of land in any one generation from putting restraints on the disposal
of it in succeeding generations. It would, therefore, have the support
of those liberals who are most jealous of any interference with freedom of contract. When we come to the relations between landlord
and tenant, we are on more difficult ground. It is agreed that as a general rule the more freedom of contract we have the better, with a view
to that more positive freedom which consists in an open field for all
men to make the best of themselves. But we must not sacrifice the end
to the means. If there are certain kinds of contract for the use of land
which interfere seriously with the public convenience, but which the
parties immediately concerned cannot be trusted to abstain from in
their own interest, such contracts should be invalid by law.[31] It is on
this ground that we justify the prohibition by the act of last session of
agreements between landlord and tenant which reserve the ground
game to the landlord. If the farmers only had been concerned in the
matter, they might perhaps have been left to take care of themselves.
But there were public interests at stake. The country cannot afford
the waste of produce and discouragement of good husbandry which
result from excessive game-preserving; nor can it rightly allow that
widespread temptation to lawless habits which arises from a sort of
half and half property being scattered over the country without any
possibility of its being sufficiently protected. The agreements in
question, therefore, were against the public interest, and as the
tenant farmers themselves, from long habits of dependence, could
not be trusted to refuse them, there was no alternative but to render
them illegal. Perhaps as we become more alive to the evil which the
Ground Game Act but partially remedied, we shall demand further
legislation in the same direction, and insist that some limit be put, not
merely to the landlord's power of reserving the game on land let to

farmers, but to his power of keeping land out of cultivation or turning it into forest for the sake of his amusement.

But while admitting that in this matter of game, from long habit of domination on one side and dependence on the other, landlord and farmer could not safely be left to voluntary agreements, and that a special law was needed to break the back of a mischievous practice, are we to allow that in the public interest the English farmer generally needs to be restrained by law from agreements with his landlord, into which he might be induced to enter if left to himself? Is he not sufficiently enlightened as to his own interest, which is also the interest of the public, and sufficiently free in maintaining it, to refuse to take land except on conditions which will enable him to make the best of it? We may wish that he were, we may hope that some day he will be, but facts show that at present he is not. The great majority of English farmers hold their farms under the liability to be turned out without compensation at six months' or a year's notice. Now it is certain that land cannot be farmed as the public interest requires that it should be, except by an expenditure of capital on the part of the farmers, which will not, as a general rule, be risked so long as he holds his land on these terms. It is true that, under a good landlord, the yearly tenant is as secure as if he held a long lease. But all landlords are not good, nor is a good landlord immortal. He may have a spendthrift eldest son, from whom under his settlement he cannot withhold the estate, and upon whose accession to the estate the temporary security previously enjoyed by yearly tenants will disappear. Whatever the reason, the fact remains that yearly tenancy under the present law is not sufficient to secure a due application of capital to the soil. 'The best agriculture is found on farms where tenants are protected by leases; the next best on farms where tenants are protected by the "Lincolnshire custom"; the worst of all on farms whose tenants are not protected at all, but rely on the honour of their landlords';[32] and this latter class of farms covers the greater part of England. Here, then, is proof that the majority of English farmers have either not been intelligent enough, or not independent enough, to insist on those contracts with their landlords which as a rule are necessary for good farming. They may in time become so, but meanwhile, with the daily increasing pressure on the means of subsistence, the country cannot afford to wait. We do not ask for any such change of the law as would hinder or discourage the farmer from making voluntary contracts with the landlord for the protection of both parties. We only wish in the public interest, which is the interest of good farming, to prevent him from taking a farm, as he now generally does, on terms

incompatible with security in the outlay of capital. In the absence of
leases, we wish a sufficient tenant-right to be guaranteed by law, such
tenant-right as would secure to the out-going tenant the full value of
unexhausted improvements. It is only thus, we believe, that we can
bring about that due cultivation of the soil which is every day becoming of greater importance to our crowded population.

   This protection, which is all that can reasonably be asked for the
English farmer, falls far short of that which the most impartial judges
believe to be necessary for the peasant farmers in Ireland. The difference between the farmers of the ^htwo countries^h may be briefly
stated thus. In Ireland, far more frequently than in England, the
tenant is practically not a free agent in the contract he makes with his
landlord. In England, during the last two or three years, the landlord
has often been more afraid of losing the tenant than the tenant of
losing his farm. It is comparatively easy for a man who does not succeed in getting a farm on terms under which he can make it pay, to get
a living in other ways. Thus in England a farmer is seldom under
such pressure as to be unable to make a bargain with a landlord which
shall be reasonably to his own advantage. In Ireland it is otherwise.
The farmers there are relatively far more numerous, and, as a rule,
far poorer. Nearly three-fourths of the Irish farmers (423,000 out of
596,000) hold less than thirty acres apiece; nearly half of them hold
under fifteen acres.[33] A tenant on that small scale is in a very different
position for bargaining with a landlord from the English farmer, as
we commonly know him, with his 200 acres or more. Apart from his
little farm the tenant has nothing to turn his hand to. With the exception of the linen-making in the north, Ireland has no industry but
agriculture out of which a living can be made. It has been said on
good authority that in many parts of Ireland eviction means starvation to the evicted tenant. This may be a strong statement, but
there is no doubt that to an Irishman of the south and west (the
districts at present disturbed) the hiring of land to till presents itself
as a necessity of life. The only alternative is emigration, and during
the recent years of depression in America that alternative was to a
great extent closed. Hence an excessive competition for farms, and a
readiness on the part of the smaller tenants to put up with any enhancement of rent rather than relinquish their holdings. Under such conditions freedom of contract is little more than a name. The peasant
farmer is scarcely more free to contract with his landlord than is a
starving labourer to bargain for good wages with a master who offers
him work. When many contracts between landlord and tenant are
made under such pressure, reverence for contract, which is the safe-

guard of society, is sure to disappear, and this I believe to be the chief reason why the farmers of southern and western Ireland have been so easily led astray by the agitation of the land league.[34] That agitation strikes at the roots of all contract, and therefore at the very foundation of modern society; but if we would effectually withstand it, we must cease to insist on maintaining the forms of free contract where the reality is impossible. We must in some way give the farmers of Ireland by law that protection which, as a rule, they have been too weak to obtain for themselves singly by contract, protection against the confiscation of the fruits of the labour and money they have spent on the soil, whether that confiscation take the form of actual eviction or of a constant enhancement of rent. To uphold the sanctity of contracts is doubtless a prime business of government, but it is no less its business to provide against contracts being made, which, from the helplessness of one of the parties to them, instead of being a security for freedom, become an instrument of disguised oppression.

I have left myself little time to speak of the principles on which some of us hold that, in the matter of intoxicating drinks, a further limitation of freedom of contract is needed in the interest of general freedom.[35] I say a further limitation, because there is no such thing as a free sale of these drinks at present. Men are not at liberty to buy and sell them when they will, where they will, and as they will. But our present licensing system, while it creates a class of monopolists especially interested in resisting any effectual restraint of the liquor traffic, does little to lessen the facilities for obtaining strong drink. Indeed the principle upon which licences have been generally given has been avowedly to make it easy to get drink. The restriction of the hours of sale is no doubt a real check so far as it goes, but it remains the case that every one who has a weakness for drink has the temptation staring him in the face during all hours but those when he ought to be in bed. The effect of the present system, in short, is to prevent the drink-shops from coming unpleasantly near the houses of well-to-do people, and to crowd them upon the quarters occupied by the poorer classes, who have practically no power of keeping the nuisance from them.[36] Now it is clear that the only remedy which the law can afford for this state of things must take the form either of more stringent rules of licensing, or of a power entrusted to the householders in each district of excluding the sale of intoxicants altogether from among them.

I do not propose to discuss the comparative merits of these methods of procedure. One does not exclude the other. They may very well be combined. One may be best suited for one kind of population, the other for another kind. But either, to be effectual, must involve a large interference with the liberty of the individual to do as he likes in the matter of buying and selling alcohol. It is the justifiability of that interference that I wish briefly to consider.

We justify it on the simple ground of the recognised right on the part of society to prevent men from doing as they like, if, in the exercise of their peculiar tastes in doing as they like, they create a social nuisance. There is no right to freedom in the purchase and sale of a particular commodity, if the general result of allowing such freedom is to detract from freedom in the higher sense, from the general power of men to make the best of themselves. Now with anyone who looks calmly at the facts, there can be no doubt that the present habits of drinking in England do lay a heavy burden on the free development of man's powers for social good, a heavier burden probably than arises from all other preventible causes put together. It used to be the fashion to look on drunkenness as a vice which was the concern only of the person who fell into it, so long as it did not lead him to commit an assault on his neighbours.[37] No thoughtful man any longer looks on it in this way. We know that, however decently carried on, the excessive drinking of one man means an injury to others in health, purse, and capability, to which no limits can be placed. Drunkenness in the head of a family means, as a rule, the impoverishment and degradation of all members of the family; and the presence of a drink-shop at the corner of a street means, as a rule, the drunkenness of a certain number of heads of families in that street. Remove the drink-shops, and, as the experience of many happy communities sufficiently shows, you almost, perhaps in time altogether, remove the drunkenness. Here, then, is a wide-spreading social evil, of which society may, if it will, by a restraining law, to a great extent, rid itself, to the infinite enhancement of the positive freedom enjoyed by its members. All that is required for the attainment of so blessed a result is so much effort and self-sacrifice on the part of the majority of citizens as is necessary for the enactment and enforcement of the restraining law. The majority of citizens may still be far from prepared for such an effort. That is a point on which I express no opinion. To attempt a restraining law in advance of the social sentiment necessary to give real effect to it, is always a mistake. But to argue that an effectual law in restraint of the drink-traffic would be a wrongful interference with individual liberty, is to ignore the essential condition under which alone every particular liberty can rightly be allowed to the individual, the condition, namely, that the allowance of that liberty is not, as a rule, and on the whole, an impediment to social good.

The more reasonable opponents of the restraint for which I plead, would probably argue not so much that it was necessarily wrong in principle, as that it was one of those short cuts to a good end which ultimately defeat their own object. They would take the same line that has been taken by the opponents of state-interference in all its forms. 'Leave the people to themselves,' they would say; 'as their standard of self-respect rises, as they become better housed and better educated, they will gradually shake off the evil habit. The cure so effected may not be so rapid as that brought by a repressive law, but it will be more lasting. Better that it should come more slowly through the spontaneous action of individuals, than more quickly through compulsion.'

But here again we reply that it is dangerous to wait. The slower remedy might be preferable if we were sure that it was a remedy at all, but we have no such assurance. There is strong reason to think the contrary. Every year that the evil is left to itself, it becomes greater. The vested interest in the encouragement of the vice becomes larger, and the persons affected by it more numerous. If any abatement of it has already taken place, we may fairly argue that this is because it has not been altogether left to itself; for the licensing law, as it is, is much more stringent and more stringently administered than it was ten years ago. A drunken population naturally perpetuates and increases itself. Many families, it is true, keep emerging from the conditions which render them specially liable to the evil habit, but on the other hand descent through drunkenness from respectability to squalor is constantly going on. The families of drunkards do not seem to be smaller than those of sober men, though they are shorter-lived; and that the children of a drunkard should escape from drunkenness is what we call almost a miracle. Better education, better housing, more healthy rules of labour, no doubt lessen the temptations to drink for those who have the benefit of these advantages, but meanwhile drunkenness is constantly recruiting the ranks of those who cannot be really educated, who will not be better housed, who make their employments dangerous and unhealthy. An effectual liquor law in short is the necessary complement of our factory acts, our education acts, our public health acts. Without it the full measure of their usefulness will never be attained. They were all opposed in their turn by the same arguments that are now used against a restraint of the facilities for drinking. Sometimes it was the argument that the state had no business to interfere with the liberties of the individual. Sometimes it was the dilatory plea that the better nature of man would in time assert itself, and that meanwhile it would be lowered by compulsion. Happily a sense of the facts and necessities of the case got the better of the delusive cry of liberty. Act after act was passed preventing master and workman, parent and child, house-builder and householder, from doing as they pleased, with the result of a great addition to the real freedom of society. The spirit of self-reliance and independence was not weakened by those acts. Rather it received a new development. The dead weight of ignorance and unhealthy surroundings, with which it would otherwise have had to struggle, being partially removed by law, it was more free to exert itself for higher objects. When we ask for a stringent liquor law, which should even go to the length of allowing the householders of a district to exclude the drink traffic altogether, we are only asking for a continuation of the same work, a continuation necessary to its complete success. It is a poor sophistry to tell us that it is moral cowardice to seek to remove by law a temptation which every one ought to be able to resist for himself. It is not the part of a considerate self-reliance to remain in presence of a temptation merely for the sake of being tempted. When all temptations are removed which law can remove, there will still be room enough, nay, much more room, for the play of our moral energies. The temptation to excessive drinking is one which upon sufficient evidence we hold that the law can at least greatly diminish. If it can, it ought to do so. This then, along with the effectual liberation of the soil, is the next great conquest which our democracy, on behalf of its own true freedom, has to make. The danger of legislation, either in the interests of a privileged class or for the promotion of particular religious opinions, we may fairly assume to be over. The popular jealousy of law, once justifiable enough, is therefore out of date. The citizens of England now make its law.[38] We ask them by law to put a restraint on themselves in the matter of strong drink. We ask them further to limit, or even altogether to give up, the not very precious liberty of buying and selling alcohol, in order that they may become more free to exercise the faculties and improve the talents which God has given them.

3

Four lectures on the English Revolution: selections*

LECTURE I

The period of which I am to speak is one of the most trodden grounds of history[1] ... But though this is so ... it may be doubted whether its character has ever been quite fairly exhibited. By partisans it has been regarded without 'dry light', by judicious historians with a light so dry as not at all to illustrate the real temper and purpose of the actors. In reaction from the latter has appeared a mode of treatment, worked with special force by Mr Carlyle,[2] which puts personal character in the boldest relief, but overlooks the strength of circumstance, the organic life of custom and institution, which acts on the individual from without and from within, which at once informs his will and places it in limits against which it breaks itself in vain. Such oversight leaves out an essential element in the tragedy of [the] human story ... The historic hero, strong to make the world new, and exulting in his strength, has his inspiration from a past which he knows not, and is constructing a future which is not that of his own will or imagination. The providence which he serves works by longer and more ambiguous methods than suit his enthusiasm or impatience. Sooner or later the fatal web gathers round him too painfully to be longer disregarded, when he must either waste himself in ineffectual struggle with it, or adjust himself to it by a process which to his own conscience and in the judgement of men is one of personal debasement. It is as such a tragic conflict between the creative will of man and the hidden wisdom of the world, which seems to thwart it, that the 'Great Rebellion' has its interest ...

It will be my endeavour in speaking of the short life of English republicanism ... to treat it as the last act in a conflict beginning with the Reformation, in which the several parties had each its justification in reason, and which ended, not simply, as might seem, in a catastrophe, but was preliminary to a reconciliation of the forces at

issue of another kind than could to an actor in the conflict be
apparent. If I seem to begin far back, I must trust to the sequel for
vindication . . .

'Justification by faith' and 'the right of private judgement' are the
two watchwords of the Reformation. Each indicates a new relation
between the spirit and outward authority . . . Raised first and in its
rudest form by Münzer's Anabaptists,[3] it worked with more subtle
influence in all the countries which felt the Reformation. The opposition between the inward and outward, between reason and authority, between the spirit and the flesh, between the individual and the
world of settled right, no longer a mere antithesis of the Schools, was
being wrought into the political life of Christendom. It gives the true
formula for expressing the nature of the conflict which issued in the
English commonwealth . . .

The Reformation in England begins simply with the substitution
of Royal for Papal power in the government of the Church. If Henry
VIII had left a successor capable of wielding his sceptre, English religion would scarcely have grown up, as it has done, in the bracing
atmosphere of schism. During the minority of Edward, a form of
Protestant Episcopacy, unique among the Reformed Churches, grew
up with a certain degree of independence, while at the same time
ideas of a different order, whose mother was Geneva, were working
undisturbed. The Marian persecution, while it strengthened the
influence of the aggressive Genevan form of protestantism on
England, completed its estrangement from the state. Thus when
'Anglicanism' – episcopal, sacramental, ceremonial – was established
by Elizabeth, it had at once to deal with an opposite system,
thoroughly formed and nursed in antagonism to the powers of this
world. This system is, so to speak, the full articulation of that voice of
conscience, of the inner self-asserting spirit, in opposition to outward
ordinance, which the Reformation evoked. In this light let us consider its action in England.

The Lutheran doctrine . . . brings the individual soul, as such,
into direct relation to God. From this doctrine the first practical cor-
ollary is the placing of the Bible in the hands of the people; the second
is the exaltation of preaching. From these again follows the diffusion
of popular education. The soul, admitted in its own right to the
divine audience, still needs a language. It must know whom it
approaches, and what it is his will to give. But as the intercourse is
inward and spiritual, so must be the power which regulates it; not a
priest or a liturgy, but the voice of the divine spirit in the Bible, interpreted by the believer's conscience. Religion being thus internalised

and individualised, preaching as the action of soul on soul, becomes the natural channel of its communication . . .

A people's Bible, then, a reading people, a preaching ministry, were the three conditions of Protestant life. The force which results from them is everywhere an unruly one. With the English . . . [i]t demanded and sought to create an outward world, a system of law, custom, and ordinance, answering to itself. Not only is the law of the Bible to be carried directly and everywhere into action; whatever is of other origin is no law for the society whose head is Christ. An absolute breach is thus made between the new and the old. Those who by a conscious, deliberate wrench have broken with the old, and lived themselves into the new, are the predestined people of God. Outside them is a doomed world. They are the saints, and their prerogative has no limits . . . The sword of the magistrate must be in their hands, or it is a weapon of offence against Christ's people . . .

Puritanism, in the Presbyterian form, had obtained supremacy in Scotland, while it was still struggling for life in England[4] . . . Without scruple or disguise it pursued 'the work of reformation' by conforming under pains and penalties the manners and opinions of men to a supposed scriptural model. In England, though the theory of Puritanism was the same speculatively, its position was happily different . . . The reforming impulse, the effort to emancipate the inward man from ceremonial bondage, was with Puritanism, rather than with the Church . . . Its limitations were its own, and happily it had no chance of fixing them finally in an outward Church. Its force belonged to a larger agency, which was transforming religion from a sensuous and interested service to a free communion of spirit with spirit, and just for this reason it kept gathering to itself elements which its own earthen vessel could not long contain.

. . . [P]olitical change corresponded to the theological. Elizabeth had ruled a nation. James and Charles never rose beyond the conception of developing a Royal interest, which religion should at once serve and justify. Thus there arose that combination, by which the Catholic Reaction had everywhere worked, of a Court Party and a Church Party, each using the other for the purpose of silencing the demands for a 'reason why' in politics and religion. Charles and Laud alike represented that jesuitical conscience (if I may be allowed the expression) which is fatal to true loyalty[5] . . . Such a conscience may be true to a cause, . . . [b]ut it dare not look into the law of liberty, or conceive the operation of God except in a system of prescribed institutions, about which no questions are to be asked, and in the maintenance of which cruelty becomes mercy and falsehood truth . . . The result, but for the Puritan resistance, must have been that freedom should yield in England ... to a despotism under priestly direction, which again could end only in the ruin of civil life, or in its recovery by the process which relegates religion to women and devotees.

The body of Protestant resistance, however, had no organic unity, but that of a common antagonism ... The men commonly reckoned as the authors of Independency or Congregationalism – an influence which more than any other has ennobled the plebeian elements of English life – bore the fitting names of Brown and Robinson[6] ... It was in 1582 ... that Brown wrote his treatise on 'Reformation, without tarrying for any', and by way of not tarrying for any in his own case, took to preaching nonconformity up and down the country ... Certain views of church polity ... were current among [the Brownists], which formed the principles of Independency in later years. The chief of these were the doctrine of the absolute autonomy of the individual congregation, and the rejection of a special order for priests or presbyters ... Such a system of church government may not in itself be of more interest than others. As giving room for a liberty of prophecy which the rule of Bishops or a Presbytery denies, its importance was immense ...

In the Long Parliament, at the time of its meeting, the only recognised representative of Independency was young Sir Harry Vane.[7] He was not, indeed, properly of the Independent or any other sect ... but he represented that current of thought which flowed through Independence, but could not be contained by it ... 'The two courses in which he had most success, and spake most plainly, were his earnest plea for universal liberty of conscience, and against the magistrate's intermeddling with religion, and his teaching his followers to revile the ministry, calling them Blackcoats, Priests, and other names which then savoured of reproach.'[8]

... The work of creation in time, [Vane] held, which did but reflect the process by which the Father begets the eternal Son, involved two elements, the purely spiritual or angelic, represented by Heaven or the light, on the one hand, and the material and animal on the other, represented by the earth. Man, as made of dust in the image of God, includes both, and his history was a gradual progress upward from a state, which would be merely that of the animals but for the fatal gift of rational will, to a life of pure spirituality, which he represented as angelic – a life which should consist in 'the exercise of senses merely spiritual and inward, exceeding high, intuitive and comprehensive'.[9] This process of spiritual sublimation ... he described as the consuming and dissolving of all objects of outward sense, and a destruction of the earthly tabernacle, while that which is from heaven is being gradually put on. In the conscience of man, the process had three principal stages, called by Vane the natural, legal, and evangelical conscience. The natural conscience was the light of those who, having not the law, were by nature a law unto themselves. It was the source of ordinary right and obligation . . . 'the source and the limit of the authority of the magistrate'. The legal conscience was the source of the ordinances and dogmas of the Christian . . . It represents the stage in which the Christian clings to rule, letter, and privilege. It too had its value, but fell short of the evangelical conscience, of the stage in which the human spirit, perfectly conformed to Christ's death and resurrection, crucified to outward desire and ordinance, holds intercourse 'high, intuitive and comprehensive' with the divine.[10]

. . . The interest of the doctrine for us lies in its application to practical statesmanship by the keenest politician of a time when politicians were keen and strong . . . 'The man above ordinances', as Vane was called by his cotemporaries,[11] was naturally not a favourite with men whom he would have reckoned in bondage to the legal conscience . . . [but from] his derided theosophy . . . Vane . . . derived certain practical principles, now of recognised value, which no statesman before him had dreamt of, and which were not less potent when based on religious ideas struggling for articulate utterance, than when stated by the masters of an elegant vocabulary from which God and spirit were excluded.

LECTURE II

In Vane first appears the doctrine of natural right and government by consent,[12] which, however open to criticism in the crude form of popular statement, has yet been the moving principle of the modern reconstruction of Europe. It was the result of his recognition of the 'rule of Christ in the natural conscience',[13] in the elemental reason, in virtue of which man is properly a law to himself. From the same idea followed the principle of universal toleration, the exclusion of the magistrate's power alike from the maintenance and restraint of any kind of opinion. This principle did not with Vane and the Independents rest, as in modern times, on the slippery foundation of a supposed indifference of all religious beliefs,[14] but on the conviction of the sacredness of the reason, however deluded, in every man, which may be constrained by nothing less divine than itself . . . Christ's spirit was not bound. A system of truth and discipline had not been written down once for all in the Scriptures, but rather was to be gradually elicited from the Scriptures by the gradual manifestation in the believer of the spirit which spoke also in them. A 'waiting', seeking attitude, unbound by rule whether ecclesiastical or secular, was that which became a spiritual Church. The application of this waiting spirit to practical life is to be found in the policy of Cromwell.

It would be unfair to ascribe the theory of Vane in its speculative fulness to the Independents as a body, . . . [but] so far as it could be represented by a sect, it was represented by [them]. It came before the world, in full outward panoply, in the army of Cromwell. The history of its inevitable conflict with the spirit of Presbyterianism on the one hand and the wisdom of the world on the other, of its aberrations and perplexities, of its brief triumph and final flight into the wilderness, is the history of the rise and fall of the English Commonwealth . . .

. . . The new-model army went to the war . . . without 'the confidence of their friends' and an 'object of contempt to their enemies'.[15] Their outward triumph it is needless to describe; we should rather seek to appreciate the nature of the spiritual triumph which the outward one involved. It used to be the fashion to treat the sectarian enthusiasm of the 'Ironsides' as created, or at least stimulated by Cromwell . . . The prevalent conception of our time, that the great men of history have not created popular ideas or events, but merely expressed or realised them with special effect, excludes such a view. The sectarian enthusiasm . . . was a necessary result of the consciousness of spiritual right elicited by the Reformation, where this consciousness had not, as in Scotland, been early made the foundation of a popular Church, but had been long left to struggle in the dark against an unsympathetic clergy and a regulated ceremonial worship. The spirit which could not 'find itself' in the authoritative utterances of prelates or express its yearnings unutterable in a stinted liturgy, was not likely, when war had given it vent and stimulus, to acquiesce in a new uniformity as exact as that from which it had broken. It had tasted a new and dangerous food. Taught as it had been to wait on God, in search for new revelations of Him, it now read this lesson by the stronger light of personal deliverances and achievements, and found in the tumultuous experience of war at once the expression and the justification of its own inward tumult.

. . . Where the Bible was not in the hands of the people, it could be regulated by priests and ceremonial. Elsewhere it was controllable by state-churches, or by ecclesiastical authority . . . which appealed to popular reason, but to this reason as regulated by fitting education and discipline. Everywhere, in ordinary times, law and custom would put a veil on the face which the believer turned towards God. But, now in England, the bands were altogether loosed. Enthusiasts, who had been waiting darkly on God while He was hidden behind established worships and ministrations of the letter, who had heard His voice in their hearts but seen no sign of Him in the world, were now enacting His work themselves, and reading His strange providences on the field of battle... Henceforth, whatever authority claimed their submission as divine, must come home to their conscience with a like directness...

... Cromwell's ... relation to the sectaries was the same practically as we have seen Vane's to have been more speculatively. Without any of Vane's theosophy, he had the same open face towards Heaven, the same consciousness (or dream, if we like) of personal and direct communication with the Divine, which transformed the 'legal conscience' and placed him 'above ordinance'. Having thus drunk of the spring from which the sectarian enthusiasm flowed, he had no taste for the reasoning which led it into particular channels, while he had, more than any man of his time, not indeed the speculative, but the political instinct of comprehension... To him, as to his men, the issues of battle were a revelation of God's purpose; the cause, which in answer to the prayers of his people, God owned by fire, had the true *jus divinum* [divine right]. The practical danger of such a belief is obvious. To Cromwell is due the peculiar glory, that it never issued, as might have been expected, in fanatic military licence, but was always governed by the strictest personal morality and a genuine zeal for the free well-being of the state and nation . . .

LECTURE III

... The question whether Charles deserved his death, is one which even debating societies are beginning to find unprofitable. His death was a necessary condition of the establishment of the Commonwealth, which, again, was a necessary result of the strife of forces, or more properly, the conflict of ideas, which the civil war involved... Beneath the confused web of personal relations ... may be seen the conflict of those religious ideas which I have spoken of as resulting from the action of the Reformation on the spirit of Christendom. On the one hand was the *jus divinum* of a sacerdotal Church, not simply appealing by ritual or mystery to the devout, but applied at once to strengthen and justify a royal interest. To this was opposed the *jus divinum* of the Presbyterian discipline, resting, not on priestly authority, but on the popular conscience, yet claiming to be equally absolute over body and soul with the other. Their antagonism elicited the *jus divinum* of individual persuasion, a right hitherto unasserted in Christendom, which, while the old recognised rights were in the suspense of conflict, became a might. In the rapture of war it felt its strength, and a master-hand gave it the form and system which it lacked ... But this might of individual persuasion, though in a revolutionary struggle it could conquer, was unable to govern. It was a spirit without a body, a force with no lasting means of action on the world around it. Even at the present day its office is to work under and through established usage and interests, rather than to control them. Much less capable was it of such control, when it was still in the stage of mere impulse or feeling, with none of the calm comprehension which comes of developed thought.

When it first faced the world in organic shape as a military republic, it already presented practical contradictions which ensured its failure. The republic claimed, and claimed truly, to be the creation of the impulse of freedom, yet found nothing but sullen acquiescence around it; it spoke in the name of the people, not half of whom, as Lady Fairfax said, it represented;[16] it asserted Parliamentary right, though Parliament had been 'purged' (nearly clean) to make room for it; it was directed by men of a 'civil' spirit, and had civil right to maintain, while it rested on the support of armed enthusiasts, who cared only for the privilege of saints. It was, in fact, founded on opinion – the opinion of a few, brought to sudden strength and maturity, as it might have been in an Athenian assembly, by debate in and about the Parliament and in the council of the army, but which had no hold either on the sentiment or the settled interests of the country... 'The inconstant, irrational, image-doting rabble', as the proud republicans called it,[17] ... was constant enough in two feelings, of which the republicans would have done well to take account, a reverence for familiar names, and a resentment against virtues which profess to be other than customary and commonplace. It was at once the merit and the weakness of the Commonweath's men that they irritated these feelings at every point.

> Before them shone a glorious world,
> Fresh as a banner bright, unfurled
> To music suddenly;[18]

and they could not wait to attain it by slow accommodations to sense and habit ... [I]n the pride of triumphant reason they took pleasure in trampling on the common feelings and interests, through which reason must work, if it is to work at all. In the writings of Milton, the true exponent of the higher spirit of the republic, we find on the one hand a perfect scorn of the dignities and plausibilities then as now recognised in England (which makes him the best study for a radical orator that I am acquainted with), on the other, a free admission of the sensual degradation of the people, which estranged them from a government founded on reason[19] ... To him, throughout, the Puritan war had seemed a crisis in the long struggle between the spirit and the flesh ... and a system of political asceticism was its proper result. Such a system to its believing supporters was the Commonwealth. Its claim was not gradually to transmute, but suddenly to suppress, the feeling of the many by the reason of the few; a claim which all the while belied itself, for it appealed to popular, and even natural right, and which implied no concrete power of political construction. It was a democracy without a *dēmos*, it rested on an assertion of the supremacy of reason, which from its very exclusiveness gave the reason no work to do.

... During more than two years, from the midsummer of 1649 to the autumn of 1651, the republican oligarchy was able to shut its eyes to the real situation. The military spirit was absorbed in the conquest under Cromwell of Ireland and Scotland, and the English Royalists, hardly recovered from their crushing failure at home, were watching the fortune of war in these other countries. The only chance for the permanence of Republicanism was that it should avail itself of this interval to establish itself on a more popular basis, and initiate practical reforms... The only hopeful line ... for the Commonwealth's men to take would have been to provide for the election of a new Parliament by reformed constituencies, to abolish all criminal prosecution not sanctioned by the common-law, to reform chancery and simplify legal process, and to resettle the Church on some plan that would admit at least the Independents and the 'moderate' or antiprelatist Episcopalians, and substitute a fixed salary for tithes. Whether this line was practicable for them is another question. They had no hold on popular feeling; a powerful Scotch army, with the young king in its keeping, was in the field against them, and the Presbyterian clergy were praying for its success...

The essential difficulty of the situation was aggravated by the oligarchical temper which it bred in the Republican leaders. With the best of them this temper took the higher form which appears in Milton's complaint, that when God has given the victory to a cause in the field of battle, 'then comes the task to those worthies which are the soul of it, to be sweat and laboured out amidst the throng and noises of vulgar and irrational men'.[20] Even in this form it cannot face facts, for it is not this pride of higher exclusion, but the higher pride, which can possess itself in sympathy and comprehension, that represents the divine reason in the world. But the pride of protected intellect, once clothed with political power, soon passes into the jealousy of a clique... [T]he leading spirits of the Long Parliament ... mistook the success of their military administration for a real faculty of Government, and hugged power for its own sake, in the mood of a self-conscious aristocracy of virtue... Thus, though their administration was singularly pure, they got credit even among their best friends, if Milton's 'Second Defence' may be taken as expressing his real mind, for a spirit of faction and obstructiveness.[21]

The one man among them who seems really to have comprehended the situation, was Sir Henry Vane. Shrinking from the touch of military violence ... [he] saw the need of popularising the Government, and stirred the question of new elections. A committee for considering the question seems to have been constantly sitting during the first year of the Commonwealth, with Vane as its Chairman, which reported at the beginning of 1650 in favour of a new Parliament of four hundred members, and a rearrangement of constituencies... On this, as on other pressing questions, Parliament could not get beyond the stage of resolutions. It resolved to deal with the question of tithes, to provide for popular education out of ecclesiastical funds, and to simplify the law, but no actual legislation was achieved... Towards facing the hostile forces which only slumbered around them – towards meeting the demands of the enthusiasm of reformation to which they owed their temporary power – they had done absolutely nothing... Cromwell, meanwhile, was riding up to London... On the 16th [Sept. 1651] ... he took his seat in the House... The question of settlement was now in the hands of one who would not allow it to tarry.

LECTURE IV

In the last lecture we saw that the immediate result of Cromwell's presence in the House after his return from Worcester was the revival of the questions of a new election and a general settlement... In pressing these questions Cromwell was true to the instinct of comprehension which had governed his course throughout... [I]n the summer of 1647 ... he was ... convinced of the difficulty of establishing a government on so narrow a foundation as was afforded either by the army or an oligarchical Parliament. His project at that time was to restore the king on the condition of his calling a new Parliament, from which he declared Royalists should be excluded ... If carried out in its completeness [Cromwell's plan] would have given England at once a genuine parliamentary government and a free national Church. Two centuries of government by borough-mongering and corruption, of Church-statesmanship and State-Churchmanship would have been saved. Charles ... rejected it, and began his game anew. No such opportunity for reconciliation could ever occur again, but Cromwell's purpose remained the same, though his mode of executing it varied with events. The anxiety for a settlement which should reconcile the old interests with the new enthusiasm is the key to his subsequent conduct. The reconciliation ... was, in fact, impossible. The new piece would not fit the old garment... The hopelessness, however, of the pacification which he contemplated was the tragedy of Cromwell's later life...

... The ultimate spring of [Cromwell's] conduct was a belief, wrought to special strength in the formation and triumphant leadership of the sectarian army, that he was the chosen champion of the despised people of the Lord. In the realisation of this belief, it was his habit (in modern language) to wait on events, and to surrender himself to temporary sympathy with men of the most various views... There is no sign that he ever committed himself to the positive maintenance of the doctrines of the men to whose sympathy he appealed. On the contrary, there is evidence that the protection of the Godly interest in its freedom of conscience, by whatever means might be available, was the only line of conduct to which he ever committed himself, and to this he was faithful throughout... What we call waiting on events, he called a recognition of the 'outward dispensation' of God ... He had that fatalism about him without which nothing great is achieved in times of political crisis; the consciousness of a divine work that must be done through him, though personal peace and honour were wrecked in the doing...

... During the campaign,[22] the direction in which the logic of events, of 'outward dispensations', was leading became more apparent, and the sense of it pervades his letters. The rapture of successful war brought back to him the old enthusiasm, the consciousness of being the chosen leader of the saints... The prosaic meaning of these new 'dispensations' ... was that the military excitement against the royal 'delinquent' had become uncontrollable, that Hamilton's invasion, instigated and aided by the Royalist Presbyterians in England, had rendered their fusion with the Commonwealth's men impossible, and that the republic must represent the latter party and

the army alone. This was no doubt the final judgement which Cromwell's practical insight had unwillingly arrived at. But we do not
really understand this judgement or its consequences, till we appreciate the 'wondrous alchemy' of the enthusiasm with which it was fused
and molten in Cromwell's own mind... [I]n Cromwell ... [en-
thusiasm] was an expansive element, in which a sympathy with the
'waiting spirit' of the sectaries, such as was necessary for their guidance, went along with a prevailing zeal for the *'salus populi'* ['...
suprema est lex' – 'the good of the people is the highest law'[23]] and a
clear judgement of its needs, is the only interpretation that will
explain the history as a whole. To the guidance of a man possessing
such a strange compound of qualities, it is due that our great religious
war ended not simply in blood, but in a real step forward of English
society.

... The possibility of a settlement, however, which should secure
the 'Godly interest', was very different now from what it would have
been if Charles's spleen and superstition had permitted him honestly
to come to terms in 1647. Then Cromwell had hoped by restoring the
king with a council, which might have been under his own direction,
to obtain that unity of initiative under a familiar name, which, important at all times, is specially necessary when order is to be rebuilt
out of a chaos of factions heated with civil war. Henceforward there
could be but two alternatives. The familiar unity might be obtained
... but only at the cost of an absolute suppression of the 'Godly interest': or an unfamiliar unity might take its place, but only on the
condition of its maintenance by a hand that could hold the sword, and
a temper that either by force or sympathy could control the sectaries –
a condition which death might at any time remove. The military ecstasy, however, was still strong upon Cromwell, and he had a spirit
for the work ... [He] had yet to learn that the providence on which
he waited wrought by a longer method, because it had a wider comprehension than was dreamt of in the Puritan philosophy.

But though Cromwell, during this period, was quite free from the
thought which Mr Peters attributed to him, 'that he would be king of
England yet',[24] still the impatience for an establishment of a 'free
church of saints' in a free state, and the 'heat of inward evidence' that
he himself was the man to achieve it, was growing constantly stronger
in him ... It was this exhilaration of energy in the Lord's work, not a
vulgar ambition of kingship, that shone in Cromwell's countenance
as he rode up from Worcester[25] ... and that made him press ... on
the first day when he resumed his seat in the House, for measures of
settlement and reform ... For a year and a half ... from September

16, 1651, to April 20, 1653, he loyally endeavoured to rouse the republican oligarchy to the necessities of the situation. If his importunity was not pressing, that of the people was, and it was clear that the Parliament must give some practical 'reason why' for its existence, or lose its prestige ... There was no result however in the way of effective legislation, and the old conviction of the army, that it was the true Parliament and judicature of the nation, was beginning to revive ... The real fact was that Parliament was once more face to face with its true, its sole constituency, the military saints, with whom its conceit of antique Republicanism would avail little, unless it could realise in the hard world of 'interests' the reforming enthusiasm which had created it ...

We have not the means of tracing in detail the conduct of Cromwell during this crisis ... He was clearly most unwilling, however, to break with the Parliament, which he had absolutely in his hands, and if its leaders could have been induced ... to invest him with a temporary dictatorship, he would have kept them at peace, as he alone had hitherto done, with the army, and worked with them constitutionally for the settlement of the nation. As it was, there are indications that he controlled the discontent of the army as long as he was able ...

By the beginning of the year 1653, Sir Henry Vane, who had hitherto been organising victory for Blake,[26] had become alive to the danger of military domination, which he specially dreaded, and was pressing forward a bill for a new Parliament.[27] It was upon this bill that the final rupture with Cromwell took place ... Cromwell's objection to the bill was that it gave the existing members the right both of sitting in the new House without re-election and of deciding on the admissibility of new members. In other words it constituted the Rump[28] a many-headed dictatorship, to regulate the work of reconstruction ...

... The rest of the story is too familiar to need repetition ... The dissolution of the Rump was clearly inevitable as soon as it broke with and sought to defy its armed constituency, which, as Cromwell had always maintained, was an equally legitimate authority with itself, and far more truly representative ...

[Having driven out the Rump Parliament, Cromwell] had now to grapple with the question which [they] had fingered in vain. The Lord's people were to be saved from themselves, and the interests of the world so reformed and adjusted that it might yield them fit habitation. The task ... was in the nature of the case a hopeless one. The claim of the saints was at once false and self-contradictory – false, for the secular world, which it sought to ignore, had rights no less divine than its own; and self-contradictory, since even amongst the most sectarian of the sectaries, it was constantly hardening into authority hostile to the individual persuasion in which it originated ... Cromwell's labour, however, was not wholly in vain. During five years,[29] by the mere force of his instinct of settlement, his commanding energy, and that absorbing sympathy miscalled hypocrisy, which enabled him to hold the hearts of the sectaries, even while he disappointed their enthusiasm, he at least kept the peace between the saints and the world, secured liberty of conscience, and placed it on ground which even the flood of prelatical reaction was not able wholly to submerge. But while protecting the Godly interest, he was obliged more and more to silence its pretension. A gradual detachment from the saints, and approximation to the ancient interests, was the necessary policy of his later years.

... The Protectorate must have the credit of having been at least perfectly true to the great end of settlement, and of having been, however arbitrary, yet perfectly honest in its arbitrariness. It was quite free from the jugglery with recognised names and institutions which is the chosen device of modern despotism. The three points of the Cromwellian programme – restoration, so far as might be, of the old constitution, reform of the law, and the protection of the Godly interest – were really inconsistent with each other, for to restore the constitution was impossible without a restoration of Royalism, and the restoration of Royalism meant the subjection of the Godly, while a reformation of the law not resting on a constitutional basis, hung only on the thread of a single life. His effort, however, to govern constitutionally was genuine and persistent. Two conditions he always announced as fundamental, the sovereignty of the Protectorate, and the maintenance of liberty of conscience ... Subject to these two conditions he would give Parliament its way, but in the first the republican minority, in the second the Presbyterian majority, would not acquiesce ...

... The unruliness of the elements which Cromwell had wrought into a system of rational government became sufficiently apparent at his death. My limits do not allow me to trace minutely the course of events which led to the restoration ... [and which] ended, apparently in simple catastrophe, the enterprise of projecting into sudden reality the impulse of spiritual freedom. Its only result, as it might seem, had been to prevent the transition of the feudal into an absolute monarchy, and thus to prepare the way for the plutocracy under feudal forms which has governed England since the death of

William III.[30] This, however, is but a superficial view. Two palpable benefits the short triumph of Puritanism did win for England. It saved it from the Catholic reaction, and it created the 'dissenting bodies'. If it seems but a poor change from the fanatic sacerdotalism of Laud to the genteel and interested sacerdotalism of modern English Churchmanship, yet the fifteen years of vigorous growth which Cromwell's sword secured for the Church of the sectaries, gave it a permanent force which no reaction could suppress, and which has since been the great spring of political life in England. The higher enthusiasm however, which breathed in Cromwell and Vane, was not Puritanic or English merely. It belonged to the universal spiritual force which as ecstasy, mysticism, quietism, philosophy, is in permanent collision with the carnal interests of the world, which, if it conquers them for a moment, yet again sinks under them, that it may transmute them more thoroughly to its service. 'Death', said Vane on the scaffold, 'is a little word, but it is a great work to die.' So his own enthusiasm died that it might rise again. It was sown in the weakness of feeling, that it might be raised in the intellectual comprehension which is power. 'The people of England,' he said again, 'have been long asleep. I doubt they will be hungry when they awake.'[31] They have slept, we may say, another two hundred years. If they should yet wake and be hungry, they will find their food in the ideas which, with much blindness and weakness, he vainly offered them, cleared and ripened by a philosophy of which he did not dream.[32]

4

On the Different Senses of 'Freedom' as Applied to Will and to the Moral Progress of Man*

========

1. [superscript a][T]hough it is important to insist that, since in all willing a man is his own object to himself, the object by which the act is determined, the will is always free – or more properly that a man in willing is necessarily free, since willing constitutes freedom,[1] and 'free will' is a pleonasm = 'free freedom' – the nature of the freedom really differs according[superscript a] to the nature of the object which the man makes his own, or with which he identifies himself. It is one thing when the object in which self-satisfaction is sought is such as to prevent that self-satisfaction being found, because interfering with the realisation of the seeker's possibilities or his progress towards perfection; it is another thing when it contributes to this end. In the former case the man is a free agent in the act because, through his identification of himself with a certain desired object – through his adoption of it as his good – he makes the motive which determines the act and is accordingly conscious of himself as its author. But in another sense he is not free, because the objects to which his actions are directed are objects in which, according to the law of his being, satisfaction of himself is not to be found. His will to arrive at self-satisfaction not being adjusted to the law which determines where this self-satisfaction is to be found, he may be considered in the condition of a bondsman who is carrying out the will of another, not his own. From this bondage he emerges into real freedom, not by overcoming the law of his being, not by getting the better of its necessity – every fancied effort to do so is but a new exhibition of its necessity – but by making its fulfilment the object of his will; by seeking the satisfaction of himself in objects in which he believes it *should be* found, and seeking it in them *because* he believes it *should be* found in them. For the objects so sought, however various otherwise, have the common characteristic that, because they are sought in such a spirit, in them self-satisfaction is to be found – not the satisfaction of this or that desire, or of each particular desire, but that satisfaction, otherwise called peace or blessedness, which consists in the whole man having found his

228

object;[2] which indeed we never experience in its fulness, which we only approach to fall away from it again, but of which we know enough to be sure that we only fail to attain it because we fail to seek it in the fulfilment of the law of our being, because we have not brought ourselves to 'gladly do and suffer what we must'.

To the above statement several objections may be made. They will chiefly turn on two points; (*a*) the use made of the term 'freedom'; (*b*) the view that a man is subject to a law of his being, in virtue of which he at once seeks self-satisfaction, and is prevented from finding it in the objects which he actually desires, and in which he ordinarily [b]seeks it. The discussion of the latter point will involve a further explanation of the real nature of the Will as varying with the objects in which self-satisfaction is sought and will help us to a settlement of the question with which we started – the question whether we are justified in speaking of the objects of virtuous will as objects which the will as reason constitutes, and as satisfying the demand of reason; of objects of various will as those which will merely adopts, as from without, and which do not satisfy the demand of reason.

2. As to[b] the sense given to 'freedom,' it must of course be admitted that every usage of the term to express anything but a social and political relation of one man to others involves a metaphor. Even in the original application its sense is by no means fixed. It always implies indeed some exemption from compulsion by others, but the extent and conditions of this exemption, as enjoyed by the 'freeman' in different states of society, are very various. As soon as the term 'freedom' comes to be applied to anything else than an established relation between a man and other men, its sense fluctuates much more. Reflecting on their consciousness, on their 'inner life' (i.e. their life as viewed from within), men apply to it the terms with which they are familiar as expressing their relations to each other. In virtue of that power of self-distinction and self-objectification, which he expresses whenever he says 'I', a man can [a]set over against himself[a] his whole nature or any of its elements, and apply to the relation thus established in thought a term borrowed from relations of outward life. Hence, as in Plato, the terms 'freedom' and 'bondage' may be used to express a relation between the man on the one side, as distinguishing himself from all impulses that do not tend to his true good, and those impulses on the other. He is a 'slave' when they are masters of him, 'free' when master of them.[3] The metaphor in this form was made further use of by the Stoics, and carried on into the doctrines of the Christian Church. Since there is no kind of impulse or interest which a man cannot so distinguish from himself as to present it as an alien

power, of which the influence on him is bondage, the particular application of the metaphor is quite arbitrary. It may come to be thought that the only freedom is to be found in a life of absolute detachment from all interests, a life in which the pure ego converses solely with itself or with a God, who is the same abstraction under another name. This is a view into which both saints and philosophers have been apt to fall. It means practically, so far as it means anything, absorption in some one interest with which the man identifies himself in exclusion of all other interests, which he sets over against himself as an influence to be kept aloof.

With St Paul the application of the metaphor has a special character of its own. With him 'freedom' is specially freedom from the law, from ordinances, from the fear which these inspire – a freedom which is attained through the communication of what he calls the 'spirit of adoption' or 'sonship'.[4] The law, merely as law or as an external command, is a source of bondage in a double sense. Presenting to man a command which yet it does not give him power to obey, it destroys the freedom of the life in which he does what he likes without recognising any reason why he should not (the state of which St Paul says 'I was alive without the law once'[5]); it thus puts him in bondage to *fear*, and at the same time, exciting a wish for obedience to itself which other desires (*phronema sarkos* [desires of the flesh]) prevent from being accomplished, it makes the man feel the bondage of the *flesh*. 'What I will, that I do not'[6]; there is a power – the flesh – of which I am the slave, and which prevents me from performing my will to obey the law. Freedom (also called 'peace,' and 'reconciliation') comes when the spirit expressed in the law – for the law is itself 'spiritual' according to St Paul; the 'flesh' through which it is weak is mine, not the law's[7]– becomes the principle of action in the man. To the man thus delivered, as St Paul conceives him, we might almost apply phraseology like Kant's. 'He is free because conscious of himself as the author of the law which he obeys.'[8] He is no longer a servant, but a son. He is conscious of union with God, whose will as an external law he before sought in vain to obey, but whose 'righteousness is fulfilled' in him now that he 'walks after the spirit'.[9] What was before 'a law of sin and death' is now a 'law of the spirit of life'.[10]

3. But though there is a point of connection between St. Paul's conception of freedom and bondage and that of Kant, which renders the above phrase applicable in a certain sense to the 'spiritual man' of St Paul, yet the two conceptions are very different. Moral bondage with Kant, as with Plato and the Stoics, is bondage *to the flesh*. The heteronomy of the will is its submission to the impulse of pleasure-

seeking,[11] as that of which man is not in respect of his reason the author, but which belongs to him as a merely natural being. A state of bondage to law, as such, he does not contemplate. It might even be urged that Kant's 'freedom' or autonomy of the will, in the only sense in which he supposed it attainable by man, is very much like the state described by St Paul as that from which the communication of the spirit brings deliverance – the state in which 'I delight in the law of God after the inward man, but find another law in my members warring with the law of my reason and bringing me into captivity to the law of sin in my members.'[12] For Kant seems to hold that the will is actually 'autonomous', i.e. determined by pure consciousness of what should be, only in rare acts of the best man. He argues rather for our being conscious of the possibility of such determination, as evidence of an ideal of what the good will is, than for the fact that anyone is actually so determined. And every determination of the will that does not proceed from pure consciousness of what should be he ascribes to the pleasure-seeking which belongs to man merely as a *'Naturwesen'* ['natural being'] or as St Paul might say 'to the law of sin in his members.' What, it may be asked, is such 'freedom', or rather such consciousness of the possibility of freedom, worth? May we not apply to it St Paul's words, 'By the law is the knowledge of sin'?[13] The practical result to the individual of that consciousness of the possibility of freedom which is all that the autonomy of will, as really attainable by man, according to Kant's view, amounts to, is to make him aware of the heteronomy of his will, of its bondage to motives of which reason is not the author.

4. This is an objection which many of Kant's statements of his doctrine, at any rate, fairly challenge. It was chiefly because he seemed to make freedom[14] an unrealised and unrealisable state, that his moral doctrine was found unsatisfactory by Hegel,[15] who holds that freedom, as the condition in which the will is determined by an object adequate to itself, or by an object, which itself as reason constitutes, is realised in the state.[16] He thinks of the 'state' in a way not familiar to Englishmen, a way not unlike that in which Greek philosophers thought of the *polis*, as a society governed by laws and institutions and established customs which secure the common good of the members of the society – enable them to make the best of themselves – and are recognised as doing so. Such a state is 'objective freedom' – freedom is realised in it – because in it the reason, the self-determining principle operating in man as his will, has found a perfect expression for itself (as an artist may be considered to express himself in a perfect work of art); and the man who is determined by the

objects which the well-ordered state presents to him is determined
by that which is the perfect expression of his reason, and is thus
free.

5. There is, no doubt, truth in this view. Last term I tried to
show[17] how the self-distinguishing and self-seeking consciousness of
man, acting in and upon those human wants and ties and affections
which in their proper human character have as little reality apart from
it as it apart from them, gives rise to a system of social relations, with
laws, customs, and institutions corresponding; and how in this
system the individual's consciousness of the absolutely desirable, of
something that should be, of an ideal to be realised in his life, finds a
content or object which has been constituted or brought into being by
that consciousness itself as working through generations of men; how
interests are thus supplied to the man of a more concrete kind than
the interest in fulfilment of a universally binding law because universally binding, but which yet are *"the product of reason,"* and in
satisfying which he is conscious of attaining a true good – a good contributory to the perfection of himself and his kind. There is thus
something in all forms of society that tends to the freedom – in the
sense of 'autonomy of will' – at least of some favoured individuals,
because it tends to actualise in them the possibility of that determination by objects conceived as desirable in distinction from objects
momentarily desired, which is determination by reason.[18] To put it
otherwise, the effect of his social relations on a man thus favoured is
that, whereas in all willing the individual seeks to satisfy himself, this
man seeks to satisfy himself, not as one who feels this or that desire,
but as one who conceives, whose nature demands, a permanent good.
So far as it is thus in respect of his rational nature that he makes himself an object to himself, his will is autonomous. This was the good
which the ideal *polis*, as conceived by the Greek philosophers,
secured for the true *politēs* – the man who, entering into the idea of
the *polis*, was equally qualified *archein kai archesthai* [to rule and be
ruled].[19] No doubt in the actual Greek *polis* there was some tendency
in this direction to rationalise and moralise the citizen. Without the
real tendency the ideal possibility would not have suggested itself.
And in more primitive forms of society, so far as they were based on
family or tribal relations, we can see that the same tendency must
have been at work, just as in modern life the consciousness of his position as member or head of a family, wherever it exists, necessarily
does something to moralise a man. In modern Christendom, with the
extension of citizenship, the security of family life to all men (so far as
law and police can secure it), the establishment in various forms of

Christian fellowship of which the moralising functions grow as those of the magistrate diminish, the number of individuals whom society awakens to interests in objects contributory to human perfection tends to increase.[20] So far the modern state, in that full sense in which Hegel uses the term (as including all the agencies for common good of a law-abiding people),[21] does contribute to the realisation of freedom, as = the autonomy of the will, = its determination by rational objects, objects which help to satisfy the demand of reason, the *b*effort*b* after self-perfection.

6. On the other hand, it would seem that we cannot significantly speak of freedom except with reference to individual persons; that only in them can freedom be realised; that therefore the realisation of freedom in the state can only mean the attainment of freedom by individuals through influences which the state (in the wide sense spoken of) supplies – 'freedom' here, as before, meaning not the mere self-determination which renders us responsible, but determination by reason, 'autonomy of the will';[22] and that under the best conditions of any society that has ever been such realisation of freedom is most imperfect. To an Athenian slave, who might be used to gratify a master's lust, it would have been a mockery to speak of the state as a realisation of freedom;[23] and perhaps it would not be much less so to speak of it as such to an untaught and under-fed denizen of a London yard with gin-shops on the right hand and on the left. What Hegel says of the state in this respect seems as hard to square with facts as what St Paul says of the Christian whom the *a*manifestation*a* of Christ has transferred from bondage into 'the glorious liberty of the sons of God'.[24] In both cases the difference between the ideal and the actual seems to be ignored, and tendencies seem to be spoken of as if they were accomplished facts. It is noticeable that by uncritical readers of St Paul the account of himself as under the law (in Romans vii.), with the 'law of sin in his members warring against the law of his reason',[25] is taken as applicable to the regenerate Christian, though evidently St Paul meant it as a description of the state from which the Gospel, the 'manifestation of the Son of God in the likeness of sinful flesh',[26] set him free. They are driven to this interpretation because, though they can understand St Paul's account of his deliverance as an account of a deliverance achieved for them but not in them, or as an assurance of what is to be, they cannot adjust it to the actual experience of the Christian life. In the same way Hegel's account of freedom as realised in the state does not seem to correspond to the facts of society as it is, or even as, under the unalterable conditions of human nature, it ever could be; though undoubtedly there is a work of moral liberation,

which society, through its various agencies, is constantly carrying on for the individual.

7. Meanwhile it must be borne in mind that in all these different views as to the manner and degree in which freedom is to be attained, 'freedom' does not mean that the man or will is undetermined, nor yet does it mean *mere* self-determination, which (unless denied altogether, as by those who take the strictly naturalistic view of human action) must be ascribed equally to the man whose will is heteronomous or vicious, and to him whose will is autonomous; equally to the man who recognises the authority of law in what St Paul would count the condition of a bondman, and to him who fulfils the 'righteousness of the law' in 'the spirit of adoption'.[27] It means a particular kind of *a*self-determination (the determination of the man by himself as object) – the state*a* of the man who lives indeed for himself, but for the fulfilment of himself as a 'giver of law universal' (Kant);[28] who lives for himself, but only according to the true idea of himself, according to the law of his being, 'according to nature' (the Stoics);[29] who is so taken up into God, to whom God so gives the spirit, that there is no constraint in his obedience to the divine will (St Paul); whose interests, as a loyal citizen, are those of a well-ordered state in which practical reason expresses itself (Hegel). Now none of these modes of self-determination is at all implied in 'freedom' according to the primary meaning of the term, as expressing that relation between one man and others in which he is secured from compulsion. All that is so implied is that a man should have power to do what he wills or prefers. No reference is made to the nature of the will or preference, of the object willed or preferred; whereas according to the usage of 'freedom' in the doctrines we have just been considering, it is not constituted by the mere fact of acting upon preference, but depends wholly on the nature of the preference, upon the kind of object willed or preferred.

8. If it were ever reasonable to wish that the usage of words had been other than it has been (any more than that the processes of nature were other than they are), one might be inclined to wish that the term 'freedom' had been confined to the juristic sense of the power to 'do what one wills': for the extension of its meaning seems to have caused much controversy and confusion. But, after all, this extension does but represent various stages of reflection upon the self-distinguishing, self-seeking, self-asserting principle, of which the establishment of freedom, as a relation between man and man, is the expression. The reflecting man is not content with the first announcement which analysis makes as to the inward condition of the

free man – viz. that he can do what he likes, that he has the power of
acting according to his will or preference. In virtue of the same principle which has led him to assert himself against others, and thus to
cause there to be such a thing as (outward) freedom, he distinguishes
himself from his preference, and asks how he is related to it – whether
he determines it or how it is determined. Is he free to will, as he is free
to act; or, as the act is determined by the preference, is the preference
determined by something else? Thus Locke begins with deciding
that freedom means power to do or forbear from doing any particular
act upon preference,[30] and that, since the will is merely the power of
preference, the question whether the will is free is an unmeaning one
(equivalent to the question whether one power has another power);[31]
that thus the only proper question is whether a man (not his will) is
free, which must be answered affirmatively so far as he has the power
to do or forbear, as above.[32] But he recognises the propriety of the
question whether a man is free to will as well as to act. He cannot
refuse to carry back the analysis of what is involved in a man's action
beyond the preference of one possible action to another, and to
inquire what is implied in the preference. It is when this latter
question is raised, that language which is appropriate enough in a
definition of outward or juristic freedom becomes misleading. It
having been decided that the man civilly free has power over his
actions, to do or forbear according to preference, it is asked whether
he has also *power to prefer*.

9. But while it is proper to ask whether in any particular case a man
has power over *his actions*, because his nerves and limbs and muscles
may be acted upon by another person or a force which is not he or his,
there is no appropriateness in asking the question in regard to a preference or will, because this cannot be so acted on.[33] If so acted on, it
would not be a will or preference. There is no such thing as a will
which a man is not conscious of as belonging to himself, no such thing
as an act of will which he is not conscious of as issuing from himself.
To ask whether he has power over it, or whether some other power
than he determines it, is like asking whether he is other than himself.
Thus the question whether a man, having power to act according to
his will, or being free to act, has also power over his will, or is free to
will, has just the same impropriety that Locke points out in the
question whether the will is free.[34] The latter question, on the supposition that there is power to enact the will – a supposition which is
necessarily made by those who raise the ulterior question whether
there is power over the will – is equivalent, as Locke sees, to a
question whether freedom is free. For a will which there is power of

enacting constitutes freedom, and therefore to ask whether it is free is like asking (to use Locke's instance) whether riches are rich ('rich' being a denomination from the possession of riches, just as 'free' is a denomination from the possession of freedom, ^{a}as $=^a$ a will which there is power to enact). But if there is this impropriety in the question whether the will is free, there is an equal one in the question which Locke entertains, viz. whether man is free to will, or has power over his will. It amounts to asking whether a certain power is also a power over itself: or, more precisely, whether a man possessing a certain power – that which we call freedom – has also the same power over that power.

10. It may be said perhaps that we are here pressing words too closely; that it is of course understood, when it is asked whether a man has power over his will, that 'power' is used in a different sense from that which it bears when it is asked whether he has power to enact his will: that 'freedom', in like manner, is understood to express a different kind of power or relation when we ask whether a man is free to will and when we ask whether he is free to act. But granting that all this has been understood, the misleading effects of the question in the form under consideration ('Is a man free to will as well as to act?' 'Has he power over his will?') remain written in the history of the 'free-will controversy'. It has mainly to answer for two wrong ways of thinking of the subject – (*a*) for the way of thinking of the determining motive of an act of will, the object willed, as something apart from the will or the man willing, so that in being determined by it the man is supposed not to be self-determined, but to be determined as one natural event by another, or at best as a natural organism by the forces acting on it; (*b*) for the view that the only way of escaping this conclusion is to regard the will as independent of motives, as a power of deciding between motives without any motive to determine the decision, which must mean without reference to any object willed. A man, having (in virtue of his power of self-distinction and self-objectification) presented his will to himself as something to be thought about, and being asked whether he has power over it, whether he is free in regard to it as he is free against other persons and free to use his limbs and, through them, material things, this way or that, must very soon decide that he is not. His will is himself. His character necessarily shows itself in his will. We have already, in a previous lecture,[35] noticed the practical fallacy involved in a man's saying that he cannot help being what he is, as if he were controlled by external power; but he being what he is, and the circumstances being what they are, at any particular conjuncture the de-

termination of the will is already given, just as an effect is given in the sum of its conditions. The determination of the will *might* be different, but only through the man's being different. But to ask whether a man has power over determinations of his will, or is free to will as he is to act, as the question is commonly understood and as Locke understood it, is to ask whether, *the man being what at any time he is*, it is still uncertain (1) whether he will choose or forbear choosing between certain possible courses of action, and (2) supposing him to choose one or other of them, which he will choose.

11. Now we must admit that there is really no such uncertainty. The appearance of it is due to our ignorance of the man and the circumstances. If, however, because this is so, we answer the question whether a man *ᵃ*has power over his will*ᵃ* in the *ᵇnegative*, instead of saying (as we should) that it is one of those inappropriate questions to which there is no answer (since a man's will is himself and 'freedom' and 'power' express relations between a man and something other than himself) – if we say that a man has *not* power over his will, is *not* free to will, we*ᵇ* at once suggest the conclusion that something else has power over it, viz. the strongest motive. We ignore the truth that in being determined by a strongest motive, in the only sense in which he is really so determined, the man (as previously explained)[36] is determined by himself – by an object of his own making, and we come to think of the will as determined like any natural phenomenon by causes external to it. (All this is the consequence of asking questions about the relation between a man and his will in terms only appropriate to the relation between the man and other men, or to that between the man and his bodily members or the materials on which he acts through them.)

12. On the other side the consciousness of self-determination resists this conclusion; but so long as we start from the question whether a man has power over his will, or is free to will as well as to act, it seems as if the objectionable conclusion could only be avoided by answering this question in the affirmative. But to say that a man has power over determinations of his will is naturally taken to mean that he can change his will while he himself remains the same; that given his character, motives, and circumstances as these at any time are, there is still something else required for the determination of his will; that behind and beyond the will as determined by some motive there is a will, itself undetermined by any motive, that determines what the determining motive shall be – that 'has power over' his preference or choice, as this has over the motion of his bodily members. But an unmotived will is a will without an object, which is nothing.

The power or possibility, beyond any actual determination of the will, of determining what that determination shall be is a mere negation of the actual determination. It is that determination as it becomes after an abstraction of the motive or object willed, which in fact leaves nothing at all. If those moral interests, which are undoubtedly involved in the recognition of the distinction between man and any natural phenomenon, are to be made dependent on belief in such a power or abstract possibility, the case is hopeless.

13. The right way out of the difficulty lies in the discernment that the question whether a man is free to will, or has power over the determinations of his will, is a question to which there is no answer because it is asked in inappropriate terms – in terms that imply some agency beyond the will which determines what the will shall be (as the will itself is an agency beyond the motions of the muscles which determines what those motions shall be), and that as to this agency it may be asked whether it does or does not lie in the man himself. In truth there is no such agency beyond the will and determining how *the will* shall be determined – not *in the man*, for the will *is* the self-conscious man; not *elsewhere* than in the man, not outside him, for the self-conscious man has no *outside*. He is not a body in space with other bodies *elsewhere* in space, acting upon it and determining its motions. The self-conscious man is determined by objects, which in order to be objects must already be in consciousness, and in order to be *his* objects, the objects which determine him, must already have been made his own. To say that they have power over him or his will, and that he or his will has power over them, is equally misleading. Such language is only applicable to the relation between an agent and patient, when the agent and the patient (or at any rate the agent) can exist separately. But self-consciousness and its object, will and its object, form a single individual unity. Without the constitutive action of man or his will the objects do not exist; apart from determination by some object neither he nor his will would be more than an unreal abstraction.

14. If, however, the question is persisted in, 'Has a man power over the determinations of his will?' we must answer both 'yes' and 'no'. 'No', in the sense that he is not other than his will, with ability to direct it as the will directs the muscles. 'Yes', in the sense that nothing external to him or his will or self-consciousness has power over them. 'No', again, in the sense that, given the man and his object as he and it at any time are, there is no possibility of the will being determined except in one way, for the will is already determined, being nothing else than the man as directed to some object. 'Yes', in the sense that

the determining object is determined by the man or will just as much as the man or will by the object. The fact that the state of the man, on which the nature of his object at any time depends, is a result of previous states, does not affect the validity of this last assertion, since (as we have seen[37]) all these states are states of a self-consciousness from which all alien *determination as from outside – all* determination except through the medium of self-consciousness – is excluded.

15. In the above we have not supposed any account to be taken of *the character of the objects willed* in the application to the will itself of the question – 'free or not free' – which is properly applied only to an action (motion of the bodily members) or to a relation between one man and other men. Those who unwisely consent to entertain the question whether a man is free to will or has power over determinations of his will, and answer it affirmatively or negatively, consider their answer, whether 'yes' or 'no', to be equally applicable whatever the nature of the objects willed. If they decide that a man is 'free to will', they mean that he is so in all cases of willing, whether the object willed be a satisfaction of animal appetite or an act of heroic self-sacrifice; and conversely, if they decide that he is *not* free to will, they mean that he is not so even in cases when the action is done upon cool calculation or upon a principle of duty as much as when it is done on impulse or in passion. Throughout the controversy as to free will that has been carried on among English psychologists[38] this is the way in which the question has been commonly dealt with. The freedom, claimed or denied for the will, has been claimed or denied for it irrespectively of those objects willed, on the nature of which the goodness or badness of the will depends.

16. On the other hand, with the Stoics, St Paul, Kant, and Hegel, as we have seen, the attainment of freedom (at any rate of the *reality* of freedom, as distinct from some mere *possibility* of it which constitutes the distinctive human nature) depends on the character of the objects willed. In all these ways of thinking, however variously the proper object of will is conceived, it is only as directed to this object, and thus (in Hegelian language) corresponding to its Idea, that the will is supposed to be free. The good will is free, not the bad will. Such a view of course implies some element of identity between good will and bad will, between will as not yet corresponding to its idea and will as so corresponding. St Paul indeed, not being a systematic thinker and being absorbed in the idea of divine grace, is apt to speak as if there were nothing in common between the carnal or natural man (the will as in bondage to the flesh) and the spiritual man (the will as set free), just as Plato commonly ignores the unity of principle

in all a man's actions, and represents virtuous actions as coming from the God in man, vicious actions from the beast.[39] Kant and Hegel, however, though they do not consider the will as it is in every man, good and bad, to be free (though Kant in his later ethical writings,[40] and Hegel (I think) always, confine the term *'Wille'* to the will as having attained freedom or come to correspond to its idea, and apply the term *'Willkür'* to that self-determining principle of action which belongs to every man and is in their view the mere possibility, not actuality, of freedom) yet quite recognise what has been above insisted on as the common characteristic of all willing – the fact that it is not a determination from without, like the determination of any natural event or agent, but the realisation of an object which the agent presents to himself or makes his own, the determination by an object of a subject which itself consciously determines that object; and they see that it is only for a subject *free in this sense* ('*an sich*' ['in itself, potentially, implicitly'] but not *'für sich'* ['for itself, actually'], *dunamei* but not *energeia*[41]) that the reality of freedom can exist.

17. Now the propriety or impropriety of the use of 'freedom' to express the state of the will, not as directed to any and every object, but only to those to which, according to the law of nature or the will of God or its 'idea', it should be directed, is a matter of secondary importance. This usage of the term is, at any rate, no more a departure from the primary or juristic sense than is its application to the will as distinct from action in any sense whatever. And certainly the unsophisticated man, as soon as the usage of 'freedom' to express exemption from control by other men and ability to do as he likes is departed from, can much more readily assimilate the notion of states of the inner man described as bondage to evil passions, to terrors of the law, or on the other hand as freedom from sin and law, freedom in the consciousness of union with God or of harmony with the true law of one's being, freedom of true loyalty, freedom in devotion to self-imposed duties, than he can assimilate the notion of freedom as freedom to will anything and everything, or as exemption from determination by motives, or the constitution by himself of the motives which determine his will. And there is so far less to justify the extension of the usage of the term in these latter ways than in the former. It would seem indeed that there is a real *"community"* of meaning between 'freedom' as expressing the condition of a citizen of a civilised state, and 'freedom' as expressing the condition of a man who is inwardly 'master of himself'. That is to say, the practical conception by a man ('practical' in the sense of *tending to realise itself*) of a self-satisfaction to be attained in his becoming what he should be, what he

has it in him to be, in fulfilment of the law of his being – or, to vary the words but not the meaning, in attainment of the righteousness of God, or in perfect obedience to self-imposed law – this practical conception is the outcome of the same self-seeking principle which appears in a man's assertion of himself against other men and against nature ('against other men', as claiming their recognition of him as being what they are; 'against nature', as able to use it). This assertion of himself is the demand for *freedom* – freedom in the primary or juristic sense, = power to act according to [b]preference[b]. So far as such freedom is established for any man, this assertion of himself is made good; and such freedom is precious to him because it is an achievement of the self-seeking principle. It is a first satisfaction of its claims, which is the condition of all other satisfaction of them. The consciousness of it is the first form of self-enjoyment – of the joy of the self-conscious spirit in itself as in the one object of absolute value.

18. It is a form of self-enjoyment, however, which consists essentially in the feeling by the subject of a possibility rather than a reality, of what it has it in itself to become, not of what it actually is. To a [a]captive[a] on first winning his liberty, as to a child in the early experience of power over his limbs and through them over material things, this feeling of a boundless possibility of becoming may give real joy; but gradually the sense of what it is not – of the very little that it amounts to – must predominate over the sense of actual good as attained in it. Thus to the grown man, bred to civil liberty in a society which has learnt to make nature its instrument, there is no self-enjoyment in the mere consciousness of freedom as exemption from external control, no sense of an object in which he can satisfy himself having been obtained.

Still, just as the demand for and attainment of freedom from external control is the expression of that same self-seeking principle from which the quest for such an object proceeds, so 'freedom' is the natural term by which the man describes such an object to himself – describes to himself the state in which he shall have realised his ideal of himself, shall be at one with the law which he recognises as that which he ought to obey, shall have become all that he has it in him to be, and so fulfil the law of his being or 'live according to nature'. Just as the consciousness of an unattainable ideal, of a law recognised as having authority but with which one's will conflicts, of wants and impulses which interfere with the fulfilment of one's possibilities, is a consciousness of impeded energy, a consciousness of oneself as for ever thwarted and held back, so the forecast of deliverance from these conditions is as naturally said to be a forecast of 'freedom' as of 'peace' or 'blessedness'. Nor is it merely to a select few, and as an expression for a deliverance really (as it would seem) unattainable under the conditions of any life that we know, but regarded by saints as secured for them in another world and by philosophers as the completion of a process which is eternally complete in God, that 'freedom' commends itself. To any popular audience interested in any work of self-improvement (e.g. to a temperance-meeting seeking to break the bondage to liquor), it is as an effort to attain *freedom* that such work can be most effectively presented. It is easy to tell such people that the term is being misapplied; that they are quite 'free' as it is, because every one can do as he likes so long as he does not prevent another from doing so; that in any sense in which there is such a thing as 'free will', to get drunk is as much an act of free will as anything else. Still the feeling of oppression, which always goes along with the consciousness of unfulfilled possibilities, will always give meaning to the representation of the effort after any kind of self-improvement as a demand for 'freedom'.

19. The variations in the meaning of 'freedom' having been thus recognised and *^aaccounted for^a*, we come back to the more essential question as to the truth of the view which underlies all theories implying that freedom is in some sense the goal of moral endeavour, the view, namely, that there is *^bsome true will^b* in a man with which many or most of his voluntary actions do not accord, a higher self that is not satisfied by the objects which yet he deliberately pursues. Some such notion is common to those different theories about freedom which in the rough we have ascribed severally to the Stoics, St Paul, Kant, and Hegel. It is the same notion which in a previous lecture [see §1] was put in the form, 'that a man is subject to a law of his being, in virtue of which he at once seeks self-satisfaction, and is prevented from finding it in the objects which he actually desires, and in which he ordinarily seeks it'. 'What can this mean?' it may be asked. 'Of course we know that there are weak people who never succeed in getting what they want, either in the sense that they have not ability answering to their will, or that they are always *wishing* for something which yet they do not *will*. But it would not be very appropriate to say of such people that they were "subject to a law, etc.", for the man's will to attain certain objects cannot be ascribed to the same law of his being as the lack of ability to attain them, nor his *wish* for certain objects to the same law of his being as those stronger desires which determine his *will* in a contrary direction. At any rate, if the proposition is remotely applicable to the man who is at once selfish and unsuccessful, how can it be true in any sense either of the man who is at once selfish and succeeds

– who gets what he wants (as is unquestionably the case with many people who live for what *a priori* moralists count unworthy objects) – or of the man who "never thinks about himself" at all? So far as the proposition means anything, it would seem to represent Kant's notion, long ago found unthinkable and impossible, the notion of there being two wills or selves in a man, the "pure" will or ego and the "empirical" will or ego – the pure will being independent of a man's actual desires and directed to the fulfilment of a universal law of which it is itself the giver, the empirical will being determined by the strongest desire and directed to this or that pleasure.[42] In this proposition the "objects which the man actually desires and in which he ordinarily seeks satisfaction" are presumably objects of what Kant called the "empirical will", while the "law of his being" corresponds to Kant's "pure ego". But just as Kant must be supposed to have believed in some identity between the pure and empirical will, as implied in the one term "will", though he does not explain in what this identity consists, so the proposition before us apparently ascribes man's quest for self-satisfaction as directed to certain objects, to the same "law of his being" which prevents it from finding it there. Is not this nonsense?'

20. To such questions we answer as follows. The proposition before us, like all the theories of moral freedom which we have noticed, undoubtedly implies that the will of every man is a form of one consciously self-realising principle, which at the same time is not truly or fully expressed in any man's will. As a form of this self-realising principle it may be called, if we like, a 'pure ego' or 'the pure ego' of the particular person; as directed to this or that object in such a way that it does not truly express the self-realising principle of which it is a form, it may be called the 'empirical ego' of that person. But if we use such language, it must be borne in mind that the pure and empirical egos are still not two egos but one ego; the 'pure ego' being the self-realising principle considered with reference either to its idea, its possibility, what it has in itself to become, the law of its being, or to some ultimate actualisation of this possibility; the 'empirical ego' being the same principle as it appears in this or that state of character, which results from its action, but does not represent that which it has in itself to become, does not correspond to its idea or the law of its being. By a consciously self-realising principle is meant a principle that is determined to action by the conception of its own perfection, or by the idea of giving reality to possibilities which are involved in it and of which it is conscious as so involved; or, more precisely, a principle which at each stage of its existence is conscious

of a more perfect form of existence as possible for itself, and is moved to action by that ^{a}consciousness. The ground for believing in the existence of such a principle must of course be that upon the analysis of our moral experience it appears to be the condition of the possibility of that experience – to afford the only means of explaining how there comes to be such a thing as this experience.[43] But before we further examine this ground, we must explain^a a little more fully how we understand the relation of the principle in question to what we call our wills and our ^{b}reason, and how^b we suppose its action to constitute the progress of morality.[44]

21. By 'practical reason' we mean a consciousness of a possibility of perfection to be realised in and by the subject of the consciousness. By 'will' we mean the effort of a self-conscious subject to satisfy itself.[45] In God, so far as we can ascribe reason and will to Him, we must suppose them to be absolutely united. In Him there can be no distinction between possibility and realisation, between the idea of perfection and the activity determined by it. But in men the self-realising principle, which is the manifestation of God in the world of becoming, in the form which it takes as will at best only tends to reconciliation with itself in the form which it takes as reason. Self-satisfaction, the pursuit of which is *will*, is sought elsewhere than in the realisation of that consciousness of possible perfection, which is reason. In this sense the object of will does not coincide with the object of reason. On the other hand, just because it is self-satisfaction that is sought in all willing, and because by a self-conscious and self-realising subject it is only in the attainment of its own perfection that such satisfaction can be found, the object of will is intrinsically or potentially, and tends to become actually, the same as that of reason. It is this that we express by saying that man is subject to a law of his being which prevents him from finding satisfaction in the objects in which, under the pressure of his desires, it is his natural impulse to seek it. This 'natural impulse' (not strictly 'natural') is itself the result of the operation of the self-realising principle upon what would otherwise be an animal system – modified, no doubt, with endless complexity in the case of any individual by the result of such operation through the ages of human history. But though the 'natural impulses' of the will are thus the work of the self-realising principle in us, it is not in their gratification that this principle can find the satisfaction which is only to be found in the consciousness of becoming perfect – of realising what it has it in itself to be. In order to any approach to this satisfaction of itself, the self-realising principle must carry its work farther. It must overcome the 'natural impulses', not in the

sense of either extinguishing them or denying them an object, but in the sense of fusing them with those higher interests, which have human perfection in some of its forms for their object. Some approach to this fusion we may notice in all good men, not merely in those in whom all natural passions – love, anger, pride, ambition – are enlisted in the service of some great public cause, but in those with whom such passions are all governed by some such commonplace idea as that of educating a family.

22. So far as this state is reached, the man may be said to be reconciled to the 'law of his being' which (as was said above) prevents him from finding satisfaction in the objects in *a*which it is his natural impulse to seek*a* it, or anywhere but in the realisation in himself of an idea of perfection. Since this law is, in fact, the action of that self-realising subject which is his self, and which exists in God as eternally self-realised, he may be said in this reconciliation to be at peace at once with himself and with God.

Again, he is 'free' (1) in the sense that he is the author of the law which he obeys (for this law, as we have seen, is the expression of that which is his self), and that he obeys it because conscious of himself as its author – in other words, obeys it from that impulse after self-perfection which is the source of the law or rather constitutes it. He is 'free' (2) in the sense that he not merely 'delights in the law after the inward man' (to use St Paul's phrase),[46] while his natural impulses are at once thwarted by it and thwart him in his effort to conform to it, but that these very impulses have been drawn into its service, so that he is in bondage neither to it nor to the flesh.

From the same point of view, we may say that his 'will is autonomous,' conforms to the law which the will itself constitutes, because the law (preventing him from finding *b*satisfaction in the objects in which he ordinarily seeks it, or anywhere*b* but in the realisation in himself of an idea of perfection) represents the action in him of that self-realising principle of which his will is itself a form. There is an appearance of equivocation, however, in this way of speaking, because the will which is liable not to be autonomous, and which we suppose gradually to approach autonomy in the sense of conforming to the law above described, is not the self-realising principle in that form in which this principle involves or gives the law. On the contrary, it is the self-realising principle as constituting that effort after self-satisfaction in each of us which is liable to be, and commonly is, directed to objects which are not contributory to the realisation of the idea of perfection – objects which the self-realising principle accordingly, in the fulfilment of its work, has to set aside. The equivocation is pointed out by saying that the good will is 'autonomous' in the sense of conforming to a law which the will itself, *as reason*, constitutes; which is, in fact, a condensed way of saying that the good will is the will of which the object coincides with that of practical reason, that will has its source in the same self-realising principle which yields that consciousness of a possible self-perfection which we call reason, and that it can only correspond to its idea, or become what it has the possibility of becoming, in being directed to the realisation of that consciousness.

23. According to the view here taken, then, reason and will, even as they exist in men, are one in the sense that they are alike expressions of one self-realising principle. In God, or rather in the ideal human person as he really exists in God, they are actually one; i.e. self-satisfaction is for ever sought and found in the realisation of a completely articulated or thoroughly filled idea of the perfection of the human person. In the historical man – in the men that have been and are coming to be – they *tend* to unite. In the experience of mankind, and again in the experience of the individual as determined by the experience of mankind, both the idea of a possible perfection of man – the idea of which reason is the faculty – and the impulse after self-satisfaction which belongs to the will, undergo modifications which render their reconciliation in the individual (and it is only in individuals that they can be reconciled, because only in them that they exist) more attainable. These modifications may be stated summarily as (1) an increasing concreteness in the idea of human perfection – its gradual development from the vague inarticulate feeling that there is such a thing into a conception of a complex organisation of life, with laws and institutions, with relationships, courtesies, and charities, with arts and graces through which the perfection is to be attained – and (2) a corresponding discipline, through inheritance and education, of those impulses which may be called 'natural' in the sense of being independent of any conscious direction to the fulfilment of an idea of perfection. Such discipline does not amount to the reconciliation of will and reason; it is not even, properly speaking, the beginning of it, for the reconciliation only begins with the direction of the impulse after self-satisfaction to the realisation of an idea of what should be, *as such* (because it should be), and no discipline through inheritance or education, just because it is only impulses that are natural in the sense defined which it can affect, can bring about this direction, which, in theological language, must be not of nature but of grace. On the contrary, the most refined impulses may be selfishly indulged; i.e. their gratification may be made an object in place of

that object which consists in the realisation of the idea of perfection. But unless a discipline and refinement of the natural impulses, through the operation of social institutions and arts, went on *pari passu* with the expression of the idea of perfection in such institutions and arts, the direction of the impulses of the individual by this idea, when in some form or other it has been consciously awakened in him, would be practically impossible. The moral progress of mankind has no reality except as resulting in the formation of more perfect individual characters; but on the other hand every progress towards perfection on the part of the individual character presupposes some embodiment or expression of itself by the self-realising principle in what may be called – to speak most generally – the organisation of life. It is in turn, however, only through the action of individuals that this organisation of life is achieved.

24. Thus the process of reconciliation between will and reason – the process through which each alike comes actually to be or to do what it is and does in possibility, or according to its idea, or according to the law of its being – so far as it comes within our experience may be described as follows. A certain action of the self-realising principle, of which individuals susceptible in various forms to the desire to better themselves have been the media, has resulted in conventional morality; in a system of recognised rules (whether in the shape of law or custom) as to what the good of society requires, which no people seem to be wholly without. The moral progress of the individual, born and bred under such a system of conventional morality, consists (1) in the adjustment of the self-seeking principle in him to the requirements of conventional morality, so that the modes in which he seeks self-satisfaction are regulated by the sense of what is expected of him. This adjustment (which it is *ª*the chief business*ª* of education to effect) is so far a determination of the will as in the individual by objects which the universal or *ᵇ*rational*ᵇ* human will, of which the will of the individual is a partial expression, has brought into existence, and is thus a determination of the will by itself. It consists (2) in a process of reflection, by which this feeling in the individual of what is expected of him becomes a conception under whatever name of something that universally should be, of something absolutely desirable, of a single end or object of life. The content of this conception may be no more than what was already involved in the individual's feeling of what is expected of him; that is to say, if called upon to state in detail what it is that has to be done for the attainment of the absolute moral end or in obedience to the law of what universally should be, he might only be able to specify conduct

which, apart from any such explicit conception, he felt was expected of him. For all that, there is a great difference between feeling that a certain line of conduct is expected of me and conceiving it as a form of a universal duty. So long as the requirements of established morality are *felt in the former way*, they present themselves to the man as imposed from without. Hence, though they are an expression of practical reason, as operating in previous generations of men, yet unless the individual conceives them as relative to an absolute end common to him with all men, they become antagonistic to the practical reason which operates in him, and which in him is the source at once of the demand for self-satisfaction and of the effort to find himself in, to carry his own unity into, all things presented to him. Unless the actions required of him by 'the divine law, the civil law, and the law of opinion or reputation' (to use Locke's classification)[47] tend to realise his own idea of what should be or is good on the whole, they do not form an object which, as contemplated, he can harmonise with the other objects which he seeks to understand, nor, as a practical object, do they form one in the attainment of which he can satisfy himself. Hence before the completion of the process through which the individual comes to conceive the performance of the actions expected of him under the general form of a duty which in the freedom of his own reason he recognises as binding, there is apt to occur a revolt against conventional morality. The issue of this may either be an apparent suspension of the moral growth of the individual, or a clearer apprehension of the spirit underlying the letter of the obligations laid on him by society, which makes his rational recognition of duty, when arrived at, a much more valuable influence in promoting the moral growth of society.

25. This process, which may be called a reconciliation of reason with itself, because it is the appropriation by reason as a personal principle in the individual of the work which reason, acting through the media of other persons, has already achieved in the establishment of conventional morality, is the condition of the *third* stage in which the moral progress of the individual consists; viz. the growth of a personal interest in the realisation of an idea of what should be – in doing what is believed to contribute to the absolutely desirable or to human perfection because it is believed to do so. Just so far as this interest is formed, the reconciliation of the two modes in which the practical reason operates in the individual is effected. The demand for self-satisfaction (practical reason as the individual's will) is directed to the realisation of an ideal object – the conceived 'should be' – which practical reason *as our reason* constitutes. The 'autonomy of the will' is

thus attained in a higher sense than it is in the 'adjustment' described under (1), because the objects to which the will is directed are not merely determined by customs and institutions which are due to the operation of practical reason in previous ages, but are embodiments or expressions of the conception of what absolutely should be as formed by the man who seeks to satisfy himself in their realisation. Indeed, unless in the stage of conformity to conventional morality the principle of obedience is some feeling (though not a clear conception) of what should be, of the desirable in distinction from the desired – if it is merely fear of pain or hope of pleasure – there is no approach to autonomy of the will or moral freedom in the conformity. We must not allow the doctrine that such freedom consists in a determination of the will by reason, and the recognition of the truth that the requirements of conventional morality are a product of reason as operating in individuals of the past, to mislead us into supposing that there is any moral freedom, or anything of intrinsic value, in the life of conventional morality as governed by 'interested motives' – by the desire, directly or indirectly, to obtain pleasure. There can be no real determination of the will by reason unless both reason and will are operating in one and the same person. A will is not really anything except as the will of a person, and, as we have seen, a will is not really determinable by anything foreign to itself. It is only determinable by an object which the person willing makes his own. As little is reason really anything apart from a self-conscious subject, or as other than an idea of perfection to be realised in and by such a subject. The determination of will by reason, then, which constitutes moral freedom or autonomy, must mean its determination by an object which a person willing, in virtue of his reason, presents to himself – that object consisting in the realisation of an idea of perfection in and by himself. Kant's view[48] that the action which is merely 'pflichtmässig' ['conformable to duty'], not done 'aus Pflicht' ['from duty'], is of no moral value in itself, whatever may be its possible value as a means to the production of the will which does act 'aus Pflicht', is once for all true, though he may have taken too narrow a view of the conditions of actions done 'aus Pflicht', especially in supposing (as he seems to do) that it is necessary to them to be done painfully. There is no determination of will by reason – no moral freedom – in conformity of action to rules of which the establishment is due to the operation of ᵃreason, of theᵃ idea of perfection in men, unless the principle of conformity in the persons conforming is that idea itself in some form or other.[49]

5

Prolegomena to Ethics: selections*

═══

BOOK III: THE MORAL IDEAL AND MORAL PROGRESS

Chapter 1: Good and Moral Good

...174. ... [Let us] recall the conclusions arrived at in an earlier stage of this treatise.[1] We saw reason to hold that the existence of one connected world, which is the presupposition of knowledge, implies the action of one self-conditioning and self-determining mind; and that, as our knowledge, so our moral activity was only explicable on supposition of a certain reproduction of itself on the part of this eternal mind, as the self of man – 'a reproduction of itself to which it makes the processes of animal life organic, and which is qualified and limited by the nature of those processes, but which is so far essentially a reproduction of the one supreme subject, implied in the existence of the world, that the product carries with it under all its limitations and qualifications the characteristic of being an object to itself' (§ 99). Proof of such a doctrine, in the ordinary sense of the word, from the nature of the case there cannot be. It is not a truth deducible from other established or conceded truths. It is not a statement of an event or matter of fact that can be the object of experiment or observation. It represents a conception to which no perceivable or imaginable object can possibly correspond, but one that affords the only means by which, reflecting on our moral and intellectual experience conjointly, taking the world and ourselves into account, we can put the whole thing together and understand how (not *why*, but *how*) we are and do what we consciously are and do. Given this conception, and not without it, we can at any rate express that which it cannot be denied demands expression – the nature of man's reason and man's will, of human progress and human short-coming, of the effort after good and the failure to gain it, of virtue and vice, in their connection and in their distinction, in their essential opposition and in their no less essential unity.

175. The reason and will of man have their common ground in that characteristic of being an object to himself which, as we have said, be-

longs to him in so far as the eternal mind, through the medium of an animal organism and under limitations arising from the employment of such a medium, reproduces itself in him. It is in virtue of this self-objectifying principle that he is determined, not simply by natural wants according to natural laws, but by the thought of himself as existing under certain conditions, and as having ends that may be attained and capabilities that may be realised under those conditions. It is thus that he not merely desires but seeks to satisfy himself in gaining the objects of his desire; presents to himself a certain possible state of himself which in the gratification of the desire he seeks to reach; in short, wills. It is thus, again, that he has the impulse to make himself what he has the possibility of becoming but actually is not, and hence not merely, like the plant or animal, undergoes a process of development, but seeks to, and does, develop himself. The conditions of the animal soul, 'servile to every skiey influence',[2] no sooner sated than wanting, are such that the self-determining spirit cannot be conscious of them as conditions to which it is subject – and it is so subject and so conscious of its subjection in the human person – without seeking some satisfaction of itself, some realisation of its capabilities, that shall be independent of those conditions.

176. Hence arises the impulse which becomes the source, according to the direction it takes, both of vice and of virtue. It is the source of vicious self-seeking and self-assertion so far as the spirit which is in man seeks to satisfy itself or to realise its capabilities in modes in which, according to the law which its divine origin imposes on it and which is equally the law of the universe and of human society, its self-satisfaction or self-realisation is not to be found. Such, for instance – so self-defeating – is the quest for self-satisfaction in the life of the voluptuary . . . It is one and the same principle of his nature – his divine origin, in the sense explained – which makes it possible for the voluptuary to seek self-satisfaction, and thus to live for pleasure, at all, and which according to the law of its being, according to its inherent capability, makes it impossible that the self-satisfaction should be found in any succession of pleasures. So it is again with the man who seeks to assert himself, to realise himself, to show what he "has it in[a] him to be, in achievements which may make the world wonder, but which in their social effects are such that the human spirit, according to the law of its being, which is a law of development in society, is not advanced but hindered by them in the realisation of its capabilities. He is living for ends of which the divine principle that forms his self alone renders him capable, but these ends, because in their attainment one is exalted by the depression of others, are not in the

direction in which that principle can really fulfil the promise and potency which it contains.

How in particular and in detail that fulfilment is to be attained we can only tell in so far as some progress has actually been made towards its attainment in the knowledge, arts, habits, and institutions through which man has so far become more at home in nature, and through which one member of the human family has become more able and more wishful to help another. But the condition of its further fulfilment is the will in some form or other to contribute to its fulfilment. And hence the differentia of the virtuous life, proceeding as it does from the same self-objectifying principle which we have just characterised as the source of the vicious life, is that it is governed by the consciousness of there being some perfection which has to be attained, some vocation which has to be fulfilled, some law which has to be obeyed, something absolutely desirable whatever the individual may for the time desire; that it is in ministering to such an end that the agent seeks to satisfy himself. However meagrely the perfection, the vocation, the law may be conceived, the consciousness that there is such a thing, so far as it directs the will, must at least keep the man to the path in which human progress has so far been made. It must keep him loyal in the spirit to established morality,[3] industrious in some work of recognised utility. What further result it will yield, whether it will lead to a man's making any original contribution to the perfecting of life, will depend on his special gifts and circumstances. Though these are such, as is the case with most of us, that he has no chance of leaving the world or even the society immediately about him observably better than he found it, yet in 'the root of the matter'[4] – as having done loyally, or 'from love of his work' (which means under consciousness of an ideal), or in religious language 'as unto the Lord', the work that lay nearest him – he shares the goodness of the man who devotes a genius to the bettering of human life.

177. It may seem that in the preceding section we have gone off prematurely into an account of virtue and vice, in respect at once of the common ground of their possibility and of their essential difference, without the due preliminary explanation of the relation between reason and will. A very little reflection, however, on what has been said will show the way in which this relation is conceived. By will is understood, as has been explained, an effort (or capacity for such effort) on the part of a self-conscious subject to satisfy itself: by reason, in the practical sense, the capacity on the part of such a subject to conceive a better state of itself as an end to be attained by action.[5] This is what will and reason are severally taken to imply in

the most primitive form in which they appear in us. A being without capacity for such effort or such conception would not, upon our theory, be considered to have will or reason. In this most primitive form they are alike modes of that eternal principle of self-objectification which we hold to be reproducing itself in man through the medium of an animal organism, and of which the action is equally necessary to knowledge and to morality. There is thus essentially or in principle an identity between reason and will; and widely as they become divergent in the actual history of men (in the sense that the objects where good is actually sought are often not those where reason, even as in the person seeking *"it"*, pronounces that it is to be found), still the true development of man – the only development in which the capabilities of his 'heaven-born'[6] nature can be actualised – lies in the direction of union between the developed will and the developed reason. It consists in so living that the objects in which self-satisfaction is habitually sought contribute to the realisation of a true idea of what is best for man – such an idea as our reason would have when it had come to be all which it has the possibility of becoming, and which, as in God, it is.

178. Such a life, as in vague forecast conceived, has always been called, according to a usage inherited from the Greek fathers of moral philosophy, a life according to reason.[7] And this usage is in harmony with the definition just given of reason at its lowest potency in us. For any truest idea of what is best for man that can guide our action is still a realisation of that capacity for conceiving a better state of himself, which we must ascribe to every child whom we can regard as 'father of the man'[8] capable of morality, to any savage to whom we would affiliate the moral life that we inherit. . .

On the other hand it must be borne in mind that this same capacity is the condition, as has been pointed out, no less of the vicious life than of the virtuous. The self-objectifying principle cannot exert itself as will without also exerting itself as reason, though neither as will nor as reason does it, in the vicious life, exert itself in a direction that leads to the true development of its capacity. That a man should seek an object as 'part of his happiness,' or as one without which in his then state he cannot satisfy himself – and this is to will – implies that he presents himself to himself as in a better state with the object attained than he is without it; and this is to exercise reason. Every form of vicious self-seeking is conditioned by such presentation and, in that sense, by reason. Why then, it may be asked, should the moralising influence in man, the faculty through which the paths of virtue are marked out, whether followed or no, be specially called reason? We answer: because it is through the operative consciousness in man of a possible state of himself better than the actual, though that consciousness is the condition of the possibility of all that is morally wrong, that the divine self-realising principle in him gradually fulfils its capability in the production of a higher life. With this consciousness, directed in the right path, *i.e.* the path in which it tends to become what according to the immanent divine law of its being it *"has it in"* it to be – and it is as so directed that we call it 'practical reason' – rests the initiative of all virtuous habit and action.

Chapter 2: Characteristics of the Moral Ideal

A. *The Personal Character of the Moral Ideal*

180. Let us pause here to take stock of the conclusions so far arrived at. It will be convenient to state them in dogmatic form, begging the reader to understand that this form is adopted to save time, and does not betoken undue assurance on the part of the writer. Through certain *media*, and under certain consequent limitations, but with the constant characteristic of self-consciousness and self-objectification, the one divine mind gradually reproduces itself in the human soul. In virtue of this principle in him man has definite capabilities, the realisation of which, since in it alone he can satisfy himself, forms his true good. They are not realised, however, in any life that can be observed, in any life that has been, or is, or (as it would seem) that can be lived by man as we know *"him. But although for this reason we cannot say with any adequacy what the capabilities are, yet,"* because the essence of man's spiritual endowment is the consciousness of having it, the idea of his having such capabilities and of a possible better state of himself consisting in their further realisation is a moving influence in him. It has been the parent of the institutions and usages, of the social judgments and aspirations, through which human life has been so far bettered; through which man has so far realised his capabilities and marked out the path that he must follow in their further realisation. As his true good is or would be[1] their complete realisation, so his goodness is proportionate to his habitual responsiveness to the idea of there being such a true good, in the various forms of recognised duty and beneficent work in which that idea has so far taken shape among men. In other words, it consists in the direction of the will to objects determined for it by this idea, as operative in the person willing; which direction of the will we may, upon the ground stated, fitly call its determination by reason. . .

182. It is clearly of the very essence of the doctrine above advanced that the divine principle, which we suppose to be realising itself in man, should be supposed to realise itself in persons, as such... [I]t is certain that we shall only fall into contradictions by substituting for persons, as the subject in which the divine self-realisation takes place, any entity to which self-consciousness cannot intelligibly be ascribed. If it is impossible that the divine self-realisation should be complete in such persons as we are or can conceive ourselves coming to be, on the other hand in the absence of self-objectification, which is at least the essential thing in personality, it cannot even be inchoate.

183. This consideration has an important bearing upon certain ways of thinking or speaking in which we are apt to take refuge when, having adopted a theory of the moral life as the fulfilment in the human spirit of some divine idea, we are called upon to face the difficulty of stating whether and how the fulfilment is really achieved. Any life which the individual can possibly live is at best so limited by the necessities of his position that it seems impossible, on supposition that a divine self-realising principle is at work in it, that it should be an adequate expression of such a principle. Granted the most entire devotion of a man to the attainment of objects contributory to human perfection, the very condition of his effectually promoting that end is that the objects in which he is actually interested, and upon which he really exercises himself, should be of limited range. The idea, unexpressed and inexpressible, of some absolute and all-embracing end is, no doubt, the source of such devotion, but it can only take effect in the fulfilment of some particular function in which it finds but restricted utterance. It is in fact only so far as we are members of a society, of which we can conceive the common good as our own, that the idea has any practical hold on us at all, and this very membership implies confinement in our individual realisation of the idea. Each has primarily to fulfil the duties of his station.[2] His capacity for action beyond the range of those duties is definitely bounded, and with it is definitely bounded also his sphere of personal interests, his character, his *realised* possibility. No one so confined, it would seem, can exhibit all that the Spirit, working through and in him, properly and potentially is. Yet is not such confinement the condition of the only personality that we know? It is the condition of social life, and social life is to personality what language is to thought. Language presupposes thought as a capacity, but in us the capacity of thought is only actualised in language. So human society presupposes persons in capacity – subjects capable each of conceiving himself and the better-

ing of his life as an end to himself – but it is only in the intercourse
of men, each recognised by each as an end, not merely a means, and
thus as having reciprocal claims, that the capacity is actualised and
that we really live as persons. If society then (as thus appears) is the
condition of all development of our personality, and if the necessities
of social life, as alone we know or can conceive it, put limits
to our personal development, can we suppose it to be in persons
that the spirit operative in men finds its full expression and
realisation?

184. It is from this difficulty that we are apt to seek an escape by
speaking as if the human spirit fulfilled its idea in the history or development of mankind as distinct from the persons whose experiences
constitute that history, or who are developed in that development;
whether in the achievements of great nations at special epochs of their
history, or in some progress towards a perfect organisation of society,
of which the windings and back-currents are too complex for it to be
surveyed by us as a whole. But that we are only disguising the difficulty, not escaping it, by this manner of speech, we shall see upon
reflecting that there can be nothing in a nation however exalted its
mission, or in a society however perfectly organised, which is not in
the persons composing the nation or the society. Our ultimate standard of worth is an ideal of *personal* worth. All other values are relative to value for, of, or in a person. To speak of any progress or
improvement or development of a nation or society or mankind,
except as relative to some greater worth of persons, is to use words
without meaning. The saying that 'a nation is merely an aggregate of
individuals' is indeed fallacious, but mainly on account of the introduction of the emphatic 'merely'. The fallacy lies in the implication
that the individuals could be what they are – could have their moral
and spiritual qualities – independently of their existence in a nation.
The notion is conveyed that they bring those qualities with them
ready-made into the national existence, which thereupon results from
their combination; while the truth is that, whatever moral capacity
must be presupposed, it is only actualised through the habits, institutions, and laws, in virtue of which the individuals form a nation.
But it is none the less true that the life of the nation has no real existence except as the life of the individuals composing the nation – a life
determined by their intercourse with each other and deriving its
peculiar features from the conditions of that intercourse.

Nor, unless we allow ourselves to play fast and loose with the terms
'spirit' and 'will', can we suppose a national spirit and will to exist
except as the spirit and will of individuals, affected in a certain way by

intercourse with each other and by the history of the nation. Since it is only through its existence as our self-consciousness that we know anything of spirit at all, to hold that a spirit can exist except as a self-conscious subject is self-contradictory. A 'national spirit' is not something in the air; nor is it a series of phenomena of a particular kind; nor yet is it God – the eternal Spirit or self-conscious subject which communicates itself, in measure and under conditions, to beings which through that communication become spiritual. It would seem that it could only mean one of two things; either (*a*) some type of personal character as at any time exhibited by individuals who are held together and personally modified by national ties and interests which they recognise as such; or (*b*) such a type of personal character as we may suppose *should* result, according to the divine idea of the world, from the intercourse of individuals with each other under the influence of the common institutions which make a particular nation, whether that type of character is actually attained or no. At any rate, if a 'national spirit' is held to be a form in which an eternal Spirit, in the only sense in which we have reason to think there is such a thing, realises itself, then it can only have its being in persons, though in persons, of course, specially modified by the special conditions of their intercourse with each other. The degree of perfection, of realisation of their possibilities, attained by these persons is the measure of the fulfilment which the idea of the human spirit attains in the particular national spirit. If the fulfilment of the idea is necessarily incomplete in them, it can be no more complete in the national spirit, which has no other existence, as national, than that which it has in them. . .

187. One of the essential implications of the idea of development is the eternal realisation for, or in, the eternal mind of the capacities gradually realised in time. Another is that the end of the process of development should be a real fulfilment of the capacities presupposed by the process. When we speak of any subject as in process of development according to some law, we must mean, if we so speak advisedly, that that into which the subject is being developed already exists for some consciousness. We express the same thing by saying that the subject is something in itself or potentially which it has not yet in time actually become;[3] and this again implies that in relation to some conscious being it is eternally that which in some other relation it is in time coming to be. A state of life or consciousness not yet attained by a subject capable of it, *in relation to that subject* we say *actually is not*; but if there were no consciousness for which it existed, there would be no sense in saying that *in possibility it is*, for it

would simply be nothing at all. Thus when we speak of the human spirit being in itself, or in possibility, something which is not yet realised in human experience, we mean that there is a consciousness for and in which this something really exists though, on the other hand, for the consciousness which constitutes human experience it exists only in possibility.

It would not be enough to say 'a consciousness *for* which it really exists'. That might merely mean that this undeveloped capability of the human spirit existed as an object of consciousness to the eternal mind, in the same way in which facts that I contemplate exist for me. Such a statement would suffice, were the subject of development merely a natural organism. But when that which is being developed is itself a self-conscious subject, the end of its becoming must really exist not merely *for*, but *in* or *as*, a self-conscious subject. There must be eternally such a subject which is all that the self-conscious subject, as developed in time, has the possibility of becoming; in which the idea of the human spirit, or all that it *"has it in"* itself to become, is completely realised. This consideration may suggest the true notion of the spiritual relation in which we stand to God;[4] that He is not merely a Being who has made us in the sense that we exist as an object of the divine consciousness in the same way in which we must suppose the system of nature so to exist, but that He is a Being in whom we exist; with whom we are in principle one; with whom the human spirit is identical in the sense that He *is* all which the human spirit is capable of becoming. . .

190. Meanwhile, as must constantly be borne in mind, in saying that the human spirit can only realise itself, that the divine idea of man can only be fulfilled, in and through persons, we are not denying but affirming that the realisation and fulfilment can only take place in and through society. Without society, no persons: this is as true as that without persons, without self-objectifying agents, there could be no such society as we know. Such society is founded on the recognition by persons of each other, and their interest in each other, *as persons, i.e.* as beings who are ends to themselves, who are consciously determined to action by the conception of themselves as that for the sake of which they act. They are interested in each other *as persons* in so far as each, being aware that another presents his own self-satisfaction to himself as an object, finds satisfaction of the other. Society is founded on such mutual interest in the sense that unless it were operative, however incapable of expressing itself in abstract formulae, there would be nothing to lead to that treatment by one human being of another as an end, not merely a means, on which

society even in its narrowest and most primitive forms must rest. There would be nothing to countervail the tendency, inherent in the self-asserting and self-seeking subject, to make every object he deals with, even an object of natural affection, a means to his own gratification. The combination of men as *isoi kai homoioi* [equals] for common ends would be impossible. Thus except as between persons, each recognising the other as an end in himself and having the will to treat him as such, there can be no society.

But the converse is equally true, that only through society, in the sense explained, is personality actualised. Only through society is any one enabled to give that effect to the idea of himself as the object of his actions, to the idea of a possible better state of himself, without which the idea would remain like that of space to a man who had not the senses either of sight or touch. Some practical recognition of personality by another – of an 'I' by a 'Thou' and a 'Thou' by an 'I' – is necessary to any practical consciousness of it, to any such consciousness of it as can express itself in act. On the origin of such recognition in the past we speculate in vain. To whatever primitive groupings, as a matter of history or of imagination, we can trace our actual society, these must already imply it. But we know that we, who are born under an established system of family ties, and of reciprocal rights and obligations sanctioned by the state, learn to regard ourselves as persons among other persons because we are treated as such. From the dawn of intelligence we are treated, in one way or another, as entitled to have a will of our own, to make ourselves the objects of our actions, on condition of our practically recognising the same title in others. All education goes on the principle that we are, or are to become, persons in this sense.[5] And just as it is through the action of society that the individual comes at once practically to conceive his personality – his nature as an object to himself – and to conceive the same personality as belonging to others, so it is society that supplies all the higher content to this conception, all those objects of a man's personal interest in living for which he lives for his own satisfaction, except such as are derived from the merely animal nature.

191. Thus it is equally true that the human spirit can only realise itself, or fulfil its idea, in persons, and that it can only do so through society, since society is the condition of the development of a personality. But the function of society being the development of persons, the realisation of the human spirit in society can only be attained according to the measure in which that function is fulfilled. It does not follow from this that all persons must be developed in the same way. The very existence of mankind presupposes the distinction be-

tween the sexes; and as there is a necessary difference between their functions, there must be a corresponding difference between the modes in which the personality of men and women is developed. Again, though we must avoid following the example of philosophers who have shown an *a priori* necessity for those class-distinctions of their time which after ages have dispensed with, it would certainly seem as if distinctions of social position and power were necessarily incidental to the development of human personality. There cannot be this development without a recognised power of appropriating material things. This appropriation must vary in its effects according to talent and opportunity, and from that variation again must result differences in the form which personality takes in different men. Nor does it appear how those reciprocal services which *ᵃ*elicit*ᵃ* the feeling of mutual dependence, and thus promote the recognition by one man of another as an *alter ego*, would be possible without different limitations of function and ability which determine the range within which each man's personality develops, in other words, the scope of his personal interests.

Thus under any conditions possible, so far as can be seen, for human society, one man who was the best that his position allowed would be very different from another who was the best that *his* position allowed. But in order that either may be good at all in the moral sense, *i.e.* intrinsically and not merely as a means – in order that the idea of the human spirit may be in any sense fulfilled in him – the fulfilment of that idea in some form or other, the contribution to human perfection in some way or other, must be the object in which he seeks self-satisfaction, the object for which he lives in living for himself. And it is only so far as this development and direction of personality is obtained for all who are capable of it (as presumably every one who says 'I' is capable) that human society, either in its widest comprehension or in any of its particular groups, can be held to fulfil its function, to realise its idea as it is in God.[6]

B. *The Formal Character of the Moral Ideal or Law.*
... 196. It is ... not an illogical procedure, because it is the only procedure suited to the matter in hand, to say that the goodness of man lies in devotion to the ideal of humanity, and then that the ideal of humanity consists in the goodness of man. It means that such an ideal, not yet realised but operating as a motive, already constitutes in man an inchoate form of that life, that perfect development of himself, of which the completion would be the realised ideal itself. Now in relation to a nature such as ours, having other impulses than those

which draw to the ideal, this ideal becomes, in Kant's language, an imperative, and a categorical imperative.[7] It will command something to be done universally and unconditionally, irrespectively of whether there is in any one, at any time, an inclination to do it. But when we ask ourselves what it is that this imperative commands to be done, we are met with just the same difficulty as when asked to define the moral ideal or the unconditional good. We can only say that the categorical imperative commands us to obey the categorical imperative, and to obey it for its own sake. If – not merely for practical purposes but as a matter of speculative certainty – we identify its injunction with any particular duty, circumstances will be found upon which the bindingness of that duty is contingent, and the too hasty identification of the categorical imperative with it will issue in a suspicion that, after all, there is no categorical imperative, no absolute duty, at all. After the explanations just given, however, we need not shrink from asserting as the basis of morality an unconditional duty, which yet is not a duty to do anything unconditionally except to fulfil that unconditional duty. It is the duty of realising an ideal which cannot be adequately defined till it is realised, and which, when realised, would no longer present itself as a source of duties, because the *should be* would be exchanged for the *is*. This is the unconditional ground of those particular duties to do or to forbear doing, which in the effort of the social man to realise his ideal have so far come to be recognised as binding, but which are each in some way or other conditional because relative to particular circumstances, however wide the range of circumstances may be to which they are relative.

197. At the same time, then, that the categorical imperative can enjoin nothing *without liability to exception* but disinterested obedience to itself, it will have no lack of definite content. The particular duties which it enjoins will *at least* be all those in the practice of which, according to the hitherto experience of men, some progress is made towards the fulfilment of man's capabilities or some condition necessary to that progress is satisfied. We say it will enjoin these *at least*, because particular duties must be constantly arising out of it for the individual, for which no formula can be found before they arise and which are thus extraneous to the recognised code. Every one, however, of the duties which the law of the state or the law of opinion[8] recognises must in some way be relative to circumstances. The rule therefore in which it is conveyed, though stated in the most general terms compatible with real significance, must still admit of exceptions. Yet is there a true sense in which the whole system of such

duties is unconditionally binding. It is so as an expression of the
absolute imperative to seek the absolutely desirable, the ideal of humanity, the fulfilment of man's vocation. Because an expression
(though an incomplete one) of this absolute imperative, because a
product of the effort after such an unconditional good, the requirements of conventional morality, however liable they may be to exceptions, arising out of circumstances other than those to which they are
properly applicable, are at least liable to no exception *ª*for the*ª* individual's pleasure. As against any desire but some form or other of that
desire for the best in conduct which will, no doubt, from time to time
suggest new duties in seeming conflict with the old – against any
desire for this or that pleasure or any aversion from this or that pain –
they are unconditionally binding.

198. Upon this view, so far from the categorical imperative having
no particular content, it may rather seem to have too much. It enjoins
observance of the whole complex of established duties as a means to
that perfection of man of which it unconditionally enjoins the pursuit. And it enjoins this observance as unconditionally as it enjoins
the pursuit of the end to which this observance is a means, *so long as
it is such a means*. It will only *ª*allow a*ª* departure from it in the interest of a fuller attainment of the unconditional end, not in the interest of any one's pleasure. The question indeed is sure to suggest
itself, what available criterion such a doctrine affords us either for distinguishing the essential from the unessential in the requirements of
law and custom, or for the discernment of duty in cases to which no
recognised rule is applicable. So far as it can be translated into practice at all, must not its effect be either a dead conformity to the code of
customary morality, anywhere and at any time established, without
effort to reform or expand it, or else unlimited license in departing
from it at the prompting of any impulse which the individual may be
pleased to consider a higher law? These questions shall be considered
in due course[9]; but before we enquire into the practical bearings of
our doctrine as to the relation between the system of duties anywhere
recognised and the unconditional ground of all duties – before we ask
how it affects our criteria of what in particular we should do or not do
– we have further to make good the doctrine itself. We have to revert
to the question, still left unanswered, how the mere idea of something
absolutely desirable – an idea which, we confess, does not primarily
enable us to say anything of its object but that there must be such a
thing – should have gradually defined itself, should have taken body
and content, in the establishment of recognised duties, in the formation of actual virtues, among men.

Chapter 3: The Origin and Development of the Moral Ideal

A. *Reason as Source of the Idea of a Common Good.*

199. That an idea of something absolutely desirable, which we cannot identify with any particular object of desire without soon discovering our mistake in the dissatisfaction which ensues upon the attainment of the particular object – that such an idea of a supreme good, which is no good thing in particular, should express itself in a system of social requirements and expectations, of which each would seem to have reference to a definite social need, may naturally at first be thought an extravagant supposition. Further consideration, however, may change our view. The idea of the absolutely desirable, as we have seen, arises out of, or rather is identical with, man's consciousness of himself as an end to himself. It is the forecast, proper to a subject conscious at once of himself as an absolute end and of a life of becoming, of constant transition from possibility to realisation and from this again to a new possibility – a forecast of a well-being that shall consist in the complete fulfilment of himself. Now the self of which a man thus forecasts the fulfilment is not an abstract or empty self. It is a self already affected in the most primitive forms of human life by manifold interests, among which are interests dependent on other persons for the means to their gratification, but interests in the good of those other persons – interests which cannot be satisfied without the consciousness that those other persons are satisfied. The man cannot contemplate himself as in a better state, or on the way to the best, without contemplating others, not merely as a means to that better state, but as sharing it with him. . .

201. We may take it . . . as an ultimate fact of human history – a fact without which there would not be such a history and which is not in turn deducible from any other history – that out of sympathies of animal origin, through their presence in a self-conscious soul, there arise interests as of a person in persons. Out of processes common to man's life with the life of animals there arise for man, as there do not apparently arise for animals,

> Relations dear and all the charities
> Of father, son, and brother[1]

and of those relations and charities self-consciousness on the part of all concerned in them is the condition. At the risk of provoking a charge of pedantry, this point must be insisted on. It is not any mere sympathy with pleasure and pain that can by itself yield the affections and recognised obligations of the family. The man for whom they are to be possible must be able, through consciousness of himself as an end to himself, to enter into a like consciousness as belonging to others whose expression of it corresponds to his own. He must have practical understanding of what is meant for them, as for himself, by saying 'I'. Having found his pleasures and pains dependent on the pleasures and pains of others, he must be able in the contemplation of a possible satisfaction of himself to include the satisfaction of those others, and that a satisfaction of them as ends to themselves and not as a means to his pleasure. He must, in short, be capable of conceiving and seeking a permanent well-being in which the permanent well-being of others is included.

202. Some sort of community, founded on such unity of self-consciousness, on such capacity for a common idea of permanent good, must be presupposed in any groupings of men from which the society that we know can have been developed. To the man living under its influence the idea of the absolutely desirable, the effort to better himself, must from the first express itself in some form of social requirement. So far as he is set on making his way to some further fulfilment of himself, he must seek to carry those in whom he is interested with him in the process. That 'better reason' (§ 179) which, in antagonism to the inclinations of the moment, presents itself to him as a law for himself, will present itself to him as equally a law for them; and as a law for them on the same ground and in the same sense as it is a law for him, *viz.* as prescribing means to the fulfilment of an idea of absolute good, common to him with them – an idea indefinable indeed in imagination, but gradually defining itself in act.

The conception of a moral law, in its strict philosophical form, is no doubt an analogical adaptation of the notion of law in the more primary sense – the notion of it as a command enforced by a political superior or by some power to which obedience is habitually rendered by those to whom the command is addressed. But there is an idea which equally underlies the conception both of moral duty and of legal right; which is prior, so to speak, to the distinction between them; which must have been at work in the minds of men before they could be capable of recognising any kind of action as one that *ought* to be done, whether because it is enjoined by law or authoritative custom, or because, though not thus enjoined, a man owes it to himself or to his neighbour or to God. This is the idea of an absolute and a common good; a good common to the person conceiving it with others, and good for him and them, whether at any moment it swers their likings or no. As affected by such an idea, a man's attitude to his likes and dislikes will be one of which, in his inward converse, the 'Thou shalt' or 'Thou must' of command is the natural expression, though of law, in the sense either of the command of a political superior or of a self-imposed rule of life, he may as yet have no definite conception.

And so affected by it he must be, before the authority either of custom or of law can have any meaning for him. Simple fear cannot constitute the sense of such authority nor by any process of development, properly so called, become it.[2] It can only spring from a conviction on the part of those recognising the authority that a good which is really their good, though in constant conflict with their inclinations, is really served by the power in which they recognise authority. Whatever force may be employed in maintaining custom or law, however 'the interest of the stronger', whether an individual or 'the few' or the majority of some group of people, may be concerned in maintaining it, only some persuasion of its contribution to a recognised common good can yield that sort of obedience to it which, equally in the simpler and the more complex stages of society, forms the social bond.

203. The idea, then, of a possible well-being of himself that shall not pass away with this, that, or the other pleasure, and relation to some group of persons whose well-being he takes to be as his own and in whom he is interested in being interested in himself – these two things must condition the life of any one who is to be a creator or sustainer either of law or of that prior authoritative custom out of which law arises. Without them there might be instruments of law and custom; intelligent co-operating subjects of law and custom there could not be. They are conditions at once of might being so exercised that it can be recognised as having right, and of that recognition itself. It is in this sense that the old language is justified, which speaks of Reason as the parent of Law.[3] Reason is the self-objectifying consciousness. It constitutes, as we have seen, the capability in man of seeking an absolute good and of conceiving this good as common to others with himself: and it is this capability which alone renders him a possible author and a self-submitting subject of law.

In saying this we are saying nothing for or against any theory of the conditions under which, as a matter of history, laws may have been first established. It is easy, and for certain purposes may be advisable, to define a sense of the term in which 'laws' do not exist till an advanced stage of civilisation, when sovereignties of ascertained range and scope have been established, and when the will of the sovereign has come to be expressed in general and permanent forms. In

proportion as we thus restrict our usage of the term 'law' we shall have
to extend our view of the effect upon human life of social requirements, which are not 'laws', but to which the good citizen renders an
obedience the same in principle as that which he renders to 'laws'; an
obedience at once willing and constrained – willing, because recognised as the condition of a social good which is his own highest good;
constrained, in so far as it prevents him from doing what he would
otherwise like to do. It is with the ground of this obedience that the
moralist is concerned, as having been rendered when as yet 'law' in
the restricted sense was not, and as still rendered equally by the good
citizen to the law which the state enforces, and to that of which the
sanction is a social sentiment shared by him.

204. This ground the moralist finds in Reason, according to the
sense explained. He will listen respectfully to any account, for which
historians can claim probability, of the courses of events by which
powers strong enough to enforce general obedience have been
gathered into the hands of individuals or groups of men; but he will
reflect that, though the exercise of force may be a necessary incident
in the maintenance of government, it cannot of itself produce the
state of mind on which social union in any of its forms depends. He
will listen, further, to all that the anthropologist can tell him of the
earliest forms in which such union can be traced; but here again he
will reflect that, when the phenomena of some primitive usage have
been duly established, the interpretation of the state of mind which
they represent is a further question and one that cannot be answered
without reference to the developed consciousness which is ours.
When the anthropologist has gathered all the results he can from a
collation of the sayings and doings of such uncivilised people as can
now be observed with records and survivals from the lives of our
ancestors, his clue for the interpretation of his material will depend in
the last resort on his analysis of that world of feeling, thought, and
desire, in which he himself lives. Unless the fragmentary indications
obtainable of the life of primitive humanity can be interpreted as
expressing a consciousness in germ or principle the same as ours, we
have no clue to their inner significance at all. They are at best no more
to us than the gestures of animals, from which we may conjecture that
the animal is pleased or pained, but by which no consciousness in its
intrinsic nature is conveyed to us, as it is conveyed in the speech of
another man. We may, of course, take this view of them. We may
hold that no inference is possible from them to any state of mind on
the part of primitive man. But we cannot interpret them as expressing
a state of mind without founding our conception of the state of mind

on our own consciousness. Even if it were possible on any other plan to read a state of mind in them at all, we certainly could not read in them a consciousness from which our own has been developed, without assuming an identity, under whatever variety of modification, between the less and the more developed consciousness.

Thus, though our information about primitive man were very different from what it is, it could never be other than a contradiction to found upon it a theory of the state of mind underlying the earliest forms of social union, which should represent this state of mind as different in kind from that which, upon fair analysis of the spiritual life now shared by us, we find to be the condition of such social union as actually exists. If we are right in ascribing to Reason a function of union in the life that we know; if we are right in holding that through it we are conscious of ourselves and of others as ourselves, through it accordingly that we can seek to make the best of ourselves and of others with ourselves, and that in this sense Reason is the basis of society because the source at once of the establishment of equal practical rules in a common interest and of self-imposed subjection to those rules; then we are entitled to hold that Reason fulfilled a function intrinsically the same in the most primitive associations of man with man, between which and the actual institutions of family and commune, of state and nation, there has been any continuity of development.

205. The foundation of morality, then, in the reason or self-objectifying consciousness of man is the same thing as its foundation in the institutions of a common life – in these as directed to a common good, and so directed not mechanically but with consciousness of the good on the part of those subject to the institutions. Such institutions are, so to speak, the form and body of reason, as practical in men. Without them the rational or self-conscious or moral man does not exist, nor without them can any being have existed from whom such a man could be developed, if any continuity of nature is implied in development. No development of morality can be conceived, nor can any history of it be traced (for that would imply such a conception), which does not presuppose some idea of a common good expressing itself in some elementary effort after a regulation of life. Without such an idea the development would be as impossible as it is impossible that sight should be generated when there is no optic nerve. With it, however restricted in range the idea may be, there is given 'in promise and potency' the ideal of which the realisation would be perfect morality, the ideal of a society in which every one shall treat every one else as his neighbour – in which to every rational agent the well-

being or perfection of every other such agent shall be included in that perfection of himself for which he lives. And as the most elementary notion in a rational being of a personal good, common to himself with another who is as himself, is in possibility such an ideal, so the most primitive institutions for the regulation of a society with reference to a common good are already a school for the character which shall be responsive to the moral ideal.

It has become a common-place among us that the moral suscepti-bilities which we find in ourselves would not exist but for the action of law and authoritative custom on many generations of our ancestors. The common-place is doubtless perfectly true. It is only misleading when we overlook the rational capacities implied in the origin and maintenance of such law and custom. The most elemen-tary moralisation of the individual must always have arisen from his finding himself in the presence of a requirement, enforced against his inclinations to pleasure but in an interest which he can recognise as being his own no less than the interest of those by whom the require-ment is enforced. The recognition of such an interest by the indi-vidual is an outcome of the same reason as that which has led to the maintenance of the requirement by the society he belongs to. All fur-ther development of morality – all articulation of duties, all education of conscience in response to them – presupposes this primary recog-nition. Of the principal movements into which the development may be analysed we shall now go on to speak in more detail, only premis-ing that the necessity of describing them separately should not lead us to forget that they are mutually involved.

B. *The Extension of the Area of Common Good*

206. The *a*first to be noticed consists*a* in a gradual extension, for the mental eye of the moral subject, of the range of persons to whom the common good is conceived as common; towards whom and between whom accordingly obligations are understood to exist.[4] What may have been the narrowest restrictions on this range within which the process of moralisation has gone on, we have no means of saying. We only know that the earliest ascertainable history exhibits to us com-munities, relatively very confined, within any one of which a common good, and in consequence a common duty, is recognised as between the members of the community, while beyond the particular community the range of mutual obligation is not understood to extend. Among ourselves, on the contrary, it is almost an axiom of popular Ethics that there is at least a potential duty of every man to

every man – a duty which becomes actual so soon as one comes to have any dealing with the other. It is true that plenty of pretexts, some under very philosophical disguise, are always forthcoming when it is wished to evade the duty; but, when we are free from private bias, we do not seriously dispute its validity. Conscience is uneasy at its violation, as it would not have been, according to all indications, in the case, let us say, of a Greek who used his slave as a chattel, though according to his lights the Greek might be as conscientious as any of us. Yet the language in which we most naturally express our conception of the duty of all men to all men indicates the school – that of tribal, or civil, or family obligation – in which we have been trained to the conception. We convey it in the concrete by speaking of a human family, of a fraternity of all men, of the common fatherhood of God; or we suppose a universal Christian citizenship, as wide as the Humanity for which Christ died, and in thought we transfer to this, under certain analogical adaptations, those claims of one citizen upon another which have been actually enforced in societies united under a single sovereignty.

207. It is not uncommon indeed with men to whom a little philosophy has proved a dangerous thing, to make much of the distinction between an obligation that admits of being enforced between persons subject to a common sovereign, and what is alleged to be due from man to man, as such; to extenuate the claims of humanity, and even to make merry over the fraternity of men and nations. The distinction is easily drawn, and so long as there continue to be men who will not observe obligations unless enforced, it cannot be considered practically unimportant. But for the moralist it is more important to observe the real fusion in the conscience of those citizens of the modern world, who are most responsive to the higher influences of their time, of duties enforced by legal penalties and those of which the fulfilment cannot be exacted by citizen of citizen or by sovereign of subjects, but is felt to be due from man to man. It is not more certain that a man would not recognise a duty, *e.g.* of educating his poor neighbours or helping to liberate a slave, unless, generations before him, equal rights had been enforced among men who could not *ª*have understood*ª* the wrong of slavery or the claim of the labourer to a chance of raising himself, than that there are men now to whom such duties present themselves with just the same cogency as legal obligations; men to whom the motive for fulfilling the latter has been so entirely purged from any fear of penalties that the absence of such fear, as a motive to the fulfilment of humanitarian duties, makes no difference to the felt necessity of fulfilling them.

No gradual modification of selfish fear or hope could yield a disposition of this kind; and if these were the sole original motives to civil or tribal or family obedience, it would be unintelligible that a state of mind should result, in which a man imposes duties on himself quite beyond the range of such obedience. But if at the root of such obedience, as well as of the institutions to which it has been rendered, there has been an idea of good, suggested by the consciousness of unfulfilled possibilities of the rational nature common to all men, then it is intelligible that, as the range of this idea extends itself – as it comes to be understood that no race or religion or status is a bar to self-determined co-operation in its fulfilment – the sense of duty which it yields, and which has gained its power over natural desires and aversions through generations of discipline in the family and the state, should become a sense of what is due to man as such, and not merely to the members of a particular community. The change is not necessarily in the strength, in the constraining power, of the feeling of duty – perhaps it is never stronger now than it may have been in an Israelite who would have yet recognised no claim in a Philistine, or in a Greek who would yet have seen no harm in exposing a sickly child – but in the conceived range of claims to which the duty is relative. Persons come to be recognised as having claims who would once not have been recognised as having any claim, and the claim of the *isoi kai homoioi* [equals] comes to be admitted where only the claim of indulged inferiors would have been allowed before.[5] It is not the sense of duty to a neighbour, but the practical answer to the question Who is my neighbour? that has varied . . .

215. . . . . [T]he rule on which the ideally just man seeks to act . . . is one that such a man gathers for himself from the lessons which law and conventional morality have taught him. It is his 'rectification of law, where law fails through being general',[6] his articulation, and application to the particulars of life, of that principle of an absolute value in the human person as such, of a like claim to consideration in all men, which is implied in the law and conventional morality of Christendom, but of which the application in law is from the nature of the case merely general and prohibitory, while its application in conventional morality is in fact partial and inconsistent. 'The recognition of the claims of a common humanity' is a phrase that has become so familiar *ato*a modern ears that we are apt to suspect it of being cant. Yet this very familiarity is proof of the extent to which the idea represented by it has affected law and institutions. The phrase is indeed cant in the mouth of any one *b*who uses it except so far as the conscientious will gives*b* vitality and application to the idea which, as

merely embodied in laws and institutions, would be abortive and dead. But if it is only the conscience of the individual that brings the principle of human equality into productive contact with the particular facts of human life, on the other hand it is from the embodiment of the principle in laws and institutions and social requirements that the conscience itself appropriates it. The mistake of those who deny the *a priori* character of such 'intuitions'[7] of the conscience as that represented by Kant's formula does not lie in tracing a history of the intuitions but in ignoring the immanent operation of idea of the reason in the process of social organisation upon which the intuitions as in the individual depend. A short summary of the view which we have been seeking to oppose to theirs will make this view clearer as it affects the intuition on which the practice of justice is founded.

216. The individual's conscience is reason in him as informed by the work of *a*reason in*a* the structure and controlling sentiments of society. The basis of that structure, the source of those sentiments, can only be a self-objectifying spirit; a spirit through the action of *b*which in and upon such beings of animal susceptibilities, and affected by such natural sympathies as we are, we become capable of effort for some bettering or fulfilment of ourselves as an absolute good, and of including a like good for others, conceived to be as ourselves, in our own.*b* Without such spiritual action, in however elementary a form, there can be no society, in the proper human sense, at all; no community of persons, however small, to whom the treatment in any respect by each of the other as himself would be intelligible.

On the other hand, given any community of persons rendered possible by such a spiritual principle, it is *potentially* a community of all men of whom one can communicate with the other as 'I' with 'Thou'. The recognition of reciprocal claims, established as between its own members within each of a multitude of social groups, admits of establishment between members of all the groups taken together. There is no necessary limit of numbers or space beyond which the spiritual principle of social relation becomes ineffective. The impediments to its action in bringing about a practical recognition of universal human *c*fellowship are the same in kind, however greater in degree, as*c* those which interfere with the maintenance of unity in the family, the tribe, or the urban commonwealth. They are all reducible to what we may conveniently call the antagonism of the natural to the spiritual man. The prime impediment, alike to the maintenance of the narrower and to the formation of wider fellowships, is selfishness: which we may describe provisionally . . . as a preference of private pleasure to common good. But the wider, the more universal the fellowship that is in question, the more serious become those impediments to it, of which selfishness may and does take advantage, but which are so far independent of it that they bring the most self-devoted members of one tribe or state into what seems on both sides inevitable hostility with those of another. Such are ignorance, with the fear that springs from ignorance; misapprehension of the physical conditions of well-being, and consequent suspicion that the gain of one community must be the loss of another; geographical separations and demarcations, with the misunderstandings that arise from them. The effect of these has often been to make it seem a necessary incident of a man's obligation to his own tribe or nation that he should deny obligations towards men of another tribe or nation. And while higher motives have thus co-operated with mere selfishness in strengthening national separation and antagonism, it would be idle to deny a large share in the process by which such influences have been partially overcome to forces – *e.g.* the force of conquest and in particular of Roman conquest – which, though they have been applied and guided in a manner only possible to distinctively ^{d}rational^d agents, have been very slightly under the control of any desire for social good on the part of the persons wielding them.

But where the selfishness of man has proposed, his better reason has disposed. Whatever the means, the result has been a gradual removal of obstacles to that recognition of a universal fellowship which the action of reason in men potentially constitutes. Large masses of men have been brought under the control each of a single system of law; and while each system has carried with it manifold results of selfish violence and seeming accident, each has been essentially an expression of reason, as embodying an idea of permanent well-being which the individual conceives ^{e}to be^e common to his nation with himself. Each has maintained alike, under whatever differences of form, the institutions of the family and of property, and there has thus arisen, along with an order of life which habituates the individual to the subordination of his likes and dislikes to social requirements, a sort of common language of right, in which the idea of universal human fellowship, of claims in man as man – itself the outcome of the same reason which has yielded the laws of particular communities – can find the expression necessary to its taking hold on the minds of men.

217. In the light of these considerations we may trace a history, if we like to call it so, of the just man's conscience – of the conscience which dictates to him an equal regard to the well-being, estimated on the same principle as his own, of all whom his actions may affect. It is

a history, however, which does not carry us back to anything beyond reason. It is a history of which reason is the beginning and the end. It is reason which renders the individual capable of self-imposed obedience to the law of his family and of his state, while it is to reason that this law itself owes its existence. It is thus both teacher and learner of the lesson through which a conscience of any kind, with the habit of conformity to conscience, is first acquired, and the individual becomes capable of a reverence which can control inclinations to pleasure. Reason is equally the medium of that extension of one system of law over many communities, of like systems over a still wider range, which, in prophetic souls reflecting on it, first elicits the latent idea of a fellowship of all, and furnishes them with a mode of expression through which the idea may be brought home to ordinary men. When it is so brought home, the personal habits which are needed to give practical effect to it, and which on their part only needed the leaven of this idea to expand into a wider beneficence, are already there. But they are there through the action of the same reason, as already yielding social order and obedience within narrower forms of community.

Thus in the conscientious citizen of modern Christendom reason without and reason within, reason as objective and reason as subjective, reason as the better spirit of the social order in which he lives, and reason as his loyal recognition and interpretation of that spirit – these being but different aspects of one and the same reality, which is the operation of the divine mind in man – combine to yield both the judgment, and obedience to the judgment, which we variously express by saying that every human person has an absolute value; that humanity in the person of every one is always to be treated as an end, never merely as a means; that in the estimate of that well-being which forms the true good every one is to count for one and no one for more than one; that every one has a *suum*[8] which every one else is bound to render him.

Chapter 4: The Development of the Moral Ideal (continued)

C. The Determination of the Idea of Common Good

218. The development of morality which we have been considering has been a development from the primary recognition of an absolute and common good – a good common as between some group of persons interested in each other, absolute as that of which the goodness is conceived to be independent of the likes and dislikes of individuals; but we have so far considered the development only with reference to

the extension of the range of persons between whom the good is conceived to be common, and who on this ground come to recognise
equivalent duties to each other. The outcome of the process, when
treated in this one-sided way, exhibits itself merely as the intuition of
the educated conscience that the true good must be good for all men,
so that no one should seek to gain by another's loss, gain and loss
being estimated on the same principle for each. It has not appeared so
far how the conscience is trained in the apprehension of what in particular the good is, and in the consequent imposition on itself of particular duties. We have treated the precept '*suum cuique*' ['To each
his own'[1]] as if the just man arrived at the idea of its applicability to all
men, and at the corresponding disposition to apply it, without any
such definite enlightenment in regard to the good proper to every one
with whom he may have to do as is necessary for his practical guidance. Some such defect of treatment is unavoidable so long as abstraction of some kind is the condition of all exposition; so long as we can
only attend to one aspect of any reality at a time, though quite aware
that it is only one aspect. We have now to make up for the defect by
considering the gradual determination of the idea of good, which goes
along with the growth of the conviction that it is good for all men
alike, and of the disposition to act accordingly...

240. ... We committed ourselves a little way back to the familiar
opinion – more likely to find acceptance than many here advanced –
that the idea of a true good first took hold of men in the form of a consideration of what was needed to keep the members of a family alive
and comfortably alive. Now between a state of mind in which the idea
of good is only operative in this form, and one which can at least naturally express itself in the proposition that the only true good is the
good will, can there be anything in common? Is it not idle to attempt
to connect them as phases in the operation of a single spiritual principle? It would be so, no doubt, if interest in provision for the necessities of a family really exhausted the spiritual demand from which it
arises. But this is not the case. It must be remembered that provision
for the wants of a family, of the kind we are contemplating, cannot
have been a merely instinctive process. It cannot have been so, at
least, on supposition that it was a process of which we can understand
the nature from our own experience, or that it was a stage in the development of the men that we are and know. It would not have had anything in common with the family interests by which we are ourselves
influenced unless it rested not on instinct but on self-consciousness –
on a man's projection of himself in thought into a future as a subject
of a possibly permanent satisfaction, to be found in the satisfaction of

the wants of the family with which he identifies himself. Now this power of contemplating himself as possibly coming to be that which he is not, and as so coming to be in and through a society in which he lives a permanent life, is in promise and potency an interest in the bettering of mankind, in the realisation of its capabilities or the fulfilment of its vocation, conceived as an absolutely desirable end.

Between the most primitive and limited form of the interest, as represented by the effort to provide for the future wants of a family, and its most highly generalised form, lie the interests of ordinary good citizens in various elements of a social well-being. All have a common basis in the demand for abiding self-satisfaction which, according to the theory we have sought to maintain, is yielded by the action of an eternal self-conscious principle in and upon an animal nature. That demand, however, only gradually exhibits what it *a*has it in*a* it to require. Until life has been so organised as to afford some regular relief from the pressure of animal wants, an interest in what Aristotle calls 'living well', or 'well-being', as distinct from merely 'living',[2] cannot emerge. Yet that primitive organisation of life through which some such relief is afforded, being rational not instinctive, would be impossible without the action of the same self-objectifying principle which in a later stage exhibits itself in the pursuit of ends to which life is a means, as distinct from the pursuit of means of living. The higher interest is latent in the lower, nor would it be possible to draw a line at which the mere living of the family ceases to be the sole object and its well-being begins to be cared for.

241. But when a supply of the means of living has been sufficiently secured to allow room for a consideration of the ends of living, what are those ends taken to be? Can any such progress be noted in men's conception of them as could justify us in speaking of a development of the idea of duty? If the idea of good were simply equivalent to the idea of a maximum of pleasure, a growth of moral ideas would simply mean a progressive discovery of means to pleasure. A development of the idea of duty, in the sense of a process affecting our conception of the ends of action, there could not be. If on this hypothesis we are to speak of a moral development at all, it can only be in the sense of an increasing enlightenment as to what should be done in order to an end of which itself the idea undergoes no modification. It is otherwise if the idea of the good is an idea of something which man should become for the sake of becoming it, or in order to fulfil his capabilities and in so doing to satisfy himself. The idea of the good, according to this view, is an idea, if the expression may be allowed, which gradually creates its own filling. It is not an idea like that of any pleasure,

which a man retains from an experience that he has had and would like to have again. It is an idea to which nothing that has happened to us or that we can find in existence corresponds, but which sets us upon causing certain things to happen, upon bringing certain things into existence. Acting in us, to begin with, as a demand which is ignorant of what will satisfy itself, it only arrives at a more definite consciousness of its own nature and tendency through reflection on its own creations – on habits and institutions and modes of life which, as a demand not reflected upon, it has brought into being. Moral development then will not be merely progress in the discovery and practice of means to an end which throughout remains the same for the subject of the development. It will imply a progressive determination of the idea of the end itself, as the subject of it, through reflection on that which, under influence of the idea but without adequate reflection upon it, he has done and has become, comes to be more fully aware of what he has it in him to do and to become.

242. Of a moral development in this sense we have evidence in the result; and we can understand the principle of it, but the stages in the process by which the principle thus unfolds itself remain obscure. As has been already pointed out [§ 240], such an end as provision for the maintenance of a family, if pursued not instinctively but with consciousness of the end pursued, implies in the person pursuing it a motive quite different from desire either for an imagined pleasure or for relief from want. It implies the thought of a possibly permanent satisfaction, and an effort to attain that satisfaction in the satisfaction of others. Here is already a moral and spiritual, as distinct from an animal or merely natural, interest – an interest in an object which only thought constitutes, an interest in bringing about something that should be, as distinct from desire to feel again a pleasure already felt. But to be actuated by such an interest does not necessarily imply any reflection on its nature, and hence in men under its influence there need not be any conception of a moral as other than a material good. Food and drink, warmth and clothing, may still seem to them to be the only good things which they desire for themselves or for others.

This may probably still be the case with some wholly savage tribes; it may have once been the case with our own ancestors. If it was, of the process by which they emerged from it we know nothing, for they have already emerged from it in the earliest state of mind which has left any record of itself. All that we can say is that an interest moral and spiritual in the sense explained – however unaware of its own nature, however unable to describe itself as directed to other than material objects – must have been at work to bring about the habits and institutions, the standards of praise and blame, which we inherit, even the remotest and most elementary which our investigations can reach. We know further that *if* that interest, even in the form of interest in the mere provision for the material support of a family, were duly reflected upon, those who were influenced by it must have become aware that they had objects independent of the gratification of their animal nature; and, having become aware of this, they could not fail with more or less distinctness to conceive that permanent welfare of the family, which it was their great object to promote, as consisting, at any rate among other things, in the continuance in others of an interest like their own; in other words, as consisting in the propagation of virtue.

243. When and how and by what degrees this process of reflection may have taken place, we cannot say. It is reasonable to suppose that till a certain amount of shelter had been secured from the pressure of natural wants, it would be impossible. The work of making provision for the family would be too absorbing for a man to ask himself what was implied in his interest in making it, and thus to become aware of there being such a thing as a moral nature in himself and others, or of a moral value as distinct from the value of that which can be seen and touched and tasted. However strong in him the interest in the welfare of his society – which, as we have seen, is essentially a moral interest – until some relief had been won from the constant care of providing for that welfare in material forms, he would have no time to think of any intrinsic value in the persons for whom the provision was made, or in the qualities which enabled it to be made. Somehow or other, however – by what steps we know not – with all peoples that have a history the time of reflection has come, and with it the supervention upon those moral interests that are unconscious of their morality, of an interest in moral qualities as such. An interest has arisen, over and above that in keeping the members of a family or tribe alive, in rendering them persons of a certain kind; in forming in them certain qualities, not as a means to anything ulterior which the possession of these qualities might bring about, but simply for the sake of that possession; in inducing in them habits of action on account of the intrinsic value of those habits, as forms of activity in which man achieves what he has it in him to achieve and so far satisfies himself. There has arisen, in short, a conception of good things of the soul as having a value distinct from and independent of the good things of the body, if not as the only things truly good, to which all other goodness is merely relative.

Already in the earliest stages of the development of the human soul, of which we have any recorded expression, this distinction is virtually recognised. Such a formal classification as that which Aristotle assumes to be familiar, between 'external goods', 'goods of the soul', and 'goods of the body',[3] is, of course, only the product of what may be called reflection upon reflection. It is the achievement of men who have not only learnt to recognise and value the spiritual qualities to which material things serve as instruments or means of expression, but have formed the abstract conception of a universe of values which may be exhaustively classified. But independently of such abstract conceptions, we have evidence in the earliest literature accessible to us of the conception and appreciation of impalpable virtues of the character and disposition, standing in no direct relation to the senses or to animal wants – courage, wisdom, fidelity, and the like. The distinction is at least apprehended between the sensible good things that come to a man, or belong or attach to him as from without, and the good qualities of the man. It may be that the latter are chiefly considered in relation to the former, as qualities contributing to the material welfare of a society; but, though there may be as yet no clear notion of virtue as a pure good in itself independently of anything extraneous that it may obtain, it is understood that prosperity and the desert of prosperity are different things. And the recognition of desert is in itself a recognition of a moral or spiritual good as distinct from one sensible or material. It is evidence that the moral nature, implied in the interest in a social well-being, has so far reflected on itself as to arrive at moral conceptions.

244. Whenever and wherever, then, the interest in a social good has come to carry with it any distinct idea of social merit – of qualities that make the good member of a family, or good tribesman, or good citizen – we have the beginning of that education of the conscience of which the end is the conviction that the only true good is to be good. This process is properly complementary to that previously analysed, of which the end was described as the conviction that the true good is good for all men, and good for them all in virtue of the same nature and capacity. The one process is complementary to the other because the only good in the pursuit of which there can be no competition of interests, the only good which is really common to all who may pursue it, is that which consists in the universal will to be good – in the settled disposition on each man's part to make the most and best of humanity in his own person and in the persons of others. The conviction of a community of good for all men can never be really harmonised with our notions of what is good, so long as anything else

than self-devotion to an ideal of mutual service is the end by reference to which those notions are formed.

245. In fact we are very far, in our ordinary estimates of good, whether for ourselves or for others, from keeping such a standard before us, and just for that reason the conviction of the community of good for all men, while retaining its hold on us as an abstract principle, has little positive influence over our practical judgments. It is a source of counsels of perfection which we do not 'see our way' to carrying out. It makes itself felt in certain prohibitions, *e.g.* of slavery, but it has no such effect on the ordering of life as to secure for those whom we admit that it is wrong to use as chattels much real opportunity of self-development. They are left to sink or swim in the stream of unrelenting competition, in which we admit that the weaker has not a chance. So far as negative rights go – rights to be let alone – they are admitted to membership of civil society, but the good things to which the pursuits of society are in fact directed turn out to be no good things for them. Civil society may be, and is, founded on the idea of there being a common good, but that idea in relation to the less favoured members of society is in effect unrealised, and it is unrealised because the good is being sought in objects which admit of being competed for. They are of such a kind that they cannot be equally attained by all. The success of some in obtaining them is incompatible with the success of others. Until the object generally sought as good comes to be a state of mind or character of which the attainment, or approach to attainment, by each is itself a contribution to its attainment by every one else, social life must continue to be one of war – a war, indeed, in which the neutral ground is constantly being extended and which is itself constantly yielding new tendencies to peace, but in which at the same time new vistas of hostile interests, with new prospects of failure for the weaker, are as constantly opening.

Chapter 5: The Development of the Moral Ideal (continued)

D. The Greek and the Modern Conceptions of Virtue
246. Our next business will be to consider more in detail how that gradual spiritualisation or dematerialisation (in the sense explained) of the idea of true good, through which alone it can come to answer the inward demand which is its source, exhibits itself in the accepted standards of virtue and in the duties which the candid conscience recognises. The conception of virtue is the conception of social merit as founded on a certain sort of character or habit of will. Every form

of virtue arises from the effort of the individual to satisfy himself with some good conceived as true or permanent, and it is only as common to himself with a society that the individual can so conceive of a good . . . But it is a falsely abstract view of virtue to take no account of the end in pursuit of which the self is devoted. The real value of the virtue rises with the more full and clear conception of the end to which it is directed, as a character not a good fortune, as a fulfilment of human capabilities from within not an accession of good things from without, as a function not a possession. The progress of mankind in respect of the standard and practice of virtue has lain in such a development of the conception of its end . . .

257. . . . On the whole the variations in the object pursued as good, though there have been periods apparently of mere loss and shrinkage, have consisted in its acquisition of greater fulness and determinateness. In like manner the differences between our standards of virtue and those recognised by the Greek philosophers arise from the greater fulness of conditions which we include in our conceptions of the perfecting of human life. The realisation of human capacities has, in fact, taken a far wider range with us than in the most advanced of ancient states. As actually achieved, it is a much more complete thing than it was two thousand years ago, and every progress achieved opens up a further vista of possibilities still unrealised. In consequence the attainment of true good presents itself to men under new forms. The bettering of human life, though the principle of it is the same now as in the Socratic age, has to be carried on in new ways; and the actual pursuit of true good being thus complicated, reflection on what is implied in the pursuit yields standards of virtue which, though identical in principle with those recognised by Aristotle, are far more comprehensive and wide-reaching in their demands . . .

266. . . . As we have more than once pointed out, while there is one sense in which moral ideas must precede practice, there is another in which they follow and depend upon it. The moral judgment at its best in any age or country – *i.e.* in those persons who are as purely interested in the perfection of mankind and as keenly alive to the conditions of that perfection as is then possible – is still limited in many ways by the degree of progress actually made towards the attainment of that perfection. It was thus the actual condition of women, the actual existence of slavery, the fact that as yet there had been no realisation, even the most elementary, of the idea of there being a single human family with equal rights throughout – it was this that rendered the Greek philosophers incapable of such an idea of chastity as any

unbrutalised English citizen, whatever his practice, if he were honest with himself would acknowledge. To outrage the person of a fellow-citizen, to violate the sanctity of his family rights, was for the Greek as much as for us a blamable intemperance. In the eye of the philosophers it meant a subjection of the higher, or civil, or law-reverencing, man to that lower man in us which knows not law,[1] and they were quite aware that not merely the abstinence from such acts, but the conquest of the lusts which lead to them by a higher interest, was the condition of true virtue. To the spirit of our Lord's re-enactment of the seventh commandment in the Sermon on the Mount, to the substitution of the rule of the pure heart for that of mere outward observance, they were no strangers. What they had still to learn was not that the duty of chastity, like any other, was to be fulfilled from the heart and with a pure will, but the full extent of that duty.

267. And this they failed to appreciate because the practical realis-ation of the possibilities of mankind in society had not then reached a stage in which the proper and equal sacredness of all women as self-determining and self-respecting persons could be understood. Society was not in a state in which the principle that humanity in the person of every one is to be treated always as an end, never merely as a means, could be apprehended in its full universality;[2] and it is this principle alone, however it may be stated, which affords a rational ground for the obligation to chastity as we understand it. The society of modern Christendom, it is needless to say, is far enough from acting upon it, but in its conscience it recognises the principle as it was not recognised in the ancient world. The legal investment of every one with personal rights makes it impossible for one whose mind is open to the claims of others to ignore the wrong of treating a woman as the servant of his pleasures at the cost of her own degra-dation. Though the wrong is still habitually done, it is done under a rebuke of conscience of which a Greek of Aristotle's time, with most women about him in slavery, and without even the capacity (to judge from the writings of the philosophers) for an ideal of society in which this should be otherwise, could not have been sensible. The sensibil-ity could only arise in sequence upon that change in the actual struc-ture of society through which the human person, as such, without distinction of sex, became the subject of rights. That change was itself, indeed, as has been previously pointed out in this treatise, the embodiment of a demand which forms the basis of our moral nature – the demand on the part of the individual for a good which shall be at once his own and the good of the others. But this demand needed to

take effect in laws and institutions which give every one rights against every one before the general conscience could prescribe such a rule of chastity, founded on the sacredness of the persons of women, as we acknowledge. And just as it is through an actual change in the structure of society that our ideal in this matter has come to be more exacting than that of the Greek philosophers, so it is only through a further social change that we can expect a more general conformity to the ideal to be arrived at. Only as the negative equality before the law, which is already established in Christendom, comes to be supplemented by a more positive equality of conditions and a more real possibility for women to make their own career in life, will the rule of chastity, which our consciences acknowledge, become generally enforced in practice through the more universal refusal of women to be parties to its violation.

268. In this matter of chastity, then, there is a serious inferiority of the highest Greek ideal to the highest ideal of Christendom, but it is important to notice where the inferiority lies. We have no right to disparage the Greek ideal on the ground of any inferiority in the motive which the Greek philosophers would have considered the true basis of this, as of every, form of temperance. There can be no higher motive to it than that civil spirit, in the fullest and truest sense, on which they conceived it to rest. But we may fairly disparage their ideal in respect of the kind of life which the realisation of this motive was considered to require. The sexual temperance which they demanded, they demanded on the true ground, but not in full enough measure. In that respect their ideal had certain inevitable shortcomings – inevitable, because no ideal can go more than a certain distance, in the detail of conduct which it requires, beyond the conditions of the given age . . .[3]

270. . . . To an ancient Greek a society composed of a small group of freemen, having recognised claims upon each other and using a much larger body of men with no such recognised claims as instruments in their service, seemed the only possible society. In such an order of things those calls could not be heard which evoke the sacrifices constantly witnessed in the nobler lives of Christendom, sacrifices which would be quite other than they are if they did not involve the renunciation of those 'pleasures of the soul' and 'unmixed pleasures', as they were reckoned in the Platonic psychology,[4] which it did not occur to the philosophers that there could be any occasion in the exercise of the highest virtue to forego. The calls for such sacrifice arise from that enfranchisement of all men which, though in itself but negative in its nature,[5] carries with it for the responsive conscience a

claim on the part of all men to such positive help from all men as is needed to make their freedom real. Where the Greek saw a supply of possibly serviceable labour, having no end or function but to be made really serviceable to the privileged few, the Christian citizen sees a multitude of persons, who in their actual present condition may have no advantage over the slaves of an ancient state,[6] but who in undeveloped possibility, and in the claims which arise out of that possibility, are all that he himself is. Seeing this, he finds a necessity laid upon him. It is no time to enjoy the pleasures of eye and ear, of search for knowledge, of friendly intercourse, of applauded speech or writing, while the mass of men whom we call our brethren, and whom we declare to be meant with us for eternal destinies, are left without the chance, which only the help of others can gain for them, of making themselves in act what in possibility we believe them to be. Interest in the problem of social deliverance, in one or other of the innumerable forms in which it presents itself to us, but in which it could not present itself under such a state of society as that contemplated by the Greek, forbids a surrender to enjoyments which are not incidental to that work of deliverance, whatever the value which they, or the activities to which they [b]are incidental[b], otherwise have.

271. There thus arise those forms of self-denial which did not enter within the horizon of the ancient moralists, and in which, if anywhere, we are entitled to trace the ethical progress of our own age. Questions whether we are better than our fathers are idle enough, but it is not so idle – indeed it is a necessity of our moral nature – to endeavour, through whatever darkness and discouragement, to trace 'some increasing purpose through the ages',[7] of which the gradual fulfilment elicits a fuller exertion of the moral capabilities of individuals. Such a purpose we may not unreasonably hold to be directed to the development of society into a state in which all human beings shall be treated as, actually or in promise, persons – as agents of whom each is an end equally to himself and to others. The idea of a society of free and law-abiding persons, each his own master yet each his brother's keeper, was first definitely formed among the Greeks, and its formation was the condition of all subsequent progress in the direction described; but with them, as has been often enough remarked, it was limited in its application to select groups of men surrounded by populations of aliens and slaves. In its universality, as capable of application to the whole human race, an attempt has first been made to act upon it in modern Christendom. With every advance towards its universal application comes a complication of the necessity, under which the conscientious man feels himself placed, of

sacrificing personal pleasure in satisfaction of the claims of human brotherhood. On the one side the freedom of every one to shift for himself – a freedom to a great extent really secured; on the other, the responsibility of every one for every one, acknowledged by the awakened conscience; these together form a moral situation in which the good citizen has no leisure to think of developing in due proportion his own faculties of enjoyment. The will to be good is not purer or stronger in him than it must have been in any Greek who came near to the philosopher's ideal, but the recognition of new social claims compels its exercise in a new and larger self-denial . . .

279. . . . . As has been previously pointed out, an explicit or reflective ideal[8] of the true good, or of virtue as a habit of will directed to it, can only follow upon a practical pursuit of the good, arising indeed out of the same spiritual demand which is the source of the ideal, but not yet consciously regulated by any theoretical form of it. In this pursuit have arisen institutions and arrangements of life, social requirements and expectations, conventional awards of praise and blame. It is in reflection upon these – in the effort to extract some common meaning from them, to reject what is temporary and accidental in them, while retaining what is essential – that there is formed such an explicit ideal of the good and of virtue as we find in the Greek philosophers. Any one who really conformed to their ideal of virtue would, no doubt, have lived a better life than any one was actually living, because he would have been pursuing, sustainedly and upon a principle of which he was aware, a line of conduct which in fact the best men were only pursuing with frequent lapses through defect either of will or judgment. But in their determinate conception, or filling up, of the ideal, and in their consequent conception of the sort of behaviour in which the virtuous will was to be exhibited, they were necessarily limited by the actual state of human society. 'Human brotherhood' had no meaning for them. They had no adequate notion of the claims in response to which the good will should be exercised. In respect of the institutions and arrangements of life, of the social requirements, etc., just spoken of, a great range of new experience has come into being for us which did not exist for them. The soul of human society has realised its capacities in new ways. We know that it can achieve, because it has done so, much of which the Greek philosophers did not dream.

280. Hence has resulted a change in the ideal of what its full realisation would be, and consequently a change in the conception of what is required from the individual as a contribution to that realisation. In particular the idea has been formed of the possible inclusion of all

men in one society of equals, and much has been actually done towards its realisation. For those citizens of Christendom, on whom the idea of Christendom has taken hold, such a society does actually exist. For them – according to their conscientious conviction, if not according to their practice – mankind is a society of which the members owe reciprocal services to each other, simply as man to man. And the idea of this social unity has been so far realised that the modern state, unlike the ancient, secures equality before the law to all persons living within the territory over which its jurisdiction extends, and in theory at least treats aliens as no less possessed of rights. Thus when we come to interpret that formal definition of the good, as a realisation of the powers of the human soul or the perfecting of man, which is true for us as for Aristotle, into that detail in which alone it can afford guidance for the actions of individuals, the particular injunctions which we derive from it are in many ways different from any that Aristotle could have thought of. For us as for him the good for the individual is to be good, and to be good is to contribute in some way disinterestedly, or for the sake of doing it, to the perfecting of man. But when we ask ourselves how we should thus contribute, or what are the particular forms of virtuous life to which we should aspire, our answer is determined by the consciousness of claims upon us on the part of other men which, as we now see, must be satisfied in order to any perfecting of the human soul, but which were not, and in the then state of society could not be, recognised by the Greek philosophers. It is the consciousness of such claims that makes the real difference between what our consciences require of us, or our standards of virtue, and the requirements or standards which Greek Ethics represent.

281. It must be borne in mind, however, that the social development, which has given the idea of human brotherhood a hold on our consciences such as it could not have for the Greeks, would itself have been impossible but for the action of that idea of the good and of goodness which first found formal expression in the Greek philosophers. It implies interest in an object which is common to all men in the proper sense – in the sense, namely, that there can be no competition for its attainment between man and man; and the only interest that satisfies this condition is the interest, under some form or other, in the perfecting of man or the realisation of the powers of the human soul. It is not to be pretended, indeed, that this in its purity, or apart from other interests, has been the only influence at work in maintaining and extending social union. It is obvious, for instance, that trade has played an important part in bringing and keeping men together;[9]

and trade is the offspring of other interests than that just described. The force of conquest, again, such as that which led to the establishment for some centuries of the *Pax Romana* round the basin of the Mediterranean, has done much to break down estranging demarcations between different groups of men; and conquest has generally originated in selfish passions. But neither trade nor conquest by themselves would have helped to widen the comprehension of political union, to extend the range within which reciprocal claims are recognised of man on man, and ultimately to familiarise men with the idea of human brotherhood. For this there must have been another interest at work, applying the immediate results of trade and conquest to other ends than those which the trader and conqueror had in view; the interest in being good and doing good. Apart from this, other interests might tend to combine certain men for certain purposes and for a time, but because directed to objects which each desires for himself alone and not for another – objects which cannot really be attained in common – they divide in spirit even when they combine temporarily in outward effect; and, sooner or later, the spiritual division must make its outward sign.

BOOK IV: THE APPLICATION OF MORAL PHILOSOPHY
TO THE GUIDANCE OF CONDUCT

Chapter 1: The Practical Value of the Moral Ideal

...298. .... [T]he comparison of our own practice, as we know it on the inner side in relation to the motives and character which it expresses, with an ideal of virtue, is the spring from which morality perpetually renews its life. It is thus that we 'lift up our hearts, and lift them up unto the Lord'.[1] It is thus alone, however insufficient, however 'dimly charactered and slight,'[2] the ideal, that the initiative is given in the individual – and it can be given nowhere else – to any movement which really contributes to the bettering of man. It is thus that he is roused from acquiescence in the standard of mere respectability. No one, indeed, who recognises in their full extent the results of disinterested spiritual effort on the part of a forgotten multitude, which the respectability of any civilised age embodies, or who asks himself what any of us would be but for a sense of what respectability requires, will be disposed to depreciate its value. But the standard of respectability by which any age or country is influenced could never have been attained, if the temper which acquiesces in it had been universal – if no one had been lifted above that acquiescence – in the past. It has been reached through the action of men who, each in his time and turn, have refused to accept the way of living which they found about them and to which, upon the principle of seeking the greater pleasure and avoiding the greater pain, they would naturally have conformed. The conception of a better way of living may have been on a larger or a smaller scale. It may have related to some general reformation of society, or to the change of some particular practice in which the protesting individual had been concerned. But if it has taken effect in any actual elevation of morality, it is because certain men have brought it home to themselves in a contrast between what they should be and what they are, which has awakened the sense of a personal responsibility for improvement.

In so doing they may not have raised the question of personal goodness in the form in which it presents itself to the self-examining conscience of one who lives among a highly moralised society and conforms as a matter of course to its standards. They may not have asked themselves, 'Have we, in doing what was expected of us, been doing it from the right motives?'. In that form the question presupposes the establishment of a definite standard of conventional morality. In the days when such morality was still in making, and in the minds of the forgotten enthusiasts to whom we owe it, this would scarcely be the way in which the contrast between an ideal of virtue and current practice would present itself. Under such conditions it would present itself less as a challenge to purify the heart than as a call to new courses of overt action, the relation of which to motives and character it would not occur to any one to consider. But in principle it is the same operation in the individual of an idea of a perfect life with which his own is contrasted, whether it take the form of a consciousness of personal responsibility for putting an end to some practice which, to a mind awakening to the claims of the human soul, seems unjust or unworthy, or the form of self-interrogation as to the purity of the heart from which a walk and conduct, outwardly correct, proceeds.

299 . . . [I]t is because, to the real reformer, the thought of something which should be done is thus always at the same time the thought of something which he should be and seeks to be, but would not be if he did not do the work, that there is a real unity between the spiritual principle which animates him and that which appears in the self-questioning of the man who, without charging himself with the neglect of any outward duty, without contemplating any particular good work which he might do but has not done, still asks himself whether he has been what he should be in doing what he has done.

300. But, granted the unity of the spiritual principle at work in the two supposed cases, is there any real unity in the effects which it produces in the person of the moral reformer and in the person of the self-questioning 'saint'? In the one case the effect is the recognition and fulfilment of certain specific duties, previously not recognised or not fulfilled, by the moral reformer and those whom he influences. He and they come to deal differently with their fellow-men. But in the other case, if we enquire what specific performance follows from the self-questioning as to purity of heart, we find it difficult to answer. Among the respectable classes of a well-regulated society there is little in outward walk and conduct to distinguish the merely respectable from the most anxiously conscientious. As a rule, it will only be to a man already pretty thoroughly moralised by the best social influences that it will occur to reproach himself with having unworthy motives even in irreproachable conduct; and, as a rule, when such a man comes thus to reproach himself in presence of some ideal of a perfect Will, he will already have been fulfilling, under the feeling that it is expected of him, all the particular duties which the consciousness of such an ideal might otherwise challenge him to fulfil. Unless he has leisure for philanthropy, or a gift of utterance, there will be little in outward act to distinguish his converted state – if we may so describe the state in which he learns to contrast his personal unworthiness with an ideal of holiness – from that of moral self-complacency in which he may have previously been living, and which is the state of most of the dutiful citizens about him.

301. If we could watch him closely enough, indeed, even in outward conduct there would appear to be a difference. Doing the work expected of him 'not with eye-service, as a man-pleaser, but in singleness of heart, as unto the Lord',[3] he will rise to a higher standard of doing it. Into the duties which he is expected to fulfil he will put much more meaning than is put by those who claim their fulfilment, and will always be on the look-out for duties which no one would think the worse of him for not recognising. But in so doing, he probably will not seem to himself to be acting according to a higher standard than those about him. And in fact, although in a certain sense he transcends the 'law of opinion',[4] of social expectation, he only does so by interpreting it according to its higher spirit. That law, being, as we have seen, the result of the past action in human consciousness of an ideal of conduct, will yield different rules according as it is or is not interpreted by a consciousness under the same influence. It speaks with many voices according as men have ears to hear, and the spirit of the conscientious man shows itself in catching the purest of them. He

is like a judge who is perpetually making new law in ostensibly interpreting the old. He extracts the higher meaning out of the recognised social code, giving reality to some requirements which it has hitherto only contained potentially. He feels the necessity of rules of conduct which, though they necessarily arise out of that effort to make human life perfect which has brought conventional morality into existence, are not yet a recognised part of that morality, and thus have no authority with those whose highest motive is a sense of what is expected of them . . .[5]

309. . . . Our conclusion, then, is that the state of mind which is now most naturally expressed by the unspoken questions, 'Have I been what I should be, shall I be what I should be, in doing so and so?', is that in which all moral progress originates. It must have preceded the formation of definite ideals of character, as well as any articulation of the distinction between outward action and its motives. It is no other than the sense of personal responsibility for making the best of themselves in the family, the tribe, or the state, which must have actuated certain persons, many or few, in order to the establishment and recognition of any moral standards whatever. Given such standards, it is the spirit which at once demands from the individual a loyal conformity to them, and disposes him, upon their suggestion, to construct for himself an ideal of virtue, of personal goodness, higher than they explicity contain. The action of such an ideal, in those stages of moral development with which we are now familiar, is the essential condition of all further bettering of human life. Its action is of course partial in various degrees of partiality. It may appear as a zeal for public service on the part of some one not careful enough about the correctness of his own life, or on the other hand in the absorbed religious devotion of the saintly recluse. In the average citizen it may appear only as the influence which makes him conscientious in the discharge of work which he would not suffer except in conscience for neglecting, or as the voice, fitfully heard within, which gives meaning to the announcement of a perfect life lived for him and somehow to be made his own. Taking human society together, its action in one mode supplements its action in another, and the whole sum of its action forms the motive power of true moral development; which means the apprehension on our part, ever widening and ever filling and ever more fully responded to in practice, of our possibilities as men and of the reciprocal claims and duties which those possibilities imply.

Chapter 2: The Practical Value of a Theory of the Moral Ideal

... 311. .... Any value which a true moral theory may have for the direction of conduct depends on its being applied and interpreted by a mind which the ideal, as a practical principal, already actuates. And it will be as well at once to admit that the value must in any case be rather negative than positive; rather in the way of deliverance from the moral anarchy which an apparent conflict between duties equally imperative may bring about, or of providing a safeguard against the pretext which in a speculative age some inadequate and misapplied theory may afford to our selfishness, than in the way of pointing out duties previously ignored. This latter service must always be rendered by the application of a mind, which the ideal possesses, to new situations, to experience newly acquired or newly analysed, rather than by reflection on any theory of the ideal. Whether a mind so possessed and applied is philosophically instructed or no, is in most circumstances matter of indifference. One is sometimes, indeed, tempted to think that Moral Philosophy is only needed to remedy the evils which it has itself caused; that if men were not constrained by a necessity of their intellectual nature to give abstract expression to their ideals, the particular misleading suggestions, against which a true philosophy is needed to guard, would not be forthcoming.

For these suggestions chiefly arise from the inadequacy of the formulae in which requirements imposed by a really valuable ideal have found intellectual expression. Under influence of such an ideal, institutions and rules of life are formed, essential for their time and turn, but not fitted to serve as the foundation of a universally binding prescription. The generalising intellect, however, requires their embodiment in universal rules; and when these are found to conflict with each other, or with some demand of the self-realising spirit which has not yet found expression in a recognised rule, the result is an intellectual perplexity, of which our lower nature is quite ready to take advantage. Blind passion is enlisted in the cause of the several rules. Egoistic interests are ready to turn any of them to account, or to find an excuse for indulgence in what seems to be their neutralisation of each other. Meanwhile perhaps some nobler soul takes up that position of self-outlawry which Wordsworth expresses in the words put into Rob Roy's mouth: –

> We have a passion – make a law,
> Too false to guide us or control!
> And for the law itself we fight
> In bitterness of soul.

And, puzzled, blinded thus, we lose
Distinctions that are plain and few;
These find I graven on my heart;
That tells me what to do.[1]

For deliverance from this state of moral anarchy, which in various forms recurs whenever a sufficient liberation of the intellectual faculties has been attained, there is needed a further pursuit of the same speculative process which have brought it about. As has just been said, no good will come of this, unless under the direction of a genuine interest in the perfecting of man; but, given this interest, it is only through philosophy that it can be made independent of the conflicting, because inadequate, formulae in which duties are presented to it, and saved from distraction between rival authorities, of which the injunctions seem at once absolute and irreconcilable because their origin is not understood.

312. But philosophy itself in its results may yield opportunity to a self-excusing egoism. The formulae in which it expresses conceptions of moral ends and virtues must always be liable to prove misleading, in the absence of that living interest in a practically true ideal which can alone elicit their higher significance. They are generated in intellectual antagonism and must always probably retain the marks of their origin. Those which have served the purpose of enabling men to see behind and beyond their own moral prejudices or some absolute authoritative assertion of a merely relative duty, have not themselves conveyed complete and final truth. If they had done so, it would still have been a truth that could only be made instructive for men's guidance in their moral vocation if applied to the particulars of life by a mind bent on the highest. But in fact the best practical philosophy of any age has never been more than an assertion of partial truths, which had some special present function to fulfil in the deliverance or defence of the human soul. When they have done their work, these truths become insufficient for the expression of the highest practical convictions operating in man, while the speculative intellect, if enlisted in the service of the pleasure-seeking nature, can easily extract excuses from them for evading the cogency of those convictions. But the remedy for this evil is still not to be found in the abandonment of philosophy, but in its further pursuit. The spring of all moral progress, indeed, can still lie nowhere else than in the attraction of heart and will by the ideal of human perfection, and in the practical convictions which arise from it; but philosophy will still be needed as the

interpreter of practical conviction, and it can itself alone provide for
the adequacy of the interpretation.

313. . . . . [A] case of perplexity as to right conduct, if it is to be one
in which philosophy can serve a useful purpose, must be one of *bona
fide* perplexity of conscience. Now the margin within which such perplexities can arise in a Christian society is not really very large. The
effort after an ideal of conduct has so far taken effect in the establishment of a recognised standard of what is due from man to man, that
the articulation of the general imperative, 'Do what is best for mankind',[2] into particular duties is sufficiently clear and full for the ordinary occasions of life. In fulfilling the duties which would be
recognised as belonging to his station in life by any one who considered the matter dispassionately, without bias by personal inclination – in fulfilling them loyally, without shirking, 'not with
eye-service as men pleasers'[3] – we can seldom go wrong; and when we
have done this fully, there will seldom be much more that we can do.
The function of bringing home these duties to the consciences of men
– of helping them to be honest with themselves in their recognition
and interpretation of them – is rather that of the preacher than of the
philosopher. *Speculatively* there is much for the philosopher to do in
examining how that ordering of life has arisen, to which these duties
are relative; what is the history of their recognition; what is the
rationale of them; what is the most correct expression for the practical ideas which underlie them. And, as we shall see, there may be circumstances which give this speculative enquiry a practical value.
These circumstances, however, must always be exceptional. Ordinarily it will be an impertinence for the philosopher to pretend either
to supplement or to supersede those practical directions of conduct
which are supplied by the duties of his station to any one who is free
from any selfish interest in ignoring them . . .

321. We have still . . . to consider the service which philosophy
may render in what we distinguished above as *bona fide* perplexities
of conscience; bona fide perplexities as distinct from those self-
sophistications, born of the pleasure-seeking impulse, in dealing with
which philosophy would be misapplied; perplexities *of conscience* as
distinct from cases like that of Jeannie Deans,[4] where conscience
speaks without ambiguity but is opposed by an impulse in itself noble
and disinterested. In cases of this latter kind philosophy may, as we
have seen, under special conditions of intellectual culture, have an
important service to render; but it will not be in the way of setting
aside apparent contradictions in the deliverance of conscience. It will
rather be in the way of vindicating the real authority of that deliver-

ance against a scepticism which might otherwise take advantage of the discovery that the forms of imagination, in which the deliverance is clothed, are not the same as statements of speculative truth. The kind of practical perplexity which we have now to consider arises not from any doubt as to the authority of conscience, nor from any attempt of selfish inclination to 'dodge' conscience by assuming its disguise, but from the fact that the requirements of conscience seem to be in conflict with each other. However disposed to do what his conscience enjoins, the man finds it difficult to decide what its injunction is.

In the crisis, for instance, through which several European states have recently passed,[5] such a difficulty might naturally occur to a good Catholic who was also a loyal subject. His conscience would seem to enjoin equally obedience to the law of the State, and obedience to the law of the Church. But these laws were in conflict. Which then was he to obey?[6] It is a form of the same difficulty which in earlier days must have occurred to Quakers and Anabaptists, to whom the law derived from Scripture seemed contradictory to that of the State, and to those early Christians for whom the law which they disobeyed in refusing to sacrifice retained any authority. In still earlier times it may have arisen in the form of that conflict between the law of the family and the law of the State, presented in the *Antigone*. Nor is the case really different when the modern citizen, in his capacity as an official or as a soldier, is called upon to help in putting down some revolutionary movement which yet presents itself to his inmost conviction as the cause of 'God and the People'.[7] This case may indeed appear different from those previously noticed, because, while those were cases of conflict between acknowledged authorities, this may seem rather to be one of conflict between private opinion and authority. But if the private opinion is more than a conceit which it is pleasant to air; if it is a source of really conscientious opposition to an authority which equally appeals to the conscience; if, in other words, it is an expression which the ideal of human good gives to itself in the mind of the man who entertains it; then it too rests on a basis of social authority. No individual can make a conscience for himself. He always needs a society to make it for him. A conscientious 'heresy', religious or political, always represents some gradually maturing conviction as to social good, already implicitly involved in the ideas on which the accepted rules of conduct rest, though it may conflict with the formulae in which those ideas have been hitherto authoritatively expressed, and may lead to the overthrow of institutions which have previously contributed to their realisation.

322. In preparation for the times when conscience is thus liable to be divided against itself, much practical service may be rendered by a philosophy which, without depreciating the authority of conscience as such, can explain the origin of its conflicting deliverances, and, without pronouncing unconditionally for either, can direct the soul to the true end to which each in some qualified way is relative. In order to illustrate this in more detail, we will suppose a philosopher, holding the doctrines previously stated in this treatise, to be called upon for counsel in difficulties of the kind just noticed. It will of course occur to every one that the counsel given goes too far back in its reasons, and in its conclusions is of too neutral a kind, to command attention in times of social or religious conflict and revolution. But, though this is so, it might have its effect upon the few who lead the many, in preparing the mind through years of meditation for the days when prompt practical decision is required.

The philosopher, then, will begin by considering how the seeming contradiction in the deliverances of conscience comes about. He will point out that, though there would be no such thing as conscience at all but for the consciousness on the part of the individual that there is an unconditional good which, while independent of his likes and dislikes, is yet *his* good – though this consciousness is as irremovable as morality – yet it does not follow that all the judgments which arise out of this consciousness are unconditionally valid. The several dicta of conscience have had their history. Passing beyond the stage of mere conformity to custom, of mere obedience to persons and powers that be – a conformity and obedience which themselves arise out of an operative, though inarticulate, idea of common good – men have formed more or less general notions of the customs and powers, as entitled to their conformity and obedience. Certain formulae, expressing the nature of the authorities to which obedience is due and their most familiar requirements, have become part of 'the *a priori* furniture' of men's minds, in the sense that they are accepted as valid independently of those lessons of experience which men are conscious of acquiring for themselves. Such are what are commonly called the 'dicta of conscience'. Certain injunctions of family duty, of obedience to the law of the State, of conformity to a law of honour or opinion, have assumed this character. So too in Christendom have certain ordinances of the Church, notwithstanding much variety of opinion as to what constitutes the Church.[8]

323. Now in all such deliverances of conscience the content of the obligation is blended with some conception or imagination of an authority imposing the obligation in a combination which only the trained

analytical intellect can disentangle. Just as to children the duty of speaking the truth seems inseparable from the parental command to do so, so to many a simple Catholic, for instance, the fact that the Church commands him to live cleanly and honestly seems the source of the obligation so to live. To give just measure and to go to Mass are to him homogeneous duties; just as to unenlightened persons in a differently ordered religious community to give just measure and to observe the Sabbath may be so. An abrogation of the authority which imposes the ceremonial obligation would seem to imply a disappearance of the moral obligation as well, because this too in the mind of the individual has become associated with the imagination of an imponent authority, the same as that which enjoins the ceremonial observance. This does not arise from the existence of a Church as a co-ordinate institution with the State. Were there no Church, the difference would only be that, as in the Græco-Roman world, the State would gather to itself the sentiments of which, as it is, the Church seems the more natural object. Moral duties would still be associated with the imagination of an imponent authority, whose injunctions they would be supposed to be, though the authority might be single instead of twofold.

Nor would any considerate member of modern society, even the most enlightened, venture to say that his sense of moral duty was independent of some such imagination of an imponent, however resolutely he might refuse to recognise either the Church or any particular personage as the imponent. If he has ceased to describe himself naturally as a good Catholic or good Churchman, he may still attach significance to the description of himself as a good Christian, and this probably implies to him the recognition of an imponent of obligation in the founder of the Christian society or the author of a Christian revelation. Or if he has ceased to recognise such an imponent, he probably still calls himself a loyal subject; and in so doing expresses the fact that he presents to himself some personal external source – some source other than a spirit working in him – of the law which he obeys; and that he obeys the law, not from fear of pains and penalties, but from reverence for the authority from which he believes it to proceed – as much, therefore, when he might evade it with impunity as when he runs the risk of punishment. Perhaps there may be no ostensible person, no emperor or king, whom he regards as the author of the law which he obeys, and he may accordingly prefer to describe himself as a loyal citizen rather than as a loyal subject,[9] but he is very exceptional if he does not still think of some association of persons, a 'sovereign people', as the authority from which law proceeds. If he ceased to present such an authority to himself, having previously discarded the imagination of Church or King or Divine Lawgiver as imponents of duty, he would be apt to find the obligation, not only of what is local and temporary in positive law, but of what is essential in the moral law, slipping away from him.

324. This imagination of an external imponent, however, is not intrinsically necessary to the consciousness of what we call metaphorically[10] moral law, while it is the source of apparent conflict between different injunctions of conscience. It is the very essence of moral duty to be imposed by a man on himself. The moral duty to obey a positive law, whether a law of the State or of the Church, is imposed not by the author or enforcer of the positive law,[11] but by that spirit of man – not less divine because the spirit of man – which sets before him the ideal of a perfect life, and pronounces obedience to the positive law to be necessary to its realisation. This actual imposition, however, of duties by man upon himself precedes and is independent of a true conception of what duty is. Men who are really a law to themselves, in the sense that it is their idea of an absolute 'should be', of some perfection to be realised in and by them, that is the source of the general rule of life which they observe, are yet unable to present that rule to themselves as anything else than the injunction of some external authority. It is this state of mind that renders them liable to the perplexities of conscience described, in which duties appear to conflict with each other.

There is no such thing really as a conflict of duties. A man's duty under any particular set of circumstances is always one, though the conditions of the case may be so complicated and obscure as to make it difficult to decide what the duty really is. That which we are apt to call a conflict of duties is really a competition of reverences for imagined imponents of duty, whose injunctions, actual or supposed, do not agree. A woman perhaps finds herself directed to act in one way by her father, in another by her confessor. A citizen may find himself similarly distracted between the law of the State and that of the Church; or between the ordinance of an ostensible sovereign and that of a revolutionary committee, claiming to act in the name of God and the People. In such cases, if the conscience were clear of prepossession in favour of this authority or that, and were simply prepared to recognise as duty the course which contributes most to the perfect life, it might yet be difficult enough to ascertain what this course of action would be, though there would be no doubt that the one duty was to pursue that course of action when ascertained. But the actual perplexity of conscience in such cases commonly arises not from this difficulty, but from the habit of identifying duty with injunctions given by external authorities, and from the fact that in the supposed case the injunctions so given are inconsistent with each other.

325. Now the task of the moral philosopher in regard to such cases would be a comparatively easy one if it simply consisted in trying to rid a man of his illusions of conscience; if he had merely to point out the work of imagination in ascribing the essential duties which conscience enjoins to an external imponent, and to show that the apparent conflict of duties is in fact merely a conflict between certain external authorities which are wrongly supposed to impose duties, whereas all that a purely external authority can impose is a command enforced by fear. If the philosopher aims at no more than this, he may succeed in his work, but its value will be doubtful. It may prove easier to convince men that duties in the moral sense cannot be imposed from without than, when this has been shown, to maintain the conviction that they exist at all. If the result of the philosopher's work is to popularise the notion that the authorities to which men have chiefly looked as imponents of duties are merely powers able to induce obedience to their commands by threat of punishment for disobedience, without substitution of any new reverence for that which must be withdrawn from the authorities so regarded, we shall have nothing to thank him for. In truth the phrase 'external authority', as applied to the imagined imponents of duty, involves something of a contradiction. If they were merely external, they would not be authorities, for an authority implies, on the part of the man to whom it is an authority, a conception of its having a claim upon his obedience; and this again implies that his obedience to it is a self-imposed obedience – an obedience which commends itself to his reason as good, irrespectively of penalties attached to disobedience. The authority, in being recognised as an authority, has ceased to be a mere source of commands enforced by fear of punishment for their violation, and in that sense to be merely external. Its injunctions now commend themselves to the subject of them, not indeed as proceeding from a spirit which is his own or himself, but as directed to the attainment of an end in which the subject is interested on his own account; which is, and is known by him to be, his true good. How the several injunctions in detail contribute to such an end he does not see, but he trusts the authority from which they proceed to have it more completely in view than he can himself. It is thus that the Church is an authority to the good Catholic, the State to the good citizen, the Bible to the orthodox Protestant. In each case the acknowledgment of the authority has become one and the same thing with the individual's presentation to

himself of a true good, at once his own and the good of others, which it is his business to pursue.

326. Now it would be a blundering and reckless procedure on the part of the moral philosopher, if he were first to construe too literally the language in which these authorities are described, so to speak, from without for rhetorical or logical purposes – to take it as if it represented their true spiritual import for those who acknowledge them – and then, in his hurry to assert the truth that a moral obligation cannot be imposed from without, were to seek to dethrone them from their place in the moral imagination, and to substitute for them an improvised conscience that should make its own laws *de novo* from within. It must rather be his object, without setting aside any of the established authorities which have acquired a hold on the conscience, to awaken such an understanding of the impulse after an ideal of conduct which, without being understood, has expressed itself in these authorities, as may gradually render men independent of the mode of its authoritative expression. One who has learnt this lesson will have a rationale of the various duties presented to him in the name of Cæsar or of God, which will help him to distinguish what is essential in the duties from the form of their imposition, and to guide himself by looking to the common end to which they are alike relative. Should an occasion arise when the duties seem to conflict, he will be prepared for the discovery that the conflict is not really between duties, but between powers invested by the imagination with the character of imponents of duty. He will be able to stand this discovery without moral deterioration, because he has learnt to fix his eye on the moral end or function – the function in the way of furthering perfection of conduct – served by the authorities which he has been bred to acknowledge. He can thus find in that end, or in the Spirit whose self-communication renders him capable of seeking it, a fit object for all the reverences claimed by those authorities, and which he now discovers to be due to them only by a derived and limited title.

327. It may thus fall to the moral philosopher, under certain conditions of society and of intellectual movement, to render an important practical service. But he will render it simply by fulfilling with the utmost possible completeness his proper work of analysis. As a *moral* philosopher he analyses human conduct; the motives which it expresses, the spiritual endowments implied in it, the history of thought, habits and institutions through which it has come to be what it is. He does not understand his business as a philosopher, if he claims to do more than this. He will not take it for a reproach to be reminded that no philosopher can supply a 'moral dynamic'. The pre-

tension to do so he would regard as a great impertinence. He finds moral dynamic enough in the actual spiritual nature of man, when that nature is regarded, as it is his business to regard it, not merely in its hitherto performance, but in its intrinsic possibilities. If he cannot help wishing for more, that is an incident of the very aspiration after perfection of conduct which constitutes the dynamic. His immediate business as a philosopher is not to strengthen or heighten this aspiration, much less to bring it into existence, but to understand it. As a man and a citizen, indeed, it is his function to serve as its organ; to give effect to it in his own conduct, to assist in communicating it to others. And since in being a philosopher he does not cease to be a man and a citizen, he will rejoice that the analysis, which alone forms his employment as a philosopher, should incidentally serve a purpose subordinate to the 'moral dynamic' – that it should help to remove any obstacle to the effort of the human soul after a perfect life.

The distraction of conscience, caused, as we have seen, by competition of reverences for authorities whose injunctions come into conflict with each other, may form such an obstacle. Its outward effect may sometimes be a paralysis of action; sometimes, on the other hand, hasty and embittered action in opposition to one of the causes or authorities between the claims of which conscience is perplexed – action hasty and embittered for the very reason that the agent is afraid to face the consequence of dispassionate enquiry into the validity of the claims to which he blindly submits. So far as the impediment to the highest living, to the free development of human capabilities, is of this kind, the philosopher by mere thoroughness and completeness of ethical analysis may help to remove it. By giving the most adequate account possible of the moral ideal; by considering the process through which the institutions and rules of life, of which we acknowledged the authority, have arisen out of the effort, however blindly directed, after such an ideal and have in their several measures contributed to its realisation; by showing that conscience in the individual, while owing its education to those institutions and rules, is not properly the mere organ or any or all of them, but may freely and in its own right apprehend the ideal of which they are more or less inadequate expressions; by thus doing his proper work as a philosopher of morals, he may help the soul to rise above the region of distraction between competing authorities, or between authorities and an inner law, to a region in which it can harmonise all the authorities by looking to the end to which they, or whatever is really authoritative in them, no less than the inner law, are alike relative.

328. That the soul, however, should derive any such benefit from

philosophy implies a previous discipline which cannot be derived
from philosophy but only from conduct regulated by the authorities
which philosophy teaches it to understand. It is a complaint as old as
the time of Plato that, in learning to seek for the rationale of the rules
which they are trained to obey – to enquire what is the ideal of human
good, which these rules serve and are justified by serving – men come
to find excuses for disregarding them. And, no doubt, as Plato saw,
till the character is set in the direction of the ideal, a theory of the
ideal can be of no value for the improvement of conduct in any sense.
It may be doubted, indeed, whether the apparent mischief, which
arises in a speculative age from the habit of asking a reason why for
the rules of respectability, does more than affect the excuses made for
acts of self-indulgence of which men, innocent of criticism or speculation, would equally be guilty. But, however this may be, it remains
true that the value of the Dialectic which asks and gives such an
account of ideal good as at once justifies and limits obedience to practical authorities, is conditional upon its finding in the individual a
well-formed habitual morality.

When it does so, it may influence life for good, by enlisting in the
real service of mankind the zeal which would otherwise become a
mis-directed loyalty or a spirit of unprofitable rebellion. It will teach
a man to question the absoluteness of the authorities which speak in
the name of Cæsar and of God – not with a view to shirking the precepts of either in the interest of his own pleasures, but in order that he
may not be led by either into a 'conscientious' opposition to the other,
obstructive to the work of which the promotion in different ways is
the true function of each. When he finds that the requirements of
Church or State, the observances of conventional morality or conventional religion, are in conflict with what some plead as their conscientious convictions, it will make him watchful to ascertain whether
these new convictions may not represent a truer effort after the
highest ideal than that embodied in the authorities which seek to suppress them. On the other hand, when he finds some conviction of his
own in conflict with authority, it will teach him not indeed to conceal
it for fear of inconvenient consequences, but to suppress all pride in it
as if it were an achievement of his own; to regard it as proceeding, so
far as it is good for anything, from the operation of the same practical
reason in society which has given rise to the authorities with which
his conviction brings him into collision. So regarding it, he will be
respectful of the prejudices which he offends by expressing it; careful
to eschew support which might be due not to an appreciation of what
is good in the new conviction, but to mere aversion from the check

put upon self-will by the authorities impugned; patient of opposition, and, in case of failure, ready to admit that there is more
wisdom than he understood in the conventions which have been too
strong for him.[12]

6

Undergraduate Essays*

═══

A. THE EFFECT OF COMMERCE ON THE MIND OF A NATION

The influence of commerce, as a national pursuit, having in most countries arisen subsequently to the diffusion of Christianity, it is sometimes difficult to separate the operations of one on the mind of a nation from those of the other. This is especially the case in the tendency to regard men as originally and practically equal, and to break down distinctions of class, which arises, to a certain extent, from commerce no less than from Christianity.[1] The pursuits of commerce and the fortunes of those engaged in it afford so clear and practical a test of the truth that, even in a worldly point of view, the value of a man resides in what he does for himself,[2] that it cannot fail to diminish the regard paid to all adventitious distinctions, except those of wealth which may enable a man to turn his innate powers to more advantageous account. And thus it is that it breaks down all notions of chivalry and feudal allegiance, for men will soon cease to render homage to one whom they equal or surpass in the power of obtaining all the appliances of life, and who yet has no other claim to their homage, while he himself will find the enjoyments, which commerce enables his superior wealth to acquire, an ample compensation for the gratification he might derive from the submission of dependents to his will.[3] And thus, in the minds of the vulgar, it substitutes a reverence for wealth for a reverence paid to birth and titles. And on the whole the substitution is probably advantageous, for the acquisition of wealth requires at any rate industry, self-control, and intelligence – qualities to which hereditary power has not generally been found to conduce – and at the same time demands that ability in its subordinate agents, and holds before them that hope of gaining commercial power themselves, which renders them at once intelligent and independent.[4] On the other hand it must be allowed that the accumulation of larger properties without any connection with the land has a tendency to absorb men in the pursuit of their own individual interests to the exclusion of those of the commonwealth, for one who has risen to wealth by foreign trade without apparently drawing on his own country naturally forgets her welfare in the plenitude and isolation of his own good-fortune, while the landowner can hardly fail to become, as it were, part and parcel of his country, when he seems to derive all that he has from its very soil. The magnitude of this evil may be learnt from the fall of the Italian Republics which at length became mere collections of individuals and ceased to be states, and it was probably with a view to strengthen as much as possible the feeling of nationality that commerce was discouraged among the Jews, and the land prevented from settling into a few hands.[5] It seems to be a modification of this feeling among us which has led to the jealousy of any centralization and the desire of achieving everything by private enterprise which is especially apparent in our most commercial districts.[6] But whatever may [be] the form or extent of this evil, it is more than counterbalanced by the perpetual spring of hope which commerce affords to every member of the community, and without which the vigour of national life would soon wither away.[7] It is not only a necessary stimulant to all material improvement, but an indispensable condition of any national cultivation of the intellect. For though there may always be some who seek learning for its own sake, yet the mass of men will only value it in its obvious application to the common affairs of life, and it is in this application that a constant aspiration to an higher sphere in life will constantly demand its aid.[8] The mere drudge of the soil who looks for nothing beyond the daily toil, which his fathers before him have undergone, and which his ignorance is sufficient to fulfil, is naturally content with his ignorance; but the trader who sees new fields of enterprise daily opening out before him, which he requires new stores of learning to explore, is naturally impelled to seek these stores, and communicates his impulse to his subordinate agents. But this same demand for knowledge in the common affairs of life, which commerce occasions, and the complexity of human action and energy which also arises from it, calls away minds of the higher stamp from those abstract branches of learning and speculation, which flourished in the ancient nations where civilization was found apart from commerce.[9] And in like manner the fine arts can never be expected to flourish in a commercial community, where men see before them in actual exertion those representations of human power and greatness which the ancients sought to exhibit in Sculpture. On the other hand the intellectual advantages of commerce are obviously great in giving the mass of men a practical knowledge of mankind at large and extending their view beyond the narrow circle of their own immediate observation,[10]

and in the regularity and calmness of thought, which they must in
some degree gain from the knowledge that their trading transactions
are governed by a natural law; while caprice and passion naturally
follow from the habit of making no provision for the morrow which
commerce tends to prevent.[11]

B. LOYALTY

In no depth of their debasement have men consented to confine the
range of the mind within the limits of the fleshy tabernacle, which is
the seat of its imprisonment.[1] The tendency to form societies, and the
reverence for super-natural beings, which even in the darkest days
have never been obliterated, are evidences that men were dimly conscious, at once, that their minds were not isolated mechanisms, but
pervaded with a life properly the same in every part, and that this life
in its turn has its foundations in the life of an higher being.[2] It is in
these instincts that loyalty has its origin, but before they attain to so
high a manifestation, they display their power in several lower forms
of the same principle. As the earliest and rudest of these we may perhaps reckon the love of home, which we find in Homer as a leading
characteristic of the early Greeks, and which we still attribute to
Indians and savage tribes. For this love of home was a great deal more
than a mere phrenological organ of habitatiousness. It could never
have bound men together as it did, had it not been closely connected
with reverence for the local or domestic shrine of God – 'the God that
maketh men to be of one mind in a house' – and with some unconscious notion of the common brotherhood of men; as displayed in
their clinging to a common hearth.[3] An higher manifestation of the
same feeling may be found in chivalry and the feudal system, for the
supposition of divine right in the king or chieftan shows that it had
other than earthly sanctions, and the acknowledgement of reciprocal
obligations between baron and retainer betokens the sense of our
common life. I call it 'an higher manifestation' than the love of home,
for ideally it requires obedience to a truly superior will, and embodies
a reverence for plighted faith. But actually a superior will was
generally confounded with a greater power of violence, faith was
often plighted for an evil end, and the reverence for it was blind and
fitful. Chivalry therefore required to be superseded by Loyalty,
which demands the same reverence and obedience regulated and controlled by being directed towards a settled law – a law which at once
proceeds from and has for its object the common nature of man, and
is therefore endowed with the authority of the Creator of that nature.

Loyalty is indeed by etymology 'legality', but its meaning has a far wider scope, for we should not have two words to signify precisely the same thing. By 'Loyalty' we mean indeed the observance of Law, but of its spirit rather than its letter – not so much the observance of laws as of the essence of Law generally, though the latter always implies the former except in those rare cases where they come actually in contact. And as Loyalty is not so much a course of outward action as an inward disposition of the mind, so it cannot consist merely in an obedience to law without a reverent consciousness of its authority, origin, and object. But it is clear that such a consciousness can only dwell in higher and more religious minds than are commonly found among men, though all, except the depraved and rebellious, feel instinctively that obedience is due to some power on earth, as the representation of the Divine authority among the affairs of men.[4] If this feeling were ever coupled with a due appreciation of human worth, it would become, I suppose, a genuine hero-worship,[5] and in our own day we may see how its accidental association with the respect due to the weaker sex prevents its complete debasement. But in their blindness, men often connect it with subjection to an existing potentate, and bow down before a king or Pope, to whom obedience may indeed in some cases be due, but not such obedience, or rather idol-worship, as they render, in irreverent forgetfulness of the source and necessary conditions of his authority. This then is mis-called loyalty, and when the object of it has ceased (as he soon must do under such influences) to bear any, the faintest, semblance of that original, whence alone can emanate the proper objects of loyalty, it too loses its semblance of the true principle of obedience, till men cry in passionate despair that there is no true law to control the impulses of the people but the fitful expression of those impulses themselves.

I spoke of chivalry, or the principle of adherence to individuals under the obligations of the law of Honour, as properly superseded by Loyalty, or the principle of reverence for law. As connected with the misplaced obedience to *a*existing*a* potentates, we may observe the way in which chivalry has been apt to reassert its claims. In the progress of mankind the law of honour is prior to that of justice, and the reverence of the persons of rulers to that of the hidden powers which they represent; nor will the feelings that have once prevailed among men, readily give up their ground. They linger in secret strength, though no longer dominant, and the written laws, which embody them, generally remain to encumber the spirit of the new generation. Thus throughout modern english history we may trace the spirit of chivalry, gradually vanishing before the advancing strength of loyalty, but supported in many cases by the letter of laws which have remained over from its days of dominant power. In the time of Charles I, if one might venture to classify parties whose motives were so mixed, one would see on the royal side the cavaliers, as the representatives of chivalry, supported by the conscientious adherents to the letter of the law, ranged against the truly loyal men who were fighting for the rules of universal law, as displayed in the spirit of English law and English religion.[6] For obedience to the royal power is but an accident of loyalty. We should indeed be loyal to the king, but only as the symbol of law – and to the Church, but only as the symbol of spiritual government. If the symbol ceases to be such, our loyalty towards it is at an end. The truly loyal man is not he who shouts for king and constitution, or who yields a blind obedience to the routine of existing institutions, but he who looks beyond them to the universal law of the common reason of men, and in reverence for this yields a willing and hearty obedience to the rules in which it embodies itself for the establishment of right dealing in society– rules which, except so far as they have been distorted by violence, have only varied to adapt themselves to the varying affairs of men.[7] And if loyalty is the natural enemy of tyranny, as that which ignores the law founded in the reason of which all are partakers, so it is no less opposed to a selfish seeking for individual gain. Recognising the duty owed by all to the supreme power and common good of the state, the loyal man is bound to his fellow-citizens in the unity of a common object, which gives to the private pursuits of his daily life their value and spiritual meaning.

C. LEGISLATIVE INTERFERENCE IN MORAL MATTERS

Many erroneous notions have been formed on this subject from false analogies between a Greek *polis* and a modern state.[1] We still speak of a nation as of a united whole, pervaded by a spirit 'one and indivisible', of which government is the controlling conscience, and legislation the highest expression. Such language is borrowed from the ancient conception of a *polis*. A Greek state might fairly be regarded as an intensified and expanded individual.[2] Its members, living generally within the narrow limits of a city wall, would be for the most part personally known to each other; sprung from a common father, of whom they were constantly reminded, with a common political-religion and a common state-property to defend, and at the same time without a spiritual religion to separate their objects in life, they had no essentially antagonistic interests. Such strife as there was among them would seem to arise from the various faculties of the same mind working and counter-working to the same end. Government might control the various members of society, just as conscience or self-love directs the exercise of the several affections to the good of the whole man.[3] Now, whatever may be our ideal of the ultimate perfection of society, we must admit that actually such language can only be applied by a kind of fiction to a modern state. Instead of being confined to the walls of a single city, a modern state generally extends over districts, in which the mere nature of the soil necessitates great diversity of character. Not only are its members descended from different races, of which indelible traces remain in the distinctions of classes, but it comprehends within itself two castes, whose interests seem essentially antagonistic.[4] In Greece, where the hired labourers were slaves destitute of personal rights, all the citizens either worked, or employed work, on their own account, and thus there was a commercial element of unity in the state. But with us, now that all men alike are recognised as members of the state, there is a perpetual internal struggle between those who have and those who wish to take, which seems irreconcilably to divide the mind of a nation. And, above and beyond all these causes of social strife, we live under the influence of a religion, which was sent as a sword upon the earth – which not only separates the many from the few, and sect from sect, by a barrier which it would seem spiritually suicidal to pass, but also sets a gulf between the inner life of the individual and his life in society. Hence it results that all analogies drawn between the relation of the state to its members and that of the father to his family, or the conscience to the faculties of the mind, are in these days essentially fallacious. There is nothing in the mind of a father which does not exist, potentially or actually, in the minds of his children. They conform to his will with sympathetic obedience, knowing that is the result of thoughts and feelings which are the same as their own, only stronger and more fully trained. But the workings and counter-workings of the conflicting forces in a nation produce a result which has no kindred with anything in the mind of the individual. We *see* the result in the shape of government and law, but we can form no conception of millions of diverse minds working to produce it. Hence the law of society presents itself to the individual as a positive rule imposed *ab extra*, not as an act of human will with which he can sympathise.[5] On the other hand, the analogy drawn from the relation of the mind to its several faculties is inconsistent with the fact that the deepest element in the life of the individual has no place in the

state. Thus we begin to see some limits of the ground on which the
legislator may not dare to tread. There are thoughts and feelings in
the individual with which only family authority may interfere, and
others still deeper with which no stranger intermeddleth[6] – which are
private to himself and God. This domain of private thought has been
much widened by Christianity. In ancient times religion was almost
entirely an outward thing, and there was no antagonism between the
law of society and that of the individual conscience. But with the
introduction of a spiritual religion began the first contest between the
apparent interests of social order and morality and the inward inspiration of 'a few poor men'.[7] Then, as now, religion and morals were so
inwoven with each other, that uniform interference with the one
involved special interference with the other, and it seemed necessary
for the preservation of society to crush the influence which was ultimately to regenerate it. The age of persecution has passed away, but
there are still men who, placing the state above the individual, would
prescribe limits to the activities both of genius and religion for the
moral good of society at large. But by such limitations society would
only rivet the chains of its own bondage. It would then indeed
become a lifeless mechanism, carried along the path of necessity by
the mere force of circumstances, and submitting unresistingly to the
effects of its past history or of physical geography. It is only the spiritual freedom of the few that releases it in any degree from this bondage. Once or twice in a century there arises some great reformer,
literary or religious, who seems placed above the earth and born of
heaven alone, and who thus exercises an independent influence on
the circumstances and destiny of mankind.[8] Such a man can scarcely
conform to the ordinary manners of man, or to the *status quo* of
society. Often he exercises rather freely the privileges of Christian
liberty. Now if the state is to interfere at all with morals, it can only
give legal effect to the moral tone of society at large, and if it thus
interferes to any wide extent, it must come in contact with such a
newly-enlightened enthusiast, and the true moral reformer becomes
an offender against state-morality. If society succeed in crushing him
it is at its own cost; if it does not, it will at any rate drive him into
fanaticism. But it would be wrong to suppose, because legislative
interference with morality must be thus narrowly limited, that therefore the state is merely a policeman on a grand scale, and its only end
is the protection of life and property against force and fraud. No state
has ever been found to confine itself to these ends; the institution of
inheritance and of property in natural production cannot be
explained as promoting them, but only as tending to the general wel-

fare of mankind. If we are told that civil rewards and penalties exist not for the punishment of evil-doers and the praise of them that do well, but only for the preservation of society, we may ask what right society has to preserve itself by such means, unless it exists for moral ends? And if society exists for such ends, so also does the state, which is but society gathered into a unit by certain common laws and institutions. But a confusion arises from identifying it with the civil government, and regarding secular laws, written on sheep-skin, as its sole expression. In reality the state in modern times operates through three organs – the civil government, the national church,[9] and the voice or usage of society. None of these powers – neither the government by legislative enactments, nor the church by excommunication, nor society by conventional exclusion – should restrain the freedom of the individual's inner life, or interfere with family authority, nor should any one of them trespass on the ground properly occupied by the other. What that ground is should be determined by experience and expediency. From the impossibility of dealing with particulars by legislation, it is best that the civil government should confine itself, in the way of repressing immorality, to the punishment of distinct overt acts, which prove necessarily and of themselves the guilt of the person who commits them, leaving other offences to the reprobation of society; and in the way of promoting morality, should merely remove obstacles which impede the free action of the church or religious bodies.[10] It is idle to say that the state refuses 'to educate her children' merely because it is found by experience (supposing such to be the case) that the voluntary action of society serves the purpose better than the interference of the civil government. The object of the civil government, in its strict sense, is to give full play to the energies, and fair room for the development, of the individual; direct interference has generally the effect of cramping the energies both of the individuals whom it is intended to benefit and of those who would otherwise confer the benefit themselves.[11]

7

Fragments on Moral and
Political Philosophy

═══

A. NOTES ON MORAL PHILOSOPHY*

1. Moral philosophy regards man in three attitudes: (1) as related to himself; (2) as related to another, but this other is also, as a person, related to self; (3) as related to himself in relation to others – as through relation to others gaining realization of the relation to himself, which is otherwise merely formal.[1]

An idea [is] *formal*, when there is no existence corresponding to it, so [the] idea of [the] absolute is *formal* [since there is] no phenomenon corresponding to it. But without [the] action of this idea, [there would be] no accounting for that [effort?] to reduce experience to a unity, without which [there can be] no knowledge.[2]

The determination *of* self – the making of oneself an object to oneself – though formal, [is the] foundation of all morality.[3] It is [the] differential between [the] natural and [the] moral. It is [the] condition of vice, for without it appetite would be simple want, which, when filled, would cease. There could be no excess unless man consciously presented to himself [the] gratification of appetite as [the] thing to be lived for... [W]ith mere wants [or] appetites [there can be] no possibility of virtue or vice, because [there are] no permanent objects [of desire]... [D]esire [must be desire for a] desired thing.[4]

This relation to self – active self-consciousness – gives man [a] conception of his good as a whole.[5] As it is [the] condition of conflict of desires, so of [the adjustment] of this conflict, of [the] subjection of immediate desire to [the] general good of the man.

This relation [is] called reason (which in Plato & Aristotle appears rather as consciousness of [the] universal than consciousness of self, but this comes to the same[6]). It rules the man, because it constitutes him [as] man – because it is that which, will he or will he [not?], makes his appetite and sensitive experience *a system*. (This makes it impossible to sin and have done with it. [It] gives [a] bilious act [a] permanent hold on [the] self-consciousness.[7] [It is therefore the] foundation of rational, as opposed to animal, habits.)

[The] virtuous [man] and [the] vicious man [is] each [an] object to himself. [The] question is, what *sort* of self is it that is the object: [the] 'empirical' or [the] 'ideal', [the] self as [the] subject of pleasures and pains, or [the] self as *free*? [There is] over and above [the] actual experience of one's acts and sufferings, a consciousness of an infinite potentiality.[8] For realisation of this, [the] man who 'lives for duty' lives. If it were actually realised [it would] no longer [be] *'duty'*. The 'should be' would be lost in the *'is'*.

2. [The] 'relation of man to himself' is that which philosophy is first able to detach from [the] complexity of life; [that is the] relation of [the] whole man to [his] subject members, of reason to desire. This [is] Platonic. In Plato, also, [is found the] conception of [a] distinction between true self and false [self, between] ideal and empirical ego, [although in Plato this distinction is not clearly formulated]. Generally, [a] vicious act [is] represented as coming from mere appetite (in which case it would be instinctive), not as acts of the man, i.e. of reason, at all.[9] Platonic philosophy has no place for [the] relation of individual wills to each other.

Aristotle comes nearer to [the] recognition of this relation, in [his] polemic against communism and [the] account of *tou adikein* [wrongdoing] as essentially consisting in violation of [the] will of another.[10] But [does he have] any corresponding theory [of the] State? [The] State, it is true, [is] sometimes spoken of as having for its object *autarchein* [the self-sufficiency] of [the] individual, and again as educating [the] individual. But generally [the State is] treated by Aristotle very much in [the] Platonic way, as [an] enlarged man, as a substance constituted by inter-relations of other independent substances.[11]

[The] relation of [the] individual to [him-]self in [the] midst of other individuals so related [is the] basis of [the] conception of rights. This [however is] an *absract* conception, i.e. it makes [an] abstraction of [the] real feelings which men have towards each other, of sympathy, in virtue of which one man enters *into* another, of [the] positive will of one man to benefit another.[12] [This abstract conception is] so far untrue, in [the] sense of being *inadequate*; men have [never] been to each other in this merely abstract [relationship], hence [the] fallacy of [the] doctrine of 'social contract' etc.[13]

At [the] same time, [the] relation of right [is the] basis of [the] moral relation (justice [comes] before generosity). [The relationship of individuals as right bearers is the] basis of moral relationships . . . As with Aristotle *phitōn ontōn ouden dei dikaiosunēs* [those who are friends have no need of justice][14] so [the] moral relation supersedes [the] legal – supersedes it, however, only as retaining it in [a] higher form; i.e. [the] relation of father to child, of [MS illegible] master to slave [is] not *moral* . . . Moral [is the] opposite of [natural].[15]

With most men, as strangers, one can only deal on [a] footing of *right*. But in such dealing the good man respects [the] right of others not merely as [a] condition of his own right being respected, but as [an] *allos autis* [other self] – as that which he has taken into himself and loves as himself. [There is] no sentiment of personal love for the strangers, but one of loyalty to a rational law.[16] At the same time [however, he] actively – positively – seeks [the] good of strangers. Though [it is] impossible *sunaisthanesthai* [to share experience in common], and *sumpaschein* [to undergo a common fate with them], yet [it is] possible *sunnoein* [to have understanding in common with them]: so far they are the *allos autis*. [The] order of [the] three relations specified [is] one of philosophical detachment – of explicit recognition – not of historical development; [they] really all exist together.

3. In what sense is [the] 'state [the] realization of freedom' and with it of [the] idea of duty?[17] We find ourselves as [a] matter of fact determined by this or that want. But even in doing [an] act prompted by want, *I* do it. The idea of self-determination [is] active. [It] appears: (1) in [the] choice between pleasures (*satisfactions*). If pleasures were mere satisfactions of want this would not be [so]. They are relative to character. 'Always obey [the] stronger motive', but my character makes it stronger, and character (as opposed to trained instinct) could not be formed without [the] action of *self*, at once distinguishing itself from wants and pleasures which determine it, and forming them to a totality. (A man's character [is the] result of all his past experiences. His experiences could not act with this cumulative force, unless there were the infinitely elastic element called self, not subject to limitations of quantity, in which each experience is preserved as [a] qualifying agent upon every other.[18])

[It appears] (2) in [the] idea of duty, of determination by something equally universal with self. Duty [is] simply [the] negative of particular motives. 'Act for Duty's sake.' But what is this? It is *not* to act for any particular pleasure or for [a] sum of pleasures. [The] idea [is] not therefore inoperative. (Even in *theories* which profess to be founded on its rejection it appears – in [the] Cyrenaic reduction of pleasures to an abstraction, in [the] Epicurean systematization of it as *ataraxia* [imperturbability], in [the] modern effort to ascertain [the] uniformity of pleasures, in [the] Utilitarian which makes [the] object to each man not his own pleasure but that of the greatest number.)[19] From [the] same *"relation of man to himself"*, from which issues [the] idea of duty, it results that his appetites become affections, and his wants a system of permanent relations. These affections and relations [are the] basis [of] sacred customs, on which rests law, on which again rests social morality. We are conscious of our consciousness; we not merely have conscious appetite, involving relation to another, but we present this consciousness as [an] object to ourselves and make it [the] object of our will, and with it not merely our own pleasures but that of another.

Thus for appetite, we have [an] active impulse towards [the] satisfaction of another as inseparable from our own, [e.g.] a basis for family custom. So [too] with wants. Each implies relation to [an] other, which is presented as [a] permanent object of consciousness. Conscious of his own universality, man seeks to organise these relations. Struggling for a *real* freedom, answering to idea, he seeks by uniform satisfaction of wants to make himself independent of this or that particular person or thing.

Thus the systematic custom and law of society [is] really [a] projection or expression of [the] universality of self, though never fully adequate. In being determined by it, man [is] determined by self, [and] thus realizes [the] idea of duty. But this implies that conforming to custom etc. be loyal, i.e. for its own sake, and according to [the] spirit not to [the] letter.[20]

B. NOTES ON ANCIENT AND MODERN POLITICAL ECONOMY*

1. [There are] connections between the doctrines of ancient political philosophy on three points, [viz.] population, property, [the] regulation of 'private life' by the state.[1]

Population. (a) [There is an] apprehension of [the] state growing too big. A state [in] which all active members could not meet on occasion in one marketplace had not [the] necessary bond of unity.[2] [The] representative system [was] not yet 'invented'; [and would, in any case, be] unsuited to [the] idea of [the] state as resting, not on [the] adjustment of interests, but on [a] common unity of sentiment.

(b) [The ancients] misunderstood [the] nature of wealth. [They were] apt to think of it as a fixed quantity, of which if one had more, another must have less, and of which, as there became more persons to divide it, each must have less.[3] [They] did not consider that,

labour being potential wealth, more labour, so long as it has [i] means
of subsistence, [ii] material to work upon, means more wealth; and
that with freedom of trade, though there is [an] ultimate possibility
of [the] world getting too full, there is virtually no limit to [the]
extension of [i] and [ii] except such as competition of other states,
more favourably situate for obtaining them, from time to time furnishes.[4] [There are] no economical reasons, e.g. why with perfect
[free trade?] Athens should not have had as large a population as
there was living room for, except [the] competition of other countries
more favourably situate for obtaining food and materials of industry,
and for exchanging the latter. This consideration did not [however]
come within [the] horizon of ancient philosophy, and if it had, it
would not have removed all their difficulties about population,
[because:] [i] Such a state of things [was] incompatible with [the]
autarkeia [self-sufficiency] of the state. [The] *autarkeia* of [the] individual or [the] *kōmē* [(unwalled) village] does not imply independence of other individuals or *kōmai* [villages]; only in [the] *state* is
[the] individual *autarchēs* [self-sufficient] – *satisfied*. But this (in
turn) implies that [the] state must not in its turn be dependent on
other states. [ii] It implies either [a] dangerous mass of slave-labour,
or multitudes of free *technitai* [artisans] unfit for political life. [iii]
To [the] ancient philosopher, looking at [the] life he saw about him it
seemed as if [the] accession of wealth meant greater antagonism of
penia [poverty] to *ploutos* [riches] – [a] few very rich, [the] multitude very poor. [They therefore failed to realise that] where labour
[is] *really* free (it is not always so where there is no legal slavery), it
compels distribution.

2. Thus, as [a] matter of fact, [the] Greek states were all of [a] very
small area, [and] with few exceptions each [was] dependent on [the]
agricultural produce of this area, on which any growth of population
caused greater pressure. This pressure again did constantly lead to
stasis [discord] which (down to a certain period) found relief in colonisation. The fact that colonisation from 'Greece proper' mainly
ceased after about 500 [B.C.] may be partly due to [a] reduction of
population by [the] heavy wars of [the] 5th century, partly to [the]
unmentionable habit[5] (quasi-approval of which by philosophers may
be partly due to their apprehensions of unlimited *teknopoia* [child
bearing]).

[The] chief states [, however, were] not dependent on [the] produce of their own territory – [e.g.?] Corinth and Athens. In them
[the] danger from [a] large slave population does not appear, nor in
Attica do we find *stasis* arising from [the] collision of *penia* and

ploutos. (This [was] more [common] in Sicilian towns). Apparently wealth [was] much distributed, and consequently that freedom from *stasis* which, Aristotle says, goes along with [a] large middle class.[6] We *do* find [, however,] in [the] case of Athens, that other political evil, which according to Plato accompanies large trade. [The Athenians'] dependence on [the] Thracian grain-trade is [a] great cause of weakness in [their] struggle with Philip.[7]

3. Thus [an] increase of population [was] a real political difficulty: and to [the] mind of [the] philosophers the incidents of that foreign trade, which could alone meet the difficulty [of providing subsistence], were inconsistent with their idea of good citizenship.[8]

... [The] example of Ireland may bring home to us [the] dangers involved in [an] increase of population, when [it is] not relieved by trade and manufacture; no population [can be] contented when it grows too fast for all to find maintenance *on the land*, and when for those who can't find such maintenance there is no alternative but emigration – unless society [is] small enough and homogenous enough to direct [the] individual internally, as in Switzerland. [The] Swiss commune does not provide *Grundbesitz* [landed property] for all whom it allows to stay at home. For [the] rest it arranges migration. It presents [the] nearest modern parallel to a Greek state as [the] philosophers conceived it – saving [the] perfect *absence* of *scholē* [leisure].[9]

4. [The] modern economist approaches [the] question of population with different preconceptions. [He is] not afraid of [the] size of states as such: [he] knows that there is no natural limit to wealth except such as arises from difficulty in providing food and warmth – a difficulty which becomes greater with [the] increase of population – which is harder in any country for [the] 21st million than [the] 20th (i.e. [the] additional labouring force which 21st million brings is not in proportion to [the] additional labour required for finding them food and fuel).[10] Of course, if at [the] same time capital has increased in [a] higher ratio still, [the] labourer will be better off not withstanding [the increase in population]. Better machinery, communications and management, too, may compensate for greater natural obstacles to [the] acquisition of necessaries. Still, however, much machinery and facilities for transport and trade may prevent us from noticing the process, yet it is true that as consumption increases, food, etc. is got with greater difficulty, labour in consequence (unless [the] condition of [the] labourer deteriorates) becomes more costly, and [there occurs the] 'tendency of profits to a minimum'.[11]

5. In England, [the] introduction of free-trade altered [the] practi-

cal aspect of [the] population question. [The] cost of subsistence has risen, but not so as to keep pace with [the] increase of [the] wage-fund . . . [Cf. the] Irish situation [where the] famine [constituted a] practical vindication of Malthus.[12] But what we have to fear now, [and] for a long time to come, is not that population in general will outgrow [the] means of subsistence in general, but the constant tendency of [the] supply of labour in particular employments and localities to grow a little too fast for the demand.

6. This tendency is [the] source of *practical* socialism in modern times[13] – which means [the] doctrine (a) that wages should be regulated otherwise than by competition ([i.e.]: competition of labourers for employment and of masters to get work done most cheaply and quickly), and (b) that accumulation of capital should be limited. [While it is] quite true that [the] vulgar antithesis between labour and capital is misleading – that capital is [the] accumulated result of labour, and that every addition to capital (unless meanwhile more capital has been diverted from wages of labour into machinery) means additional demand for labour *somewhere* – [it is equally true that] capital [is] much more elastic – more easily shifted – than labour which attaches to human persons. A certain trade goes on flourishing, with [a] consequent increase of labourers in it, for a time; then comes a check from changes in fashion or greater difficulty of obtaining [the] raw material. Capital (though limited to some extent by machinery) can leave the trade more quickly than labourers can follow. Meanwhile capital in other trades and districts is perhaps yielding [a] larger return than before. Thus labourers in impoverished districts may often have [the] spectacle before them of [a] capitalist still flourishing and flaunting [the] ostentation of wealth in their eyes while they are half-starved. [In those circumstances] of course they do not believe (what yet is true *in the general* [sense]) that [the] interests of capital and labour are identical.

7. Hence socialism [is] always strongest in a place like Paris where capitalists go to enjoy themselves – to spend in luxuries that part of their income which is not reinvested productively in labour. [The] local trades of Paris may mostly be languishing while [the] presence of great capitalists in it becomes more and more obvious – for it is not reproductive expenditure but expenditure on luxuries that catches the eye – and makes [the] cost of living there higher and higher. Hence [the] folly of Louis Napoleon in trying to keep socialists quiet by attracting rich people to Paris.[14] [The] only people who gained were builders and shopkeepers. [Most of the luxuries consumed by the rich were produced with little or no labour, and many were made

elsewhere than in Paris.] ... [There was] thus no permanent improvement in [the] condition of [the] labouring classes and everything to provoke them to jealousy of [the] rich. [The] same remarks apply partially to London and Berlin.

NOTES

INTRODUCTION

1. Green's pupils and those influenced by him (a group variously described as 'British', 'English' or 'Oxford' Idealists or Neo-Hegelians) played a prominent role in late nineteenth- and early twentieth-century political philosophy in Britain. This group included Bernard Bosanquet (1848–1923), Sir Henry Jones (1852–1922), John Henry Muirhead (1857–1940), and D. G. Ritchie (1853–1903). These men held a number of chairs at British universities in the period 1882–1922, and were extremely productive writers. Systematic accounts of post-Greenian political Idealism can be found in H. Haldar, *Neo-Hegelianism* (London, 1927); F. P. Harris, *The Neo-Idealist Political Theory* (New York, 1944); Jean Pucelle, *L'Idéalisme en Angleterre: De Coleridge à Bradley* (Neuchatel, 1955); Peter Robbins, *The British Hegelians, 1875–1925* (New York, 1982). It is perhaps a measure of Green's lasting influence in the twentieth century that both J. P. Plamenatz, *Consent, Freedom and Political Obligation* (Oxford, 1938) and H. A. Prichard, *Moral Obligation* (Oxford, 1949) thought it worth attempting to demolish aspects of Green's political philosophy more than half a century after his death. Plamenatz recanted somewhat in the second edition (1968) of his work (p. 166). The relationship between Green's work and that of later Idealists is problematic and complex and cannot be considered here; see the works mentioned above and in note 3, and the more thematic studies by Gerald Gaus, *The Liberal Theory of Man* (London, 1983), John Morrow, 'Liberalism and British Idealist Political Philosophy: A Reassessment', *History of Political Thought* 5 (1984), pp. 91–108, and Andrew Vincent and Raymond Plant, *Philosophy, Politics and Citizenship: Idealism and the Welfare State* (Oxford, 1984).

2. See Richter, pp. 315, 323n; Vincent and Plant, *Philosophy, Politics and Citizenship*, ch. 7.

3. Peter Clarke, *Liberals and Social Democrats* (Cambridge, 1978) pp. 22–7; Stefan Collini, *Liberalism and Sociology: L. T. Hobhouse and Political Argument in England 1880–1914* (Cambridge, 1979), pp. 125–8, 161–5; Vincent and Plant, *Philosophy, Politics and Citizenship*, ch. 5; cf. Michael Freeden, *The New Liberalism: An Ideology of Social Reform* (Oxford, 1978), who argues that organic language was far more important to New Liberalism than Idealist influences.

4. The best accounts of Green's life are Nettleship's *Memoir*, and Richter; the paragraphs which follow draw extensively on these sources.
5. See W. G. Addison, 'Academic Reform at Balliol, 1854–1882. T. H. Green and Benjamin Jowett', *The Church Quarterly Review* (Jan. 1952), pp. 89–98.
6. Among Green's papers at Balliol College, Oxford are lists headed 'Sales Figures', running up to 1928. The figures for the *Prolegomena* are 14,776 copies, while those for the *Lectures* and the *Works* (separate volumes) are 2,775 and 1,572 respectively. These last two sets of figures are clearly not total sales figures. Richter (p. 294n) reports that Longmans originally printed 2,000 sets of the *Works*, and mentions a figure of 15,602 for the *Lectures*; it is not clear if this latter figure is for more than one printing. In any case, since both the *Works* and the *Lectures* went through numerous editions and reprints, it is clear that the figures in the Green Papers do not represent total sales; if they did, there would have been no reason for Longmans to keep re-issuing both the *Works* and the *Lectures*. One explanation for the discrepancy between the two sets of figures is that the returns in Balliol represent only Mrs Green's share of the sales; the remainder, not credited to Mrs Green for royalty purposes, may have been split between Longmans and Nettleship and his estate. Publishers' figures suggest that the sales of Green's writings (other than the *Prolegomena*, about which we can be reasonably clear) were extensive.
7. Green's influence on educational thought and practice is discussed in Peter Gordon and John White, *Philosophers as Educational Reformers: the Influence of Idealism on British Educational Thought and Practice* (London, 1979).
8. The best account of Green's interest in temperance reform is Peter P. Nicholson, 'T. H. Green and State Action: Liquor Legislation', paper presented to the Commemorative Conference on T. H. Green, Balliol College, Oxford, 1982; Green's most complete statement of his views on 'the drink problem' is in 'Liberal Legislation and Freedom of Contract', see pp. 209–12 below.
9. *Works*, I, pp. 1–310.
10. *Ibid.*, pp. 12–13, 52; *Prolegomena* §§ 9, 13, 18, 69–70.
11. 'Essay on Christian Dogma', *Works*, III, p. 184; see also *Prolegomena*, §§ 90–120.
12. *Prolegomena*, § 293.
13. For interesting accounts of Green's theology see Bernard M. G. Reardon, *From Coleridge to Gore. A Century of Religious Thought in Britain* (London, 1971), pp. 305–8, and Vincent and Plant, *Philosophy, Politics and Citizenship*, ch. 2. Green was however, very critical of many forms of institutionalised worship and the dogma which accompanied it – see, for example, the remarks on church reform quoted below in note 9 to 'Legislative Interference', and 'Essay on Christian Dogma', pp. 161–85.

14. Richter, p. 131.
15. See David Newsome, *Two Classes of Men: Platonism and English Romantic Thought* (London, 1974), pp. 80–2; Reardon, *From Coleridge to Gore*, p. 27.
16. 'Fragment on Immortality', *Works*, III, p. 199.
17. 'Faith', *Works*, III, p. 264.
18. Nettleship, *Memoir*, p. xxxvii; Richter, pp. 80, 97; Vincent and Plant, *Philosophy, Politics and Citizenship*, pp. 8–9.
19. Cf. Vincent and Plant, *Philosophy, Politics and Citizenship*, pp. 8–17.
20. Nettleship, *Memoir*, pp. xiv, xxv; Newsome, *Two Classes of Men*, *passim*.
21. See Anthony Manser, *Bradley's Logic* (Oxford, 1983), ch. 1; Robbins, *The British Hegelians*, chs. 2–3.
22. See *Prolegomena*, §§ 155–70.
23. *Ibid.*, § 171.
24. *Ibid.*, § 293.
25. *Ibid.*, § 190.
26. *Ibid.*, § 245.
27. *Ibid.*, § 184.
28. *Ibid.*, § 198; cf. Green's remarks on resistance, *Lectures*, ch. H.
29. *Lectures*, § 15; cf. Green's support for temperance legislation ('Liberal Legislation', below pp. 209–12) with his attitude towards property, *Lectures*, ch. N.
30. See *Lectures*, §§ 9–15.
31. 'Freedom', § 24; cf. *Lectures*, § 121.
32. 'Freedom', § 25.
33. See for example Vincent and Plant, *Philosophy, Politics and Citizenship*, pp. 10–11, 20.
34. See Maurice Mandelbaum, *History, Man & Reason. A Study in Nineteenth-Century Thought* (Baltimore, 1971), pp. 221–2. On Green's interest in Fichte see Nettleship, *Memoir*, pp. xxv, cxxv.
35. See Morrow, 'Liberalism and British Idealist Political Philosophy', pp. 96–7.
36. C. B. Macpherson, for example, brackets Green with J. S. Mill as a proponent of a developmental conception of human nature; see *Democratic Theory: Essays in Retrieval* (Oxford, 1973), chs. I, IX–X.
37. Green discussed Austin's conception of sovereignty in *Lectures*, ch. F.
38. See John Austin, *Lectures on Jurisprudence* (1863), 3rd edn, 2 vols. (London, 1869), vol. I, pp. 226–7; cf. Green, *Lectures*, §§ 81–3. On nineteenth-century views on sovereignty see Mark Francis, 'The Nineteenth-Century Theory of Sovereignty and Thomas Hobbes', *History of Political Thought* 1 (1980), pp. 517–40.
39. *Lectures*, § 137; cf. H. L. A. Hart, *The Concept of Law* (Oxford, 1961), pp. 80–1, 236.
40. *Lectures*, §§ 86, 132.

41. *Ibid.*, § 84.
42. *Ibid.*, § 86.
43. *Ibid.*, §§ 21–31; see also *Prolegomena*, §§ 199–205 and cf. Austin, *Lectures*, vol. I, pp. 275–6 and note.
44. *Lectures*, § 148.
45. *Ibid.*
46. *Ibid.*, §§ 216–21, 228–30; see also 'Liberal Legislation', below pp. 199–209.
47. *Lectures*, § 37.
48. See 'English Revolution', below pp. 213–27.
49. *Lectures*, § 62.
50. *Ibid.*, §§ 144–7.
51. See for example 'Liberal Legislation', below pp. 198–212.
52. *Lectures*, § 86.
53. See 'Liberal Legislation', below pp. 198–212.
54. See 'English Revolution', below pp. 224–5.

1. LECTURES ON THE PRINCIPLES OF
POLITICAL OBLIGATION

* From *Works*, II, pp. 334–553. Green lectured on 'The Principles of Political Obligation and the Social Virtues' at Balliol in the October term 1879 and the Hilary term 1880, following lectures on Moral Philosophy in the summer term of 1878 and on 'The Theory of Duty' in the three following terms (*Memoir*, p. cxxv). The *Lectures* were first published in *Works*, II; they and 'Freedom' were issued in one volume in 1895 with a Preface by Bernard Bosanquet, and this was reprinted eleven times from 1901–1950. The last three reprints (1941, 1948, 1950) contained an Introduction by A. D. Lindsay; this version was reissued in paperback in the United States in 1967. Selections from the *Lectures* are in Rodman.

A. The Grounds of Political Obligation

1. That is, in the lectures posthumously published under the title *Prolegomena to Ethics*; see below for extracts from these lectures.
2. *The Theory of Moral Sentiments* (1759) was the title of Adam Smith's major work on moral philosophy. Green's reference to 'moral approbation or disapprobation' may echo Smith's fourth chapter heading 'On self-approbation and self-disapprobation'. The distinction between 'civil law' and 'law of opinion or reputation' appears in John Locke's *Essay on Human Understanding* (1690), ed. Peter H. Nidditch (Oxford, 1975), Bk II, ch. 28, §§ 7–13. Cf. 'Freedom', § 24.
3. All but the first sentence of this section have been added by Nettleship, but in doing so he followed Green's note in the MS to 'Quote from course of Lent Term the acc[oun]t of these capacities.' The passages which appear as § 6 follow those which became §§ 183–191 of the *Pro-*

legomena, which in turn follow those which became 'Freedom'; see 'Freedom', note to the title and note 49. Nettleship did, however, omit some sentences from § 6 which are important in placing these various passages in context. *Prolegomena*, § 191 ends: 'to realise its idea as it is in God. [MS continues] Have endeavoured now to answer, upon one and the same principle, the following questions (1) how it comes to pass that there is such a thing as moral action – action to which the predicates morally good and morally bad are applicable; in other words, how moral action is possible, what is implied in its possibility: (2) on what ground the distinction of morally good and morally bad is to be applied to actions that admit of being so distinguished: (3) what is the general nature of the progress on the part of mankind and of individuals in the direction of realising the capacity for doing actions morally good; in other words, what is the origin and course of development (a) of moral ideas, (b) of the disposition through which these ideas take effect in action. The answers given to these questions may be summarized as follows: to (1) the condition of the possibility of moral action is the existence in man of will and reason, as expressions of one self-realising principle which in themselves, or according to the divine idea of that principle, harmonise with each other, but which as they appear in the historical man – in man as existing in time – only show a capacity for gradually coming to do so. [§ 6 extract begins] Will is the capacity ... object to be attained by action. [MS continues] The existence of a will, in the sense explained, carries with it the possibility of its determination by reason, in the sense explained; and an action which proceeds from will, as carrying with it this possibility, is susceptible of moral attributes – of being good or bad. Answer to (2) The ground for reckoning it good or bad must lie in its relation to that realisation of the moral capacity, which consists in the complete harmony of the will with, or its determination by, reason. This realisation is *the* moral good or end. The action will be good in the most proper or strict sense according to the degree to which in the will represented by it this realisation is attained. In a less direct (*alt*. proper) sense, and considered apart from a will from which it proceeds, it will be good in so far as it tends to promote in the agent or any other person the harmony of the will with reason. Answer to (3) [§ 6 continues] All moral ideas have their origin in reason ... dominant interest of the character.'

4. See also *Prolegomena*, §§ 154–6.
5. Thomas Hobbes, *Leviathan* (1651), ed. Michael Oakeshott (Oxford, 1960), Part II, ch. 18, pp. 115–16.
6. See also *Prolegomena*, §§ 154–6.
7.*There are two definitions of '*Recht*' or '*jus naturae*' quoted by [Herman] Ulrici [*Gott und der Mensch*, II: *Grundzüge der praktischen Philosophie, Naturrecht, Ethik und Aesthetik* (Leipzig, 1866–73)], (p. 219) which embody the truths conveyed in these statements.

(1) Krause defines '*Recht*' as 'the organic whole of the outward conditions necessary to the rational life'.

(2) Henrici says that '*Recht*' is what (or 'that is properly matter of legal obligation which') 'in the outward intercourse of men corresponds to the idea of the inviolability of the essential material conditions of a moral humanity, i.e. of the human personality in respect of its existence and its perfection'; or more simply, 'Right is that which is really necessary to the maintenance of the material conditions essential to the existence and perfection of human personality.' Cf. [Friederich Adolf] Trendelenburg, [*Naturrecht auf dem Grunde der Ethik* (Leipzig, 1860)] § 46. 'In the moral whole, right is the sum total of those general determinations of action through which it comes about that the moral whole and its organization is able to maintain itself and develop further.' Afterwards he emphasises the words 'of action', and adds: 'No doubt action cannot be thought without the will which underlies it: but determinations of right are not determinations of the will such as would devolve upon the inner realm, the ethics of intention. Will that does not become deed shuns right. When right draws into its domain guilt and transgression, *dolus* and *culpa*, they are to be regarded as inner but characteristic qualities of action.'

8. For the importance Green placed on liberty of conscience see 'English Revolution', below pp. 213–27. An example of (b) might include the 'prohibitions and restraints' on bequests dealt with below in §§ 224–5. See also 'Liberal Legislation', pp. 205–9 and note 24.

9. Cf. J. S. Mill, *On Liberty* (1859), chs. 3 and 4, and see also Green's 'Liberal Legislation', below pp. 199–200.

10. See for example David Hume, *Essays, Moral, Political, and Literary*, 2 vols., ed. T. H. Green and T. H. Grose (London, 1875), vol. I, Essays IV, V, IX.

11. See Green's critique of John Austin's doctrine of sovereignty, §§ 81ff below.

12. Perhaps an oblique reference to J. S. Mill's attempt to qualify the hedonistic version of Utilitarianism, e.g. *Autobiography* (1873), ch. 5; see also *Prolegomena*, §§ 199–205.

13. For Green's critiques of Utilitarianism and its philosophical antecedents, see *Prolegomena*, §§ 219–39, 329–82; 'Popular Philosophy in its Relation to Life', *Works*, III, pp. 92–125; 'Introduction to the Moral Part of the *Treatise*', in David Hume, *A Treatise of Human Nature* (1739–40), 2 vols., ed. T. H. Green and T. H. Grose (London, 1874), vol. II, pp. 1–71 (also in *Works*, I, pp. 301–71). See also note 12 to *Prolegomena*, § 328, below.

14. Cf. *Prolegomena*, Bk III, *passim*.

15. See § 149 below and note.

16. Aristotle, *Politics*, 1252a–1253a.

B. Spinoza

1. We have replaced Green's Latin quotations from the *Tractatus Politicus* (1677) with the translations in Spinoza, *The Political Works*, trans. and ed. A. G. Wernham (Oxford, 1958); references in the text are to chapter number and section number. Similarly, quotations from Spinoza's *Ethic* (1677) are from W. Hale White's translation, revised by A. H. Stirling, 4th edn (Oxford, 1910); references are to part number and proposition number.

2. 'For example, nobody can give up his power of judgement; for by what rewards or threats can a man be led to believe that a whole is no greater than its part, or that God does not exist, or that a body which he sees to be finite is an infinite being; and, in general, to believe anything contrary to what he perceives or thinks? Similarly, by what rewards or threats can a man be induced to love someone he hates, or to hate someone he loves? Among such actions we must also include those which are so repugnant to human nature that it considers them the worst of all evils; for example, bearing witness against oneself, torturing oneself, killing one's own parents, making no attempt to avoid death, and things of that sort, which no man can be induced by rewards or threats to do. If we still wish to say that a commonwealth has the right or power to command such actions, we shall find it impossible to conceive of this right in any other sense than that in which it might be said that a man has a right to be a raving lunatic; for what else but raving lunacy would such a right be, when nobody can be bound by it? I am here speaking expressly of those actions which cannot fall under the right of the commonwealth, and which are repugnant to ordinary human nature. No doubt fools and madmen cannot be induced to carry out commands by any reward or threat; no doubt devotion to some religious faith may lead one or two men to regard the laws of the state as the worst of all evils. But this does not invalidate these laws, since most of the citizens are bound by them. It follows that, since those who have neither hopes nor fears are to that extent in possession of their own right..., they are enemies of the state..., and the state may restrain them by right.' *Tractatus Politicus*, III.8.

3. *For the definition of *fortitudo*, see *Ethic*, III.59, Schol. 'All the actions which follow from the affects which are related to the mind in so far as it thinks I ascribe to *fortitude*, which I divide into *strength of mind* [*animositas*] and *generosity* [*generositas*]. By *strength of mind*, I mean the desire by which each person endeavours from the dictates of reason alone to preserve his own being. By *generosity*, I mean the desire by which from the dictates of reason alone each person endeavours to help other people and to join them to him in friendship.'

4. *Certainly this is so if we apply to the 'free people' the definition of freedom applied to the 'free man'. 'I call a man completely free in so far as he is guided by reason, for then he is determined to action by causes which

can be understood adequately through his own nature alone. But he is necessarily determined to action by them; for freedom ... does not remove the necessity of acting but imposes it.' (II.11)

5. Cf. § 35 above, and see also II.19: 'obedience is the steadfast will to do what the law declares to be good, and the common decree requires'.

6. On the importance of pre-political institutions in relation to the recognition of rights, see below §§ 117, 134, 141, 148ff.

7. We have translated *'polis'* as 'state', as Green himself does later in this section. In *Prolegomena*, § 264, however, he writes: 'We must not conclude, because to a Greek all duty was summed up in what he owed to his *polis*, that he recognised no duties but such as we should naturally call duties to the state. The term "state" is generally used by us with a restricted meaning which prevents it from being a proper equivalent for *polis*.' See also 'Freedom', § 4; 'Legislative Interference in Moral Matters', below pp. 306–7.

8. Cf. Aristotle, *Politics*, 1277b; 1284a.

9. *Ibid.*, 1252a–1253a; 1283b.

10. This is the number of Spinoza's letter to Boxel (October, 1674) in *The Correspondence of Spinoza*, ed. A. Wolf (London, 1928), pp. 286–90, following the numbering in Van Vloten and Land's memorial edition of 1882. Green cited it as Letter LX, its number in the *Posthumous Works* (1677).

11. Immanuel Kant, *Grundlegung zur Metaphysik der Sitten* (1785), *The Moral Law*, trans. H. J. Paton (London, 1948), pp. 67–9.

12.*Cf. *Ethic*, IV, Appendix, xxxii. 'Nevertheless we shall bear with equanimity these things which happen to us contrary to what a consideration of our own profit demands, if we are conscious that we have performed our duty, that the power we have could not reach so far as to enable us to avoid those things, and that we are a part of the whole of nature, whose order we follow. If we clearly and distinctly understand this, the part of us, which is determined by intelligence, that is to say, the better part of us, will be entirely satisfied therewith, and in that satisfaction will endeavour to persevere; for, in so far as we understand, we cannot desire anything excepting what is necessary, nor, absolutely, can we be satisfied with anything but the truth. Therefore in so far as we understand these things properly will the efforts of the better part of us agree with the order of the whole of nature.' 'By *good* ..., I understand in the following pages everything which we are certain is a means by which we may approach nearer and nearer to the model of human nature we set before us ... Again, I shall call men more or less perfect in so far as they approach more or less nearly to this same model' (*Ethic*, IV, Preface).

C. Hobbes

1. Spinoza to Jelles, 2 June 1674. *The Correspondence of Spinoza*, ed. A. Wolf (London, 1928), p. 269. This letter has the same number in earlier editions.
2. Ed. Michael Oakeshott (Oxford, 1960), p. 112. Green only noted down the first and last phrases of this quotation. The MS also contains the words 'Cap 18. Passages marked', but none of the relevant passages from this chapter (treating 'Of The Rights of Sovereigns by Institution') were included in Nettleship's edition.
3. *Leviathan* (1651), Part II, ch. 17, p. 113.
4. *Ibid.*, Part II, ch. 17, p. 112.
5. *Ibid.*, Part II, ch. 18, p. 113.
6. In the MS there is a note, probably in A. C. Bradley's hand, instructing a copyist to add material here from 'Conybeare's notes of the lectures'; these additions were not incorporated in Nettleship's edition of the *Lectures*. Frederick Cornwallis Conybeare (1856–1924) 'was a disciple of T. H. Green, and it is recorded of him that he invited other enthusiasts to meet together and compare their lecture-notes, so as to obtain a correct text of their master's words'. Albert C. Clark, 'F. C. Conybeare, 1856–1924', *Proceedings of the British Academy*, 11 (1924–5), p. 470. Conybeare was a Fellow of University College, Oxford, 1880–7, and became a noted Armenian scholar.
7. *'Jus naturale*, is the liberty each man hath, to use his own power, as he will himself, for the preservation of his own nature; that is to say, of his own life; and consequently, of doing anything, which in his own judgment, and reason, he shall conceive to be the aptest means thereunto' (*Leviathan*, Part I, ch. 14 [p. 84]).
8. *Leviathan*, Part I, ch. 13, p. 82.
9. *Ibid.*, Part I, ch. 15, p. 93.
10. *Ibid.*, Part I, ch. 14, p. 84.
11. Spinoza, *Tractatus Politicus*, in *The Political Works*, trans. and ed. A. G. Wernham (Oxford, 1958), II.5. See § 36 above.
12. *'[R]eason*, when we reckon it amongst the faculties of the mind ... is nothing but *reckoning*, that is adding or subtracting, of the consequences of general names agreed upon for the *marking* or *signifying* of our thoughts; ...' (*Leviathan*, Part I, ch. 5, pp. 25–6).
13. See Spinoza, *Tractatus Politicus*, II.15, § 32 above.

D. Locke

1. E.g. The Virginian Declaration of Rights – 12 June 1776: 'That all men are by nature equally free and independent, and have certain inherent rights, of which, when they enter into a state of society, they cannot by any compact deprive or divest the posterity; ...' The Declaration of Independence of the United States of America – 4 July 1776: '... We hold these truths to be self-evident, that all men are created equal, that

they are endowed by their Creator with certain unalienable Rights...'
These extracts appeared as an Appendix in one of the works of D. G.
Ritchie (1853–1903), a pupil and colleague of Green; see *Natural Rights*
(London, 1894), pp. 287–9.

2. *Locke, *Second Treatise* [1690], § 87: 'Man being born ... with a Title
   to perfect Freedom, and an uncontrouled enjoyment of all the Rights
   and Priviledges of the Law of Nature, equally with any other Man, or
   Number of Men in the World, hath by Nature a Power, not only to preserve his Property, that is, his Life, Liberty and Estate, against ...
   other Men; but to judge of, and punish the breaches of that Law in
   others... [T]here, and there only is *Political Society*, where every one
   of the Members hath quitted this natural Power, resign'd it up into the
   hands of the Community in all cases that exclude him not from appealing for Protection to the Law established by it.' [Green used the sol-
   ecism *Treatise of Civil Government* as the title of Locke's work,
   abbreviated *Civil Government*. We have preferred the title and abbrevia-
   tion shown, and have used the version in John Locke, *Two Treatises of
   Government*, ed. Peter Laslett, 2nd edition (Cambridge, 1967).
   References in the text of this chapter are to the *Second Treatise*.]

3. *'Laws therefore humane, of what kind soever, are available by consent',
   Hooker, *Eccl. Pol.* 1.10 (quoted by Locke § 134, note). '[T]o be com-
   manded we do consent when that Society, whereof we be a part, hath at
   any time before consented, without revoking the same after by the like
   universal agreement.' Hooker; *ibid*.

4. *[Hugo Grotius] *De Jure belli et pacis* [1625], *Proleg.* §§ 15 and 16.

5. Locke writes of the 'inconveniences' of the state of nature in § 13; cf. § 58
   below.

6. Hobbes, *Leviathan* (1651), ed. Michael Oakeshott (Oxford, 1960), Part
   I, ch. 13, p. 82.

7. E.g. in Bk I of *Du Contrat Social* (1762), and Part I of the *Discours sur
   l'origine et les fondements de l'inégalité parmi les hommes* (1755).

8. These words do not appear in Hooker or in Locke's citation of him.
   However, the sentiment is expressed in a quotation from Hooker (*Eccl.
   Pol.* 1.7) with which Locke concludes § 5: 'there being no reason that
   others should shew greater measure of love to me, than they have by me,
   shewed unto them...'

9. Hobbes, *Leviathan*, Part I, chs. 14, 16; Part II, chs. 17, 18, 21.

10. *Ibid.*, Part II, ch. 19, p. 121.

11. *According to Hobbes, tyranny = 'monarchy misliked'; oligarchy = 'aris-
    tocracy misliked' [*Leviathan*, Part II, ch. 19, p. 121].

12. See Green, 'English Revolution', *Works*, III, pp., 310–26, 333–5. Cf.
    Richard Overton's *An Appeal from the Commons to the Free People*
    (1647): 'While the betrusted are dischargers of their trust it remaineth in
    their hands, but no sooner the betrusted betray and forfeit their trust but
    ... it returneth from whence it came... For all just human powers are

betrusted, conferred, and conveyed by joint and common consent; for to
every individual in nature is given an individual propriety by nature, not
to be invaded or usurped by any...'; *Puritanism and Liberty*, ed. A.
S. P. Woodhouse (London, 1951), p. 327.

13. Alexander Pope, *The Dunciad*, Bk IV, l. 188.
14. Cicero, *De Legibus*, III (iii), 8.

E. Rousseau

1. Cf. §§ 51, 55.
2. The translations from *Du Contrat Social* (1762) appear to be Green's
   own; the references in the text are to book number and chapter number.
   His translations have been compared to several modern ones; they are
   very close to those in Jean-Jacques Rousseau, *The Social Contract*,
   trans. Maurice Cranston (Harmondsworth, 1968).
3. A variant of George Wither's *Vox Pacifica* (1645), canto 4. The original
   reads 'And, know, there is, on earth, a *greater-thing* / Than an un-
   righteous *Parliament* or King.' The version reproduced by Green
   appears in Samuel Taylor Coleridge's *On the Constitution of the Church
   and State* (1830), ch. XI. Green may be recalling Coleridge's variant.
4. Immanuel Kant, *Grundlegung zur Metaphysik der Sitten* (1785), *The
   Moral Law*, trans. H. J. Paton (London, 1948), p. 91.
5. Green ignores Rousseau's footnote: 'This should always be understood
   to refer only to free states, for elsewhere family, property, lack of
   asylum, necessity or violence may keep an inhabitant in the country
   unwillingly, and then his mere residence no longer implies consent
   either to the contract or to the violation of the contract', *The Social Contract*, p. 155n.
6. The United Provinces, comprising roughly modern Holland and Bel-
   gium, were formed out of those provinces of the Spanish Netherlands
   which ratified the Edict of Abjuration (1581) by which Philip II was
   deposed. The constitution of the state was, in the words of a modern his-
   torian, 'something of a mystery even to its creators', but there was no
   doubt that it left the United Provinces 'with much of the Swiss and
   Venetian in their constitution'. J. H. Elliot, *Europe Divided 1559–1598*
   (London, 1968), p. 294.
7.*'If it happened that the prince had a private will more active than that of
   the sovereign, and that he made use of the public force placed in his
   hands as the instrument of this private will, there would result, so to
   speak, two sovereignties, one *de jure*, the other *de facto*; but from that
   moment the social union would disappear, and the body politic would be
   dissolved' (III, i). 'When the prince ceases to administer the state according to the laws, and usurps the sovereign power ... then the state in the
   larger sense is dissolved, and there is formed another within it, composed only of the members of the government ... the social pact is
   broken ... and all the ordinary citizens return as a matter of right to

their state of natural liberty, and are merely forced, but not obliged, to obey' (III, x).

F. Sovereignty and the General Will

1. John Austin (1790–1859), Professor of Jurisprudence in the University of London from 1826 to 1832, and an associate of Bentham and the Mills.

2. John Austin, *Lectures on Jurisprudence* (1863), 3rd edn, 2 vols. (London, 1869), vol. I, p. 88. Subsequent references in the text are to volume and page number of this edition.

3. *Cf. Maine's lecture on the subject in *The Early History of Institutions* [(London, 1875), Lecture XII], pp. 349–50. [Maine says he is here restating 'Austin's doctrine of Sovereignty in another way – more popularly, though without, I think, any substantial inaccuracy. It is as follows:] There is, in every political community – that is, in every political community not in the habit of obedience to a superior above itself – some single person or some combination of persons which has the power of compelling the other members of the community to do exactly as it pleases. This single person or group – this individual or this collegiate Sovereign (to employ Austin's phrase) – may be found in every independent political community as certainly as the centre of gravity in a mass of matter. If the community be violently or voluntarily divided into a number of separate fragments, then, as soon as each fragment has settled down (perhaps after an interval of anarchy) into a state of equilibrium, the Sovereign will exist and with proper care will be discoverable in each of the now independent portions. The Sovereignty over the North American Colonies of Great Britain had its seat in one place before they became the United States, in another place afterwards; but in both cases there was a discoverable Sovereign somewhere. This Sovereign, this person or combination of persons, universally occurring in all independent political communities, has in all such communities one characteristic, common to all the shapes Sovereignty may take, the possession of irresistible force, not necessarily exerted but capable of being exerted. According to the terminology preferred by Austin, the Sovereign, if a single person, is or should be called a Monarch; if a small group, the name is an Oligarchy; if a group of considerable dimensions, an Aristocracy; if very large and numerous, a Democracy. Limited Monarchy, a phrase perhaps more fashionable in Austin's day than it is now, is abhorred by Austin, and the Government of Great Britain he classes with Aristocracies. That which all the forms of Sovereignty have in common is the power (the power but not necessarily the will) to put compulsion without limit on subjects or fellow-subjects.' [Sir Henry Maine (1822–88) was an eminent jurist who held chairs at Cambridge (1847–54, 1877–8) and Oxford (1869–78), and was a legal member of Council in India from 1862–9.]

4. Spinoza, *Tractatus Politicus* (1677) in *The Political Works*, trans. and ed. A. G. Wernham (Oxford, 1958), V.2. Cf. § 35 above.
5. Cf. *Prolegomena*, § 324.
6. Austria ruled Venetia from 1815 until driven out by Prussia in alliance with Piedmont in 1866.
7. Cf. *Prolegomena*, §§ 206–17, 218–45.
8. A reference to the collapse of Louis Napoleon's regime and the establishment of the Third Republic in 1870–1. The birth of the Third Republic was accompanied by the Paris Commune, which hardly seems a conspicuous example of the sort of transition which Green has in mind. The 'temporary foreign conquest' refers to the German occupation after the Battles of Metz and Sedan (1870).
9. *Leviathan* (1651), ed. Michael Oakeshott (Oxford, 1958), Part II, ch. 18, p. 115.
10. *Social Contract* (1762), trans. Maurice Cranston (Harmondsworth, 1968), Bk II, ch. 4.
11. *Ibid.*, Bk IV, ch. 2; but cf. *Lectures*, ch. E, note 5.
12. Green wrote on a facing pace: 'case of Quakers & Ch[urch] rate'. The church rate was levied on parishioners and occupiers of land within a parish for the maintenance of church buildings, and gave rise to much opposition from Dissenters and others who were not members of the Church of England. It was made voluntary in 1868. See also *Prolegomena*, § 321.
13. See also *Prolegomena*, §§ 321–4.
14. Austin is quoting Article 5 of the U.S. Constitution.
15. Spinoza, *Tractatus Politicus*, III. 9; see above § 33.
16. Giuseppe Mazzini (1805–72), Italian patriot, republican, and leader of the movement for Italian unification. Green is said to have 'venerated' him (Christopher Harvie, *The Lights of Liberalism* (London, 1976), p. 104), and defended Mazzini in the Oxford Union in 1861. Nettleship quotes a letter Green wrote in 1860 about the events in Italy in the autumn of that year which bears on the point made in the *Lectures*: 'Garibaldi is evidently not strong enough to take at all a high tone, and thus I fear the Mazzinian or federal program, which I have no doubt is really the best, will have to give way, for want of public virtue, to Cavour's. I can't think that a Piedmontese king of all Italy, without federal limitations, would ever be trustworthy, or that Italy can ever be permanently safe with Rome and Venetia in the hands of foreigners. But of course there is no good in attempting plans which there is not enough national spirit to carry out. The southern Italians are clearly a feeble folk' (*Memoir*, p. xlii).
17. Cf. *Prolegomena*, §§ 85–153.
18. Cf. *ibid.*, § 304.

G. Will, Not Force, is the Basis
of the State

1. See also above §§ 25–31, and *Prolegomena*, Bk III, chs. II–V.

2. Cf. Rousseau: 'The passage from the state of nature to the civil society produces a remarkable change in man; it puts justice as a rule of conduct in place of instinct, and gives his actions the moral quality they previously lacked'. *The Social Contract*, trans. Maurice Cranston (Harmondsworth, 1968), Bk I, ch. 8, p. 64.

3. See also § 2 above, 'Freedom' §§ 24–5, and *Prolegomena* §§ 85–153, 180–91.

4. E.g. Rousseau, *Social Contract*, Bk II, ch. 10; see also Green's discussion of Plato and Aristotle in 'Notes on Moral Philosophy', below pp. 310–11.

5. Rousseau actually uses the term 'Prince' to identify the collective body of magistrates; see *Social Contract*, Bk III, ch. 1.

6. Cf. §§ 170, 174 below and notes.

7. On Green's theory of property see §§ 211–32 below, 'Liberal Legislation' pp. 206–8 below.

8. Cf. 'English Revolution' below pp. 220–7, and 'The Force of Circumstances', *Works*, III, pp. 3–10.

9. Although Green proceeds to discount (§§ 124, 127–30) the moral significance of a *prima facie* account of origins, he argues in the chapter on property (below §§ 228–30) that important aspects of modern states (namely those having to do with the distribution and use of landed property, and the relationship between proprietors and the propertyless) have been vitiated by the lingering influences of their coercive origins.

10. 'Publicist': 'writer on law of nations' (*O.E.D.*).

11. A reference to the 'Dual Monarchy' of Austro-Hungary established in 1867, by which the head of the House of Hapsburg was the personal sovereign of each state.

12. Cf. *Prolegomena*, Bk I, *passim*.

13. See also 'The Force of Circumstances' and 'The Influence of Civilisation on Genius', *Works*, III, pp. 3–10, 11–19.

14. By the Treaty of Pressburg (1805) Austria recognised Napoleon as King of Italy, her Italian possessions going partly to the new Italian kingdom and partly to France; a centralised system of *préfectures* was established in France in 1799, and the civil code (or *Code Napoléon*) was drawn up between 1800–4. Although it actually eroded the position of women and restored paternal authority, some of the social gains of the Revolution were incorporated within it: most notably, equality before the law and the abandonment of privileged orders and seigneurial rights. The 'French system along the Rhine' was institutionalised in 1805 by the Confederation of the Rhine which was under the protection of Napoleon, and embraced the rulers of the various Rhineland Duchies and Kingdoms.

15. Source not identified. Cf. *Prolegomena*, § 295: '[I]f we look ... closely, we shall find that the selfish political leader was himself much more of an instrument than of an originating cause, and that his action was but a trifling element in the sum or series of actions which yielded the political movement. The good in the effect of the movement will really correspond to the degree of good will which has been exerted in bringing it about; and the effects of any selfishness in its promoters will appear in some limitation to the good which it brings to society. It is seldom indeed that the most conspicuous actors on the world's stage are known to us enough from the inside, or that the movements in which they take part can be contemplated with sufficient completeness, to enable us very certainly to verify this assurance in regard to them. But the more we learn of such a person, for instance, as Napoleon, and of the work which seemed to be his, the more clearly does it appear how what was evil in it arose out of his personal selfishness and that of his contemporaries, while what was good in it was due to higher and purer influences of which he and they were but the medium.'

16. Cf. Green's critique of Austin, §§ 81–112 above.

17. Cf. Hobbes, *Leviathan*, Part II, chs. 18–19, 21, 26, and Rousseau, *Social Contract*, Bk II, chs. I–IV; the latter, however, does maintain that 'the sovereign ... cannot impose on its subjects any burden which is useless to the community ...' (ch. IV).

18. '*Suum cuique* principle': 'to everyone his own'; cf. *Prolegomena*, § 217, note 8. Many Oxford and Cambridge colleges had the right to nominate their members as incumbents of parishes, and to control the income from tithes. These livings were invariably held by Fellows or by those whose marriages precluded them from continuing as Fellows.

H. Has the Citizen Rights Against the State?

1. Hobbes, *Leviathan* (1651), ed. Michael Oakeshott (Oxford, 1960), Bk II, ch. 18, p. 115.

2. Above, §§ 100–1.

3. See also *Prolegomena*, §§ 206–17; in the remainder of that work Green argues that the common good evolves qualitatively as well as in terms of the range of those who are included within it; as A. C. Bradley succinctly put it in his Analytical Table: 'moral progress is not only the widening of the range of persons whose common good is sought, but the gradual determination of the content of the idea of good' (*ibid.*, p. xxiii).

4. The MS is difficult to follow at this point. Nettleship took the rest of § 143 from the verso although Green's version appears to jump from 'well-being?' to 'he has no rights' in the first sentence of § 144. Since Nettleship's insertion maintains the continuity of the argument (e.g. the discussion of social good in the additional passages ties in with the line of argument in § 144) it has been retained.

5. Cf. Green's remarks on the gap between the aspirations of the English

Republicans and those of the ordinary citizens in 'English Revolution', pp. 220–1 below.

6. Green was reported as having told the Oxford Reform League on 23 March 1867: 'We are the last people to threaten physical force. But if we took our opponents, the "philosophical liberals", at their word we should have to resort to it, for they tell us it is absurd to claim representation as a right; but if the plea of right is not listened to, the plea of force alone remains.' *Oxford Chronicle*, 30 March 1867; cited Christopher Harvie, *The Lights of Liberalism* (London, 1976), p. 118.

7. Cf. Green's remarks on the conflict of duties, *Prolegomena*, §§ 314–27.

I. Private Rights. The Right to Life and Liberty

1. Henry John Stephen (1787–1864), *New Commentaries on the Laws of England, (Partly founded on Blackstone)*, 4 vols. (London, 1841–5), vol. I, p. 126. The MS does not include this quotation, but contains the words 'cf. Classification in Stephen's Commentaries (p. 136 Ed./ [18]58) . . .' An editorial note added to the MS contains the instruction 'Give the Classification from Stephen' and adds 'Our concern is with the first three classes, which we proceed to consider.' This addition was not included in Nettleship's edition of the *Lectures*.

2. *Tacitus speaks of it as a peculiarity of the Jews and Germans that they did not allow the killing of younger children (*Hist.*, V, 5; *Germ.* 19). Aristotle (*Pol.* 1335b [21]) provides that 'no deformed child' shall be brought up, but seems to condemn exposure, preferring that the required limit of population should be preserved by destruction of the embryo, on the principle that 'what is lawful and what is not lawful turns on having sensation and being alive.') [*Pol.* 1335b 25–6] Plato's rule is the same as regards the defective children and the procuring abortion, but he leaves it in the dark whether he meant any healthy children, actually born, to be put out of the way (*Rep.* 460c and 461c).

3. E.g. Sir Henry Maine, *Ancient Law* (1861) (Boston, 1963), ch. III, where (1) and (2) are discussed; (3) is Green's own.

4. Cf. *Prolegomena*, §§ 206–17.

5. The MS says 'three' questions, but Green later added no. 3 without altering 'Three' to 'Four'; Nettleship did this for him. The four categories listed relate to the chapters which follow: (1) and (2) to chapter K (on war), (3) to L (on punishment), while although (4) most obviously refers to M (on the promotion of morality), it may also be thought to include N and O (on property and the family) which are aspects of the 'nature and extent of the individual's claim . . .'

K. The Right of the State over the Individual in War

1. We have not found a source where Green might have known of this phrase used in connection with war. It was used in a different context by

Rev. Richard St John Tyrwhitt, in the Preface to the first edition of his *Our Sketching Club. Letters and Studies in Landscape Art* (London, 1874), p.v.: 'For luxurious butchery of domestic pigeons, and multitudinous murder of tame pheasants, I have never shared in or witnessed either, and I loathe the idea of both.' Tyrwhitt (1827–95) was vicar of St Mary Magdalen in Oxford from 1858 to 1872; perhaps he also used the phrase in the context Green mentions. It is given that association in Wilfred Owen's 1918 poem *Mental Cases*, line 12.

2.*[Sir William] Markby, *Elements of Law [Considered with Reference to Principles of General Jurisprudence* (1871), second edition (Oxford, 1874)], § 226n, [p. 111. Markby is quoting Sir William Oldnall Russell, *A Treatise on Crimes and Misdemeanours* (1819), 4th edn, 3 vols., by C. S. Greaves, vol. 1, p. 668 note (Bk III, Ch. 1)].

3. Probably a reference to the rescue of two prisoners by Irish Nationalists in Manchester, September 1867, when a policeman was shot dead.

4. The Second Afghan War of 1878–9; see also note 16 below.

5. Cf. Plato, *Protagoras*, 358c.

6. Cf. 'Liberal Legislation', below pp. 194–212.

7. Cf. 'The Force of Circumstances', *Works*, III, pp. 3–10.

8. The Dutch Republic's struggle with Spain in the early seventeenth century finally ended with the Spanish recognising the Republic's independence by the Treaty of Munster (1648); the War of the League of Augsberg (1689–97) in which the Dutch and other Protestant powers were engaged against Louis XIV concluded with the Treaty of Ryswick. The German nations and their allies defeated Napoleon at the battle of Leipzig, October 1813. Hungarian nationalists fought to expel the Austrians between 1848–9, while the Italians were engaged against the same foe at various times between 1848–66.

9. Germany was finally unified as a result of the Franco–German War of 1870–1 following earlier successes against the Danes (1864) and Austria (1866). The Balkan provinces of the Turkish Empire were a constant source of international tension in the second half of the nineteenth century, because their strategic position, the weakening of Turkish control, the existence of large Christian populations, and the growth of Slavic self-identity, involved the Great Powers directly or indirectly in the area. The major attempt to produce stability in the area occurred in the year before Green wrote the *Lectures*, at the Congress of Berlin (1878), when a number of the Provinces were recognised as independent states.

10. Cf. *Prolegomena*, §§ 321–8. The example of attempted Papal interference which Green probably had in mind here was the so-called *Kulturkampf* in Germany, a clash between papal pretensions (typified by the decree of papal infallibility issued by Pius IX in 1870), and German unity and power recently cemented and affirmed by the defeat of France in 1870–1. The Imperial Government responded to lay acceptance of

the decree by a series of measures directed against the Jesuits and the church's educational and disciplinary role, enacted 1871–5.

11. The arguments developed by Green in §§ 167–9 were echoed by his pupil Bernard Bosanquet in response to claims about the relationship between the Idealist conception of the state and the outlook which produced the First World War. For an account of this controversy see John Morrow 'British Idealism, "German Philosophy" and the First World War.' *Australian Journal of Politics and History*, 28 (1982), pp. 380–90.

12. Russia tended to champion the cause of the Balkan Christians, partly for strategic and political reasons, but partly also because they were Orthodox; see note 9.

13. Penal laws against Catholics in Ireland were widely believed to generate Anglo–Irish antagonisms. Green may have known of the interesting critique of these laws by Edmund Burke in his *Letters to Sir Hercules Langrishe* (1792).

14. The Russian government adopted a hard line against Polish Catholics after the suppression of the Second Polish Revolt 1863–5; in some respects the Catholic Church in Poland had the same status *vis-à-vis* national aspirations as did its sister church in Ireland. The 'ultramontane movement' incorporated Catholics who accepted the papal claim to infallibility; see note 10.

15. France was forced to relinquish Metz to Germany following her defeat in 1870–1.

16. Great Britain was involved in a series of conflicts in Afghanistan in the nineteenth century because of its strategic importance on the border between India to the south, and Russia's Asian provinces to the north. The situation deteriorated after 1870 when the Afghans began to look to Russia as a counterweight to British influence, and when the British began to fear Russian designs on Afghanistan. The last few words are abbreviated in the MS ('acq.sc. frontier') and the correct construction is not clear. Another interpretation would be 'acquisition, i.e. [a] frontier'. Perhaps Nettleship chose to refer to the frontier as 'scientific' because it marked artificially created zones of influence.

17. A reference to Locke's theory of the state of nature; see §§ 55–8 above.

18. Green probably has Kant's scheme in mind. There are some interesting parallels between Green's treatment of international relations and that of Kant, e.g. the references to national independence (Preliminary Art. 2 of Kant's 'Perpetual Peace: a Philosophical Sketch'), standing armies (Prelim. Art. 3), the importance of the internal rectitude of states (First Definitive Art.). For a full account of the British Idealists' views on international relations, see Peter P. Nicholson, 'Philosophical Idealism and International Politics: Reply to Dr Savigear', *British Journal of International Studies*, 2(1976), pp. 77–83.

19. The struggles between the German states and Napoleon are often thought to have stimulated German nationalism. Fichte's *Addresses to*

the *German Nation* (1807–8), which Green is almost certain to have known, are frequently seen as part of the revival.

20. The view that free trade provided one of the best ways of forging common interests between states was an important part of the platform of the radical liberals Richard Cobden and John Bright, both of whom Green greatly admired. Cf. Cobden: 'I believed Free Trade would have the tendency to unite mankind in the bonds of peace, and it was that, more than any pecuniary consideration, which sustained and activated me ... in that struggle'. *Speeches on Questions of Public Policy by Richard Cobden, M.P.*, ed. John Bright and James E. Thorold Rogers (London, 1878), p. 518; see also Richter, pp. 79, 80, 89, 269–76; *Prolegomena*, § 281; 'The Effect of Commerce on the Mind of a Nation', below pp. 302–4.

L. The Right of the State to Punish

1. Cf. §§ 25–7, 213. Green's view that animals are not moral beings is nicely illustrated by a story recounted by Graham Wallas who heard Green lecture at Oxford. 'Green asked for questions ... I, being fresh from reading Darwin, asked him whether his arguments applied to the conscious mind of a dog, and Green answered that he was not interested in dogs'; cited in Peter Clarke, *Liberals and Social Democrats* (Cambridge, 1978), p. 14.

2. See also *Prolegomena* § 381 and cf. A. J. M. Milne, *The Social Philosophy of English Idealism* (London, 1962), p. 150.

3. For example, Jeremy Bentham argued that punishment controlled action ('either that of the offender or of others...') by '*reformation*', '*disablement*', or '*example*'; it could also be beneficial where it afforded 'pleasure or satisfaction' to the injured or those whose 'ill-will ... has been excited by the offence'. 'Introduction to the Principles of Morals and Legislation' (1760) in Bentham, *A Fragment on Government with An Introduction ... Legislation*, ed. Wilfred Harrison (Oxford, 1967), p. 281n.

4. See above, §§ 32–78.

5. The first phrase is from Titus Maccius Plautus, *Asinaria (The Comedy of Asses)*, line 495; cf. 'Popular Philosophy in its Relation to Life', *Works*, III, p. 97.

6. Cf. Green's unpublished 'Notes (various) on Moral Philosophy. Lectures Apparently', Green Papers, Balliol College (catalogue no. RLN 15): 'In early state of society individual a chattel of family ... Harm to him is harm to family. Compensation to family accordingly.'

7.*Social right, i.e. right belonging to a society of persons recognising a common good, and through membership of the society to the several persons constituting it. The society to which the right belongs, is in principle or possibility a society of all men as rendered capable of free intercourse with each other by the organisation of the state. *Actually* at first it is only this or that family; then some association of families; finally the state, as including all other forms of association, reconciling the rights which arise out of them, and thus the most perfect medium through which the individual can contribute to the good of mankind and mankind to his.

8.*'Happy shall he be that rewardeth thee as thou has served us.' [Psalm 137. Green refers here to the French determination to regain territories lost to Germany as a result of the Franco–Prussian War.]

9. Cf. G. W. F. Hegel, *Philosophy of Right* (1821), trans. T. M. Knox (Oxford, 1942), § 100: 'Further, what is involved in the action of the criminal is not only the concept of crime, the rational aspect present in the crime as such whether the individual will it or not, the aspect which the state has to vindicate, but also the abstract rationality of the individual's *volition*. Since that is so, punishment is regarded as containing the criminal's right and hence by being punished he is honoured as a rational being.'

10. Nettleship added the following gloss to the MS at this point: 'after "society" add "and therefore are a means to morality, not the end to which morality is the means" & please put a pencil note to show that these words are my addition'. This addition was not included in the printed version of the *Lectures*.

11.*'The just' = that complex of social conditions which for each individual is necessary to enable him to realise his capacity of contributing to social good. Justice is the habit of mind which leads us to respect those conditions in dealing with others – not to interfere with them so far as they already exist, to bring them into existence as far as they are not found in existence.

12. Cf. Bentham, 'An Introduction . . . Legislation', who argues that the fact of extreme hunger suggests 'the depravity of a man's disposition is less conclusive' than if the act had been committed by someone in different circumstances, where the temptation was weaker (p. 263). However, he goes on to argue that the strength of the temptation does not excuse punishment because to do so would provide encouragement to those who may be tempted (p. 268).

13. A reference to the Acts which reserved to landlords the rights to game on lands which they had let to tenant farmers; see 'Liberal Legislation', pp. 206–7 below.

14. Cf. 'Liberal Legislation', pp. 209–12 below and note 35.

15. See William Edward Hearn, *The Aryan Household. Its Structure and Its Development* (Melbourne, 1878), ch. xix; Sir Henry Maine, *Ancient Law* (London, 1861), ch. x.

16. Henry John Stephen, *New Commentaries on the Laws of England (Partly founded on Blackstone)*, 4 vols. (London, 1841–5), vol. III, p. 356.

17.*See [Sir William] Markby, *Elements of Law [Considered with Reference*

to *Principles of General Jurisprudence* (1871), 2nd edn (Oxford, 1874)],
chap. XI, especially [§ 434], note 1, pp. 242–3; and [John] Austin [*Lectures on Jurisprudence* (1863), 3rd edn, 2 vols. (London, 1869), vol. I],
Lecture XXVII. 'Between crimes and civil injuries the distinction, as it
actually exists, is merely one of procedure (as stated by Austin [vol. I] p.
518). The violation of right in one case is proceeded against by the
method of indictment, in the other by an 'action'. The distinction that in
one case *punishment* is the object of the process, in the other redress, is
introduced in order to explain the difference of procedure; and to justify
this distinction resort is had to the further distinction that civil injury is
considered to affect the individual merely, crime to affect the state. But
in fact the action for civil injury may incidentally have a penal result
(Austin, [vol. I] p. 521), and if it had not, many violations of right now
treated as civil injuries would have to be treated as crimes. As an explanation therefore of the distinction between crimes and injuries as it
stands, it is not correct to say that for the former punishment is sought,
for the latter merely redress. Nor for reasons already given is it true of
any civil injury to say that it affects, or should be considered as affecting,
injured individuals *merely*. The only distinction of principle is that between violations of right which call for punishment and those which do
not; and those only do not call for punishment in some form or other
which arise either from uncertainty as to the right violated, or from inability to prevent the violation.' [Green added a note to the MS: 'But
how about adultery?' Cf. §§ 243–5 below.]

M. The Right of the State to Promote Morality

1. See § 156 above.
2. Cf. §§ 6–13 above.
3. Cf. Adam Smith, *The Theory of Moral Sentiments* (1759), Part I, section 1, chs. I and II.
4. See also 'Liberal Legislation', below pp. 194–212.
5. Cf. *Prolegomena*, §§ 206–17.
6. See also §§ 224–32 below.

N. The Right of the State in Regard to Property

1. In the MS the passage 'Each ... them' appears *after* 'It is owing ...
acted on.' (in § 212) but is enclosed in square brackets suggesting that
these two passages should be rearranged. Although it is not possible to
determine if the brackets are Green's or Nettleship's, the present editors
have followed the order which appears in Nettleship's version since it
makes the best sense.
2. E.g. by David Hume, *A Treatise of Human Nature* (1739–40), 2 vols.,
ed. T. H. Green and T. H. Grose (London, 1874), Bk III, Part II, sect.
III (vol II, pp. 349–58).
3. E.g. by Sir Henry Maine, *Ancient Law* (1861) (Boston, 1963), ch. VIII.

4. Hugo Grotius, *De Jure Belli* (1625), trans. Francis W. Kelsey, 3 vols. (Oxford, 1925), vol. II, Book II, ch. II, ii. § 5 (pp. 189–90), ii. § 4 (p. 189), ii. § 1 (p. 186). These passages appear on a separate sheet; Nettleship put them in a footnote, but Green's use of > suggests they should be incorporated in the text as was done in other cases.

5. *'[There] is annexed to the sovereignty, the whole power of prescribing the rules, whereby every man may know, what goods he may enjoy, and what actions he may do, without being molested by any of his fellow-subjects; and this is it men call *propriety*. For before constitution of sovereign power, . . ., all men had right to all things; which necessarily causeth war: and therefore this propriety, being necessary to peace, and depending on sovereign power, is the act of that power in order to the public peace.' 'The nature of justice, consisteth in keeping of valid covenants: but the validity of covenants begins not but with the constitution of a civil power, sufficient to compel men to keep them; and then it is also that propriety begins.' Hobbes, *Leviathan* [(1651), ed. Michael Oakeshott (Oxford, 1960),] Part II, ch. 18 [p. 117]; Part I, ch. 15 [p. 94].

6. See above §§ 46–8.

7. Hobbes, *Leviathan*, Part I, ch. 15, p. 94.

8. John Locke, *Second Treatise of Government* (1690), in *Two Treatises of Government*, ed. Peter Laslett, 2nd edn (Cambridge, 1967), § 27.

9. Cf. G. W. F. Hegel, *Philosophy of Right*, trans. T. M. Knox (Oxford, 1942), §§ 45–6, 52, 57, 59, 62, 64.

10. See also §§ 2–7 above; cf. *Prolegomena*, §§ 248–9, 266–8, and 'Freedom' §§ 23–5.

11. This sort of account of wage labour under capitalism is usually associated with Karl Marx; although there is no evidence that Green knew of Marx's ideas, it is possible that he may have done so from his friend and colleague Arnold Toynbee (1852–83) who discussed Marx in his *Lectures on the Industrial Revolution . . . Popular Addresses, Notes and Fragments* (London, 1908), pp. 38 n. 1, 109, 113, and in '*Progress and Poverty': A Criticism of Mr Henry George* (London, 1883), p. 22. See also I. M. Greengarten, *Thomas Hill Green and the Development of Liberal–Democratic Thought* (Toronto, 1981), p. 10 n31. There were, however, a number of non-Marxist sources for the account which Green offers at this point; see, for example, Mill, *Political Economy*, vol. II, Bk II, ch. ii, §§ 5–7, and Robert Owen, *Observations on the Effects of the Manufacturing System* (1815). Mill's *Political Economy*, Bks II and IV (ch. xi) are generally useful sources to consult in relation to Green's economic ideas.

12. The phrase comes, of course, from P. J. Proudhon, *Q'est ce que la propriétié?* (1840). Green's unpublished papers indicate that he had some knowledge of French socialism. See also 'Notes on Ancient and Modern Political Economy', below pp. 316–17.

13. Aristotle, *Politics*, 1256b–1257a, 1328a–1330b.
14. Cf. Locke, *Second Treatise*, § 73; Green perhaps has in mind the provisions of the *Code Napoléon*. Although the *Code* did much to restore paternal power, it stipulated that except for a certain disposable proportion, property was to be divided equally between all legitimate children.
15. That is, the power to determine how an estate will be transmitted in the future. Settlements, which were designed to guard against gross extravagance and to ensure that the heir fulfilled responsibilities to other beneficiaries, tended also to keep landed estates intact, because alienation was difficult, if not impossible.
16. Cf. Green's criticism of Aristotle's economic ideas in 'Notes on Ancient and Modern Political Economy', below pp. 313–15.
17. This section shows the gap which separates Green's analysis of capitalism from that of, e.g., Marx. Green is concerned about the way that capital is used rather than about the harmful effects of capitalism *per se*. Some commentators (e.g. Greengarten, *Thomas Hill Green and the Development of Liberal–Democratic Thought*, ch. 5, and C. B. Macpherson, *Property. Mainstream and Critical Positions* (Toronto, 1978), pp. 199–207) regard Green's analysis as at best short-sighted, and at worst as a species of bourgeois apologetics. These criticisms miss the point: Green regards property as justified because of its importance for self-development; this does not necessarily preclude a consideration of alternatives to capitalism provided that it could be shown to extend opportunities for self-realisation. For a discussion of these issues see John Morrow, 'Property and Personal Development: an interpretation of T. H. Green's Political Theory', *Politics* 18 (1983), pp. 84–92.
18. For a further statement of Green's views on landed property, see 'Liberal Legislation', below pp. 205–9 and *Memoir*, p. cxii. Green's remarks on property rights in land must be considered against the background of contemporary debate on British and Irish land reform. Participants represented a variety of positions reflecting a concern to free land from outmoded restrictions on the alienation of land (party dealt with by the Encumbered Estates Act of 1848), to maximise productivity by allowing for a free trade in land, to protect tenants' claims for compensation for improvements at the termination of their tenancies (which was acknowledged, if not satisfied, by the Agricultural Holdings Act of 1865). The debate also involved more radical demands for peasant proprietorship, the taxation of the 'unearned increment' (i.e. the improvement in land values due to factors other than those wrought by the action of the owner), and schemes for land nationalisation and home colonisation advanced by the Land and Labour League (founded in 1869) to which J. S. Mill belonged. Like Mill (see *Political Economy*, vol. II, Bk II, chs. vi–vii) Green assumes that land is not merely a factor of production, and must be treated differently from other objects of property rights. Green's ideas on land reform were fairly moderate, although his criti-

cisms of proposals to tax the unearned increment (see below, § 232) were based on practical difficulties rather than on principles. In 'Liberal Legislation' he expressed sympathy with the idea of peasant proprietorship – at least for Ireland; see below p. 209, and cf. Mill, *Political Economy*, vol. II, Bk II, chs. vi–vii.

19. See 'Liberal Legislation', below pp. 199–204 and notes.

20. Almost certainly a reference to the unearned increment schemes of the American radical Henry George (1839–97). Green was probably aware of George's ideas through Arnold Toynbee, who published a critique of George's ideas a year after Green's death; see note 11 above.

O. The Right of the State in Regard to the Family

1. This phrase is the title of Bk III of Stephen's *New Commentaries* (1841–5) which Green used elsewhere in the *Lectures*; see § 149 and note above.

2. E.g. Hegel: 'The absolute goal, or, if you like, the absolute impulse, of free mind ... is to make its freedom its object ...' *Philosophy of Right* (1821), trans. T. M. Knox (Oxford, 1942), § 27.

3. John Austin, *Lectures on Jurisprudence* (1863), 3rd edn, 2 vols. (London, 1869), vol. I, p. 378; vol II, p. 736. Austin seems to have disapproved of the German terminology: 'Now I think it extremely probable, that they were led into this strange jargon by that use of the term *subject* ... Inasmuch as the person having *a* right is the *subject* of the right, the term *Recht*, as meaning *a* right, must (they fancied) have something to do with the *subjectivity* of Kant ...' Austin thought Kant's terminology had been misapplied (vol. II, p. 737).

4. See *Lectures*, §§ 213–18.

5. Cf. Hegel, *Philosophy of Right*, § 163.

6. The economic basis of the family plays a significant role in Hegel's account (*Philosophy of Right*, §§ 170–2); it also provided the basis for Bernard Bosanquet, a pupil of Green's, to reject various welfare proposals on the grounds that they would undercut the economic basis of the family as a moral unit; see John Morrow, 'Liberalism and British Idealist Political Philosophy: A Reassessment', *History of Political Thought* 5 (1984), pp. 91–108. Interestingly enough, one of the sources Green used in the present chapter was sceptical about the legal basis of property in the modern family: 'the modern family has no separate legal existence ... has no present property, but only expectations, which may be defeated by the caprice of its master ...' William Edward Hearn, *The Aryan Household. Its Structure and Its Development* (Melbourne, 1878), p. 64. For Green's use of Hearn see note 12 below.

7. Cf. Green's earlier discussion of origins, *Lectures*, §§ 124, 127–30, 211–12; cf. §§ 228–30.

8. See also the discussion of Austin in *Lectures*, ch. F.

9.*'Marriage is the joining of husband and wife, the sharing of an entire life, the making common by divine and human law.' *Digest* xxiii, 2.1. 'Matrimony is the joining of man and woman comprising an indivisible common life.' *Inst.*, i.9,2. (Quoted by [Friedrich Adolf] Trendelenburg, *Naturrecht [Auf dem Grunde Der Ethik* (Leipzig, 1860)], p. 208).

10. Cf. Hegel, *Philosophy of Right*, § 167, for a different formulation of this point.

11. See also *ibid.*, § 173.

12.*Her position among the Greeks is well illustrated by a passage from the speech of Demosthenes (?) against Neæra, § 122 (quoted by W. E. Hearn, *The Aryan Household*, p. 71), 'Mistresses we keep for pleasure, concubines for daily attendance upon our persons, wives to bear us legitimate children and to be our faithful housekeepers.'

13. Cf. Hegel, *Philosophy of Right*, § 163.

14. The Matrimonial Causes Act of 1857 had ended the need to obtain a private act of parliament in order to secure a divorce and made divorce an economically feasible option for members of the middle classes. However it was still easier for men to sue for divorce than women, and in any case, the cost of litigation was such that it effectively prevented divorce for the lower classes; see Judith Ryder and Harold Silver, *Modern English Society*, 2nd edn. (London, 1977), pp. 131–2.

15. Cf. *Lectures*, § 154.

16. This argument may also apply to adultery: 'A husband impatient for the time of the restraint of marriage may be tempted to passing adultery as a means of ridding himself of it.'

P. Rights and Virtues

1. Green's statement here suggests that this aspect of the 'inquiry into rights' has not been dealt with, despite the fact that the remainder of this chapter actually deals with preliminary matters related to the discussion of social virtues which Green suggests comes last on the list. It is not possible, of course, to tell what Green would have done had *he* completed and revised the *Lectures* for publication, but it is not obvious that the chapter on 'Rights and Virtues' has been wrongly placed by Nettleship. Although Green discusses the matters such as property and the family which have been dealt with above, he refers *back* to these discussions by using the past tense (e.g. § 249, 'As we have seen...'); in any case, his treatment differs in that the focus is now on the way in which individuals exercise rights, rather than the character of rights themselves. The distinction between rights antecedent to, and those which arise out of, the state relates to the functions of *government* rather than to the functions of the *state*. The preceding chapters (I–O) deal, as Green pointed out in § 149, with *personal rights*, but in doing so this is seen as contributing to an account of the 'nature and functions of the state' (see §§ 137, 148). For example, in his discussion of punishment

Green discusses the extent to which the state is justified in interfering in the liberty of the subject, but he also considers the purposes of punishment in relation to the promotion of the common good.

2. Green's discussion in the following passages is very reminiscent of Aristotle's remarks in the *Nicomachean Ethics*, Bks II–IV.

3. Nettleship omitted the uppercase Ds; Green's use of them suggests that he may have had in mind the fourth essay in F. H. Bradley's *Ethical Studies* (1876). The point that Green makes here could perhaps be seen as a rejoinder to the conclusion of Bradley's treatment: 'So we see "duty for duty's sake" says only, "do the right for the sake of the right"; it does not tell us what right is'; *Ethical Studies*, 2nd edn. (Oxford, 1962), p. 159. Cf. *Prolegomena*, § 183 note 2.

2. LECTURE ON 'LIBERAL LEGISLATION AND FREEDOM OF CONTRACT'

*From *Works*, III, pp. 365–86; corrected against the MS. The lecture was delivered on Tuesday 18 January 1881 in the Temperance Hall, Leicester under the auspices of the Leicester Liberal Association. An abridged version appeared in *Alliance News*, the organ of the temperance organisation the United Kingdom Alliance, on 29 January 1881. *Alliance News* published letters generated by Green's lecture on 5 February and on 12 February; other letters appeared in the *Leicester Chronicle* on 29 January and 5 February. Green was originally identified by *Alliance News* as a Cambridge professor but this error was corrected on 12 February. A full version of the lecture was published as a pamphlet in Oxford and London in February 1881. In a preface dated 8 February Green wrote that 'There is nothing original about it in the way either of information or of theory. It only attempts to set forth clearly and succinctly a view of which the statement seems to the writer to be just now of some importance.' Whatever one thinks of the originality of the lecture, it is generally regarded as significant in understanding the theoretical basis and the practical import of Green's political theory. The lecture was republished in Rodman.

1. That is, the summer session of 1880.

2. Various elements of the argument presented here can be discerned in contemporary *Hansards*, most clearly in Lord Bradbourne's speech to the House of Lords on 24 August 1880 (*Hansard*, series 3, vol. CCLV, pp. 1975–89, esp. p. 1986) which relates closely to the last part of the paragraph.

3. For example the Factory Acts of 1867 and 1878, the Elementary Education Act of 1870, and the Public Health Act of 1875.

4. The Agricultural Holdings Act of 1875 stipulated that tenants were entitled to compensation for improvements, but effectively allowed land-

lords to oblige tenants to contract out of its provisions by entering into tenancy agreements which precluded claims for compensation.

5. Cf. *Lectures*, §§ 224–7; Mill, *Political Economy*, vol. II, Bk II, ch. ii, §§ 4–5.

6. A 'local option' would allow ratepayers to vote their own localities 'dry'. The best account of Green's attitude to 'the drink problem' is that of Peter P. Nicholson, 'T. H. Green and State Action: Liquor Legislation', paper presented to the Commemorative Conference on T. H. Green, Balliol College, Oxford, 1982.

7. Probably a reference to the radical M.P.s John Bright (1811–89) and Richard Cobden (1804–65); see Richter, pp. 269–76. In notes for an (undelivered) introduction to a speech to be given by Mr William Partridge, 15 March 1882, Green describes the return of Bright as M.P. for Birmingham in 1857 as 'one of the most remarkable events in the internal political history of England during the last 30 years' (Green Papers, Balliol College Library).

8. The measures which Green probably had in mind were the Municipal Corporations Act of 1835, the Charitable Trusts Act 1842, a series of acts (1837–51) relating to non-resident clergymen and plural livings, and administrative reforms instigated by the Ecclesiastical Commission Reports of 1834 and 1835.

9. Source not identified; Peter Nicholson has pointed out to the editors that the expression may have been used with reference to slave-owners whose slaves were to be emancipated, or to land-owners subject to compulsory purchase orders, or to publicans who had to surrender their licences.

10. Between 1842 and 45 a third of the duties were abolished and the remaining two thirds were reduced; Gladstone introduced the first of his reforming budgets in 1853; he continued to reform the fiscal machinery during ten years as Chancellor of the Exchequer (1852–5, 1859–66).

11. The Factory Act of 1867, unlike early legislation, extended regulation to all workshops employing more than fifty people; it also covered a wide range of named occupations. The consolidation of which Green writes was 'An Act to Amend and Extend the Acts Relating to Factories and Workshops' of 1870 (33 and 34 *Vic.*)

12. Anthony John Mundella (1827–97), Liberal statesman, M.P. for Sheffield 1868–97 (*D.N.B.*).

13. Cf. Green's account of the history of this Act in 'Two Lectures on the Elementary School System of England', *Works*, III, pp. 413–33. W. E. Forster (1818–86), M.P. for Leeds (1859–86), was Vice President of the Council, the body responsible for education.

14. Education Acts of 1876 and 1880 transformed the facilitating aspects of the 1870 Act into those of a compulsory nature. See 'Two Lectures...', *Works*, III, pp. 433–55.

15. That is in Leicester, a textile manufacturing town where the effects of the legislation under discussion would be widely appreciated.

16. Green's language in this and the following passages – especially the account of freedom in relation to 'powers' – seems to have had a significant impact on the work of C. B. Macpherson, a modern scholar who offers an account of Green's political philosophy in which sympathy and criticism are nicely balanced; see C. B. Macpherson, *Democratic Theory. Essays in Retrieval* (Oxford, 1973); *The Life and Times of Liberal Democracy* (Oxford, 1977); and *Property. Mainstream and Critical Positions* (Toronto, 1978). For a critical account of Macpherson's treatment of Green's property theory, see John Morrow, 'Property and Personal Development: An Interpretation of T. H. Green's Political Philosophy', *Politics* 18 (1983), pp. 84–92.

17. See also *Lectures*, §§ 84, 92, 114–26.

18. Cf. J.–J. Rousseau, *Discours sur l'origine et les fondements de l'inégalité parmi les hommes* (1755).

19. Cf. *Prolegomena* §§ 218, 241, 244–6, 257, 266, 270.

20. See also *Lectures*, §§ 213, 216, 220–32.

21. Cf. J. S. Mill, *On Liberty* (1859), ch. v.

22. See for example Mill's *Political Economy*, vol. II, Bk I, chs. i–ii, x; Bk III, ch. iv.

23. Cf. *Lectures* §§ 207–10.

24. That is, Sir William Vernon Harcourt (1827–1904), Liberal statesman, M.P. for Oxford 1869–80, and Derby 1880–1904 (*D.N.B.*). In a speech delivered in 1873, Harcourt had spoken of 'grand-maternal government'. Green responded by contrasting 'that liberty ... which is compatible with the real freedom of others and that which merely means freedom to make oneself a social nuisance'. Harcourt's speech and Green's response were reported in the *Alliance News* and *Oxford Chronicle* respectively (4 Jan. 1873); see Brian Harrison, *Drink and the Victorians* (London, 1971), p. 210. Green's letter to the *Chronicle* provoked a correspondence with Harcourt in which Green, although principally concerned with the 'drink question', produced a defence of limiting freedom of contract similar to that expounded in the present lecture. 'That the law cannot make men good – that its business is to set them free to make themselves good – I quite agree. The question is, how these truisms are to be applied. I am no advocate of beneficent despotism. No tendency, inconsistent with recognised principles of English legislation, lurks under my use of the phrases "constructive Liberals" and "organic reforms" ... As instances of what I mean by "organic social reforms" I should specify compulsory education, restraint on the power of settling real estate and on freedom of contract in certain respects, specially in respect of Game, between landlord and Tenant, the inspection of dwelling houses, the compulsory provision of them in certain cases, the prevention of landlords from building them and of tenant from agreeing to

live in them unless they are of a certain size; the compulsory reservation of a certain amount of allotments . . .

All of these measures, though it may be fairly said that in the long run and on the whole they are essential to individual liberty, would be excluded by the mere 'laissez-faire' application of the doctrine that Government has only to provide for the protection of person and property.' Undated draft (early January 1873) in Green Papers, Balliol College Library.

25. Cf. the opening paragraph of this lecture.

26. Green's willingness to acknowledge that the state may relieve the head of a family of certain responsibilities, and thus allow other functions to be more satisfactorily fulfilled, would perhaps provide grounds for accepting state provision of certain material services. To the extent that this was the case, his position differs significantly from that of his pupil Bernard Bosanquet, who was an adamant opponent of such provisions. See, for example, Bernard Bosanquet, 'Character and its Bearing on Private Property', and 'Socialism and Natural Selection', in *Aspects of the Social Problem*, ed. Bernard Bosanquet (London, 1895), pp. 19–22, 109, 291, 300, 311, and John Morrow, 'Liberalism and British Idealist Political Philosophy: A Reassessment', *History of Political Thought* 5 (1984), pp. 91–108.

27. For example, the reports on textile factories (1833), handloom weaving (1838–41), mines (1842) and Edwin Chadwick's *Report on the Sanitary Condition of the Labouring Poor* (1842).

28. See also *Lectures*, §§ 226–32; cf. Mill, *Political Economy*, vol. II, Bk I, ch. xii; Bk II, chs. ii–x.

29. Edward Henry Stanley, 15th Earl of Derby (1826–93), a leading Liberal statesman, was much concerned with land reform; he contributed articles on the question to periodicals such as *Nineteenth Century*; see Roy Douglas, *Land, People and Politics* (London, 1976), pp. 17, 33. Thomas William Coke, 2nd Earl of Leicester (1822–1909) is described by the *D.N.B.* as a 'prominent agriculturalist', although he does not appear to have spoken on this (or any) subject in the House of Lords in the period 1870–80. The point which Green is making may have been raised in relation to discussions of the so-called 'New Domesday' survey of land ownership which was debated in the Lords in 1872; *Parliamentary Papers*, 1874, LXXII, parts 1–3, Return of Landowners 1873 (c. 1097), *Hansard*, series 3, vol. CCIX (19 Feb. 1872).

30. Hugh McCalmont Cairns, 1st Earl Cairns (1819–85), Conservative statesman, and a leading member of the Bar (*D.N.B.*). Green is referring to the Land Settlement Act, introduced by Cairns in February 1880 and passed into law in 1882. It was designed to balance a public concern that land be effectively utilised with familial interests expressed in settlements (see *Lectures*, §§ 224–7 and notes 14, 15). Life-tenants were to be

given the powers previously vested in the Court of Chancery, but the original spirit of the settlement in question was to be preserved. For a critical contemporary account of Cairns' Bill with which Green was familiar, see George C. Broderick, *English Land and English Landlords* (London, 1881), pp. 138–41. Green addressed a meeting of agricultural labourers on Broderick's behalf during the election campaign of 1868; see *Memoir*, p. xcii.

31. See note 4 above for a similar case.

32. A slightly modified quotation from Broderick, *English Land and English Landlords*, p. 378. Under 'Lincolnshire custom' tenants were compensated for unexhausted improvements at the end of their tenancies on the basis of a customary arrangement; it covered a proportion of money expended on manure, fertiliser, drainage, seed and certain buildings; see G. M. Williams, 'On the Tenant's Right to Unexhausted Improvements, according to the Custom of North Lincolnshire', *Journal of the Royal Agricultural Society of England* 6 (1845), pp. 44–6; a communication from Charles Stokes in the same issue refers to a similar agreement between landlords and tenants in Loughborough; *ibid.*, pp. 46–8.

33. Green's figures may come from contemporary discussions of the land problem in Ireland; a *Report Into Workings of Landlord and Tenant (Ireland) Act* (Bessborough Report) was presented to Parliament in 1881 (c. 2779, xvii).

34. The Irish National Land League, founded in October 1879, had close links with the party of Nationalist M.P.s at Westminster; Parnell was party leader and president of the League. The League's immediate goal was to secure what were known as the 'three Fs', namely fair rents, fixity of tenure, and the free sale of rights of occupancy; Gladstone's Irish Land Act of 1881 went some way to meeting these demands. The agitation to which Green refers was associated with the League, but was not publicly endorsed by leading members of the Irish Nationalist party in Parliament. The most notorious tactic in the League's campaign was 'boycotting': the organised and sometimes violently enforced ostracism of people deemed to have contravened the League's code of fair conduct.

35. See the paper by Nicholson cited in note 6 above.

36. Cf. 'Freedom', § 6: 'To an Athenian slave, who might be used to gratify a master's lust, it would have been a mockery to speak of the state as a realisation of freedom; and perhaps it would not be much less so to speak of it as such to an untaught and under-fed denizen of a London yard with ginshops on the right hand and on the left.'

37. Cf. Mill, *On Liberty*, ch. iv, which may be Green's target.

38. See also *Lectures*, § 119. Green exaggerates here; in 1881 there were about three million qualified voters out of an adult male population of three times that size. Cf. p. 197 above, where Green refers more circumspectly to the 'more democratic parliament of 1868.'

3. FOUR LECTURES ON THE ENGLISH REVOLUTION: SELECTIONS

*From *Works*, III, pp. 277–364, reissued with an introduction by Kenneth Bell (London, 1912). These lectures were delivered before the Edinburgh Philosophical Institution in 1866. *The Jubilee Book of the Philosophical Institution* (Edinburgh, 1897) refers to Green's lectures ('by good fortune or wise guidance, it often happened that the Institution listened to young men who afterwards became distinguished'), but does not explain how Green came to be invited to lecture. It is possible that Green may have visited Scotland on business connected with the Snell Exhibitions offered to Glasgow students who wished to continue their studies at Balliol. Green's only other recorded visit to Scotland took place in April 1875 when he received the degree of Doctor of Laws from Glasgow University; this award is not mentioned in the *Memoir* or in Richter, but is reported in John Henry Muirhead, *Reflections by a Journeyman in Philosophy* (London, 1942), p. 37; this is supported by *University of Glasgow Degree, Prize, and Certificate of Honour List Session 1874–5* (Glasgow, 1875), p. 6. Green's friend and former Oxford colleague Edward Caird was a Professor at Glasgow when Green received the degree; it may have been awarded for Green's work on the Green and Grose edition of Hume. The lectures were not published during Green's lifetime, but were included by Nettleship in vol. III of the *Works*, on the advice of C. A. Fyffe, J. Frank Bright and C. H. Firth. Fyffe suggested that certain phrases be 'softened' on the grounds that they may, after the passage of a number of years, have struck Green as 'unduly sharp or sarcastic' and recommended that a passage relating to Bishop Juxon be omitted (Fyffe to Mrs Green, 1 January 1883); it would have appeared in *Works*, III, p. 325. The passage in question refers to the conduct of Dr William Juxon (1582–1663), Bishop of London and subsequently Archbishop of Canterbury. On being asked to attend the King just prior to his execution, Juxon became flustered and, in the words of Edmund Ludlow (whom Green quotes), 'broke out into these Expressions, *God save me, what a Trick is this, that I should have no more Warning, and I have nothing ready*'. Edmund Ludlow, *Memoirs*, 3 vols. (London 1698–9), vol. I, pp. 282–3. Presumably Fyffe suggested that this passage be omitted because of the barbed nature of Green's introduction to it: 'Since all Englishmen are bred to the belief that Juxon carried himself on the occasion as became a Bishop and a confessor of the Royal Martyr, I shall ask leave to read an extract from Ludlow that might give a different impression.' (Green Papers, Balliol College Library, MS of 'Four Lectures on the English Revolution'.)

1. Green drew on a number of works, most of which have been identified

by the present editors in notes. His major sources appear to have been Thomas Carlyle's *Oliver Cromwell's Letters and Speeches with Elucidations* (London, 1845), John Forster's *Sir Henry Vane the Younger, 1612–1662* (London, 1838), vol. 4 of *Lives of Eminent British Statesmen*, and also the third volume of *The Statesman of the Commonwealth of England*, 5 vols. (London, 1840). Green's reliance on Forster is particularly heavy; most of the quotations from Vane's writings, along with other material, are identified in Forster's *Vane*.

2. Carlyle, *Cromwell's Letters and Speeches*.

3. Early in 1534 the Anabaptists gained control of the city of Münzer (Munster) and established a communitarian and polygamous 'New Jerusalem'; the city was retaken in 1535 by what Elton describes as the 'significantly odd alliance between a catholic bishop and protestant prince'; G. R. Elton, *Reformation Europe 1517–1559* (London, 1968), p. 101. The Anabaptists were suppressed with great cruelty.

4. Presbyterianism was a system of church government designed to secure the freedom of the church from outside interference. Each parish was part of a system of authority which culminated in the supreme governing body, the General Assembly. The freedom embodied in the Presbyterian system was not that of individuals or groups, but 'of the church itself to instruct, admonish, and discipline all sinners...' William Haller, *Liberty and Reformation in the Puritan Revolution* (New York, 1955), p. 105. By contrast many Puritans in England were Independents; that is to say, they upheld the autonomy of individual congregations, and were fearful of national systems of church government.

5. William Laud (1573–1645), a leading churchman and Archbishop of Canterbury from 1633. Laud was infamous for his advocacy of episcopal authority over the lesser clergy and their congregations (*D.N.B.*).

6. Robert Brown[e] (1550–1633) first attracted the unfavourable notice of the church authorities as the leader of a sect at Norwich; he fled to Holland in 1581, and was excommunicated in 1586. John Robinson (1576?–1633) was the pastor of the Pilgrim Fathers (*D.N.B.*). Although Green's account of Robinson's ideas has been omitted, it should be noted that he described Robinson's address to those embarking for America as exhibiting 'a higher spirit of christian freedom than anything that had been heard since christianity fixed itself in creeds and churches', *Works*, III, p. 281.

7. Sir Henry Vane the Younger (1613–62) was M.P. for Hull in the Long Parliament (1640–53). A leading political figure of the revolutionary period, Vane served with distinction on a series of committees responsible for ecclesiastical, military, naval and civil affairs. Vane was arrested at the Restoration and executed in June 1662, despite the fact that he was not one of the men who had signed Charles' death warrant (*D.N.B.*).

8. Richard Baxter, *Reliquiae Baxterianae* (London, 1696), p. 75; Forster, *Sir Henry Vane*, pp. 76–7 note.

9. [Sir Henry Vane], *A Retired Man's Meditations* (London, 1655), p. 45; Forster, *Sir Henry Vane*, p. 83.

10. The distinctions between 'natural', 'legal', and 'evangelical' conscience are discussed in chs. 15–17 of Vane's *Retired Man's Meditations*.

11. The phrase is in Forster, *Sir Henry Vane*, pp. 69, 77 note, who quotes Clarendon, *History of the Rebellion and Civil Wars in England* (London, 1702–4), Bk XVI, sect. 88. Clarendon's statement referred to Vane's religious views, but this is not clear from Green's use of the quote.

12. Support for this claim can be found in [Anon] *The Tryall of Sir Henry Vane... Also his Speech and Prayer etc. on the Scaffold* (London, 1662), pp. 123–4, 296, and in Vane's *The Peoples Case Stated*, written during his imprisonment from 1660 to 1662 and reproduced by Forster as Appendix B of *Sir Henry Vane*.

13. The phrase comes from the title of ch. 15 of Vane's *Retired Man's Meditations*.

14. Perhaps a reference to J. S. Mill's *On Liberty*, which had been published in 1859.

15. John May, *Breviary of the History of the Long Parliament* (1650) in *Maseres Tracts*, 2 parts (London 1812), pt 1, p. 74. The New Model Army developed out of a troop of horse raised by Cromwell in Huntingdon in the second half of 1642. By 1645 the entire parliamentary army had been 'new modelled'. Cromwell described his troops as being 'well armed within by the satisfaction of their conscience, and without by good iron arms'; cited Christopher Hill, *God's Englishman* (Harmondsworth, 1972), p. 62.

16. Lady Fairfax (1618?–1665), wife of Sir Thomas, 3rd Lord Fairfax (1612–1671), Lord General at the time of the trial of Charles I (1649). Green's reference is to an incident at the trial; the source is probably *The Fairfax Correspondence: Memoirs of the Reign of Charles the First*, ed. George W. Johnson (London, 1848), vol. 1: '... when the clerk began to read the charge, "In the name of the good people of England – " she interrupted him by crying out, "No, nor half of them; it is false; where are they or their consents? Oliver Cromwell is a traitor"' (p. cv). Other sources (e.g. Clarendon, *History*) turn this into 'No, nor the hundredth part of them'; see Clement R. Markham, *A Life of the Great Lord Fairfax...*, 2 vols. (London, 1870), vol. 1, pp. 349–50n.

17. John Milton, *Eikonoclastes* (1649), *Works of John Milton*, 18 vols. (New York, 1931–8). vol. 5, p. 328.

18. William Wordsworth, *Ruth*, lines 169–71; Green substitutes 'them' for 'me' in the first line.

19. Milton, *Eikonoclastes*, p. 69.

20. A slightly modified quotation from Milton's *Tenure of Kings and Magistrates* (1649), *Works of John Milton*, vol. 5, p. 3.

21. See Milton's *Defence of the People of England* (1654), *Works of John Milton*, vol. 8, esp. pp. 225–55.

22. That is, Cromwell's campaign against the Scottish forces led by the Duke of Hamilton; the invading army was routed at the Battle of Preston in August 1648.

23. Cicero, *De Legibus*, III (iii), 8.

24. The phrase 'that he would be king of England yet' is Green's; it appears earlier in a part of the lectures which has been omitted – see *Works*, III, p. 345. The source of this view is Edmund Ludlow's *Memoirs*, vol. 2, p. 114: 'and that he [Peter] told a friend with whom he then quartered on his return to London, that he was inclined to believe Cromwell would endeavour to make himself king'. Peter's modern biographer disputes reports in Royalist circles that Peter himself was an advocate of a Cromwellian monarchy; see Raymond P. Strearns, *The Strenuous Puritan. Hugh Peter, 1598–1660* (Urbana, 1954), pp. 393–4. The Rev. Hugh Peter who was Cromwell's chaplain, was often referred to as 'Peters', presumably because of the title of a work, *Mr Peters* [sic] *Last Report of the English Warres* (1646).

25. The Battle of Worcester took place on 2 September 1651.

26. Robert Blake (1599–1657), a highly successful admiral and general at sea under the Commonwealth (*D.N.B.*). The victory referred to was that over the French fleet in April 1652.

27. The bill provided for a parliament of four hundred, representation being based on population and wealth. The borough franchise was to rest on a uniform rental qualification applied to householders, while in the counties tenants subject to their landlords were to be excluded; voters had to possess freehold land valued at forty shillings, a copyhold of five pounds, or a leasehold of twenty pounds per annum.

28. 'The Rump' refers to members of the Long Parliament remaining after 'Pride's Purge' of 1648 when many members of the leading families of England were excluded from the Long Parliament.

29. That is, during Cromwell's Protectorate, 1653–8.

30. 1702.

31. The first lines Green quotes are from Forster, *Sir Henry Vane*, p. 237, who draws on *The Tryall*, p. 88. 'The people ... awake' is also from Forster (p. 196) but was not uttered by Vane on the scaffold, which for dramatic purposes is surely a pity. Forster cites 'Burton's Diary', i.e. Thomas Burton M.P., *Diary of Thomas Burton*, 4 vols., ed. John Towill Rutt (London, 1828), vol. 4, p. 105 which relates a speech given by Vane in the House of Commons, 9 March, 1659. Green misquotes; the original (which is faithfully reproduced by Forster) runs 'when a man is asleep, he finds no hunger till he wake. I doubt the people of England will be hungry when they awake.'

32. A reference to the introduction of idealist philosophy in nineteenth-century England.

4. ON THE DIFFERENT SENSES OF 'FREEDOM' AS APPLIED
TO WILL AND TO THE MORAL PROGRESS OF MAN

*From *Works*, II, pp. 307–33. These were part of the lectures Green gave in 1879 on 'The Theory of Duty', most of which were used for the *Prolegomena*; see § 100n, and *Lectures*, § 6n. The analysis of freedom in the MS follows that which became § 154 of the *Prolegomena*: '. . . a vocation conceived as given by God, makes the object what it really is. [MS continues] In like manner (as has been before said) the real nature of the will in any man – his character – depends on the nature of the objects in which he mainly tends to seek to satisfy himself. And the same remark will apply to national will and to human will – if we are justified in speaking of such entities. (Whether we are or not will be considered shortly.)

In like manner, though it is important to insist that, since in all willing a man is his own object to himself . . .'

1. *In that sense in which 'freedom' expresses a state of the soul, as distinct from a civil relation.
2. Cf. Green, 'Lectures on the Philosophy of Kant. II. The Metaphysics of Ethics', *Works*, II, p. 95; *Prolegomena*, § 171.
3. E.g. *Republic*, 561, 573, 577d, 590c.
4. Rom. viii: 15.
5. Rom. vii: 9.
6. Rom. vii: 15; cf. Green, 'Extract from lectures on the Epistle to the Romans', *Works*, III, pp. 192ff.
7. Rom. vii: 14.
8. Cf. Kant, *Grundlegung zur Metaphysik der Sitten* (1785), *The Moral Law*, trans. H. J. Paton (London, 1948), pp. 115–16; Green, 'Lectures on the Philosophy of Kant', pp. 106–9.
9. Rom. viii: 4.
10. Rom. viii: 2.
11. Kant, *Grundlegung*, Paton pp. 81, 109–10; *Kritik der Praktischen Vernunft* (1788), in *Kant's Critique of Practical Reason,* trans. T. K. Abbott, 6th edn (London, 1909), p. 214; *Die Religion innerhalb der Grenzen der blossen Vernunft* (1793), *ibid.*, pp. 341–4. Cf. Green, 'Lectures on the Philosophy of Kant', p. 107.
12. Rom. vii: 22–3.
13. Rom. vii: 7.
14. *In the sense of 'autonomy of rational will', or determination by an object which reason constitutes, as distinct from determination by an object which the man makes his own – which latter determination Kant would have recognised as characteristic of every human act, properly so called. [Cf. n. 8 above.]
15. Hegel, *Philosophy of Right* (1821), trans. T. M. Knox (Oxford, 1942), §§ 15, 33, 135.
16. *Ibid.*, §§ 33, 142–57, 257–360 *passim*.

17. See *Prolegomena*, §§ 199–217.
18. This last clause is queried in the MS.
19. Cf. Aristotle, *Politics*, 1277b, 1284a.
20. Cf. *Prolegomena*, §§ 206–17.
21. *Philosophy of Right*, §§ 258, 267n.
22. Cf. *Prolegomena*, § 205; *Lectures*, § 7.
23. Cf. Green's discussion of 'temperance' and 'self-denial' in Greek morality, *Prolegomena*, §§ 261–72.
24. Rom. viii: 21.
25. Rom. vii: 23.
26. Rom. vii: 3, 19.
27. Rom. viii: 4, 15.
28. Kant, *Grundlegung*, Paton pp. 98–107. Cf. Green, 'Lectures on the Philosophy of Kant', p. 121.
29. E.g. Zeno, *On the Nature of Man*, quoted in Diogenes Laertius, *Lives of Eminent Philosophers*, 2 vols., trans. R. D. Hicks (London and Cambridge, Mass., 1925), vol. 2, Bk VII, p. 195.
30. John Locke, *An Essay Concerning Human Understanding* (1690), ed. Peter H. Nidditch (Oxford, 1975), Bk II, ch. 21, § 10.
31. *Ibid.*, § 16.
32. *Ibid.*, § 21.
33. Cf. the discussion of freedom of the will in *Prolegomena*, §§ 85–114.
34. Locke, *Essay*, Bk II, ch. 21, § 16.
35. *Prolegomena*, § 107.
36. *Ibid.*, § 105.
37. *Ibid.*, § 102.
38. I.e. Locke, Berkeley, Hume.
39. *Republic*, 379c, 571c–572b.
40. Cf. *Kant's Critique of Practical Reason*, trans. Abbott, p. 268n.
41. Cf. *Prolegomena*, § 187, and note.
42. Kant, *Grundlegung*, Paton pp. 58, 121; Green, 'Lectures on the Philosophy of Kant', pp. 98–105.
43. See *Prolegomena*, Bk I, 'Metaphysics of Knowledge'.
44. There follow two MS pages in which Green argues that the principle (which 'we may call, in a certain sense truly, the universal human will or universal practical reason') is realised in individual self-conscious men living in community; cf. *Prolegomena*, §§ 180ff. Green restates the problem set out at the end of § 20 before continuing as shown; the phrase noted in variation *b–b* is in that restatement.
45. Cf. *Lectures*, § 6; *Prolegomena*, § 177.
46. Rom. vii: 22.
47. Locke, *Essay*, Bk II, ch. 28, § 7.
48. Kant, *Grundlegung*, Paton pp. 57–8, 65, 74. Cf. Green, 'Lectures on the Philosophy of Kant', p. 149.
49. Green then proceeds to discuss the relationship between personal devel-

opment and a 'national spirit' in passages incorporated into the *Prolegomena*, §§ 183-91. See also *Lectures*, § 6, note.

5. PROLEGOMENA TO ETHICS: SELECTIONS

*Ed. A. C. Bradley, 4th edn (Oxford, 1899). This book was based on
Green's lectures from 1878 to 1882. He was close to completing it at the
time of his death, and the MS passed into Bradley's care. He divided it
into books, chapters and sections and composed their titles, provided
the useful 'Analytical Table of Contents' and some references, altered
punctuation, and reworked some sentences, but on the whole he wielded
a light editorial hand. All of Book I and part of Book II were published in
Mind 7 (1882), pp. 1-29, 161-85, 321-48. The book itself was first
published in 1883; 17,000 copies were sold in five editions before it went
out of print in 1949 (Richter, p. 294n).

Book III, Chapter 1: Good and Moral Good
1. I.e. Book I ('Metaphysics of Knowledge') and Book II ('The Will').
2. Shakespeare, *Measure for Measure*, act 3, scene 1, line 9.
3. Cf. 'Loyalty', pp. 304-6 below.
4. Job xix: 28.
5. Cf. *Lectures*, § 6; 'Freedom', § 21.
6. John Milton, *On the Morning of Christ's Nativity*, Hymn, stanza 1, line 29.
7. E.g. Plato, *Philebus*, 11b, 66e; cf. 'Freedom', *passim*.
8. William Wordsworth, *My Heart Leaps Up*, line 7.

Book III, Chapter 2: Characteristics
of the Moral Ideal
1. *We say that his true good *is* this complete realisation when we think of
the realisation as already attained in the eternal mind. We say that it
would be such realisation when we think of the realisation as for ever
problematic to man in the state of which we have experience.
2. This is a clear echo of the famous title of ch. 5 of F. H. Bradley's *Ethical
Studies* (1876), 'My Station and Its Duties'; cf. *Lectures*, § 251 and
note. F. H. Bradley was the older brother of the editor of the *Prolegomena* and a Fellow of Merton College, Oxford, from 1870 until his
death. One who knew him well writes: 'There are characteristic differences between [*Ethical Studies* and the *Prolegomena*], traceable to
differences in the personality of their authors, but it has always been
rightly felt by their readers that the attitude of the writers to the moral
life and the moral ideal is at bottom the same; the differences discoverable are chiefly differences in emphasis. It should be noted that the two
works seem to be virtually independent. Bradley had attended Green's
lectures at Oxford and shared the veneration with which Green's character inspired all who came even remotely under his influence, but there

seems to have been little or no further personal contact between the two philosophers; in later life Bradley used to express the view that Green's close dependence on Kant had an unfortunate effect on the permanent value of his work. The *Prolegomena*, on the other side, takes no account of work already done for moral philosophy in *Ethical Studies*. It must be remembered that Green's book was a posthumous one.' A. E. Taylor, 'Francis Herbert Bradley, 1846–1924', *Proceedings of the British Academy*, 11 (1924–5), p. 464; see also Richter, p. 160n. On Bradley's political thought see Peter Nicholson, 'Bradley as a Political Philosopher', *The Philosophy of F. H. Bradley*, ed. Anthony Manser and Guy Stock (Oxford, 1984), pp. 117–30.

3. The contrast between 'actuality' and 'potentiality' is important for Green's theory of development and self-realisation. See 'Freedom', § 16; 'The Philosophy of Aristotle', *Works*, III, pp. 75–6, 79–80, 83–4; 'Fragment of an Address on the text "The Word is Nigh Thee"', *Works*, III, pp. 224–7. Cf. Aristotle, *Metaphysics*, 1048a–1048b (Book θ, ch. 6); *De Anima*, trans. D. W. Hamlyn (Oxford, 1968), 412ab (Bk II, ch. 1) and Hamlyn's note; Hegel, *The Philosophy of Right* (1821), trans. T. M. Knox (Oxford, 1942), § 301; Craig A. Smith, 'The Individual and Society in T. H. Green's Theory of Virtue', *History of Political Thought* 2 (1981), pp. 191–4.

4. Cf. 'Fragment of an Address on the text "The Word is Nigh Thee"', pp. 224–7; 'The Witness of God', *Works*, III, pp. 239–40.

5. Hence parents have a moral duty to educate their children, which ought to be enforced by the state (*Lectures*, § 209; 'Liberal Legislation', below pp. 202–3). In 'Two Lectures on the Elementary School System of England' (*Works*, III, pp. 413–55), Green writes of the duty of educating his children as one which a man 'owes to his neighbours, and of which his neighbours are entitled to exact the fulfilment' (p. 447). For the detail of Green's views about education and his influence on educational practice, see Peter Gordon and John White, *Philosophers as Educational Reformers: The Influence of Idealism on British Educational Thought and Practice* (London, 1979).

6. See note to *Lectures*, § 6.

7. Kant, *Grundlegung zur Metaphysik der Sitten* (1785), *The Moral Law*, trans. H. J. Paton (London, 1948), p. 82.

8. John Locke, *An Essay Concerning Human Understanding* (1690), ed. Peter H. Nidditch (Oxford, 1975), Bk II, ch. 28, § 7. Cf. *Lectures*, § 4; 'Freedom', § 24.

9. In Book IV.

Book III, Chapter 3: The Origin and
Development of the Moral Ideal

1. John Milton, *Paradise Lost*, Bk IV, lines 756–7; cf. 'Popular Philosophy in its Relation to Life', *Works*, III, p. 112.

2. Cf. *Lectures*, ch. G, 'Will, not force, is the basis of the state.'
3. E.g. Sir Edward Coke (1552–1634), *First Institutes* (1628), ed. Francis Hargrave and Charles Butler, 19th edn (corrected), 2 vols. (London, 1832), vol. 1, sect. 138: 'And this is another strong argument in law, *Nihil quod est contra rationem est licitum* [nothing is lawful which is contrary to reason]; for reason is the life of the law, nay the common law itselfe is nothing else but reason; which is to be understood of an artificiall perfection of reason, gotten by long study, observation, and experience, and not of every man's naturall reason; for, *Nemo nascitur artifex* [no-one is born a skilled workman] This legall reason *est summa ratio* [is of very great weight]. And therefore if all the reason that is dispersed into so many severall heads, were united into one, yet could he not make such a law as the law in *England* is; because by many successions of ages it hath beene fined and refined by an infinite number of grave and learned men, and by long experience growne to such a perfection, for the government of this realme, as the old rule may be justly verified of it, *Neminem oportet esse sapientiorem legibus*: no man out of his own private reason ought to be wiser than the law, which is the perfection of reason'.
4. Cf. *Lectures*, §§ 151–4.
5. Green says that this extension of the range of persons recognised as having claims may be brought about through conquest and trade (see § 281 below; *Lectures*, § 174; and 'The Effect of Commerce on the Mind of a Nation', pp. 302–4 below); through common education ('the true social leveller. Men and women who have been at school together, or who have been at schools of the same sort, will always understand each other, will always be at their ease together, will be free from social jealousies and animosities, however different their circumstances in life may be.' 'Lecture on the Work to be done by the New Oxford High School for Boys', *Works*, III, pp. 457–8); and through the novel ('An Estimate of the Value and Influence of Works of Fiction in Modern Times', *Works*, III, pp. 20–45). This last essay won Green the Chancellor's Prize in 1862. In it he argues that the novel is 'an inferior work of art' (p. 36) compared to the poem and the tragedy since 'the aspect of things' which the novelist shows us 'is merely the outward and natural, as opposed to the inner or ideal' (p. 30) revealed by the poet or the tragedian. Nevertheless, the novel 'has a proper work of its own which, if modern progress be anything more than a euphemism, must be a work of good' (p. 39); the novelist is 'a great expander of sympathies; . . . he . . . carries our thought into many a far country of human experience, which it could not otherwise have reached . . . In the progressive division of labour, while we become more useful as citizens, we seem to lose our completeness as men . . . There is less of human interest to touch us within our calling, and we have less leisure to seek it beyond. Hence it follows that one who has made the most of his profession is apt

to feel that he has not attained his full stature as a man; that he has faculties which he can never use, capacities for admiration and affection which can never meet with an adequate object ... [The] alleviation [of this feeling], if not its remedy, is to be found in the newspaper and the novel ... The personal experience and the fictitious act and react on each other, the personal experience giving reality to the fictitious, the fictitious expansion to the personal ... It is the twofold characteristic, of universal intelligibility and indiscriminate adoption of materials, that gives the novel its place as the great reformer and leveller of our time ... Every good novel, therefore, does something to check what may be called the despotism of situations; to prevent that ossification into prejudices arising from situation, to which all feel a tendency' (pp. 40–1).

6.*Aristotle, *Nicomachean Ethics*, V, x, 6.
7.*I use the term 'intuition' here, in the sense commonly attached to it by recent English writers on morals, for a judgement not derived deductively or inductively from other judgements. The reader should be on his guard against confusing this sense of the term with that in which it is used as an equivalent for the German '*Anschauung*', or apprehension of an object.
8. In *Prolegomena*, § 211, Green quotes 'the famous definition of Justice in the Institutes: – "*Justitia est constans et perpetua voluntas suum cuique tribuendi.*" ['Justice is the set and constant purpose which gives to every man his due.' *The Institutes of Justinian*, trans. J. B. Moyle, 5th edn (Oxford, 1913), Bk I, Title 1, p. 3.] Every man both by law and common sentiment is recognised as having a "*suum*", whatever the "*suum*" may be, and is thus effectively distinguished from the animals (at any rate according to our treatment of them) and from things. He is deemed capable of having something of his own, as animals and things are not.' The phrase '*suum cuique*', 'to each his own', comes from Cicero, *Tusculanae Disputationes*, V. 22; see also *Lectures*, § 135.

Book III, Chapter 4: the Development of the Moral Ideal (continued)
1. See § 217 above, note 8.
2. Aristotle, *Politics*, 1280b; see also Andrew Vincent and Raymond Plant, *Philosophy, Politics and Citizenship: Idealism and the Welfare State* (Oxford, 1984), pp. 59–61.
3.*Aristotle, *Nicomachean Ethics*, I, viii, 2.

Book III, Chapter 5: the Development of the Moral Ideal (continued)
1. Cf. 'Freedom', §§ 2–3.
2. Cf. *Lectures*, § 219, and 'Liberal Legislation', pp. 195–9 below.
3. The last clauses of this sentence are queried in the MS.
4. *Philebus*, 46ff.
5.*ᵃAmounting, i.e., merelyᵃ to the denial to any one of a right to use others as his instruments or property.

6. Cf. Green's comparison of the 'Athenian slave' and the 'untaught and underfed denizen of a London yard' in 'Freedom', § 6.
7. An adaptation from Alfred, Lord Tennyson's *Locksley Hall*, line 137: 'Yet I doubt not thro' the ages one increasing purpose runs.'
8.*I.e. an ideal which the persons affected by it have reflected on.
9. Cf. § 207 above and note.

Book IV, Chapter 1: the Practical Value of the Moral Ideal
1. *Book of Common Prayer* (1549), Communion Service.
2. Alfred, Lord Tennyson, *In Memoriam*, LXI, 6.
3. Eph. vi: 5–6; Col. iii: 22.
4. John Locke, *An Essay Concerning Human Understanding* (1690), ed. Peter H. Nidditch (Oxford, 1975), Book II, ch. 28, § 7.
5. Cf. 'Loyalty' and 'Legislative Interference in Moral Matters', pp. 304–9 below; 'The Force of Circumstances', *Works*, III, pp. 9–10: 'If we look at the state of European nations, it would seem that the effect of external influences upon them, though various, has not been unequal, and that their political constitutions have been alike as powers of evil, but very different in the amount of living beneficial power which they have received from men who were raised above them. The spiritual energy of the liberated few introduces an element of good into the force to which the many are subject. We see everywhere – in the abolition of serfdom, in the reconcilement of nations, in the general recognition of personal equality – how Christianity, as an external influence, has lightened the worldly burden of multitudes who were ignorant of its inward power. The men whose souls its positive truths have liberated exercise a negative influence in removing the most oppressive evils from the outward circumstances of life. From time to time – in a crusade of reformation – their enthusiasm opens some new spring of national life, which in its turn mingles with the onward stream of national progress. But they must themselves be wholly free from the dominion which they only modify for others. It is one of the effects of our fondness for excessive generalisation that we identify the reformers of bygone days too much with the spirit of their age, and seldom sufficiently appreciate the independence of their position, or the isolated eminence of their greatness. The world is ever claiming as its own those who have indeed been in it but not of it. The very essence of a true reformer consists in his being the corrector and not the exponent of the common feeling of his day. The breath of his life is inspired from above, not drawn up from below. Those flashes of religious enlightenment which from time to time break on the slumbers of mankind often resemble in their history the discoveries of scientific truth. The wants of the age, or some unknown influences from above, set the minds of thinking men in motion, they know not whither, till at last the master mind among them reaches the wished-for light, and reflects it on his fellows. Immediately they recog-

nise it as that after which they have been striving, while the world at large finds its darkness broken, but knows not whence the light has come. It has its own way; its antagonistic forces work along the winding pathway of "human progress", but they move on a different plane from the spiritual energy which animates the true reformer. Its rival parties adopt him as their own, or cast him from them, as may suit their purpose; but he is fulfilling a work which they know not of, a work which has many points of contact with the political and social movements of the day, but which is yet distinct from them both in origin and end. He must needs be raised above that atmosphere of circumstances, on which he throws the light of his own being, penetrating even to those who still wander beneath it'. This essay was first published in the Old Mortality Society's journal *Undergraduate Papers* (1857–8).

Book IV, Chapter 2:
the Practical Value of a Theory of the Moral Ideal

1. William Wordsworth, *Rob Roy's Grave*, lines 25–32.
2. *I use this as a fair equivalent of Kant's formula – 'Treat humanity, whether in your person or in that of another, never merely as a means, always at the same time as an end.' [*Grundlegung zur Metaphysik der Sitten* (1785), *The Moral Law*, trans. H. J. Paton (London, 1948), p. 96.]
3. Eph. vi: 6.
4. The heroine of Sir Walter Scott's novel *The Heart of Mid-Lothian* (1818), based on the true story of Helen Walker. Jennie's half-sister Effie has borne an illegitimate child, which has disappeared. The law provided that those circumstances would be taken as proof that the mother has killed the child unless she has told someone of her pregnancy. Jennie is convinced of Effie's innocence, but she refuses on conscientious grounds to swear that Effie gave the smallest indication of her pregnancy. Effie is convicted and sentenced to death, but Jennie walks to London and successfully petitions Queen Caroline for a pardon for Effie – whose child subsequently turns out to be alive. Green uses the example to introduce the problem of the philosopher's advice 'according to the principles advocated in this treatise' in 'cases . . . in which the difficulty felt in adhering to a general rule, such as that of veracity, arises from an impulse entitled in itself to as much respect as the conscientious injunction to adhere to the rule' (§ 315).
5. E.g. the *Kulturkampf* and 'ultramontane movement' in Germany, and the position of Polish Catholics; see *Lectures*, § 167 note 10, and § 168 note 14.
6. Cf. *Lectures*, §§ 100–12, 142–7, 167–8.
7. Nettleship quotes one of Green's letters to his family, written when he was an undergraduate at the time of the formation of a volunteer rifle corps: 'Fools talk at Oxford of its being desirable, in order that the

gentry may keep down the chartists in the possible contingency of a rising. I should like to learn the use of the arm that I might be able to desert to the people, if it came to such a pass. After all we do not know what may arise from the hunger produced by a European war' (*Memoir*, p. xxiv).

8. For example, S. T. Coleridge distinguished between the National Church, which was part of the political structure of a particular community and had a specific social and educational role, and the Christian Church, a universal, spiritual unity of all believers without institutional or legal trappings. See *On the Constitution of Church and State* (1830), ed. John Colmer, *Collected Coleridge*, vol. 10, pp. 102–28.

9. Cf. 'Loyalty', pp. 304–6 below.

10.*I say 'metaphorically', because what we primarily understand by 'law' is some sort of command, given by a superior in power to one whom he is able to punish for disobedience; whereas it is the essence of moral 'law' that it is a rule which a man imposes on himself, and from another motive than the fear of punishment.

11. Cf. Green's analysis of Austin, *Lectures*, §§ 81–6.

12. In the final two chapters of the *Prolegomena*, Green discusses 'The Practical Value of a Hedonistic Moral Philosophy' (ch. 3) and compares it with that of his theory of the ideal good (ch. 4). He writes: 'Whatever the errors arising from its Hedonistic psychology, no other theory has been available for the social or political reformer, combining so much truth with such ready applicability. No other has offered so commanding a point of view from which to criticise the precepts and institutions presented as authoritative' (§ 329). The particular contribution of Utilitarianism has been that 'it has most definitely announced the interest of humanity, without distinction of persons or classes, as the end by reference to which all claims upon obedience are ultimately to be measure ... Impartiality of reference to human well-being has been the great lesson which the Utilitarian had to teach' (§ 333), and 'it is precisely this that has brought the Utilitarian into conflict with every class-prejudice, with every form of family or national pride, with the inveterate and well-reputed habit of investing with a divine right the cause of a friend or the party or the institution which happens to interest us most, without reference to its bearings on the welfare of others more remote from our sympathies' (§ 213). But the Hedonistic conception affords no 'definite conception of the claims of mankind'; although it 'insists ... on the claim of every man to have as much pleasure as is compatible with the attainment of the greatest possible amount on the whole ... this claim cannot be translated into a claim to be or to do, or to have a chance of being or doing, anything in particular. We cannot found upon it even a claim of every man to be free' (§ 380; cf. *Lectures*, § 18). See also Green's 1868 essay 'Popular Philosophy in its Relation to Life' (*Works*, III, pp. 92–125), which Nettleship regards as 'perhaps the most preg-

nant and eloquent of his writings' (*Memoir*, p. lxxiii). Green there locates the origin of Utilitarianism in 'the philosophy of nature and knowledge inherited from Bacon and Locke' (p. 96), and traces its influence on philosophy, poetry, and religion. He concludes that 'the modern spirit is being schooled out of its individual egoism' since 'man, above all the modern man, must theorise his practice, and the failure adequately to do so, must cripple the practice itself ... Art, religion, and the political life have outgrown the nominalistic logic and the psychology of individual introspection; yet the only recognised formulae by which the speculative man can account for them to himself, are derived from that logic and psychology. Thus the more fully he has appropriated the results of the spiritual activity of his time, the more he is baffled in his theory ... The prevalence of such a state of mind might be expected at least to excite an interest in a philosophy like that of Hegel, of which it was the professed object to find formulae adequate to the action of reason as exhibited in nature and human society, in art and religion' (pp. 124–5). See also the present editors' 'Introduction', above pp. 5–6, and A. J. M. Milne, 'The Idealist critique of Utilitarian social philosophy', *Archives Européennes de Sociologie* VIII (1967), pp. 318–31.

6 UNDERGRADUATE ESSAYS

*From 'Undergraduate Notebooks', Green Papers, Balliol College. These essays were written between 1855 and 1859; they are arranged here in chronological order. Parts of 'Loyalty' are in *Memoir*, pp. xxii–xxiii; otherwise they are published here for the first time.

A. *The Effect of Commerce on the Mind of a Nation*

1. See *Prolegomena*, §§ 275, 280, 285, for Green's account of the universalising implications of Christianity. David Hume connected the rise of commerce with greater equality in 'Of Commerce', *Essays, Moral, Political and Literary*, 2 vols., ed. T. H. Green and T. H. Grose (London, 1875), vol. I, pp. 296–7.

2. Cf. Green's treatment of the realisation of self through interaction with the material world, *Lectures*, ch. P.

3. The idea that commerce broke down the relations of subordination which characterised feudal society and facilitated freedom was a common theme in eighteenth-century literature; see for example Albert O. Hirschman, *The Passions and the Interests. Political Arguments for Capitalism before Its Triumph* (Princeton, 1977) and J. G. A. Pocock, 'The Political Economy of Burke's Analysis of the French Revolution', *Historical Journal* 25 (1982), pp. 332–4. Green may have come across the idea in any number of sources; one possibility is S. T. Coleridge, whose influence may be seen elsewhere in the present essay; see notes 4, 5, 7, 9 below.

4. The benefits listed here may reflect Green's acquaintance with Coleridge's writings; see for example the '*Rifacciamento*' edition of the journal *The Friend*, issued in 1818, ed. Barbara E. Rooke, *Collected Coleridge*, vol. 4, part II, p. 128.

5. Examples drawn from pre-exilic Israel appeared in Coleridge's *Lay Sermons* (1816–17), ed. R. J. White, *Collected Coleridge*, vol. 4, pp. 17, 33, and *On the Constitution of Church and State* (1830), ed. John Colmer, *Collected Coleridge*, vol. 10, pp. 39–40.

6. Cf. Green's remarks on centralisation in 'Liberal Legislation', above p. 202.

7. In *The Friend* (part I, p. 253) Coleridge identified hope as one of the ends of the state.

8. Cf. Green, 'Lecture on the Grading of Secondary Schools', *Works*, III, p. 405.

9. Coleridge discussed the stifling intellectual effects of 'the spirit of commerce' in *Lay Sermons*, pp. 191–5 and *On the Constitution of Church and State*, pp. 42–8; cf. Hume, 'Of Commerce', p. 289.

10. Cf. *Prolegomena*, §§ 207 and note, 281; *Lectures*, § 174.

11. Cf. *Lectures*, ch. P.

B. Loyalty

1. See 'Freedom', § 3 for the Pauline sources of this view.

2. This may represent an early formulation of the idea of the unfolding of the eternal consciousness which Green developed in the 'Introduction to Hume' (*Works*, I, pp. 12–13) and in the *Prolegomena*, §§ 9ff; see the Introduction to the present volume, pp. 4–6.

3. Cf. Green's account of the domestic source of conceptions of rights, *Lectures*, §§ 24, 30, 91, 134–5, 236–8.

4. In the *Lectures*, § 86, Green argued that the 'real determinant of the habitual obedience of the people' resided in 'that impalpable congeries of the hopes and fears of a people bound together by common interests and sympathy, which we call the general will'; compare with the discussion of Green's treatment of Austin in the Introduction to this volume, pp. 8–12.

5. Probably a reference to Thomas Carlyle's notion of hero-worship in *On Heroes, Hero-Worship, and the Heroic in History* (London, 1841); Carlyle's position may be seen as insufficiently appreciative of 'human worth'.

6. Cf. Green's later characterisation of the major actors in 'English Revolution', above pp. 219ff.

7. These themes are developed at length in ch. G of the *Lectures*.

C. Legislative Interference in Moral Matters

1. Cf. Green's discussion of Hegel in 'Freedom', §§ 4–6.

2. See also 'Notes on Moral Philosophy', below pp. 310–13.

3. Probably a reference to Plato's discussion of the classes in the state and the elements of the soul, *Republic*, 427c–445b.

4. Cf. Green's account of the lasting impact of feudalism on modern class relationships, *Lectures*, §§ 228–9.

5. See also the discussion of Austin in *Lectures*, ch. F.

6. Prov. xiv: 10.

7. This is one of the central strands of Green's discussion of the English Revolution; see above pp. 214–5.

8. Cf. Green's treatment of Cromwell and Vane, 'English Revolution', above pp. 219ff; see also *Lectures*, §§ 3–4; *Prolegomena*, §§ 298–301 and the extract from 'The Force of Circumstances' included there in § 301, note 5. In the light of Green's later treatment of Cromwell, it is significant that 'great reformers' are here literary or religious figures and not politicians or statesmen.

9. The National Church does not play a significant role in Green's mature writings; that it is mentioned here may reflect Green's early interest in Coleridge, whose influence may be discerned elsewhere in the undergraduate essays – see 'Effects of Commerce', above pp. 302–4 and note 3. In later life Green's attitude to the Church of England was exceptionally cool. Although he subscribed to the Thirty Nine Articles in order to take the M.A., he did so in a way which was intended to signify membership of the Church, not a statement of faith in all its doctrines (see Richter, p. 86). Phyllis Grosskurth reports John Addington Symonds, Green's brother-in-law, as saying that when Green signed the Thirty Nine Articles 'he had to justify his action with the rationalisation that "one kiss does not make a marriage"'; *John Addington Symonds, A Biography* (London, 1964), p. 104. People wishing to teach at the University invariably took Holy Orders; Green declined to do so, partly because of an unwillingness to accept the formulae of the Church but also, Nettleship says, because of the 'repugnance' felt by 'a political and religious republican to the systems of social and ecclesiastical privileges with which he associated the English establishment' (*Memoir*, pp. xxxv–xxxvi). In a speech on Church Reform given at Merton College on 7 December 1881, Green gave a sympathetic account of those whose scruples concerning the Thirty Nine Articles, and whose dislike of the 'exclusive' and 'hierarchical tone of clerical opinion', alienated them from the Church. Green went on to refer to the almost complete absence of congregational life in the Church, which he attributed to a gulf between ordinary laymen and the clergy engendered by the absence of lay control over clerical appointments. Despite this antipathy to the Church, Green argued that disestablishment was not likely to be beneficial: it would generate great bitterness, leave the field open for a counter-productive struggle between those with 'catholicising' and 'evangelical' tendencies, and, perhaps more tellingly in the light of Green's early interest in Coleridge's ideas, it would 'make the clergyman of the future either a mere

priest or a mere preacher, instead of the leader in useful social work. . .'
Green thought that the best solution was to 'congregationalise' the
Church, that is, give the laity ('subject to general control by Bishops') a
clearly formulated and significant role in clerical appointments and in
determining ceremonial questions; this would eliminate the need for
subscription to the Thirty Nine Articles since congregations would
decide if the views of applicants for livings were compatible with theirs.
Green's 'Notes for a Speech on Church Reform' (and Mrs Green's copy
of them) are in the Green Papers at Balliol College; Nettleship quoted
liberally from them in the *Memoir* (pp. cxxii–cxxiii), but did not include
Green's remarks about the lack of congregational life in the Church, or
the suggestion that congregations should have a veto on clerical appointments.

10. Cf. *Lectures*, §§ 12–17.
11. *Ibid.*, §§17–18, 207–10.

7. FRAGMENTS ON MORAL AND POLITICAL PHILOSOPHY

A. *Notes on Moral Philosophy*
*From Green Papers, Balliol College (catalogue no. RLN 15); not pre-
viously published.

1. The formal character of the idea of the good is discussed in *Prolegomena*, §§ 192–8.
2. Cf. *ibid.*, §§ 55–73.
3. Cf. *ibid.*, §§ 85–114.
4. Cf. *ibid.*, §§142–5.
5. *Ibid.*, § 129.
6. E.g. Aristotle, *Politics*, 1332a; Plato, *Republic*, 608c–612a.
7. Cf. *Prolegomena*, §§ 101–14.
8. Cf. *Prolegomena*, § 193: 'the desire for the object will be founded on a
conception of its desireableness as a fulfilment of the capabilities of
which a man is conscious in being conscious of himself'. See also 'Freedom', *passim*.
9. See Plato, *Republic*, 434d–441c, 576b–589.
10. Aristotle, *Politics*, 1260b–1264b. Cf. Green's account of the shortcomings of Greek political philosophy, especially its failure to conceive of
'the relationship of wills' except in terms of an excessively narrow conception of humanity, *Prolegomena*, §§ 246–85.
11. Aristotle, *Politics*, 1252a.
12. Cf. *Lectures*, § 25: 'No one. . .can have a right except (1) as a member
of a society, and (2) of a society in which some common good is recognised by the members of the society as their own ideal good, and that
which *should be* for each of them.'
13. In *Lectures* Green describes the natural rights of social contract

theorists as 'abstracted from social function and recognition' (§ 49); the account here is compatible with that of the *Lectures*, but differs from it in laying more stress on the sympathetic basis of social recognition.

14. Cf. Aristotle, *Nicomachean Ethics*, VIII–IX and *Politics*, 1252a–1260b.
15. Aristotle, *Politics*, 1252a.
16. Cf. *Prolegomena*, § 286: 'Thus the ideal of virtue which our consciences acknowledge has come to be the devotion of character and life, in whatever channel the idiosyncrasy and circumstances of the individual may determine, to a perfecting of man, which is itself conceived not as an external end to be attained by goodness, but as consisting in such a life of self-devoted activity on the part of all persons.'
17. Cf. *Lectures*, ch. G; 'Freedom', §§ 4–7.
18. Cf. *Prolegomena*, Bk II.
19. The Cyrenaics 'reduced pleasure to an abstraction' by transforming the Socratic doctrine that happiness served as a motive for virtue into the idea that pleasure itself was the end of life. They thus 'seized on the one side of the Socratic teaching and disregarded all the rest'; Frederick Copleston, *A History of Philosophy*, 8 vols. (London, 1961), vol. I, p. 121; Green uses the term 'abstraction' as equivalent to onesidedness. The Epicurean poet T. Lucretius Carus (19–51 BC) aimed to liberate man from the fear of the gods and of death and to lead them to 'peace of soul'; Copleston, *History*, vol. I, pp. 401–2. For Green's critical analysis of various sorts of hedonism, see *Prolegomena*, §§ 219–39, 329–82.
20. Cf. *Lectures*, ch. G; *Prolegomena*, §§ 199–217; and 'Loyalty', below pp. 304–6.

B. Notes on Ancient and Modern Political Economy

*From Green Papers, Balliol College (catalogue no. RLN 19); not previously published. Nettleship gave it the title 'Notes on Political Economy'. This fragment also contains remarks on sovereignty, but since these add little to ch. F. of the *Lectures* they have been omitted. The present selection from RLN 19 is of interest as it enlarges upon points made in the *Lectures* and indicates Green's familiarity with contemporary economic doctrines.

1. In fact Green deals only with the first two points.
2. For example Aristotle, *Politics*, 1327a.
3. *Ibid.*, 1265b.
4. Cf. Mill, *Political Economy*, vol. II, Bk I, chs. i and ii, and 'Liberal Legislation', above pp. 195–212.
5. The reference may be to infanticide (see the works cited by Green in the note to *Lectures*, § 152), or to 'Greek love' (see the discussion of Greek notions of 'temperance' and 'chastity' in *Prolegomena*, §§ 261–78).
6. Aristotle, *Politics*, 1295–1296b.
7. In 340 BC Philip the Second of Macedon seized the Athenian grain fleet

in the Dardenelles, and managed to provoke the Athenians into a war in which they were decisively defeated by 338.

8. Aristotle, *Politics*, 1326b–1327a.

9. The case of Ireland would have been an obvious one to draw; it was mentioned, for example, by Mill, *Political Economy*, vol. II, Bk I, ch. viii, §4. Although Switzerland was frequently discussed by nineteenth-century writers (there are numerous references in Mill's *Political Economy*, and in Joseph Kay's, *The Social Condition of the People in England and Europe* (London, 1850), which Mill used) the editors have been unable to locate a reference to the points Green makes in this section. The use of the term *Grundbesitz* suggests perhaps a German language source.

10. This doctrine, associated with the Rev. Thomas Malthus, author of *Essay on Population* (1798), is commonly expressed in terms of the declining marginal productivity of land.

11. The phrase and the line of argument which proceeds it originate in David Ricardo's *Principles of Political Economy and Taxation* (1817), ed. R. M. Hartwell (Harmondsworth, 1971), ch. VI: 'The natural tendency of profits then is to fall; for in the progress of society and wealth, the additional quantity of food required is obtained by the sacrifice of more and more labour' (pp. 139–40). Mill used the phrase as a chapter heading in *Political Economy*, vol. III, Bk IV, ch. iv.

12. Cf. Mill, *Political Economy*, vol. I, Bk II, ch. ii, § 1.

13. Cf. *ibid.*, vol. II, Bk II, ch. ii, § 2, and ch. xii, §§ 1–2.

14. Presumably a reference to the rebuilding of parts of central Paris by Louis Napoleon; this programme, carried out by Georges Haussman, Prefect of the Seine (1853–70), generated large scale employment in the building industries and attracted large numbers of people from all social classes to the capital. See David H. Pinkney, *Napoleon III and the Rebuilding of Paris* (Princeton, 1958).

VARIANTS

These variants record the original editors' signifiant departures from Green's MSS; see 'Preface', p. vii. '*Alt.*' signifies an unresolved choice in the MS.

1. LECTURES ON THE PRINCIPLES OF POLITICAL OBLIGATION

§1. *a–a* The subject of this course of lectures is the principles of political obligation; and that term is intended to include the obligation of the subject towards the sovereign, the obligation of the citizen towards the state, and the obligation of individuals to each other as enforced by a political superior. *b–b* this being *c–c* the law; and throughout I distinguish moral duty from legal obligation; *d–d* a

2. *a–a* Our results on this question may be briefly stated as follows. *b–b alt.* passion *c–c* be a character *d–d* this ideal would be

3. *a–a* standard certainly *b–b* character.

4. *a–a* good – may be called by the name of 'a theory of

6. *a–a alt.* to be expected by one of another *b–b alt.* general *c–c alt.* morality. This embodiment, again, constitutes the moral progress of mankind. This progress, however, is only a *moral* progress in so far as it tends to bring about the harmony of will and reason, in the only form in which it can really exist, viz. in the characters of persons. And this result is actually achieved,

7. *a–a* capacities of will and reason, and *b–b* exercised. In their *c–c* forces, and thus they give

9. *a–a* duties may be said to exist, *b–b alt.* men

10. *a–a* is such as *b–b* may have *c–c* and *d–d* 'Recht'; a moral ground which *e–e* that established system.

12. *a–a* in which case there is an act, but it is not mine (e.g. if another . . . is shot); or (2) *b–b* or (3)

13. *a–a* relations

15. *a–a* acts only should

18. *a–a alt.* misconceives

20. *a–a alt.* attainment *b–b* man

21. *a–a* man's

28. *a–a* a servant),

31. *a–a alt.* natural
36. *a–a alt.* To begin with,
37. *a–a* traced to
39. *a–a* life determined
40. *a–a alt.* human
46. *a–a* obligation to observe
47. *a–a* the absolute
49. *a–a alt.* something *b–b alt.* are not
50. *a–a* Thus the only . . . 'social contract', is that of Spinoza. *b–b* like that of Spinoza
55. *a–a* and is consequently able to distinguish the
58. *a–a* As to the second point, from his own conception
59. *a–a* of the
60. *a–a* sovereignty
61. *a–a* Locke's theory *b–b* It
62. *a–a* the irrevocableness of the original act by which any government was established
63. *a–a* chapter (XIX) on the 'dissolution of government' *b–b* 'It often
65. *a–a* some pact
66. *a–a* individual
68. *a–a* sense: in the sense of *b–b* A reader of him who is
72. *a–a* officer according
79. *a–a alt.* manifested *b–b* explained
81. *a–a* (1) laws set by God to men, or the law of nature; and (2) laws set by men to men, or human law. *b–b* latter, the human laws. These are
84. *a–a* upon the fact that the superior is so *b–b* or less
85. *a–a* is perfectly *b–b alt.* statute *c–c* with determinate persons, or
88. *a–a* [the word is unclear in the MS and is queried in Nettleship's directions] *b–b alt.* compel their application for
90. *a–a* probably there was never any political system more *b–b* The
91. *a–a alt.* guarantees men these *b–b* will *c–c* the political freedom which
93. *a–a alt.* determinate person or persons, with whom sovereignty is vested, must *b–b* disapprovingly
95. *a–a* second question raised concerning Rousseau's theory: Is there any truth in speaking of a sovereign 'de jure' founded upon the 'volonté générale'? *b–b* in the sense of a
99. *a–a* under most popular sovereignties *b–b* person has such a right, no number of persons have it.
100. *a–a* recognised
101. *a–a alt.* possible *b–b* the maintenance
103. *a–a alt.* no right *b–b alt.* powers *c–c* falling
107. *a–a* particular) contrary *b–b* unless on the ground

108. *a–a alt.* prevalent
111. *a–a* since, as argued elsewhere [*Proleg. to Ethics*, II, i and ii], it *b–b* bad. But
112. *a–a* more *b–b* complication. Appearances *c–c* while *d–d* set *e–e* those *f–f* rights, interest
114. *a–a* way, a life of *b–b alt.* they should be masters of themselves
117. *a–a alt.* proportionate
118. *a–a* for to this
120. *a–a* made to; (i.e from being frightened at the consequences of not conforming, not consequences which follow *b–b* Is then the conception of common good which is alleged a conception *c–c* misleading, when the requirements of the state have so largely arisen out of force directed by selfish motives, and when the motive to obedience to those requirements is determined by fear, to speak of them as
121. *a–a* The idea the original citizen has of the common good served by the state is *b–b* that of his wife.
122. *a–a alt.* come to take as a matter of course,
124. *a–a* that of their neighbours, to
125. *a–a alt.* fulfil
127. *a–a* individual desires
132. *a–a* law. The
133. *a–a* are harmonised,
135. *a–a* in it (1) through
136. *a–a* derived from the Roman state, if not on institutions actually handed down from it; and *b–b* operation. [Chapter G ends here.]
137. *a–a* in my last course *b–b* In the last course *c–c* represent itself as a right, and claim obedience to itself as such. .
139. *a–a alt.* power; *b–b* a power given by it to the individual of putting the claim in force.
140. *a–a* good. Now that capability
141. *a–a* of some society, the state
143. *a–a alt.* proposed sub[version?]
144. *a–a* Thus to the question, Has the individual no rights against enactments founded on imperfect views of social well-being? *b–b* a duty prohibiting the import
145. *a–a alt.* correlative to
147. *a–a* general anarchy, not merely
148. *a–a* Returning from this digression, we resume our consideration of the nature and functions of the state. In order to understand this nature,
151. *a–a* use *b–b* any other
158. *a–a* agency and intentional *b–b* absence of

161. *a–a* for a more humbling sense (as the preachers would say)
163. *a–a* good-will
165. *a–a* brought about;
167. *a–a* defending against aggression what *b–b* organisation. *c–c* in matters which the state treats as belonging to itself, take their direction
168. *a–a* arts
175. *a–a* necessary
178. *a–a alt.* society
183. *a–a alt.* analogy with *b–b alt.* very
186. *a–a alt.* conduct
187. *a–a alt.* real
189. *a–a alt.* concrete
196. *a–a* The answer is that there are two *b–b* implies. (1) *c–c* any
197. *a–a* of good
198. *a–a alt.* ‘culpable
199. *a–a* all depravity
200. *a–a* for
201. *a–a* to associate *b–b* be a breach,
202. *a–a* the *b–b* is rightly treated criminally when its *c–c* negligently. As *d–d alt.* wilful *e–e alt.* a crime
204. *a–a* and
206. *a–a alt.* primary *b–b* the *c–c alt.* in the name *d–d alt.* taint
207. *a–a* life is constantly gaining on its negative side *b–b* good. We treat *c–c* possible. Is this reasonable? Yet are *d–d* acting? Are they not allowing
213. *a–a* knowledge (conception *b–b alt.* feelings
214. *a–a* it. Hobbes
216. *a–a alt.* ascribes *b–b alt.* common
217. *a–a alt.* ethical
219. *a–a* which, though the alternative course is left open to him, the individual submits, because
220. *a–a* upon the free moral life, and his provision with means for it.
231. *a–a* special
248. *a–a alt.* maintained *b–b* a dominant interest
249. *a–a* right
250. *a–a* some

2. LECTURE ON 'LIBERAL LEGISLATION AND FREEDOM OF CONTRACT'

a–a is only *b–b* with. In *c–c alt*. least restrained *d–d* should *e–e* rules *f–f* of the *g–g* feeling, saves *h–h* Irish counties

4. ON THE DIFFERENT SENSES OF 'FREEDOM' AS APPLIED TO WILL AND TO THE MORAL PROGRESS OF MAN

§1. *a–a* Since in all willing a man is his own object, the will is always free. Or, more properly, a man in willing is necessarily free, since willing constitutes freedom,[1] and 'free will' is the pleonasm 'free freedom'. But while it is important to insist upon this, it is also to be remembered that the nature of the freedom really differs – the freedom means quite different things – according *b–b* seeks it. 2. As to

2. *a–a alt.* put himself in antagonism to

5. *a–a alt.* strictly rational, *b–b alt.* impulse

6. *a–a alt.* revelation

7. *a–a* self-determination; the state

9. *a–a* in the sense of

11. *a–a alt.* is free to will *b–b* negative,[2] we [note 2: Instead of saying . . . other than himself]

14. *a–a* determination, all

17. *a–a alt.* identity *b–b alt.* choice

18. *a–a alt.* slave

19. *a–a alt.* justified *b–b* some will

20. *a–a* consciousness. We must now explain *b–b* reason, – the will and reason of this man and that, – and how

22. *a–a* which he ordinarily seeks *b–b* satisfaction anywhere

24. *a–a* the business *b–b* national

25. *a–a* reason or the

5. PROLEGOMENA TO ETHICS: SELECTIONS

§176. *a–a* has in

177. *a–a* them

178. *a–a* has in

180. *a–a* him; and for this reason . . . capabilities are. Yet,

187. *a–a* has in

191. *a–a alt.* occasion

197. *a–a* for the sake of the

198. *a–a* allow such a

206. *a–a* first of the movements into which the development of morality may be analysed consists
207. *a–a alt.* understand
215. *a–a* in *b–b* in whom there is no conscientious will giving
216. *a–a* reason without him in *b–b* which beings such as we are, endowed with certain animal susceptibilities and affected by certain natural sympathies, become capable of striving after some bettering or fulfilment of themselves, which they conceive as an absolute good, and in which they include a like bettering or fulfilment of others. *c–c* fellowships, though greater in degree, are the same in kind as *d–d alt.* spiritual *e–e alt.* as
240. *a–a* has in
270. *a–a* Negative, because amounting merely *b–b* belong,

6. UNDERGRADUATE ESSAYS

B. Loyalty

a–a alt. unworthy

7. FRAGMENTS ON MORAL AND POLITICAL PHILOSOPHY

A. Notes on Moral Philosophy

§1. *a–a alt.* by
3. *a–a alt.* reflexion in himself

BIBLIOGRAPHY

The works listed below deal in whole or in part with T. H. Green's political or social philosophy. The bibliography is intended as a guide to the literature rather than a definitive listing. No mention is made of the extensive thesis or dissertation literature; this is well referenced in standard bibliographical sources.

A. BOOKS

Barker, Ernest, *Political Thought in England, 1848 to 1914*, 2nd edition, revised (London, 1947).

Bowle, John, *Politics and Opinion in the 19th Century* (London, 1954).

Brinton, Crane, *English Political Thought in the 19th Century* (London, 1933).

Cacoullos, Anne R., *Thomas Hill Green: Philosopher of Rights* (New York, 1974).

Chin, Y., *The Political Theory of Thomas Hill Green* (New York, 1920).

Clarke, Peter, *Liberals and Social Democrats* (Cambridge, 1978).

Copleston, F. C., *A History of Philosophy*, paperback edition, 8 vols. (New York, 1964), vol. 8, Parts I and II.

Cunningham, G. Watts, *The Idealist Argument in Recent British and American Philosophy* (New York and London, 1933).

Dewey, John, 'The Philosophy of Thomas Hill Green', and 'Green's Theory of the Moral Motive', both in *The Early Works, 1882–1898*, 5 vols. (Carbondale, Ill., 1969), vol. 3, *1889–92*.

'Self-realization as the moral ideal', in *The Early Works, 1882–1898*, 5 vols. (Carbondale, Ill., 1971), vol. 4, *1893–94*.

Fairbrother, W. H., *The Philosophy of Thomas Hill Green*, 2nd edition (London, 1900).

Gaus, Gerald F., *The Modern Liberal Theory of Man* (London, 1983).

Gordon, Peter and White, John, *Philosophers as Educational Reformers: The Influence of Idealism on British Educational Thought and Practice* (London, 1979).

Greengarten, I. M., *T. H. Green and the Development of Liberal–Democratic Thought* (Toronto, 1981).

Greenleaf, W. H., *The British Political Tradition*, 4 vols. (London, 1983–), vol. 2, *The Ideological Heritage*.

Haldar, H., *Neo-Hegelianism* (London, 1927).

373

Harris, F. P., *The Neo-Idealist Political Theory: Its Continuity with the British Tradition* (New York, 1944).

Harvie, Christopher, *The Lights of Liberalism. University Liberals and the Challenge of Democracy, 1860–86* (London, 1976).

Inglis, Fred, *Radical Earnestness. English Social Theory, 1880–1980* (Oxford, 1982).

Kemp, J., 'T. H. Green and the ethics of self-realisation', in *Reason and Reality*, ed. G. N. A. Vesey (London, 1972).

Lamont, W. D., *Introduction to Green's Moral Philosophy* (London, 1934).

Lewis, H. D., *Freedom and History* (London, 1962).

Lindsay, A. D., 'T. H. Green and the Idealists', in *The Social and Political Ideas of Some Representative Thinkers of the Victorian Age*, ed. F. J. C. Hearnshaw (London, 1933). Reprinted as the 'Introduction' to the *Lectures* (London 1941 et seq.; Ann Arbor, 1967).

MacCunn, John, *Six Radical Thinkers* (London, 1910).

Macpherson, C. B., *Property. Mainstream and Critical Positions* (Toronto, 1978).

Mandelbaum, Maurice, *History, Man and Reason. A Study in Nineteenth Century Thought* (Baltimore, 1971).

Manser, Anthony, *Bradley's Logic* (Oxford, 1983).

Marcuse, Herbert, *Reason and Revolution. Hegel and the Rise of Social Theory* (New York, 1941).

Milne, A. J. M., *The Social Philosophy of English Idealism* (London, 1962).

Muirhead, J. H., *The Service of the State. Four Lectures on the Political Teaching of T. H. Green* (London, 1908).

Mukhopadhyay, A. K., *The Ethics of Obedience: A Study of the Philosophy of T. H. Green* (Calcutta, 1967).

Plamenatz, John, *Consent, Freedom and Political Obligation*, 2nd edition (Oxford, 1968).

Prichard, H. A., *Moral Obligation and Duty and Interest* (Oxford, 1968).

Pucelle, Jean, *L'Idéalisme en Angleterre: De Coleridge à Bradley* (Neuchâtel, 1955).
    La Nature et l'Esprit dans la Philosophie de T. H. Green: La Renaissance de l'Idéalisme en Angleterre au XIXe siècle, 2 vols. (Paris and Louvain, 1960 and 1965).

Reardon, Bernard M. G., *From Coleridge to Gore. A Century of Religious Thought in Britain* (London, 1971).

Richter, Melvin, *The Politics of Conscience: T. H. Green and His Age* (London, 1964).

Robbins, Peter, *The British Hegelians, 1875–1925* (New York, 1982).

Rodman, John, 'Introduction' in *The Political Theory of T. H. Green: Selected Writings*, ed. Rodman (New York, 1964).

Schneewind, J. B., *Sidgwick's Ethics and Victorian Moral Philosophy* (Oxford, 1977).

Sidgwick, Henry, *Lectures on the Ethics of T. H. Green, Mr Herbert Spencer, and J. Martineau* (London, 1902).

Thakurdas, Frank, *The English Utilitarians and the Idealists. An Introductory Study of the Development of English Political Theory in the 18th & 19th Century* (New Delhi, 1978).

Ulam, A. B., *The Philosophical Foundations of English Socialism* (Cambridge, Mass., 1951).

Vincent, Andrew and Plant, Raymond, *Philosophy, Politics and Citizenship: Idealism and the Welfare State* (Oxford, 1984).

Walsh, W. H., *Hegelian Ethics* (London, 1969).

B. JOURNAL ARTICLES AND CONFERENCE PAPERS

Addison, W. G., 'Academic Reform at Balliol, 1854–1882. T. H. Green and Benjamin Jowett', *The Church Quarterly Review* (Jan. 1952), pp. 89–98.

Bishirjian, R. J., 'Thomas Hill Green's political philosophy', *Political Science Reviewer*, 4 (1974), pp. 29–53.

Chapman, Richard A., 'Thomas Hill Green (1836–1882)', *Review of Politics*, 27 (1965), pp. 516–31.

Collini, Stefan, 'Sociology and Idealism in Britain, 1880–1920', *Archives Européennes de Sociologie*, XIX (1978), pp. 3–50.

'Idealism and "Cambridge Idealism"', *Historical Journal*, XVIII (1975) pp. 171–7.

Hansen, Philip, 'T. H. Green and the moralization of the market', *Canadian Journal of Social and Political Theory*, 1 (1977), pp. 91–117.

Harris, H. S., 'Hegelianism of the "Right" and "Left"', *Review of Metaphysics*, 11 (1958), pp. 603–9.

Harris, Paul, 'Green's theory of political obligation and disobedience', paper presented to the Commemorative Conference on T. H. Green, Balliol College, Oxford, 1982.*

Hoover, Kenneth R., 'Liberalism and the idealist philosophy of Thomas Hill Green', *Western Political Quarterly*, 26 (1973), pp. 550–65.

Jenks, Craig, 'T. H. Green, the Oxford philosophy of duty and the English middle class', *British Journal of Sociology*, 28 (1977), pp. 481–97.

Knapp, V. J., 'T. H. Green and the exorability of property', *Agora*, 1 (1969), pp. 57–65.

Martin, Rex, 'T. H. Green on natural rights in Hobbes, Spinoza, and Locke', paper presented to the Commemorative Conference on T. H. Green, Balliol College, Oxford, 1982.*

Mehta, V. R., 'T. H. Green and the problem of political obligation', *Indian Political Science Review*, 7 (1973), pp. 115–24.

'T. H. Green and the revision of English liberal theory', *Indian Journal of Political Science*, 35 (1974), pp. 37–49.

'The origins of English Idealism in relation to Oxford', *Journal of the History of Philosophy*, 13 (1975), pp. 177–87.

Milne, A. J. M., 'The Idealist critique of Utilitarian social philosophy', *Archives Européennes de Sociologie*, VIII (1967), pp. 318–31.

'The common good and rights in T. H. Green's ethical and political theory', paper presented to the Commemorative Conference on T. H. Green, Balliol College, Oxford, 1982.*

Monson, Charles H., 'Prichard, Green and moral obligation', *Philosophical Review*, 63 (1954), pp. 74–87.

Morrow, John, 'British Idealism, "German Philosophy" and the First World War', *Australian Journal of Politics and History*, 28 (1982), pp. 380–90.

'Property and personal development: an interpretation of T. H. Green's political philosophy', *Politics*, 18 (1983), pp. 84–92.

'Liberalism and British Idealist Political Philosophy: A Reassessment', *History of Political Thought*, 5 (1984), pp. 91–108.

Nicholls, David, 'Positive Liberty 1880–1914', *American Political Science Review*, LVI (1962), pp. 114–28.

Nicholson, Peter P., 'Philosophical Idealism and international politics: reply to Dr Savigear', *British Journal of International Studies*, 2 (1976), pp. 77–83.

'T. H. Green and state action: liquor legislation', paper presented to the Commemorative Conference, Balliol College, Oxford, 1982.*

Pant, Nalini, 'Political authority and individual liberty in Rousseau and Green: an autopsy', *Journal of Political Studies*, 7 (1974), pp. 70–7.

Quinton, A. M., 'Absolute Idealism', *Proceedings of the British Academy*, 57 (1971), pp. 303–29.

Randall, J. H., Jr, 'T. H. Green: the development of English thought from J. S. Mill to F. H. Bradley', *Journal of the History of Ideas*, 27 (1966), pp. 217–44.

Richter, Melvin, 'T. H. Green and his audience: liberalism as a surrogate faith', *Review of Politics*, 18 (1956), pp. 444–72.

Ritchie, D. G., 'The political philosophy of the late Thomas Hill Green', *The Contemporary Review*, 51 (1887), pp. 841–51.

Rodman, John, 'What is living and what is dead in the political philosophy of T. H. Green', *Western Political Quarterly*, 26 (1973), pp. 566–86.

Sankhdher, M. M., 'T. H. Green: the forerunner of the welfare state', *Indian Journal of Political Science*, 30 (1969), pp. 149–64.

'T. H. Green's concept of the welfare state', *Journal of Political Studies*, 3 (1970), pp. 1–21.

Smith, Craig A., 'The individual and society in T. H. Green's theory of virtue', *History of Political Thought*, 2 (1981), pp. 187–201.

Weinstein, W. L., 'The concept of liberty in nineteenth century English political thought', *Political Studies*, 13 (1965), pp. 145–62.

*To be included in *The Philosophy of Thomas Hill Green*, ed. Andrew Vincent (Gower Press, forthcoming).

INDEX

action, free, 73, 99, 159–62, 235ff; and
  intention, 18–19; moral, 3, 199–200
actuality, *see* potentiality
agency, free, 159; human, 122ff
Agricultural Holdings Act (1875), 195,
  343
Anabaptists, 214, 293, 349
Aristotle, 2, 36, 37, 57, 275, 278, 280–1,
  285, 310–12, 315, 324, 325, 333, 340,
  343, 353, 355, 357, 364, 365, 366
army, New Model, 218, 220–4, 350;
  standing, 135
Austin, John, 8–10, 12, 66ff, 320, 321,
  323, 329, 330, 332, 338, 341, 360, 362,
  363; *see also* law(s); morality;
  obedience; sovereignty; superiors

Bentham, Jeremy, 336, 337
Bible, 214–5, 217–9
Blake, Robert, 225, 351
Bosanquet, Bernard, 318, 321, 335, 341,
  346
Bradbourne, Lord, 343
Bradley A. C., 332, 354
Bradley, F. H., 343, 354
Bright, John, 336, 344
Broderick, G. C., 347
Brown(e), Robert, 216, 349

Caesar, Julius, 101, 128–9
Caird, Edward, 348
Cairns, Lord, 205, 346
capital, capitalists, 174–5, 316
Carlyle, Thomas, 213, 349, 362
categorical imperative, 261–2
Charitable Trusts Act (1842), 196, 344
Charles I, 215, 219, 224, 306, 348, 350
chastity, Greek conception of, 281–2,
  365
Christianity, 1, 3–4, 153–6, 202, 229,
  308; moral progress and, 283–5, 358–9
Church, Catholic, 215–6, 227, 293, 295,
  297–8; of England, 215, 294, 330,
  363–4; national, 309, 360, 363; rate,

330; Reformed, 214–5, 218–20, 349;
  state and, 293, 295
civil injury, 153–6
civil institutions, common good and,
  91ff; general will and, 74; morality
  and, 14–16, 112, 232, 300; (*see also*
  freedom; government; law; rights;
  sovereignty; state)
class interests, 196
Cobden, Richard, 336, 344
Coke, Sir Edward, 355–6
Coleridge, Samuel Taylor, 5, 8, 328,
  360, 361, 362, 363
commerce, 126, 302–4, 361, 362
common good, *see* good, common
conscience, 4, 215, 217, 268, 271–3, 278,
  350; liberty of, 214, 216–18, 226;
  perplexity of, 289, 292–300
consciousness, 3, 5–7, 232, 310–13;
  common good and, 108; eternal, 3, 9,
  101, 243–4, 250ff, 275; human, 90–1;
  modern and primitive, 266–7;
  property and, 164, 167–8; of right, 91;
  rights and, 26–7, 107ff; self-, 263
contract, freedom of, 162, 194ff, 345;
  political obligation and, 89; social, *see*
  government by compact
Cromwell, Oliver, 11, 218ff, 350, 351,
  363
custom, 213, 232, 262, 264–6, 268

democracy, 12, 52, 93–4, 96–7, 119, 212,
  347
Derby, Lord, 205, 346
desire, 228–30, 232, 244, 251, 310
duty, duties, conflict of, 290–8;
  development of idea, 275–9; external
  authority and, 295–7; moral, 7, 13ff,
  17, 87, 159–61, 191–3, 296; particular,
  261–2; sense of, 270; socially
  recognised, 254, 263; unconditional,
  261

education, 161, 175, 177, 211, 259, 319,

377

Printed in the United States
1547200002B/85-186